BY MANY A
HAPPY
ACCIDENT

Comments on the book

This book, *By Many a Happy Accident: Recollections of a Life* written by Shri Hamid Ansari, offers an informative and engaging account of the life and work of an outstanding public servant of our times. Shri Ansari's career spans almost four decades—as an officer in the Indian Foreign Service, Vice Chancellor of the Aligarh Muslim University, Chairman of the Minorities Commission and thereafter, as the Vice President of India and Chairman, Rajya Sabha. Shri Ansari has brought an exceptionally high degree of integrity and dedication to every position he has occupied and his talented wife, Salma ji, has been a great support to him in the discharge of his duties. Shri Ansari's account of his life and career is an inspiration to us all.

—**Dr Manmohan Singh**, Former Prime Minister of India

Hamid Ansari's autobiography will enthral readers by the breadth of his vision. It is brilliantly entertaining, rising to great nobility of feeling and expressions.

—**K. Natwar Singh**, Former External Affairs Minister

The life experiences of this man of integrity, humility and sustained progressive spirit—who found opportunities and rewards come his way virtually unsought—are recollected in tranquillity in this sensitively crafted book. But this autobiography of a distinguished diplomat, educationist, public intellectual and writer who went on to become the Vice President of India, is not just a personal story: that itself holds a great deal of interest. It can also be read as a poignant reflection on the erosion of the constitutional values of liberty, equality and fraternity, and the fading away of the secular, democratic and liberating spirit of India's freedom struggle.

—**N. Ram**, Former Editor-in-Chief, *The Hindu*

Shri Hamid Ansari is a deeply thoughtful and dignified public figure. He tells his own life story clearly, interestingly, with restraint and an admirable absence of rancour. It will be a resource for those interested in India's relations with West Asia, the workings of parliament and the conduct of public life.

—**Pratap Bhanu Mehta**, Professor of Political Science and Former Vice Chancellor, Ashoka University

BY MANY A
HAPPY ACCIDENT
RECOLLECTIONS OF A LIFE

M. Hamid Ansari

RUPA

First published by
Rupa Publications India Pvt. Ltd 2021
7/16, Ansari Road, Daryaganj
New Delhi 110002

Sales Centres:

Allahabad Bengaluru Chennai
Hyderabad Jaipur Kathmandu
Kolkata Mumbai

Copyright © M. Hamid Ansari 2021

Photograph copyright vests with the respective photographer or
the owner of the photograph

All online references provided in this book have been retrieved
by the author on or before 4 December 2020.

The views and opinions expressed in this book are the author's own
and the facts are as reported by him which have been verified to the
extent possible, and the publishers are not in any way liable for the same.

All rights reserved.

No part of this publication may be reproduced, transmitted,
or stored in a retrieval system, in any form or by any means,
electronic, mechanical, photocopying, recording or otherwise,
without the prior permission of the publisher.

ISBN: 978-93-90356-27-0

Second impression 2021

10 9 8 7 6 5 4 3 2

The moral right of the author has been asserted.

Printed at Thomson Press India Ltd, Faridabad

This book is sold subject to the condition that it shall not,
by way of trade or otherwise, be lent, resold, hired out,
or otherwise circulated, without the publisher's prior consent, in any
form of binding or cover other than that in which it is published.

Salma
Sulaiman
Nuriya
Osman
Who together made this possible

~

Manzoor hai guzaarish-e-ahwal-e-waaqaee
Apna bayan husn-e-tabiat nahin mujhe

(True expression of experience is what I really seek
I do not care to display my skill at speech.)

∼

Contents

Foreword by Pranab Mukherjee   *xi*
Preface   *xiii*

1. Growing Up   1
2. Cultivation of the Mind   10
3. In Harness   20
4. Representing India   52
5. 'And Wilderness is Paradise enow'   137
6. Vice President of India and Chairman, Rajya Sabha   182
7. Vice Presidency   228
8. Away from Routine   318
9. The Family   330
10. In Lieu of a Conclusion   333

Acknowledgements   343
Index   345

Foreword

Recollection is a conscious exercise of bringing back to mind something that happened in the near or distant past. Hamid Ansari has facilitated my and perhaps the reader's task by a candid admission in the Urdu couplet on the first page: a frank narration of unplanned happenings that shaped his journey through life in its three periods: professional diplomacy, intermittent academia and miscellaneous public duties, and a long spell of holding the second-highest public office in the Republic.

When he was elected for his first term as Vice President of India in August 2007, a Kolkata daily called him a 'Calcutta boy'. He admits to having imbibed what Nirad Babu in his *Autobiography* called a general propensity among Calcutta students of attending meetings and listening to speeches!

I saw Hamid Ansari at work in the early eighties as Chief of Protocol. He was part of the core team that shouldered the onerous responsibility, at short notice, of organizing the 7th Non Aligned Conference in New Delhi and for which he was rewarded the Padma Shri. In later years, his services as our ambassador in different lands were appreciated by the government and furthered bilateral relations. He was among the early architects of our relations with some of the countries in the Persian Gulf littoral. I personally saw him at work as our Permanent Representative to the United Nations when I led our delegation in 1994 at a time when, on account of the troubles in

J&K, we were under pressure globally and weathered it successfully.

There was wide-ranging consensus in the UPA about his candidature in 2007 notwithstanding apprehensions in some sections about his unfamiliarity with parliamentary life. These were soon put to rest by the judicious manner in which he conducted the proceedings of the Rajya Sabha and his insistence on being an umpire in cricket or a referee in hockey, conducting the game by the rules, being inclusive and accommodative but without becoming a player. He displayed these qualities in the normal day-to-day conduct of the proceedings as also at certain critical moments like the Women's Reservation Bill and the Lokpal Bill and in the quiet consultation in quest of a consensus on proposed legislation relating to mines and minerals, land acquisition, etc. He made a concerted effort to save the Question Hour as an essential ingredient of accountability of the executive. He insisted that the practice of passing a bill *in the din* be forsaken and legislative approval obtained by prescribed procedures.

Apart from his responsibilities as Chairman, Rajya Sabha, Hamid Ansari made a conscious effort to be a 'bully pulpit' on questions of public interest or concern—'teasing questions' as he called them—in our polity. To this end, he made good use of university convocations, memorial lectures and anniversaries. Some of these are mentioned in this volume. He spoke within the framework of the Constitution and its core values, and about the rights bestowed on minorities and weaker sections but awaiting realization in good measure. In these, he was candid without being polemical. He avoided controversy and the few partisan attempts at involving him in contentions exposed themselves.

By Many a Happy Accident is an interesting account by a close observer of aspects of our public and parliamentary life in recent years.

Pranab Mukherjee
Former President of India
27 July 2020

Preface

It is said that the age to write an autobiography is reached only when one has lost all curiosity about the future. A life in retirement, someone wrote a few centuries back, 'was ever safe and to the studious mind never unpleasant but now by so much the better as the world is worse'. Both dicta may have a grain of veracity, but neither dampens optimism about life in general; hence, the impulse to recollect episodes from one's own past.

An autobiography is a difficult piece of writing, it being a record of half-forgotten things. Memory is a tricky wench; it attempts to be candid as well as dissertate. It is a recollection, not an apologia. It must out of necessity commence with family history, of how, when and where the story began. My effort can be no different.

I begin with a correction. In response to a question asked in August 2017, I had said that I had no intention of writing my memoirs. How then did this 'transcendent realization' come about? A simple answer is a complex one—to change neither the beginning nor the end, but to tell our three children what the journey, my own and with Salma, has been like; to record some happenings where I was a witness; to reflect however inadequately on some of what transpired.

Chapter 1

Growing Up

I was born on 1 April 1937 in Calcutta (now Kolkata), where my father Mohammad Abdul Aziz Ansari—Abba to his children—worked as Resident Director of an insurance company. We were a largish family; an elder brother and sister, Khalid and Naseem, and two older sisters, Fatima and Saleha, from Abba's first wife, who died early. Younger to me was another brother, Haris, and two sisters, Safia and Zakia. The family's roots are in eastern Uttar Pradesh (UP) in Yusufpur, a modest-sized *qasba* (bigger than a village, smaller than a town) in Mohammadabad tehsil of Ghazipur district. Family history, genealogical tables[1] and *District Gazetteer*[2] of the British period bear witness to a continuous presence there of almost seven centuries as office holders and modest-sized landholders. The family lands and mango gardens were jointly managed by a designated senior member and every member got his or her proportionate share of the proceeds.

---

[1] Mohammad Samiuddin, *Tazkira-e Ganj-hai Giran-maya: Tarikh-e-Doodman-e-Aali* (Aligarh, 2012) pp. 329–38, Ansariyan-e-zila Ghazipur.
[2] H.R. Nevill, *Ghazipur: A Gazetteer being volume xxix of the District Gazetteers of the United Provinces of Agra and Oudh* (Allahabad, 1909) pp. 99–100. Some more details, including the date of the foundation of the village, 730 Hijri or AD 1329, are given in Irwin's Settlement Report of 1884–85.

My mother, Aasiya Farooqi, hailed from Muhammadabad Gohna in the adjacent district of Azamgarh (now Mau). She was much younger than her husband. Her father, Abdul Rauf, a barrister at law, died in a poisoning accident while on a visit to Hyderabad when she was very young. She was brought up by her maternal aunt and given the traditional education for girls in Muslim families in that period.

My paternal grandfather, Moulavi Abdul Karim, received traditional education, perhaps at Deoband, and was for some time the manager of a small raja's estate in eastern UP. The only thing noteworthy of that assignment, according to family legend, was the single-handed capture of a proclaimed outlaw for which deed he received from the British Indian government a Sword of Honour bearing the imperial insignia. I have inherited this as an heirloom. He performed the Hajj at an early age and helped with the construction of a mosque across the road from the entrance of our ancestral family house. This double-storeyed structure stands to this day and has been renovated recently thanks to an initiative taken by Haris and executed under the supervision of our nephew, Abdul Malik, whose house is adjacent to ours.

By the turn of the century and the first decade of the twentieth century, perceptions about modern education for boys were sufficiently evolved in middle-class families in UP for my father and others older and younger than him in the family to be sent for modern school and college education. After his initial schooling, Abba was sent to Mohammedan Anglo-Oriental (M.A.O.) College, Aligarh for his master's and law degrees. Teaching was undertaken in the college in Aligarh, but the examinations were conducted by the Allahabad University. While still a student there, he and some of his contemporaries—Abdul Rahman Siddiqi, Shuaib Qureshi, Chaudhry Khaliquzzaman, Abdul Rahman Peshawari and a few others—responded to Dr Mukhtar Ahmad Ansari's call for volunteers to join his Medical Mission to Ottoman Turkey during the Balkan

Wars (1912–13).³ Abba returned to Aligarh to complete his studies and then commenced the practice of law at Barabanki near Lucknow. Like many others of his generation, he kept alive his interest in the developing political scene in UP and in the country.

The outbreak of World War I and Ottoman Turkey's involvement in it had its impact on Muslim opinion in India, sections of which had not reconciled itself to British rule. The Silk Letter Conspiracy and the attempt to form a Muslim Salvation Army (Al Junood-ul-Rabbaniya) by inciting frontier tribes and seeking help from Turkey, took shape in 1915–17 in Deoband, Kabul and Madina.⁴

The Khilafat movement emerged a few years later, in 1919. An internal report of the British Indian government testified candidly to its impact.

> The success which attended the Non-cooperation and Khilafat movements in India is undoubtedly attributable to the Great War, for neither agitation could have attained the dimensions which it did but for the economic pressure which the people were subjected [to] in consequence to the prolonged and widespread hostilities. This pressure aggravated and magnified local grievances and spread the spirit of unrest, thus making, for a time, the work of agitators easy... Although the Khilafat movement ostensibly had the purely religious object of compelling the maintenance of spiritual and temporal Muslim control over the Holy Places of Islam, yet there is no doubt that the real aims of its most revolutionary and active leaders was the destruction of the British rule in India, an aim which was justified on the ground that Britain is the most powerful rival

---

[3] A full account of this is given in Burak Akcapar, *People's Mission to the Ottoman Empire: M.A. Ansari and the Indian Medical Mission, 1912–13* (Oxford University Press, New Delhi, 2014). Also, Mushirul Hasan, *M.A. Ansari: Gandhi's Infalliable Guide* (New Delhi, 1987, 2010) pp. 72–87.

[4] Details of this case, as presented in courts of law by the home department, are given in *The Silk Letter Movement* by Maulana Mohammad Miyan Deobandi (English translation, Deoband, 2013).

to Muslim influence in the Near East. Gandhi quickly realized this and, appreciating the value of a common object for Non-cooperation and Khilafat movements, provided them with a common platform... In consequence of Gandhi's influence, the two organizations became for a time largely interdependent and although maintained separate machinery, yet their methods and products were identical.[5]

Given the climate of opinion of the period and also that among his contemporaries, Abba joined the Khilafat Non-cooperation Movement and was sentenced to a jail term of a year. He spent most of that period in the Mianwali jail (now in Pakistan). In the early 1980s, I was able to obtain with the help of Saidullah Khan Dehlavi, a senior Pakistani diplomat posted in New Delhi and the son of an old family friend, a copy of the jail register indicating his period of internment.[6]

On return to normal life, Abba resumed his law practice but retained his interest in the Freedom Movement. He was one of 100 signatories to an *Appeal for Inter-Communal Harmony* issued in Delhi on 6 October 1923. The list of those who affixed their signatures to that document included Lala Lajpat Rai, Mufti Kifayatullah, Pandit Madan Mohan Malaviya, Maulana Abul Kalam Azad, Swami Shraddhanand, Maulana Shabbir Ahmad Usmani, C.R. Das, Maulana Mohammad Ali, Motilal Nehru, Mukhtar Ahmad Ansari, Pandit Jawaharlal Nehru, Rajendra Prasad, Sardar Vallabhbhai Patel, C. Rajagopalachari, Subhas Chandra Bose, Kasturba Gandhi and Sarojini Naidu.

The Appeal argued that:

> ...if any individual or group of individuals belonging to any community commits an act of violence against, or attacks the

---

[5]P.C. Bamford, *Histories of the Non-Cooperation and Khilafat Movement* (Government of India Press, Delhi, 1925) p. xiii. Bamford wrote this report as Deputy Director, Intelligence Bureau, Home Department, Government of India.
[6]Zafar Ahmad Nizami, *Role of Muslims in the Indian Freedom Struggle 1857–1947* (Institute of Objective Studies, New Delhi, 2011) Volume I, p. 209.

person, property or honour of women or places of worship (mandir, mosque, church or gurdwara, etc), of his neighbours or fellow townsmen or helps those who indulge in such misdeeds, he is, from the religious point of view, guilty of a great sin; and that it is the duty of co-religionists of such offenders to stand up and resist such miscreants and to protect those who are so attacked.[7]

This line of argument against communal violence has rarely if ever been used subsequently.

Dr Mukhtar Ahmad Ansari presided over the 1927 Madras (now Chennai) session of the Indian National Congress (INC) and Abba accompanied him to it.[8] In an article in the *Modern Review* in July 1929, Dr Ansari wrote that 'communalism is too harmful to be left to itself in the hope that it will die a natural death some day in the definite future... Your first duty, therefore, is to carry a relentless crusade against communalism as an active guiding principle of Indian political life'.[9]

In 1930, Abba accepted an offer to be a judge in the Rampur State and remained there till 1935 when his Aligarh roommate, Abdul Rahman Siddiqi, invited him to join a newly formed insurance company in Calcutta. After the outbreak of World War II, some apprehension of continuing Japanese military successes in the Northeast made the company shift its headquarters to Lucknow. We remained there till the end of 1945.

STARTING SCHOOL

I have only the haziest recollections of that period. On our return to Calcutta, I had my first experience of a proper school. It was run

---

[7]Text in *Selected Works of Motilal Nehru*, Vol. 4, pp. 496–503. It gives the names and the background of the signatories. M.A. Aziz Ansari's name is at serial number 70.
[8]Mushirul Hasan, op. cit., chapters 7 and 8 for a detailed account of Dr Ansari's leadership of the Indian National Congress (INC).
[9]ibid. p. 202.

by the Seventh-Day Adventist and was located on Park Street. We stayed in an apartment in the Khaleeli Mansion on Lower Circular Road. Khaleeli sahib, of Iranian origin and well settled in Calcutta in the tea business, was a family friend and his elder son, Habib, was in school with my brother, Khalid. Later, we moved to a more spacious flat in Siddiqi Mansion on Suhrawardy Avenue. The landlord was Dr Zubair Siddiqi, Sir Ashutosh Professor of Islamic Culture at the University of Calcutta. He, too, was a close friend of Abba.

My earliest impressions and recollections of my father are that of a strict, but not stern paterfamilias—methodical, orthodox in a traditional sense, very regular in his habits and addicted to punctuality in all matters including meal timings at the family table. There was no tradition of morning tea; breakfast was early and no concessions given to late-risers! Abba's lunch was at around nine, before he left for office. He dispensed with lunch at work and instead had tea and some biscuits. Dinner was punctually after Maghrib (sunset) and before Isha (evening) prayers. Some of these traits were imbibed by me, in greater measure by my younger brother, Haris and much less by the elder one, Khalid.

In the summer of 1946, Abba was appointed Superintendent (later designated Controller) of Insurance in the Government of India (GoI) with his headquarters in Simla (now Shimla). So the whole family moved there to stay in a spacious bungalow of the colonial period. Haris and I were admitted mid-term to the Harcourt Butler School. We all have happy recollections of that period; it was, however, short-lived. In July 1947, with the impending formation of Pakistan, Abba, like other senior Muslim officers in the central government, received a letter from Mohammed Ali Jinnah asking him to proceed to Pakistan to assume the same responsibility there. He thanked Jinnah for the offer, but expressed the inability 'to change my country'.

Like many other places in northern India, Simla, too, experienced the trauma and bloodshed in the aftermath of Partition. An overwhelming number of Muslim civil and military government officers stationed there left for Pakistan; our family was one of the two at the senior level who opted to remain. I recall one afternoon Abba came back from office early and, with a note of urgency, said the family had to move to a hotel. There, food for all of us and milk for the youngest member of the family was found to be a problem; so, after a few days, we moved to a better one. Before leaving the house that afternoon, he made a trunk call to Maulana Azad in Delhi to tell him about the situation in Simla. The Maulana said Delhi knew nothing about it, but that he would tell the prime minister (PM) about it. That night, a contingent of soldiers of a British battalion from a cantonment in the vicinity of Simla was posted at the Auckland House (Girls) School across the road from our house. Given the general security situation, it was decided that the family would leave Simla and travel to Delhi on the way to Yusufpur. The journey, with the whole family crammed into a first-class railway compartment along with four policemen, remains etched in my memory and so do the images of refugees on both sides of the railway track. Abba, of course, had to stay back.

In Delhi, we stayed with Rafi Ahmed Kidwai sahib, an old family friend, who was a member of Jawaharlal Nehru's cabinet. His official residence was at 6, King Edward Road, later renamed Maulana Azad Road. At that point, it was a mini-refugee camp with many other families seeking shelter there. Some were accommodated in tents in the rear lawns around a small mosque[10] that was very much in use. My mother had vivid recollections of that sojourn and so does my elder sister, Naseem. Destiny does play games with individuals. Six decades later, in August 2007, I returned to this house as Vice President of India and stayed there for two weeks short of 10 years! The mosque, which fell within the ambit of The Places of Worship (Special Provisions) Act, 1991, and had reportedly been put to other uses in some of the intervening years, was diligently restored at my wife Salma's initiative and put to regular use till we were there. I

---

[10]S. Tanvirul Hasan, *Freedom and Partition and the Seasons Changed: Life and Times of Sir S. Sultan Ahmad* (New Delhi, 2007), p. 126.

have no idea of its present condition.

The next year and a half were spent in Yusufpur, where Haris and I were admitted to the local high school. Many of the classrooms had thatched roofs. I learnt to play hockey there and relished it. The larger family, with many uncles, aunts and cousins, added considerable diversity and fun to our daily life. Shikar trips along the Ganges, wedding feasts and many mango-eating competitions in the innumerable mango orchards of the family added to it. Decades later, when I visited Yusufpur as Vice President, the school (now a higher-secondary school) honoured me with a reception which was attended by one of the teachers of my time.

We returned to Simla by the middle of 1949 and Haris and I were admitted to St Edwards School, run by the Irish Christian Brothers. They were good and inspiring teachers and strict disciplinarians. I did well in studies and in sports and altogether enjoyed the period of two years spent there as a student of fifth and sixth standards. Sporting activities, principally hockey and cricket, were diligently indulged in. A few classmates of that period, Pramod Kapoor and Kailash Sood, still remain in touch. On a visit to Simla in 2010, I visited the school and revived many memories of those happy years. A family photograph taken by Asadur Rahman sahib, a college friend of my elder brother Khalid, is a reminder of that happy period.

Abba's term of office as Controller of Insurance ended in the summer of 1951 and he went back to his old job in Calcutta. He became the president of the Muslim Institute in 1952–53 and also represented the Muslim Chamber of Commerce in the West Bengal Assembly in 1951–55.[11]

The move to Calcutta posed a problem for my education since the school board in West Bengal required four years of a classical language (Sanskrit, Arabic or Persian) for matriculation. This ruled out admission in a school in Calcutta. As a solution, I was sent to

---

[11]West Bengal Legislative Assembly Proceedings, 17 September–2 November 1951, Volume 4, Alphabetical List of Members, Sl. No. 76.

Aligarh, where Ammi's first cousin, Dr Islamul Haq Ansari, was professor of pathology in the Tibbiya College of the university. His elder son Ziaul Haq and I were of the same age and I joined him as a Class IX and X student in the University High School, popularly known as the Minto Circle. Zia and I became close friends, and studied and played cricket together. Zia was an excellent batsman and went on to lead the Aligarh Muslim University (AMU) cricket team. Other friends of those years with whom contacts were retained in later years were Rashiduzzafar, Ziaul Hasan, Rifaqat Ali Khan, Anwar Ali Beg, Hakim Mahboob Alam, Khwaja Shamim and Habib Ahmad. Ehsan Haider was a good headmaster who, sometime later, left Aligarh to take up an assignment with the British Broadcasting Corporation (BBC) in London. The one teacher whose memory is very clear in my mind is Syed Mohammad Tonki. He was pious in his own way as well as an ardent nationalist and communist of an earlier vintage; a teacher who taught by example and was not overbearing. He introduced me to Christopher Caudwell's *Studies in a Dying Culture*, a book whose real worth I learnt to appreciate only later in life.

I obtained a first division in the high-school examination in 1952, said goodbye to Zia, his younger brother Ansar and their parents and rejoined the family in Calcutta. So, despite disruptions of place and quality, and of going to four schools which were different in their operating systems, my school education ended on a reasonably satisfactory note.

∽

Chapter 2

Cultivation of the Mind

After school, the momentous decision confronting me was that of choosing subjects to take up for study in college. My preference was geology and the college where it was on the curricula of studies was Presidency. This fancy was thwarted right at the beginning, because though I had a first division in high school, the cut-off percentage for geology was higher than what I had obtained. The next choice was St Xavier's with physics, chemistry and mathematics. It was on Park Street, not very far from the Park Circus area, where we stayed; an added benefit was its proximity to the Maidan and to the Mohammedan Sporting Club, where I could go for cricket practice. This arrangement was altogether congenial. My elder sister, Naseem, went to Lady Brabourne College in the Park Circus area and younger brother, Haris, to St James's School for Boys.

An unanticipated happening, troublesome at that time but eventually blissful, surfaced when halfway through the first year of college, my interest in the subjects I had opted for seemed to diminish. One tangible reason for it was that I had come across, and read with much interest, Harold J. Laski's *An Introduction to Politics*. The conviction took root in my mind that I had erred in choosing the Science stream! I discussed my predicament with my elder brother, Khalid, who was then in Calcutta University studying philosophy and also preparing for the Indian Administrative Service (IAS) examination. He pleaded my case, but that did not save me from a stern lecture or two on how not to waste parents' hard-earned monetary resources.

The switchover to Intermediate (Arts) was nevertheless allowed and I plunged into my new subjects with much enthusiasm. My particular fancy was for logic, civics, ancient history and economic geography, and in these, I scored handsomely. This induced Father Rector to concede that my decision to switch was a wise one. These new subjects, I must confess, became a lifelong passion. Formal logic was fun and helped train the mind. I took a fancy to ancient Greek and Roman history too and read a good deal on these subjects.

My time at St Xavier's was enjoyable, rewarding and well spent. The dedication of the Jesuit teachers was exemplary; their motivation emanated from impulses that I understood later in life. I played cricket for college. The student body was disinclined to be politically active; the joke was that a police station across the road from the college entrance was obviously misplaced!

Decades later, in January 2008, I went back to St Xavier's as the Vice President of India to deliver the first convocation address. The feeling of homecoming was difficult to articulate. I used the occasion to express my gratitude to the institution for initiating me to disciplines that became a lifelong passion. I referred to 'the national objective of building a knowledge society, an inclusive society, a humane society' and urged that 'the national effort directed at the educational pyramid' must respond to a qualitatively new situation, harmonize the objectives and develop synergies.

Calcutta of that period remains a very pleasant memory. Park Circus, Syed Amir Ali Avenue, Park Street, Esplanade, College Street, Chowringhee, Maidan, Victoria Memorial, Eden Garden, Dalhousie Square and many other locations still ring a bell. I started reading Marxist literature that was easily available. Looking back, I can testify to Nirad C. Chaudhuri's observation that 'there was nothing that a student in Calcutta was more fond of than attending meetings and listening to speeches'.[12] In March 1953, I attended a massive memorial meeting for Joseph Stalin in the Maidan at which one of the speakers, I recall, was the Gandhian, Pandit Sunderlal. The world, at that point, did not know enough about the other side of Stalin's record of governance.

Much to the joy of everyone in the family, Khalid cleared the IAS examination in 1954 and was allotted the Andhra Pradesh cadre. The following year, he got married to a cousin in Yusufpur. He remained unconventional in his service life, 'eccentric but relied upon to give sane advice' as one of his superiors put it.

I finished my Intermediate (Arts) examination in the summer of 1955. Abba's retirement from the insurance company was pending later that year and tough decisions had to be taken for the future, particularly about the further education of myself, Haris and my two younger sisters, Safia and Zakia. The roll of the dice indicated Aligarh, where I wanted to go to do an honours course in political science and have the guidance of the historian Prof. Mohammad Habib, who also headed what was for our universities a newer field of study in political science. His own preference was for history of political thought.

Later that year, the family moved to Aligarh, where we rented a modest house in Ammar Manzil on Marris Road. The local dignitary Kunwar Ammar Ahmad Khan's ancestors were Lalkhani Rajputs, who had embraced Islam. He was a genial person, very fond of dogs. Many years later, he became the Secretary of the AMU Old Boys' Association.

Dr Zakir Husain was the Vice Chancellor (VC) of AMU. One day, Abba's old friend from Calcutta, Prof. Zubair Siddiqi, came to deliver a lecture in the university and was the house guest of the VC. He called on Abba, who complained about Zakir sahib not having returned his call on him, a more senior person among Aligarhians. This apparently was conveyed by the guest to his host and the next

---

[12]Nirad C. Chaudhuri, *Autobiography of an Unknown Indian* (London, 1951), p. 366.

morning, without prior notice, Zakir sahib came to our house to express his regret over the lapse. Such was the etiquette amongst people of an earlier generation!

Abba had a few friends of his generation in Aligarh. These included former professor of Persian, Hamiduddin Khan sahib.

On the whole, however, Abba did not fancy living in Aligarh, and after three years, we decided to go back to our ancestral home in Yusufpur, where he established the Dr Mukhtar Ahmad Ansari School (now a co-ed, higher-secondary institution) and obtained an initial donation for it from PM Nehru. He spent time reading his collection of books and in taking peripheral but lively interest in local affairs. He even got arrested in one local agitation and was released when the UP Chief Minister (CM) Pandit Govind Ballabh Pant was told about his role in the Freedom Movement! Abba passed away on 10 June 1985 at the ripe age of 96. Almost till the very end, he would walk to the mosque just outside our house in Yusufpur. He remains an excellent example of a life based and spent on principles.

THE FORMATIVE YEARS

Rasheed Ahmad Siddiqi's account of the Aligarh of an earlier period, *Aashufta Bayani Meri,* remains a classic. Aligarh in my time had a student body of around 5,500 students and about two-thirds of these were in university halls of residence. The campus had sought to overcome with much success some vestiges of its own past.[13] There were iconic figures in the faculty; apart from Prof. Mohammad Habib, there were professors Shaikh Abdul Rasheed, Noorul Hasan and Khaliq Ahmad Nizami in history; Hadi Hasan in Persian; Maqbool Ahmad in Islamic studies; D.P. Mukerji in economics; Rasheed Ahmad

---

[13]Mushirul Hasan, 'Negotiating with its Past and Present: The Changing Profile of the Aligarh Muslim University,' pp. 136–56 in Mushirul Hasan (ed.) *Inventing Boundaries: Gender, Politics and the Partition of India* (New Delhi, 2000). This essay depicts in graphic details the ease with which segments of the university community were misled by organized, emotive and political propaganda.

Siddiq and Aal-e-Ahmad Suroor in Urdu; Mohammad Baber Mirza in zoology; Tahir Rizvi in geography; and Abrar Mustafa Khan in botany. It was intellectually vibrant; some of the political inclinations, particularly of the Left, were fully reflected among the teachers and students; perhaps a larger segment was unconcerned, while some subscribed to conservative viewpoints including the Jamaat-e-Islami. The contestations were strident yet civilized and the students' union was active. The traditions of the institution were fully respected. A delightful book by Dr Athar Parvez, *Aligarh Se Aligarh Tak,* captured the ambiance of the early and mid-'50s and the centrality of the university's Shamshad market. He makes the point that an Aligarh person, no matter how modern, is also a traditionalist. He recalled the legends and superstitions relating to an innocent functionary in the office of the Duty Society by the name of 'Moed Khan', who was known for his unfailing memory but the sight of whom was considered inauspicious in the season of examinations! Most of the students did not see the evident malice in such typecasting.

The three-year honours course in political science was comprehensive and two areas of study—history of western political thought and contemporary West Asia—ignited interests that became lifelong pursuits. Plato, Aristotle, Marsilius of Padua, Thomas Hobbes, Machiavelli, John Locke, Rousseau, T.H. Green, Karl Marx and Harold Laski were read, re-read and imbibed. Laski's *A Grammar of Politics* and George Sabine's *A History of Political Theory* did become for me biblical texts for many years and still retain their relevance. Prof. Habib considered the core of political philosophy to lie in Plato, Aristotle, Hobbes, Rousseau, Marx, T.H. Green and Mao Tse Tung and most of the lectures were devoted to them. He was perhaps the first teacher in the country to add Chairman Mao's thought to the political science curriculum. The papers I opted for did not cover Ancient Indian and Islamic political thought; these were discovered and explored later in life and with much benefit.

Prof. Habib was a historian of eminence with a focus on the history of the Delhi Sultanate. His writings shed much light on the theory of kingship in that period. 'Muslim political consciousness did not recognize any king as sovereign *de jure*... So long as a Muslim king was sovereign *de facto,* he was hedged by a sort of pseudo-divinity and people prostrated themselves before him. But when his power vanished, his divinity also vanished.'[14] His tutor at Oxford was Sir Ernest Barker and he bore the imprint of the latter's liberal ideas. He had close personal relations with his generation of leaders of the Freedom Movement. In 1952, he led a goodwill delegation to the People's Republic of China (PRC) and was fulsome in his admiration for the achievements of the Chinese revolution. When I was leaving the university after completing my studies, he gave me a character certificate that was embarrassingly generous. In 1967, he contested the office of the Vice President of India as a candidate of the combined opposition, 'partly because he was critical of government policies, and partly because, as he cheerfully told press correspondents, he was going to lose'.

I was the only student in the honours course to opt for the paper on West Asia, which was taught by Dr Hashim Kidwai. The classes were, therefore, in the nature of tutorials, mostly taken in the garden outside the Aasman Manzil block and were thoroughly enjoyable. This background in the region's history and politics was of immense benefit to me later as a diplomat in the region. Dipping into the rich collection of books in the Lytton Library (before it shifted to its new building to become the Maulana Azad Library) was always rewarding.

Two important foreign dignitaries came to the university with much fanfare. The first was King Saud bin Abdulaziz Al Saud of Saudi Arabia and the second was Reza Shah Pahlavi, Shahanshah Aryamehr, the Shah of Iran. Both visits were reflective of the centrality attached to the AMU by the GoI.

I spent almost five years in AMU, in different capacities (and

---

[14]Decades later, I came across Mohammed Arkoun's epigram in relation to the historical and doctrinal situation of Islam: 'Islam is theologically Protestant and politically Catholic.' (M. Arkoun, *Islam: To Reform or To Subvert?* Saqi Books, p. 379.)

not counting the period in Minto Circle in 1951–52 and by virtue of which my enrolment number, D-14, makes me a very senior alumnus in the AMU Old Boys' fraternity). This also saved me from the ritual of having to undergo the 'introduction' ceremony in the hostel—pleasant and good fun at most times, but could be nasty at others! For a good part of this time, I was in 74, Aftab Hostel, the only one in the university then with single-seater rooms. Haris was in the same hostel studying geology and so was Yedullah Kazmi, a newcomer who attracted the attention of seniors for his seemingly insatiable appetite. The food in the dining hall was passable, with biryani served on Fridays; those with more resources joined the foreign students' mess. My pocket money every month was ₹30; it sufficed for occasional tea in the famous Cafe de Phoos and for a newspaper. In the family storeroom in Yusufpur, I discovered, and used, a Primus stove that had been used by Abba in his time in Aligarh!

These were the formative years in every sense. My circles were academic and sports oriented, occasionally social and generally low key. I did not have the honour of being mentioned in the New Year *namak-daan* (salt cellar), drawn up in the dead of night at year end by a group of senior-most socially active students to mention in pithy Urdu couplets those of their peers of both sexes who made the grade of being 'notorious' in various fields! My group of friends included Desh Raj Singh and Shahid Mehdi, both of whom were in history and joined the IAS; Nejatullah Siddiqi, who went on to earn a name in Islamic economics; Hisamuddin Farooqi of the zoology department; Ayub Syed, who moved from West Asian studies to journalism and edited the Bombay weekly *Current*; hockey captain Asjad Husain Khan; Students' Union President Abidullah Ghazi, who continues to devote himself to good causes based in Chicago; Rafaqat Ali Khan, who later taught history in Jamia Millia; Riding Club Captain Habib Ahmad; Zamiruddin and his brother Sharfuddin Alvi; Islam Ahmad, who spent many years in the Board of Control for Cricket in India (BCCI) and is now in Chicago, and many others.

Many decades later, Abidullah Ghazi depicted the mood of the times in an evocative poem recited in an Old Boys' gathering in Washington.

Khayalaat-e-pur-shauq ka silsila tha
Badal dain zamane ko woh hosla tha
Har ek dil main paida naya walwala tha
Hare ek gaam ahbaab ka qafila tha
Idhar duwa karna udhar kar dikhana
Bahot yaad aata hai guzra zamana

(The memory of past days is compelling. They bore in every mind a string of vibrant thoughts, new fervour in every heart, to stake a claim and implement it to change the world.)

The University Tarana, penned by the poet Israrul Haq Majaz in 1936, was sung with gusto (as it is to this day in all parts of the world where Aligarhians gather). The cultural life was rich but participation in youth festivals, and participation of girls in the university's contingent, unavoidably became a source of contention between the traditionalists and the modernizers. Despite it, AMU participants made their mark. They did likewise in inter-university debating competitions. In sports, Aligarh excelled in hockey and to a lesser extent in other sports. Niazul Latif of Hyderabad shone in inter-university tennis. I played in inter-hall cricket matches and generally kept wickets. In one match, I was fielding at short leg and a loose delivery allowed the batsman to pull the ball which hit me on my nose and landed me in the university hospital for a few days. I must have been a sight, judging from the number of visitors who came to see me and sympathize! I took to cricket umpiring seriously in inter-hall and inter-university matches. A good deal of my time was, therefore, spent at the university cricket ground, in the Willingdon Cricket Pavilion and in 13, SS East, the earmarked room for the university cricket captain. I helped organize a farewell match for an eminent cricketer and Old Boy Syed Mushtaq Ali and wrote a brochure for the occasion. A team from Roshanara Club, Delhi, was invited. A star attraction of the match was Mansoor Ali Khan, the Nawab of Pataudi. I stood as umpire in the match and earned some notoriety for giving him the benefit of the doubt in an LBW (leg before wicket) appeal on the first ball he faced! We raised a princely sum of ₹10,000 and presented it to Mushtaq Ali sahib.

I was attracted for a while to a girl a year senior to me in political science and, not getting much of a chance to talk to her, wrote a letter citing a sentence in Aristotle's essay on friendship: 'wishing to be friends is quick work but friendship is a slow ripening fruit'. It elicited no response and my fancy seemed to vanish quickly!

The examination result gave me a first-class first in honours; this carried with it the award of the Sir William Marris medal. Thereafter, the one-year MA course in political science was smooth sailing and there, too, a First came my way.

I then had to decide on what to do next. My preference was a career in academia. I had done some reading on the Pluralistic Theory of the State first suggested by Otto von Gierke and in pursuit of it, enrolled as a PhD candidate to work on Laski's theory of sovereignty and on his remark in *An Introduction to Politics* that 'we cannot leave the hinterland between states unorganized; and as soon as we envisage its organization, it is obvious that the sovereignty of the state means anarchy'.[15] I obtained a university scholarship and applied for a University Grants Commission (UGC) Fellowship (that was awarded but not taken since by then I was preparing for the UPSC [Union Public Service Commission] examination). As part of the conditions for the university fellowship, I was asked to take undergraduate classes in political science in the university's Women's College for a few weeks. While there, I had my first encounter with Yadullah's sister, Salma Kazmi. She was the president of the college union—assertive and very much the mistress in her own turf. I had no idea then that she would resurface later in my life!

---

[15]P. 102.

Naseem apa got married to a cousin, Iqbal Farooqi, who was in the first batch of geologists selected for the Oil and Natural Gas Corporation (ONGC). Haris continued his master's course in geology and after leaving Aligarh took an emergency recruitment commission in the Indian army. He however did not fancy it much, so left it midway and became an insurance man where he made a name for himself and eventually became a member of the Insurance Regulatory and Development Authority (IRDA). Safia and Zakia, after the family's move to Yusufpur, continued their studies as private students and completed their bachelor's courses. Safia married Moinuddin, a geologist also with the ONGC and Zakia got married to Hasan Kidwai, a banker. Hasan died in 1982 and Zakia, with great determination and courage, remade her life and is now a Trustee of the Krishnamurti Foundation's Rajghat Besant School in Varanasi.

My preference for a life in academia was not shared by Abba, who thought otherwise and suggested the civil services. Sensing reluctance on my part, he wrote to Prof. Habib, who lectured me on the virtues of being an obedient son and doing no more than taking another examination! And so it came about; the examination was taken half-heartedly and when the results were declared, I found my name way down in the list of the selected candidates. A letter of appointment to the IAS arrived in due course with instructions to proceed to the National Academy of Administration (later renamed Lal Bahadur Shastri National Academy of Administration) in Mussoorie and duly report on 1 June 1961. A few days prior to it, I was in Khalid's office in the Ministry of Agriculture in Shastri Bhawan when the then deputy secretary (appointments) in the home ministry, Bishan Tandon, called him and enquired if I would opt for the Foreign Service, since someone higher up in the list had preferred IAS instead. This incidental happening decided the course of my life for the next 37 years!

Chapter 3

In Harness

At least we'll die with a harness at our back.

FOREIGN SERVICE: THE EARLY YEARS

I arrived at the National Academy of Administration and settled down to the drill early and easily. The Indian Foreign Service (IFS) contingent consisted of nine others: Bhupat Oza, Madhav Mangalmurti, Krishan Mohan Lal, Gajendra Singh, Prakash Shah, J.N. Doddamani, J.N. Puri, Vinod Grover and Kamal Bakshi. We became friends and these became lifelong friendships. There were many others in the IAS and other central services. Early rapport was forthcoming with Kamal Bakshi, Gajendra Singh, Moni Malhotra, Sitakant Mahapatra, K.S. Bains, Narendra Naik, J.P. Singh, R.U. Singh, T.S.R. Subramanian, Sardar Joginder Singh, Arun Bhagat, S.N. Mathur, Vineet Nayyar and many others. We were a happy bunch of 270, freshly out of university life but not quite *au fait* with being officers of the government. We were inclined to be frivolous at times and altogether enjoyed the surroundings of Charleville. The directing team was headed by Dr A.N. Jha, Indian Civil Service (ICS). He was assisted by R.K. Trivedi and Brig. Mohammad Sheriff as deputy directors. The latter, in the best traditions of the Royal Military

Academy, Sandhurst, was a disciplinarian and ensured attendance in the early morning physical training and riding classes.

An interesting instance of rules and their inbuilt limitations surfaced when one of our somewhat pedantic lecturers noticed absentees and decided to report it. The director, a senior member of the ICS fraternity, considered sending the absentees on a day's 'extraordinary leave' only to be told by the accountant that the procedures involved were such that the trainees concerned would not be paid for many weeks, and, in turn, they would not be able to clear their mess bills, resulting in the mess itself becoming non-functional. Confronted with this impasse, the contemplated action was converted into a reprimand and a modest fine, whose proceeds were to be sent to the PM's Relief Fund.

The Foundation Course for the IFS probationers was for three months. This included an attachment of about a week to an army unit. A few others and I were sent to the 16 Dogra regiment, then on duty outside Baramulla in Jammu and Kashmir (J&K). An accidental mention in the Officer's Mess of Brigadier Mohammad Usman, MVC, who I discovered was one of the regiment's war heroes, evoked admiration. It resulted in the rare honour of being invited to the Junior Commissioned Officer's Club. Decades later, as Vice President, I was invited to unveil a memorial in his honour at Jangar in Jammu. On arrival, I was presented a bouquet by two youngsters, aged 9 and 11. After the function and at the helipad, the same youngsters were there. The elder, a boy, responded to a question by saying that 'we are from a very poor family; please help us with our education'. Our son Sulaiman, who was with me, said, 'This is the best one-liner I have heard in business.' I turned to the senior general present on the occasion and he generously offered to take them in the nearest Sainik School. For many years after that, I got regular annual reports about their progress.

Next came the district training intended to familiarize new entrants to the way India was governed. K.M. Lal and I were assigned to Andhra Pradesh. I spent most of those three months in Warangal.

My first exposure to Andhra cuisine was somewhat disconcerting and forced me to resort to a diet of eggs in various forms resulting in my penning an Urdu poem in praise of eggs! The district collector was an elderly Hyderabadi gentleman, Mohsin Bin Shabbir, who was impeccably correct and generous and had no objection to my spending most of my time with the Superintendent of Police (SP) Sushil Kumar, a younger officer holding his first charge as SP. He went on to become Joint Director of the Intelligence Bureau (IB) and Director General (DG) and Inspector General of Police (IGP), Andhra Pradesh.

My district attachment period coincided with the general elections of 1962 and there was high tension in Warangal because the contending candidates, a sitting minister belonging to the Congress and his opponent belonging to the Communist Party of India (CPI), were from the same family. On polling day, the Deputy Inspector General (DIG) of police himself was camping in the constituency and asked Sushil Kumar if he had called on the minister. The answer was a firm no because the minister was there as a candidate. The senior person did not take kindly to the response but swallowed it! One wonders if this rectitude is the norm today in the civil services.

While in Hyderabad, I made the acquaintance of a distant cousin who had done her master's in political science from the University of Delhi. A common friend suggested a more serious interest; we corresponded for some time, but the 'interest' went no further.

District training over, and after a couple of weeks in the state secretariat in Hyderabad, where the then chief minister mistook the designation IFS to mean Indian Forest Service, the two probationers—Lal and I—were back in Delhi for desk attachment in the Ministry of External Affairs (MEA) and to be trained in a somewhat haphazard process about the dos and dont's of the path ahead.

I was given Arabic as my compulsory language and posted as Third Secretary in a yet-to-be opened mission in Algiers, Algeria. A misunderstanding about the timing of our formal recognition of the new Algerian government (despite our principled and long-standing support to the Algerian national movement) resulted in a considerable delay in the agrément being given to our ambassador-designate; this resulted in a delay in my departure for Algiers. I finally set eyes on the capital city, in a very different capacity, more than half a century later, in 2016, and laid a wreath at the tomb of Ahmed Ben Bella, the first president of Algeria.

After a couple of months or so, the joint secretary responsible for Personnel and Postings got irritated at my regular tap on his office door and said: 'Stop pestering me; you can go anywhere you like, even Baghdad.' This turned out to be another 'happy accident' for reasons that will become evident as this narrative proceeds!

BAGHDAD

I flew to Baghdad via Tehran in the last week of December 1962. On arrival there, I was taken to the Semiramis Hotel located on the banks of the river Tigris. As a language trainee and the youngest member of the mission's team of diplomats, I was told that accommodation for earlier probationers (Peter Sinai and Akbar Khaleeli of the 1957 and 1959 batches of the IFS, respectively) had been surrendered and that a new place would be rented in due course. Sadat Ali Khan, a former Member of Parliament (MP) and parliamentary secretary to PM Nehru, was the ambassador to Baghdad. He and Begum Sakeena Khan represented the best in the old culture of Hyderabad. The first secretaries were Jagdish Ajmani, a senior member of the IFS, and Yogeshwar Sahni from the Cabinet Secretariat. Both became lifelong friends. Yogeshwar, in particular, treated me like a younger brother. He was affectionate but a hard taskmaster; I learnt much of the niceties of diplomatic work under his tutelage.

An unusual happening was experienced early by this student of political theory, who tended to explain in a bold and graphic manner the meaning of Prof. Laski's observation that 'revolutions are footnotes to the problem of sovereignty'. 8 February 1963 was a Friday and the previous evening, a young German engineer staying in the hotel and whom I had befriended, offered to take me for a drive outside the city, an offer I had readily accepted. Accordingly, early the next day, we left the hotel in his Volkswagen and drove to the southern end of the city in the direction of the Al Rasheed cantonment. We noticed a good deal of military activity there and my friend suggested that we take refuge in a nearby beer factory, whose manager was a German. On arrival there, we were warmly greeted, offered refuge, informed that a military coup was in progress and that beer in abundance was available but not food! We spent a day there before road conditions allowed us to return safely to the city.

Iraq had a previous experience of a coup d'état. The one on 8 February put an end to the government of Brigadier General Abd al-Karim Qasim, who had on 14 July 1958, dethroned the post-World War I, British-crafted Hashemite dynasty and proclaimed that the 'Iraqi people consist of brotherly nationalities [that] have amalgamated in order to defend the Republic', that strength lies in unity, that 'the army and the people have merged into a single entity' and that 'we cooperate with our brotherly Arab states on the basis of the individual interests of those Arab states'. It was also, as a historian was to write later, 'a watershed in the Cold War in the Middle East. ...Within weeks, (it) had gone from being a US ally central to its security architecture to joining its opponents, Nasser and the Soviets.'[16] Land and social reforms were enunciated, polygamy was outlawed and far-reaching steps were initiated on women's rights and much greater emphasis given to education. Relations with India improved meaningfully with Indian assistance being sought in planning and in the training of the Iraqi air force.

Qasim's four-and-a-half years in power were to show a sharpening of disagreements with the Kurdish leader Mulla Mustafa Barzani over Kurdish autonomy, resulting in a resumption of the military operations against the Kurds in the north, in dissent within the army over the union with Nasser's Egypt, and in internal suppression

---

[16]Odd Arne Westad, *The Cold War: A World History* (New York, 2017) pp. 455–56.

of dissent. Iraq's dissociation from the Baghdad Pact led to a deterioration of relations with Western powers, as also with Iran on regional differences. All these were aggravated by the nationalization of the oil industry and the resultant dispute with the formidable Iraq Petroleum Company (IPC). The misadventure of reigniting Iraq's claims on Kuwait added to these. Domestic, regional and global problems thus resulted in the regime's problems and isolation and set the stage for its overthrow by the Ba'ath Party. The role of the United States (US) in the turn of events was widely suspected then and has subsequently been confirmed by credible American sources.[17]

My work as a probationer was cut out so that I could study Arabic and learn the functioning of the different wings of the embassy. A tutor for Arabic, Shakir Al-Hitti, who worked in the Ministry of Planning, was engaged. I made progress but was also confronted by his occasional absence, allegedly on account of his Communist leanings and the resultant problems with the intelligence agencies! Training in the consular wing, which rendered consular service to many stations in the Persian Gulf still as British protectorates, included writing a few dozen passport booklets (to understand how the work is actually done). A more interesting aspect of work related to the quarterly disbursement of Oudh Bequest pensions in Najaf and Karbala. This related to the loan taken by the British East India Company from the King of Oudh (Awadh), which was converted after 1857 into a payment of interest thereon to the king's descendants, most of whom had migrated for reasons of piety to these places of pilgrimage. Government records that I came across many years later indicated that after Independence, legal opinion suggested that the successor government had no legal obligation to continue these

---

[17] Eric Jacobsen, 'A Coincidence of Interests: Kennedy, U.S. Assistance and the 1963 Iraqi Ba'ath Regime,' *Diplomatic History*, Vol. 37, Issue 5, 1 November 2013, pp. 1029–59: 'US policy makers provided the Ba'ath regime with military and economic assistance, including sale of military equipment...' Also, Bryan R. Gibson's article, 'The Secret Origins of the U.S.-Kurdish Relationship Explain Today's Disaster,' available at https://foreignpolicy.com/2019/10/14/us-kurdish-relationship-history-syria-turkey-betrayal-kissinger/.

pension payments. However, PM Nehru's decision in the matter was cryptic: 'Legal no, moral yes'.

Another interesting aspect of consular work was the quarterly tour to Bahrain to service the requirement of the largish and reasonably prosperous Indian community there. Its leading figure was Atma Jashanmal, whose ancestors, competent traders, had migrated to Basra during World War I and then gradually extended their business to Kuwait and Bahrain (and later to other Arab sheikhdoms of the Persian Gulf).

The most substantive part of my work, and to my liking, was the drafting of political reports. In the process, I was able to update my reading on the politics of Iraq and the Arab national movements. An excellent initiation to the latter was at hand in George Antonius's classic work, *The Arab Awakening*, which I had acquired a couple of years earlier and Stephen Longrigg's *Four Centuries of Modern Iraq*. Notwithstanding my meagre salary as a third secretary in those pre-Finance Commission days, I also managed to acquire a few books to sustain my readings in political philosophy as also three volumes of Leon Trotsky's *The History of the Russian Revolution* and Isaac Deutscher's trilogy on Trotsky; they remain precious possessions.

The coup of 8 February 1963, which brought the Ba'ath Party, led by Abdul Salam Arif, to power also highlighted internal dissent and power struggles. These had deeper roots in inter-Arab politics of pro-Nasser and pro-Syrian Ba'ath elements. 18 November 1964 thus saw another resort to force in which the pro-Nasser faction, led by Iraqi president Ahmad Hasan al-Bakr and assisted by the Iraqi National Guard, prevailed. Much of the scene of action, including bombardment by the air force, was in a building in the al-Aadhamiya district adjacent to our ambassador's residence and chancery. My own house was not very far from there. First Secretary K.R. Krishnaswamy telephoned me and suggested that I walk the distance of about a kilometre and ascertain position. This I did. I was glared at on my way by a tank commander. Once I reached the residence, I was greeted like a long-lost friend and treated to a sumptuous dinner.

The ambassador candidly narrated that when the first shots were fired in the morning, a bullet went through the bedroom window whereupon he took to the precaution of proceeding to the basement with a bottle of cognac to keep him company.

The antipathy in official circles to vestiges of the British period became evident when I initiated (along with three other junior diplomats, two British and one Sri Lankan) an effort to arrange a cricket match, something that had not been undertaken in Baghdad since the 1958 Revolution. Permission to use a soccer ground, initiated by the British mission, was declined; a reiteration of the request by an Indian third secretary brought better results. One of the British colleagues, Richard Long, has mentioned this cricketing venture in his book *Bygone Heat: Travels of an Idealist in the Middle East* (London, 2001).

I recollect meeting an interesting visitor to the embassy. He and a few others from the Kurdish area of Iraq came to deliver a letter addressed to PM Nehru, in which they sought his help, as they put it, in the Kurdish people of Iraq being given their rights. Given the sensitivity of the matter in the context of our excellent relations with the Government of Iraq, it was decided that the junior-most official should give them a pro forma meeting and receive their communication. I did, as directed. The leader of the delegation was Jalal Talabani, who gave me a booklet *Kurdistan: Divided Nation of the Middle East* by S.S. Gavan, which was published in London in 1958. It had a Marxist orientation and urged the unification of all regions inhabited by the Kurds. I still have this publication personally signed by him. He went on to become the president of Iraq for two terms, from 2005 to 2014.

Baghdad had a few Indian families, principally United Nations (UN) experts on deputation to the Iraqi government departments. Their doyen was Dr Asadullah Kazmi, father of Yedullah Kazmi, my hostel mate from Aligarh, who headed the United Nations Educational, Scientific and Cultural Organization's (UNESCO) mission to Iraq. He was highly respected in local and Indian community circles and his residence was often the venue for multinational gatherings. It was there that a few months later I once again met his youngest daughter, Salma, who had returned from Aligarh and was teaching in a women's college of Baghdad University. She was also her father's official hostess. Her charm and social graces were much in evidence, as was her youthful confidence in being cigarette-smoking and sherry-sipping in fairly conservative surroundings. I was bewitched and the fancy soon became an obsession that could only be expressed inadequately given my own diffidence. She, on her part, seemed disinterested. Weeks and months followed, alternating between agony and ecstasy. Gradually, the light became steadier and added much meaning to my life. With my time in Baghdad being limited to the schedule of language examinations in the summer of 1964, I picked up enough courage one morning to go to Dr Kazmi's office to ask for Salma's hand in marriage and was subjected to searching questions about what can only be described as 'pedigree of horses'! When I mentioned this to my ambassador, he exclaimed 'excellent alliance'. Intimation of this to my own parents was more difficult and led to what my elder brother Khalid later described as 'storm in a tea cup'.

I went ahead nevertheless and our wedding was scheduled for 25 August 1964. It was an event in the social calendar of all those associated with the Indian embassy in Baghdad and the Kazmi family. My most prized wedding gift is a portrait of Salma in charcoal done by a friend of hers, Cynthia Stewart, spouse of the then general manager of the all-powerful IPC. It remains on the wall in my study.

After the wedding, we were instructed by the elders to visit the shrine of Sheikh Abdul Qadir Jilani in central Baghdad. We decided to spend our honeymoon in the Kurdish areas of northern Iraq, where there was an interregnum in fighting. Getting permission was a problem; a friend in the Iraqi foreign office promised to help and did produce a permit allowing us to travel to Kirkuk, Erbil and beyond, up to the summer resort of Salahuddin. We travelled by train to Kirkuk and noticed the remarkable similarity between the railway infrastructure of Iraq and that of our own country. I later discovered that much of Iraq's railways system was built by Indian railway engineers. From Kirkuk, we hired a car to take us to the hotel in Salahuddin. This proved to be eventful as, on the outskirts of Erbil, the National Guard checkpoint declined to accept our foreign office travel permit and detained us for a few hours in one of their offices. Mercifully, a senior man happened to surface and let us off after an admonition. Few newly married couples on honeymoon could have had a more disconcerting experience. This notwithstanding, our stay in Salahuddin was blissful; it included a visit to the picturesque gorge, Gali Ali Beg. We returned to Baghdad after a week. There was much curiosity in the diplomatic community about permission given to an Indian diplomat; an elderly Soviet colleague remonstrated about it to the Chief of protocol, only to be told that he too could go for the same purpose.

The next two months or so spent in Baghdad were busy. I cleared the departmental exams in Accounts on the third attempt. In Arabic, it was smooth going. There was much socializing and work to be done for the next station of posting, Rabat in Morocco, after a spell of leave-cum-training in India.

The charms of Baghdad were many, replete with history at every turn. Frequent weekend trips to the ruins of Babylon near Al Hillah and Ctesiphon in the vicinity of Baghdad gave some glimpses; much of the glorious past, however, remained unvisited. The centrality of the river Tigris was and remains legendary. Travellers such as Ibn Jubayr in 1184 and Ibn Battuta around the year 1333 sang praises of it; they and others also dwelt on its misfortunes through history. The neighbourhood of Baghdad testifies to its pre-Islamic glory at Ctesiphon. Above all, the ruins of Babylon and of innumerable other historic sites in different parts provided opportunities for excursions. So did destinations for pilgrimage such as Najaf, Karbala and Samarra.

For personal and professional reasons, Baghdad remains a very pleasant memory. Gregariousness and generosity characterize the Iraqi character as does a deep-rooted duality, which the Iraqi scholar

Ali Al-Wardi calls *izdiwaj* (split personality) of a value system of a sedentary population on the one hand and the nomadic Bedouin.[18] Inheritors of a great past, the people of Iraq have suffered grievously because of the misfortune bestowed on them in our times by their own rulers and by the outside world. Founded as Madinat al-Salamor or City of Peace, Baghdad has rarely known peace, and the ninth-century poet Abu Tammam's depiction of 'death's loud herald over the city' has come true again and again.

Despite its demographic profile in ethnic and sectarian terms,[19] and apart from the Kurdish insurgency in the north, Iraq in that period was a society more or less at peace with itself and did not exhibit the horrendous social tensions and conflicts that became so prominent a few decades later.

The journey from Basra to Bombay (now Mumbai) was enjoyable and every morning, the ship would halt in a port in the principalities of the Persian Gulf, the peace of whose waters was maintained by the British for seven decades in terms of Lord Curzon's proclamation of 1903 at Sharjah. Muscat was still in its traditional practices, where the failure to carry a lantern after sunset identified an individual as a mischief-maker or a thief.

The training spell in Delhi gave us the opportunity to visit our family in Yusufpur. It was an event, a novelty, an experience, for the bride and for the in-laws. Salma adapted smoothly to the new surroundings and survived the test pretty well, including a spell in the kitchen to demonstrate the skill or absence thereof of making chapatis under the watchful eyes of the family cook.

---

[18]Raphael Patai, *The Arab Mind* (New York, 1986) pp. 201–02. There are said to be about 150 tribes, and the tribal sheikhs exercise much authority in the settlement of local disputes.

[19]In ethnic terms, 70 per cent Arabs, 15 per cent Kurds, 10 per cent Turkomans and 5 per cent others. In sectarian terms, 60 per cent Shias, 31 per cent Sunnis, 2–5 per cent Christians and about 2 per cent Yazidi and others. According to Yitzhak Nakash (*The Shi'is of Iraq*, pp. 25–28), most of the conversions to Shi'ism took place in the nineteenth century.

RABAT

After the home leave, we resumed our travel to take up my assignment in Rabat, as third, and later, second secretary (commercial). It commenced on a worrying note with Salma landing up in hospital for an appendicitis operation.

Ambassador Y.K. Puri, a senior member of the ICS, was a stern but considerate head of mission, who insisted that officers' meeting be conducted in French; as a result, I had to learn the basics of the language. Other colleagues included Syam Sunder Nath, a senior and somewhat eccentric member of the IFS, Shiv Kumar, D.R. Kwatra and Pyare Lal Santoshi. Anxious to get a formal confirmation in the service, I made haste to clear the second part of the Arabic language examination in a few weeks. The Moroccan and western Arabic dialect are very different from the Iraqi and the eastern one, so much so that the US State Department runs separate language schools for them.

Once settled down in the new surroundings, we travelled a good bit in our newly acquired Volkswagen Beetle to many parts of northern and eastern Morocco, where history, culture and good cuisine make it a visitor's paradise. Casablanca, Fez and Meknes were frequently visited by us and so was Tangiers on the way to Gibraltar. Visits to Marrakesh were planned several times, but did not materialize; we finally visited that city half a century later as Vice President.

My regular beat was to Casablanca, the country's commercial capital. My work as commercial secretary of the mission did not make much headway since there was, at that time, an embargo on imports from India, except for raw silk from Mysore for the king of Morocco's ceremonial robes.

Morocco's long history and its liberation from over four decades of being a French protectorate was a subject of interest to me. Historians explain it in terms of African, European and West Asian influences; an 'object' of history as historian and novelist Abdallah

Laroui put it, than its own indigenous influences. The Arab and Islamic impact helped forge a specific Maghrebi identity. This process was accelerated with the establishment of regional centres of learning across North Africa; in Morocco, it was at Fez, a city of sanctity, learning and commerce. The period of the French protectorate left an impact of 'psychic dualism' on the minds of the elite, as it did in other colonial destinations. I acquired early a copy of Allal al-Fassi's classic[20] on the subject and learnt more from a young journalist friend who was a member of the Istiqlal Party. I also educated myself somewhat on the role of the Berbers in the history of the Maghreb. Salma and I also met and became good friends with an Iraqi scholar in the university, Dr Mohammad Mishat, and his very pleasant German wife. He was a Ba'athist, but did not belong to the faction then out of power. He returned to Iraq when Saddam Hussein came to power. Successively, he became the VC of a university, education minister, ambassador to France and then to the US. He was in Washington at the time of the 1990–91 Kuwait War. He was asked to return, travelled to Vienna en route home and then disappeared into thin air. It was rumoured that the US intelligence had given him a new identity and a new home.[21]

Another friend in Rabat was Sulaiman Dajani, counsellor in the Jordanian mission. He had served earlier as private secretary to King Hussein of Jordan. He and his wife, Huzaimah, became our close friends and this affiliation of the two families continues to this day. Huzaimah and Sulaiman were a source of great strength to us when our first child, Sulaiman, was born on 17 February 1966. In fact, the evening Salma had to move to the clinic, I was hosting a few friends

---

[20] *The Freedom Movements in North Africa.*

[21] Perhaps this was another manifestation of the inroads that Western intelligence agencies had made in the Ba'ath Party. Many years later, a declassified British dispatch of 20 December 1969 from the embassy in Baghdad gave a graphic account of the ambassador's first meeting with Saddam Hussein: 'I should judge him, young as he is, to be a formidable, single-minded and hard-headed member of the Ba'ath hierarchy but one with whom, if one could see more of him, it would be possible to do business.'

for dinner and it was Sulaiman who drove her to the clinic. Half a century later, in June 2016, when we were on an official visit to Rabat and thanks to the gracious spouse of the then Moroccan PM, Salma was able to locate and visit the clinic where our child was born.

Our stint in Rabat, brief but immensely enjoyable, was cut short with orders from the headquarters to move to the mission in Jeddah to replace Syed Shahabuddin as head of chancery. Given a mix of Saudi and Indian perceptions and the requirements of work relating to the Hajj pilgrimage, Ambassador Puri's efforts to defer the transfer made no headway when the standard phraseology 'exigencies of service' was invoked. So we left Rabat in April with a two-month-old baby, unimaginable today. We travelled by air to Marseille and then by a very comfortable Messageries Maritimes ship to Bombay. It was an enjoyable journey and we divided our time between looking after the baby and having fun. The cuisine was superb and so was the French wine with the waiters replacing a bottle as soon as it was half empty.

JEDDAH

After a period of home leave divided between Yusufpur and Allahabad, I proceeded to Jeddah. The prescribed route was by sea from Bombay and so in early July, I boarded a Mogul Line passenger-cum-cargo ship at the peak of the monsoon season. The first few days of the journey were distinctly uncomfortable on account of the high seas. It calmed down nearer Aden, still a British colony, where the state of emergency was very much in evidence. Then we travelled across the Red Sea to Port Sudan before a horizontal crossing to the port city of Jidda, said to have been sanctified by the third Caliph Uthman as the access point for overseas pilgrims to Makkah.[22]

A posting to Jeddah at that time was considered something of a punishment, for being 'a Muslim officer' in the IFS. However,

---

[22]F.E. Peters, *Mecca: A Literary History of the Muslim Holy Land* (Princeton, 1994) pp. 108–10.

having acquired a copy of Sir Richard Burton's *Personal Narrative of a Pilgrimage to Al-Madina and Meccah* and read St John Philby's *Forty Years in the Wilderness* and *the Empty Quarter*, I was sufficiently 'indoctrinated' about life and work in Saudi Arabia and looked forward to it.

Jeddah then was a modest-sized city devoid of many civic facilities, particularly piped water that had to be obtained through water tankers or donkey-drawn carts mounted with a barrel of water. It was then, as now, the commercial nerve centre of the country. It was also the seat of the foreign office, the principal port and the point of entry and exit for most of the Hajj and Umrah pilgrims from all over the world. Our mission was a small one and I was assigned all work other than commercial, which was looked after by the only other diplomat. It was a learning experience in every sense.

In 1966, the Kingdom of Saudi Arabia had recovered from the domestic political turmoil in the Saudi royal family and the acute financial crisis that preceded and accompanied it. King Faisal resisted the pressures from within the royal family for modest institutional reforms (including the suggestions for a type of constitutional monarchy made by his half-brother Talal bin Abdulaziz in his *Risala Ila al-Muwatineen* [Message to the Citizens]) but did bring about administrative correctives and financial discipline. On the external front, the revolution in Yemen was viewed as an existential crisis aggravated by pressure from Nasser's Egypt and the Egyptian military involvement on the side of the Yemeni republicans.[23] It was to ward off and counter the pressure of Arab nationalism that the seeds of an Islamic alliance were sown through the King Faisal–Shah of Iran statement of 1965. A semi-official dimension to the use of

---

[23] Saeed M. Badeeb, *The Saudi-Egyptian Conflict over North Yemen 1962–1970* (Washington, 1986):

> Saudi Arabia views Yemen from three different perspectives: the political, security and strategic standpoints... Saudi Arabia also watches the regional foreign policies of North Yemen with interest because of their effect on the Arabian Peninsula and the Gulf (and) believes that its internal security can be seriously affected by events elsewhere in the Middle East. (pp. 96–98)

Islam as a foreign policy tool was given earlier when the Muslim World League (Rabitat al-Alam al-Islami) was established in 1962 with its headquarters at Makkah. (Its executive council included two Indians: Maulana Abul Hasan Ali Nadwi of Nadwatul Ulama university, Lucknow and Maulana Manzoor Nomani. Official Delhi had some misgivings about the new entity [Rabitat al-Alam al-Islami] and passports to the two gentlemen were issued after intervention at senior levels going up to PM Nehru).[24] Alongside, steps were taken with the assistance of the US and the UK to strengthen Saudi defence capabilities. To dilute the impression of total reliance on the Western Bloc, the Saudi government also initiated defence training cooperation with Pakistan and some details of this were shared with me by a friend in the defence wing of the US embassy.

The difficulties of political reporting from a station where open sources are negligible were evident in Jeddah. Much depended on a discerning study of the local media and of the occasional cartoons that conveyed a message to the initiated. Like most communicators in closed societies, chance remarks had to be noted. A Jeddah businessman briefed me about social mores and said that only some families would socialize together. Contacts, therefore, had to be on an individual basis. Official documents, available elsewhere, were generally inaccessible. One such case was that of the Arbitration Agreement of 1954 concerning the Buraimi Oasis[25] dispute with the British acting on behalf of the Sheikhdom of Abu Dhabi. The people concerned on the Saudi side, including the legal advisor in the foreign ministry Sheikh Abdul Rahman Al-Mansoori (later permanent under-secretary and advisor to the King), were not very communicative; so was the case with the Arab League Secretary-General Azzam Pasha, who gave me an appointment under the mistaken impression that

---

[24]Experience in subsequent decades was to show that the League essentially functioned as the cultural wing of the Saudi government.
[25]J.B. Kelly, *Eastern Arabian Frontiers* (London, 1964) gives details of the Arbitration. More information on boundary drawing in Arabia is given in Richard Schofield (ed.), *Territorial Foundations of the Gulf States* (New York, 1994).

my voice sounded feminine on the telephone! A friend in the British mission loaned me for three days the voluminous text of the *Saudi Memorial* and, in those pre-photocopier days, the relevant pages had to be diligently typed by a very competent and hard-working typist in the embassy.

Indo-Saudi bilateral relations, traditionally cordial, came under strain on account of Saudi tensions with Egypt and our own good relations and defence cooperation with Egypt. Friendship with an Egyptian counsellor, Saaduddin Murtada (who was later Egypt's first ambassador to Israel) earned me some unwelcome attention from the local intelligence. Saudi authorities also took a number of steps to signal their displeasure. These included, under instigation from our neighbour (Pakistan), a ban on visas to Sikhs and a directive against the employment of Indians in government departments. King Faisal's counsellor Sheikh Mohammad Ali Reza (who was also the Saudi ambassador to Egypt) told Ambassador Midhat Kidwai in a private conversation that 'an enemy's friend becomes an enemy'. The situation, however, changed after the Egyptian defeat in the Six-Day War of 1967 (5–10 June).

For about five months every year, the embassy's and my own preoccupation was with the Hajj 'bandobast'. Compared to what it is today, the size of operations and Saudi facilities were modest and so were the resources. Our pilgrims were in the range of 15,000–16,000 and the logistics of arrangements were divided between the Hajj Committee in Bombay and the embassy. Barring a small number, around 1,000, who travelled by air, our pilgrims travelled in Mogul Line ships and stayed in Makkah and Madina in modestly priced accommodation rented for them. The syndicates of pilgrim guides (Moallims) were critical for the accommodation of pilgrims. By tradition, each Moallim catered to one country or to one region or province in the country. This had the advantage of familiarity with local languages; its drawback was exploitation, since pilgrims had very limited choice. To minimize it, we introduced a system of restricting their canvassing by giving visas whose validity ended before the pilgrims starting arriving in Bombay, the port of embarkation. This was frequently bypassed since many of them would go to the local police and seek extension on account of the approaching confinement of an Indian spouse and since the extension could only be granted by the Ministry of Home Affairs (MHA), the papers had to be forwarded to Delhi by the postal system. This gave the applicant the few weeks he required. During the core pilgrimage period of four days in Arafat and Mina, they stayed in tents, prayed for salvation and stoned the devil as per ritual.

The Hajj pilgrimage has multiple dimensions. To the Muslims, it is a religious duty 'for those who can afford the journey' (Qur'an 3:97). To them and to others, it has profound political and economic implications and historical records of the medieval and modern times testify to it in ample measure. In the old days, it contributed substantially to the livelihood and prosperity of the people of Makkah and is reflected in the old sayings attributed to a Meccan: 'we sow no wheat or sorghum, the pilgrims are our crop' and that 'the Hajj is the bread of Hijaz'. This is testified to by available details of India's trade with the region and a historian's observation that 'as much as two-third of the Gujarati exports to the Red Sea were sold at Mecca'.[26] Above all, the annual gathering of pilgrims from all over the world differing from each other in every way except that of faith offers opportunities for fascinating sociological perspectives.

King Faisal's annual banquet during the Hajj was always an occasion to gather prominent personalities from the Muslim world. Guests, on one occasion, included the judge of the International Court of Justice and former Pakistani foreign minister, Sir Muhammad Zafarullah Khan who, being of the Ahmadiyya faction, had become controversial in the domestic politics of his country. He, as an honoured guest, was seated next to the King. I asked a Saudi newspaper editor if

---

[26]M.N. Pearson, *Pious Passengers: The Hajj in Earlier Times* (New Delhi, 1994) p. 146. Many earlier European travellers such as Burckhardt wrote about Jeddah's relevance in the trade with India–Cf: F.E. Peters, *Mecca: A Literary History of the Muslim Holy Land* (Princeton, 1994) pp. 238–45.

this reflected a Saudi view on the controversy and he said 'it was a big mistake' and that the king received a large number of telegrams from Pakistan protesting it.

Many family members, including my own parents, came for the Hajj. Two very erudite colleagues from the MEA, Syed Nazir Hussain and Dr Barakat Ahmad, came to assist us in countering Pakistan's propaganda onslaught; the time spent with them resulted in lifelong friendships. Other prominent non-official Indians who came for Hajj during that period were Begum Akhtar and Maqbool Fida (M.F.) Husain. The latter gave me a folder of his Hajj drawings and did not collect it before his departure. It was I who had to remind him about it. A common friend later called me a fool and a simpleton for having done so. Another eminent visitor was Ustad Bismillah Khan, who came for Umrah after a performance in Moscow. I requested him to introduce the Saudi public to the virtues of the shehnai, and he readily agreed to do so for Saudi TV, besides a private performance arranged by the embassy. It was enchanting!

Makkah in that period was still a very traditional city and so was Madina. The traditional system of marking time with sunset being 12 o'clock was still in vogue; it was initially disconcerting and so was the practice of government offices beginning work two hours after sunset. The imprint of Indian contacts was very visible, particularly in the endowments created by erstwhile princely states. Most of these were in adverse possession of their Saudi caretakers and years of litigation in Sharia courts produced but partially the desired results and the people of Makkah lived up to their age-old reputation of adroitness.

An educational institution with an Indian pedigree was Madrasa Saulatiya, established by Indian scholars who migrated after the events of 1857. It was established thanks to a donation given by Begum Saulat un-Nisa of Calcutta in the year 1873. On a visit there in 1966, the then head of the institution Maulana Mohammad Saleem Usmani Kairanvi gave me a graphic account of what happened in the Islamic Conference convened by King Ibn Saud at Makkah in

1926 when the Indian delegation proposed a de facto international regime for the Holy Cities.[27] (Some details of this are given in the section on my tenure as Ambassador to Riyadh, many decades later.)

A consular visit to Dhahran gave me the opportunity to call on the legendary and much-feared governor of the Eastern Province, Abdullah bin Jiluwi. He was stern but correct and said he regarded Indian nationals as his children 'who when the need arises need to be punished'.

The Indian community in Jeddah was small but cohesive, with a predominance of people from Bombay and Hyderabad. Apart from individual gatherings, cultural life was confined to weekly film shows in the embassy compound. Local nationals were excluded from these though. On one occasion, I received in my office a junior member of the royal family who wished to borrow, as he put it, *aflam al hub* (films of love). Another unusual visitor was the head of the local unit of the Committee for the Promotion of Virtue and the Prevention of Vice (commonly known as *Mutawa*) wanting to have a book on a theological subject published in Hyderabad. Given their nuisance value, I hastened to oblige.

The absence of schooling for our children was acutely felt and Salma decided to establish a school for community children in the chancery premises. A discarded ambulance originally used by the medical mission during the Hajj was used to ferry the children. Years later, the Saudi government gave land for a school building whose foundation stone was laid by PM Indira Gandhi in 1981.

An event with wider and later ramifications was the convening of the Rabat Islamic Summit/Summit Conference of Islamic Countries on 22–24 September 1969 following the attack on the Masjid-e-Aqsa in Jerusalem. Ambassador T.T.P. Abdullah was instructed by Delhi to call on King Faisal and put forth the point that the incident affected Muslims the world over and not only the Muslim states.

---

[27]Martin Kramer, *Islam Assembled: The Advent of the Muslim Congresses* (New York, 1986) pp. 106–21.

India, with its very large Muslim population, had to be represented. The Saudi monarch concurred and instructed his minister of state for foreign affairs, Omar Saqqaf, to project this in the preparatory meeting of foreign ministers. Pursuant to this, and at the invitation of the King of Morocco, who chaired the conference, Ambassador to Morocco Gurbachan Singh addressed the meeting in its preliminary session. A few months later when I was at the ministry headquarters in Delhi, Ambassador Singh was my immediate superior, having been called back from Rabat for his alleged mishandling of the conference episode. To clarify matters, he obtained the transcript of the afternoon proceedings from his contacts in Rabat and gave it to me to translate.[28]

Despite the politically motivated uproar in our political circles, I learnt from well-informed Saudi friends that King Faisal's decision to include India in the conference was taken after careful deliberation. However, things went astray when the president of Pakistan Yahya Khan, acting on domestic pressure in the wake of the Ahmedabad riots of September 1969, threatened to walk out of the conference. Faced with this situation, a few participants, particularly Egypt and Malaysia, suggested an observer status to India. This was rejected by

---

[28]British documents relating to the Rabat Islamic Summit (*Islam: Political Impact 1908–1972 [British Documentary Sources]–Volume 12 1962–1972*) (Editor: Jane Priestland; Archives Edition 2004) substantiate the point that it was King Faisal who insisted on the Indians being invited (pp. 725–37).

The minutes of the Second Session of the Conference record the following remarks of King Faisal: '...my second observation, if his Majesty and my brothers agree, is that I would like to propose that His Majesty the Chairman should extend an invitation to our brothers, the representatives of India, to participate in this gathering, provided there is agreement regarding this among our brothers. (Applause)' The chairman of the conference then spoke: 'Morocco will extend an invitation to an Indian Government Delegation to represent here by our side that great community of Muslims in India so that our brother Muslims in India feel that we are with them heart and soul. The presence of the esteemed Government of India here will be part of our obligation to them. It will also preserve the freedom of religion and the freedom of Muslims in her area. Morocco will immediately extend the invitation.'

the leader of our delegation. The final communiqué of the conference then resorted to a factual distortion and depicted our delegation as 'Representatives of the Muslim community in India'. Ambassador Singh's detailed account of the incident was published in the Oral History section of the *Indian Foreign Affairs Journal* (April 2006). A Pakistani version of Yahya Khan's role in Rabat was given later by his then aide-de-camp, Ambassador Arshad Sami Khan, in his book *Three Presidents and an Aide: Life, Power and Politics* (2008).

Altogether, my stint of over three years in Jeddah was productive and rewarding. Friends, Indians as well as Saudi, made in that period became lifelong friends. Among them were Fazalbhai and Rafibhai, who attended to the Mogul Line's work in Jeddah, Dr Osman and his wife Dr Shahinshah, both attached to the Royal Court and Mohammad Salahuddin, editor of the daily Arabic newspaper *Al Madina*. Salahuddin was critical of Indian policies and an early adherent to Islamist perceptions of the Muslim Brotherhood. He obtained for me a copy of Prince Talal bin Abdulaziz's *Risalahila al-Muwatineen*, a 1961 appeal for converting an absolute monarchy into a constitutional one, and for which he was dismissed from his post and had to spend many years in exile in Cairo.

NEW DELHI

We returned to Delhi in October 1969. It was my first stint at the headquarters after the initial training period. With three postings in the Arab world, I was considered fit for the West Asia and North Africa (WANA) division as Deputy Secretary. At that point of time, WANA covered the whole region from Afghanistan and Iran to Morocco and Mauritania.

Around the time I joined the Foreign Service, there was a serious internal debate in the MEA about priorities in our West Asian policy in the context of the internecine conflict in the Arab world. Gamal Abdel Nasser, President of Egypt, and the version of Arab nationalism championed by him was at one end of the ideological pole; the conservative regimes led by King Faisal of Saudi Arabia was another. The then ambassador to Cairo, Azim Hussain, advocated unambiguous primacy to a pro-Cairo approach. The secretary concerned, Badruddin Tyabji, suggested a more even-handed policy, given the totality of our interests. The debate settled on the traditional Indian approach of calibrated bilateralism, with nuances, but without overt entanglement in wider controversies.

My posting in the WANA division also coincided with the British announcement of withdrawal from 'East of Suez'. This policy of Pax Britannica, premised on the command of the sea and control over routes to India, had led to the treaties of 1820, 1839 and 1853 with the Rulers of the Arab Sheikhdoms and whose dimensions were spelt out in the Viceroy of India Lord Curzon's edict of 1903 in Sharjah: 'The peace of these waters must be maintained; your independence will continue to be upheld; and the influence of the British Government must remain supreme.' This dispensation continued till after World War II and the discovery of oil in the region added an impetus to it. The Political Resident in Bahrain and Political Agents in the Trucial States[29] were the symbols of British power and control and the arbiter of the destinies of the ruling dynasties.[30]

Political developments elsewhere in West Asia and financial constraints compelled London to announce an abdication from these imperial responsibilities on 30 November 1970. The GoI was concerned about its implications on Indian interests in the erstwhile Trucial States of the Persian Gulf and initiated political contacts with rulers of these emerging states whose familiarity with India and Indians was well known. I accompanied Surendra Pal Singh, Minister of State in the MEA, on a tour of the Gulf region. As the desk officer, I also participated in the preparation of policy papers, and in the process, discovered the wealth of records of the British period, some

---

[29]British-controlled Sheikhdoms in the Persian Gulf.
[30]One of the last Political Agents in Dubai, Sir James Craig, whom I met in Jeddah in 1968, left for posterity a very readable account of the Political Agent's work-Cf: Matthew Parris and Andrew Bryson (eds.) *Parting Shots* (London, 2010) pp. 328–33.

with security classification that had not been reviewed for decades! These included John Gordon Lorimer's invaluable compendium the *Gazetteer of the Persian Gulf, Oman and Central Arabia;* it was on the 'secret' list of books in the MEA library and my effort to have it declassified required the intervention of the then director of the Historical Division, Dr S. Gopal. After some delving into the records, I prepared a comprehensive note that eventually became a Policy Paper.

Living in Delhi, and that too on a meagre salary, had its own share of problems. With no prospect of government accommodation, we rented a ground-floor apartment in Safdarjung Enclave. At that time, we were fortunate enough to have Salma's family cook for us, and we also admitted Sulaiman, our son, to a nursery school on Hailey Road.

My area of work as Deputy Secretary covered Afghanistan and Iran. A tiger shoot safari by the Crown Prince of Afghanistan, agreed upon by the two governments, ran into avoidable trouble when the then chief of protocol in the MEA, Ambassador Prithi Singh, tendered private advice to the Afghan side resulting in the cancellation of the official part of the visit and its replacement by a private one. Ambassador Ashok Nandlal Mehta, then in Kabul, was visibly annoyed and in his characteristic style, prevailed upon the government to undo the misunderstanding.

My work included representing the government on the board of directors of Mogul Line Ltd, the nationalized shipping company entrusted with the transportation of Hajj pilgrims. This also included the management of the government quota of seats (given on compassionate grounds) for which there was much demand, particularly from people who had the right kind of access. One such request came from the president of the Kerala Muslim League. It was not conceded because he had undertaken the journey in the preceding five years. Little did I realize the implications of this straight-forward administrative decision which was endorsed by the minister of external affairs. The next day, I was summoned by the foreign secretary and was told to take the file to the PM's secretary. I did so diffidently, fearing a reprimand for a sin not committed. I did not have to wait for long; it was back with me after a few minutes with orders recorded in long hand: 'five seats should be given. This does not constitute a precedent.' The significance of the pilgrimage in the domestic politics of India was thus unambiguously driven home to me.

A case of crass interference by a foreign mission in the run-up to the general election of 1971 came to light when our agencies traced to the Israeli consulate in Bombay an advisory suggesting to intending voters a community-wise preference. Appropriate action was taken.

Relations with Imperial Iran came under stress during the Bangladesh crisis of 1971. Foreign Secretary T.N. Kaul paid a quiet visit to Tehran to explain our position. While the Shah's response was statesmanlike, Foreign Minister Ardeshir Zahedi was strident and menacing. Reporting on the latter meeting, Ambassador Ataur (Ishi) Rahman suggested that allowance be made for the lateness of the hour and the host having imbibed several rounds of vodka.[31]

The government decided to send special emissaries to West Asian countries to explain the emerging situation. I accompanied General Shah Nawaz Khan (formerly of the Indian National Army) on his visit to Yemen and Saudi Arabia. The Saudi response, by Deputy Foreign Minister Sheikh Ibrahim Masood, was terse and totally unhelpful.

After the 1971 war, a good number of Bangladeshi Hajj pilgrims were stranded in Saudi Arabia since they had made their outward journey by Pakistani ships and, as per standard Saudi regulations, were told to return the same way. The Government of Bangladesh was understandably apprehensive and sought our advice. Since Hajj arrangements were part of my official responsibilities, the head of the

---

[31] On Indo-Iran relations, with which I had to do more many years later, I recall being told by the historian Prof. Nurul Hasan (later Minister of Education, Ambassador to USSR and Governor of West Bengal) about the sophistication of diplomatic exchanges between the Mughal and Safawi courts in the sixteenth and seventeenth centuries.

Bangladeshi mission, Humayun Rashid Choudhury (to whom I was of some help a few months earlier in his previous incarnation) sought my advice. I suggested a direct communication from Sheikh Mujibur Rahman to King Faisal, invoking Islamic compassion. This worked out and we had to provide Mogul Line ships for their transportation.

Work on the West Asian desk gave me the opportunity to familiarize myself with the material on the region in our Archives. The rules of access were far from easy and I recall a conversation with Prof. Aghwani of the School of International Studies (later Dean of Jawaharlal Nehru University [JNU]) who expressed himself candidly on the procedural obstacles deterring Indian scholars from pursuing research in the very rich material available in the records of the British period.

After three postings in West Asia followed by the desk dealing with the region, the normal practice of rotation seemed to decide my next assignment. It was to be in the mission in Brussels. However before leaving, the problem of our substantial collection of books, including many inherited from Salma's father, had to be solved. It was suggested to me that the ministry had storage space in the basement of the South Block that could be availed of. We packed the books in two, big steel trunks, deposited them in the store and obtained a receipt. That I thought was a cast iron guarantee of safety, only to discover many years later that the basement had been flooded in one rainy season and what was left of the books was only a pile of soiled paper!

BRUSSELS

In my new assignment, political reporting on Belgium, Luxembourg and the European Economic Community (EEC) was one aspect of my work; press and culture was another. Both provided ample opportunities to meet new people and understand the world beyond India and West Asia. Brussels was culturally rich; it was also a gourmet's delight and was evolving tentatively as the political hub of a new Europe. A sharper focus existed on trade-related issues; Ambassador K.B. Lall, who succeeded B.R. Patel in 1973, was successful in negotiating a Cooperation Agreement to replace the earlier Trade Agreement. Lall was an inspiring team leader, erudite and innovative, whose vast experience in administration and diplomacy was beneficial to all members of his team: Kant Kishore Bhargava, two successive Cabinet Secretariat officers Naresh Kumar and R. Govindarajan, Mani Shankar Aiyar, Farouk Kapadia, Rajan Abhyankar and Randhir Singh; the latter was head of chancery.

Lall was a patrician of the old school, a senior member of the ICS and an expert on trade-related matters who was serving his second term as Ambassador to Belgium and the EEC. He was a hard taskmaster but unstinting in praise of work he considered worthwhile.

One of the communes in Brussels had a statue of Mahatma Gandhi and an annual ceremony was held there on 2 October every year. Lall asked me to coordinate arrangements with the local mayor, who suggested that after the ceremony in the park, the ambassador and his entourage would adjourn to the town hall for a glass of champagne. This I thought would be disrespectful to the memory of the Father of the Nation and conveyed this in suitable terms to the mayor. When I reported this to Lall, he disapproved of my initiative and suggested that I correct it. When I sought to argue citing government practices, he said, 'I have retired and this would not reflect adversely on you!' On another occasion, on an official visit to the city of Antwerp, he was asked to sign the Golden Book in the mayor's office not in English but in his mother tongue. My mother tongue, he said, is Urdu, and proceeded to write his full name accordingly.

My own work was essentially away from the Community headquarters at Berlaymont, except for the EEC's foreign policy coordination and energy policy. The former was focused on the follow-up to the 1970 Davignon Report that included common reporting by EEC ambassadors. These, in the words of the then Belgian ambassador to New Delhi, were 'sexless'. Energy policy, on the other hand, had acquired political priority in the wake of the

1973 oil crisis emanating from the embargo by the Organization of the Petroleum Exporting Countries (OPEC) in the wake of the Arab-Israeli war.

Cultural and press relations gave me ample scope to make new friends. Rik Leanart, editor of a Flemish language newspaper, who had visited India in 1972, became a good friend and so did Janine Schotsman, who was head of the Indian section of the Royal Museum of Art and History. Apart from the regular work relating to the promotion of Indian culture, I helped organize two events of cultural significance. The first was our participation in the Middelheim Biennale in Antwerp, where Amar Nath Sehgal's sculpture *Combat* is an exhibit in a remarkable 25-acre open-air park of sculptures. The park owed its creation to the city's long-serving mayor Lode Craeybeckx, whose personal popularity in the city's working class was such that he remained mayor from 1947 till his death in 1976. The second event, a first for Europe, was an exhibition of Indian miniatures in our National Museum's collection. It was held under the joint patronage of the President of India and the King of Belgium.

Early in 1973, a message from the Prime Minister's Office (PMO) informed us of a visit by V.K. Krishna Menon to participate in a gathering of Democratic Lawyers. The ambassador assigned me the responsibility of attending to him. His requirements were frugal and he just wished to avoid a cold buffet, which was the standard fare for such gatherings; I therefore took him home for lunch the next day and also tried to talk to him about his political and diplomatic career. He was reticent, said he lived from day to day and kept no notes.

Our second child, Nuriya, was born in July 1973. When I took Salma for her confinement to the Edith Cavell clinic very early on the morning of 5 July, the receptionist there insisted on seeing our marriage certificate. Since the document issued by the authority concerned in Baghdad was not readily available, I had to wake up Randhir Singh, who generously agreed to go to office and bring forth a certificate from the embassy.

Despite Salma's confinement and childbirth, we did a lot of

travelling in the Belgian countryside. Luxembourg was part of my beat and I enjoyed my visits there. Sulaiman, at the age of 7, was admitted to a local community school, where no one spoke English. After an initial period, he picked up French and became fluent in it, so much so that when at the end of our stay I went to the school to take leave of the principal and thank him, he said, 'Your son speaks French like a Belgian child.'

Salma and I met and became good friends with the journalist Brajesh Khandaria and with his sister, painter Usha Bhalla, who presented one of her paintings to Salma. Salma also took to Transcendental Meditation and visited Maharishi Mahesh Yogi in his headquarters in Switzerland.

A visit to a Flemish village near Antwerp to attend a function to welcome back after 25 years one of its residents who had joined the Order of Jesuits and spent the period in St Xavier's College, Ranchi, drove home to me the commitment to what his elderly mother described as 'God's work'.

In June 1975, a pleasant surprise from Delhi came in the form of a message appointing me as Ambassador to Kuwait. After a few weeks, this was superseded by another message transferring me to the headquarters. A few hours after I had left Brussels for a spot of ex-India leave with Salma's brother and sisters in Karachi, another advisory instructed me to go to Tehran instead to replace a commercial counsellor, who had suddenly passed away. Unaware of it, I reached Delhi after a week, only to be told that instead of Tehran, I should proceed to Jeddah as chargé d'affaires because the Saudis had refrained from responding to our request for an agrément for my colleague Syed Shahabuddin. Foreign Minister Y.B. Chavan instructed me to ascertain whether the Saudi reticence was individual or India specific.

JEDDAH AGAIN

My first port of call was on Shaikh Salim Sunbul, the long-serving chief of protocol in the Saudi foreign office, whom I had known earlier. He was reticent. On my insistence, his response was elliptical and related to his personal relations with his only sister, who lived in Madina. She was very dear to him but with whom he occasionally disagreed. This did not result in the exchange of sharp words, but, in an unstated, mutual agreement, to stop talking. Despite traditional reluctance to elaborate on matters deemed sensitive, an answer to the external affairs minister's query was finally made available by a close Saudi friend; it shed light on the Saudi style of communication. The authorities concerned, they conveyed, were uncomfortable with Shahabuddin's 'activism' during the 1965 Indo-Pak conflict and did not wish to repeat the experience at the level of a senior diplomatic representative. This cleared the air on the technicalities of the matter and Delhi soon sought agrément for a senior member of the civil service.

1975 was a difficult year for the Kingdom. King Faisal, who had ruled the country since 1964 and was responsible for controlled reforms and a measure of modernization, was assassinated by his nephew on 25 March. He was succeeded by his younger brother Khalid bin Abdulaziz. King Faisal had helped tide over the crisis emanating from the end of monarchy in Yemen (1962–64), and the resulting Egyptian threat through republican Yemen, internal dissent in the Saudi armed forces, the compact with the Shah of Iran against the tide of Arab nationalism, the creation of the Organisation of Islamic Cooperation (OIC) in 1969, the Arab-Israeli War of 1973 and the oil crisis of 1973–74.[32]

The Hajj in December 1975, shortly after our arrival in Jeddah, was eventful in an unpleasant manner. A fire in a pilgrim's tent spread

---

[32]Faisal's 'most enduring legacy,' according to his biographer, 'was his successful defence of faith, which empowered Riyadh and legitimized Al Saud. It may be said that this characteristic of Saudi foreign policy featured both moral as well as pragmatic aspects. To be sure, and while it was true that Saudi rulers always relied on Islam to rule with justice, Faisal elevated the trait to new heights. Faith and its defence became the essence of his behaviour and most of his policies.' — Joseph A. Kéchichian, *Faysal: Saudi Arabia's King for All Seasons* (University Press of Florida, 2008) p. 199.

quickly in the direction of our camp, which had to be abandoned. A few of our pilgrims suffered in the fire. In the melee of evacuation, our eldest son Sulaiman was lost for a few hours; a Pakistani doctor in Makkah who knew us escorted him back to our camp.

I attended, as head of the Indian mission, the King's Hajj banquet in Mina. Sitting across the aisle among guests was a person in traditional Moroccan attire. I walked up to him and mentioned the time I had spent in Rabat. He turned out to be none other than Gen. Muhammad Oufkir, the dreaded head of Moroccan intelligence who was accused of abducting dissident intellectual Mehdi Ben Barka from a Paris street (with the help of the French secret service) and subsequently murdering him in a villa in the suburbs. Decades later, a pang of conscience induced the French on the fortieth anniversary of the event to name the spot of abduction La Place Mehdi Ben Barka.

I participated in the 'Washing of the Kaaba' ceremony along with Abdul Rahman Antulay, the leader of our Hajj delegation that year. The rarity of the privilege was evident; so was the opportunity to satisfy one's individual curiosity. The cube-like room, with no inlet of light except through the heavily ornate door, is empty but for two or three supporting pillars and a few vessel-like objects hanging from the roof.[33] The 'Kiswah' or the outer covering of the Kaaba has its own history and politics associated with it. Its colour has changed over time: from green to red and now black. It is changed once a year, and by well-established tradition is given to the Banu Shayba (traditional custodian of the Kaaba) and in turn to the rulers of the day. The present-day custom is for the King to give pieces of it to eminent pilgrims from different lands. Since the Kiswah is now made in Makkah itself, unlike earlier times, reliable rumour has it that cut-pieces are also made for wider distribution to lesser beings among pious pilgrims, whose reverence remains undented.

---

[33]Over the years, subsequent readings enabled me to learn more about this sanctum sanctorum. An early description of the same was given in *The Travels of Ibn Jubayr* (AD 1183) pp. 76–90. Also, *First Encyclopaedia of Islam,* Volume IV, pp. 585–92 and F.E. Peters, *The Hajj,* pp. 230–40.

Three decades later, on 17 December 1996, a tablet was affixed (in Arabic) to the interior wall of the Kaaba:

> In the name of God Most Gracious Most Merciful
>
> All praises to Allah and peace be upon Prophet Mohammad, the noblest of prophets and messengers, upon his family and companions.
>
> With the help of Allah, comprehensive renovation of Holy Ka'ba was carried out during the reign of the Custodian of the Two Holy Mosques, King Fahad Bin Abdul Aziz Al Saud. The comprehensive work included, three pillars, outer and inner walls of the Ka'ba, floor, internal marble covering of the wall, terrace, stairs and small-driven gadget of the wall of Prophet Ismail's room as well as Mizab (roof drain) of the Holy Ka'ba.
>
> May Allah accept it and bestow his reward.
>
> Work carried out in the month of Rajab 1417 AH.

There were other figures in history, some with sullied reputations in other fields, who also rebuilt the Kaaba. The advent of new technologies and of 'Islamic' television channels now makes it possible for the pious to see the modernized interior of this hallowed structure.

Chapter 4

Representing India

ABU DHABI

With my job done in Jeddah, I was asked to proceed as Ambassador to the United Arab Emirates (UAE), with residence in Abu Dhabi, in June 1976. When I conveyed this to my father, he asked me to send him a new atlas, since these lesser-known places did not figure on the atlases in his collection of books. While being a head of the mission at the age of 39 was a matter of some pride and satisfaction to me, the importance of the assignment and its proximity to India did ensure diligence in all aspects of work, particularly commercial and consular. In the wake of the oil crisis of 1973, the priority of crude oil supplies from all the producers in the Persian Gulf had assumed centrality in our external relations.

The UAE, a union of the rulers of seven sheikhdoms, took shape through the Independence Agreement of 2 December 1971. This was in the wake of the British government's announcement of 1968 for a military withdrawal by the end of 1971 and the resultant termination of the General Maritime Treaty of 1820 and the Exclusive Agreement of 1892. The purpose of these treaties, besides maintaining 'the peace of these waters', was to ensure British supremacy in the waterway, the exclusion of other European powers near the entrance to the Persian

Gulf and exploration of sites for naval bases.[34] The new state came into existence with unsettled borders (with Saudi Arabia and Iran), barely settled internal boundaries (tribal grazing zones converted into provincial boundaries by the British diplomat Julian Walker) and unbalanced internal political and financial arrangements (oil wealth with Abu Dhabi, trade and much else with Dubai and the rest dependent on Abu Dhabi's largesse).

The emergence of the new international entity was preceded, on 30 November, by the use of force by the Shah of Iran (after the failure of inducement and enticement) to settle his claim to the two Tunb islands. Iraq and Libya took the matter to the UN Security Council (UNSC), where, after an inclusive debate on 9 December, the matter was shelved. There is, however, some contemporary evidence to suggest that the Iranian action was part of a wider deal with the Western powers in which Iran relinquished its claim to Bahrain and acquiesced to its independent status.[35]

Security and status, and security through status, were thus the immediate objectives of the Rulers of the Emirates when they embarked upon statehood and weaved themselves into an entity that sought to preserve their traditional authority. This was while taking away from them no more than what they had in effect surrendered to British paramountcy, thus replacing, in a sense, the Political Resident with a constitutional president and a constitutional authority. The division of powers in a Provisional Constitution (that remains provisional to this day) was a delicate one and arbitrariness was sought to be checked through collegiate responsibility at the highest level and reinforced by a notional power of veto, at least for the bigger units.

---

[34]Muhammad Morsy Abdullah, *The United Arab Emirates: A Modern History* (London, 1978) pp. 26-29.

[35]Sir Denis Wright, who was the British ambassador to Iran from 1963 to 1971, has cited (in *The English amongst the Persians*, pp. 68-69) the British documentary evidence in favour of the Iranian claim. The UAE side of the argument was given in some detail by Ambassador Ali Humaidan in a series of six articles in the Saudi newspaper *Asharq Al-Awsat* (15 and 26 June and 6, 13, 20 and 27 July 1997).

My initial round of calls on the rulers of the federal units and meetings with the business community was educative in bringing home to me the depth and intensity of individual as well as collective bonds of affinity and nostalgia they had with India and Indians. Bombay Hindustani was the lingua franca in the bazaars, and to the rulers and the general public of the lower Gulf, India, particularly the area around Bombay and Kerala, was the embodiment of knowledge, prosperity, medical expertise and publishing and a market for the pearl fishing industry. Almost a dozen proverbs relating to India, in very complimentary terms, were imbibed in colloquial usage. The Banya community settled there, as well as a few Sindhi families from India, were highly respected for their commercial and entrepreneurial skills, and they, in turn, intermingled with ease and learnt the local dialects, mannerism and customs. Despite this, they retained their identity and did not allow it to become an impediment to the cultivation of fraternity.

My tenure in the UAE coincided with the Emergency at home, the subsequent general elections and the installation of the Janata Party government. The first phase of this witnessed a good deal of activity relating to individuals in Dubai involved in smuggling activities and listed in documents of the Conservation of Foreign Exchange and Prevention of Smuggling Activities Act (COFEPOSA), 1974.

A few months after our arrival in Abu Dhabi, President Fakhruddin Ali Ahmed paid a visit to the UAE (in November 1976). It was a return on our side, a return visit to Sheikh Zayed's visit to India in 1975. The president and First Lady Begum Ahmed were received with great warmth by the hosts and by the Indian communities in Abu Dhabi and Dubai. The head of the presidential palace in Abu Dhabi, closer to the rituals of the desert, scoffed at some of my standard schedule refinements and enquired if I doubted their capacity to look after a guest. In the official talks led from our side by Minister Accompanying Shafi Qureshi, the question of smuggling was forcefully raised. Foreign Minister Ahmad Khalifa Al Suwaidi's response left us with very little room to pursue the matter: he said that while he understood and sympathized with the Indian government's concern and wished to extend the fullest cooperation, a procedural impediment prevented him from doing so since local laws did not impose any restrictions on export trade. He further added that 'if however anything illegal had been exported to India, it should be returned forthwith'.

The fancy of Abu Dhabi sheikhs for bustard hunting in the Rajasthan desert areas adjacent to Pakistan was a matter of sensitivity and was frowned upon by PM Indira Gandhi and her ire was conveyed to me personally. Permission with some reluctance was eventually given to the Crown Prince of Abu Dhabi Sheikh Khalifa. Local tradition and opposition to this sport eventually prevailed and this was perhaps the last occasion when it was permitted.

After the general election of 1977 and the installation of the Janata Party government, the pace of visits by our senior dignitaries to the UAE picked up. External Affairs Minister Atal Bihari Vajpayee, Information and Broadcasting Minister L.K. Advani and Petroleum Minister H.N. Bahuguna visited Abu Dhabi and Dubai. Vajpayee's meeting with Sheikh Zayed was instructive; full of proverbs, it focused on our economic problems arising out of the oil crisis, and a friend's response to it. Vajpayee described wealth as dirt on one's hand that should be washed off; in response, Sheikh Zayed cited an Arab proverb describing wealth as water in a boat that must be taken out to save the boat from sinking. It was an object lesson in the use of traditional idioms in diplomatic discourse!

On wider perspectives, my conversations with the Ruler of Sharjah, Sheikh Sultan, were always enlightening. He had studied in Baghdad University and was familiar with the nuances of opinion in Arab nationalism. I was his guest for a few days in the picturesque surrounding of Khor Fakkan on the Gulf of Oman and travelled by a dhow to the Ras Al Khaimah enclave of Dibba.

The cultural advisor to the UAE president, Dr Ezzeddin Ibrahim, who earlier had affiliations with the Muslim Brotherhood in Egypt and had been in Abu Dhabi for many years, was a person of knowledge and old-fashioned charm. He called me one day to seek help in resolving a dispute within the largish community of Indians from Kerala, to whom the Ruler of Abu Dhabi had given land many years back to build a church and a community centre. They professed adherence to the different factions within the Syriac Orthodox Church, some to the Patriarch of Antioch and others to the Malankara Catholicos. Not knowing much about it, I sought clarification from Delhi and was told that the matter had been adjudicated by the Supreme Court of India. Dr Ezzeddin appreciated this clarification, and in the process, we became good friends. Another Arab expatriate of eminence in the circle of advisors to Sheikh Zayed was Dr Adnan Pachachi, a former foreign minister of Iraq and twice Permanent Representative (PR) to the UN. He was to play a role in Iraqi politics many years later.

The importance of adherence to traditional ritual was driven home to me on an occasion when additional supplies of crude oil became critical to us and were not forthcoming in response to requests through normal channels. Sheikh Tahnoun bin Mohammed was the governor of Al Ain and the chairman of the Abu Dhabi National Oil Company. It was the month of Ramadan and I joined him one evening, though uninvited, for the Iftar party and spent several hours socializing and even playing some volleyball. When we sat down for dinner, he enquired about India. My response was that our country was thirsty. This puzzled him and he said that the monsoon brings enough water. I clarified that our 'thirst' was for crude oil; he responded handsomely and resolved our problem.

Apart from Dubai's disinclination to act on our COFEPOSA requests, its penchant for trading came to the fore after the Iranian Revolution and the various embargoes that came into play. A leading Indian businessman briefed me, in some detail, about the ease with which country crafts (dhows) could be loaded in the Dubai harbour for overnight delivery in Bandar Abbas, with payment in bags of cash in US dollars!

The Ruler of Dubai's fondness for India was legendary. In my farewell call on him, I raised the question of the then aggressive Iraqi propaganda against south Asians alleging 'dilution of Arabness of the Emirates' by their presence in large numbers. His response was forceful: 'Tell your government that Rashid Al Maktoum does not retire for the night till he is satisfied that his gate is guarded by an Indian.'

Mohan Jashanmal, whose brother Atma I had met a few years earlier in Bahrain, became a close friend and remains so to this day. He possessed a film projector and very often brought it home to show us movies. He moved with ease in local circles, spoke the dialect and was regarded by Abu Dhabians 'as one of us'. In a special gesture, Crown Prince Sheikh Zayed had given him and his family permanent status; it continues to this day.

During the visit of Queen Elizabeth II to the UAE in 1979, Salma and I were invited to dine with the Queen and the Duke of Edinburgh on the royal yacht. This puzzled the Crown Prince of Abu Dhabi, Sheikh Khalifa, who enquired why of all the ambassadors in town, only the Indian was invited. The Commonwealth was the explanation given by my British colleague, but a sense of intrigue seemed to linger.

A friendly Indian telephone supervisor in Abu Dhabi alerted me one morning in November 1979 about an 'unusual' telecom blackout in Saudi Arabia. I conveyed this to Romesh Bhandari, Secretary in the MEA; it was the first that Delhi had heard about. This, it transpired the next day, arose out of the occupation of the Grand Mosque by Islamist students.

The Indian community in the UAE (then numbering around 200,000) was the largest among expatriates and, according to my British colleague, was critical to every walk of life. Our expatriates, dispersed in all branches of activity, were generally content but with occasional problems relating to conditions in labour camps, visa status and a breach in the contracted terms of their employment contracts. Regular efforts by local authorities to check their visa status resulted in a few thousand of our citizens coming to the embassy and the consulate general in Dubai on one occasion, to seek regularization through new passports. My colleagues and I decided that we would respond positively after an ad-hoc scrutiny process of interrogation by teams of officers. This required considerable replenishment of our stock of passport booklets. An urgent message to Delhi regarding this caused an alarm about my intentions, but the alarm subsided when the matter and its implications were explained.

Salma was instrumental in initiating a weekly open house at our residence. It proved to be a great success. The attendance was mainly from blue-collar members with grievances and these were attended to, to the extent possible, by officers of the mission who were invariably present. Two other initiatives undertaken by Salma have endured. She started the Indian Ladies Association and nursery, as well as the Special Care Centre for differently abled children. Both catered to a community requirement and received patronage at the highest levels locally through Shaikha Fatima, spouse of the president. Both continue to function to this day. Nuriya was one of the first students of the nursery.

The absence of a proper, and affordable, school for Sulaiman (then over 10 years of age) led to the decision to send him to Lawrence School, Sanawar. Our third child, Osman, was born in November 1979, barely 10 weeks before our departure.

Indo-UAE relations at the end of 1979 displayed maturity and diversity that was reflective of the realization of India's industrial, technological and human power potential and a growing respect for our political system and its stability. We left Abu Dhabi in January 1980 with the satisfaction that the tasks entrusted for the assignment had been accomplished.

NEW DELHI: THE CHIEF OF PROTOCOL

Back in Delhi the choice, I was told, was to assign me either the West Asian desk or of protocol. I was familiar with the first but barely so with the second; the roll of the dice took me to the latter and I remained involved in it for five days short of five years—a record in the annals of the modern Indian state. During this period, I worked with two presidents, Neelam Sanjiva Reddy and Giani Zail Singh, with Indira Gandhi as PM till 31 October 1984 and then with Rajiv Gandhi as PM till 30 January 1985.

The practices of civility in interstate discourse, to facilitate peaceful interaction and 'of finding the right word where sword might be the alternative', have been observed in all periods of history. These practices have crystallized over time and are summed up as diplomatic protocol and subscribed to by all governments. Sir Ernest Satow's *A Guide to Diplomatic Practice* has history and precedents, but every incumbent has to learn the job on the ground. In our system, the Chief of Protocol (CoP) in the MEA is the point person for interaction with the diplomatic and consular corps in the country. He oversees the management of their privileges, facilities and immunities in terms of the Vienna Conventions on Diplomatic and Consular Relations of 1961 and 1963, respectively. The responsibilities of the office extend to the procedural facilitation of the external contacts and travel of the president, the vice president, the PM and the members of the council of ministers in the MEA. The CoP is entrusted with arrangements for government hospitality as also with the organization of international conferences and gatherings in India at the head of state/government and foreign minister levels. Coordination of work with the president's and vice president's secretariats, and with the PMO, is part of the daily routine. In the course of this work, the CoP, rarely privy to the secrets of state, nevertheless has a ringside view of some interesting happenings in the conduct of foreign affairs and interaction of our leaders with foreign dignitaries. In the process, there are occasions that provide a glimpse of the human side of high dignitaries and sometimes their frailties too.

Following the general elections for the Seventh Lok Sabha, Indira Gandhi was sworn in as PM in January 1980. Unrelated to it and emanating from the process of internal transfers in the MEA, my induction as CoP on 5 February confronted me with a new set of personalities at the political level in the government. My first official function in Rashtrapati Bhavan was a lunch hosted by the PM in honour of the King of Bhutan. My job was to introduce to the visitor the invitees in the line-up, but not knowing most of them, I fumbled and the PM graciously took over.

Mrs Gandhi was punctilious about hospitality arrangements. She expressed herself candidly about the drop in standards in her absence and set up a committee for refurbishing the public areas of Rashtrapati Bhavan. The CoP was named the secretary of the committee. I, however, had little to contribute, given its membership: Mrs Sonia Gandhi, Mrs Ram Sathe, Mrs Natwar Singh, Mrs Rina Singh, Mrs Sunita Kohli and Mrs Usha Bhagat. It is another matter that the high-ranking resident of that palatial edifice was less enamoured of some of the recommendations and the Military Secretary and I had to do some deft tip-toeing around them.

An important event for the new Indira Gandhi-led government was the Soviet foreign minister Andrei Gromyko's visit to India in February 1980. Coordination of positions on Afghanistan after the Soviet intervention of December 1979 was an obvious purpose of the visit. After the first day of talks, the visitor delayed his departure and sought a second meeting with the PM that ended with the following exchange: 'Madame Prime Minister, can I tell Comrade Brezhnev that we agree?' 'I am afraid not,' was the cryptic response. This position was reiterated later, in October 1982, when Mrs Gandhi visited Moscow and the Soviet leader asked her about the way out of Afghanistan. Foreign Secretary M.K. Rasgotra has recorded her terse response: 'The way out is the same as the way in.'[36]

Mrs Gandhi was a protocol person's delight. Her knowledge of procedures and diplomatic etiquette was amazing and so was her

---

[36]M.K. Rasgotra, *A Life in Diplomacy* (New Delhi, 2016) pp. 336–37. Brezhnev's remark was: 'Now there are 1,10,000 Russian soldiers in Afghanistan. I do not know what they are doing there. I want to get out of Afghanistan. Madam, you know the region well! Show me a way to get out of Afghanistan; Show me the way.' Her response was: 'Mr General Secretary, it is a good idea to withdraw your forces from Afghanistan. The way out is the same as the way in.'

eye for detail; for the same reason, faults were invariably detected and frowned upon. She could be gracious as well as unforgiving. She had some misgivings about the Warrant of Precedence and the placement in it of MPs; it was clarified to her that the Warrant had the *imprimatur* of our first PM. She nevertheless wanted it reflected in matters such as seating priorities at the dinner table in state banquets at Rashtrapati Bhavan and on one occasion wished to have it conveyed through the CoP. I demurred, knowing fairly well that, as B.K. Nehru later put it in a somewhat similar scenario, relations between the PM and president were 'hardly cordial'.[37] My diffidence, in a very difficult moment, seemed to induce a rethink. 'Let it be; it would upset Rashtrapati ji,' she said to my great relief.

Mrs Gandhi was hugely amused when, in August 1982, at the time of the Iranian Majlis speaker Hashemi Rafsanjani's visit, the Iranian ambassador requested, through me, that the visitor wished to greet the PM in the Indian fashion of doing namaste rather than the normal handshake, which the new Iranian etiquette avoided with ladies on religious grounds. 'They are coming round,' was her cryptic response!

Mrs Gandhi's four-day visit to Saudi Arabia in 1982 was an interesting experience and instructive about her attention to details. It was the first since Jawaharlal Nehru's visit in September 1956. She was sensitive to Saudi dress norms, made searching queries about them and observed them impeccably. Her discussions with Crown Prince Fahd were substantive. When Foreign Minister Saud al-Faisal called on her, he enquired about her diplomatic style; 'I look for the minimum area of agreement and build upon it,' she said. Elsewhere, she described her approach as striving 'to strengthen friendships, to change indifference into friendship and to lessen the hostility where it exists'. This mix of pragmatism and flexibility was much in evidence in her leadership of the Non-Aligned Movement (NAM).

It is true of all humans that no mood can be maintained unaltered. For those working around her, judging the PM's moods was thus a

---

[37] B.K. Nehru, *Nice Guys Finish Second* (New Delhi, 1997/2012) p. 656.

functional necessity. I summed it up to a close friend, but dare not do so elsewhere, in a couplet of Ghalib:

Hai tevrii charhi hui ander niqab ke
Hai ik shikan pari hui tarf-e-naqab main

(A scowl there is inside the veil
A crease fold there is on the side of the veil.)

The late Rishi Kumar (R.K.) Mishra of the Observer Research Foundation (ORF) related an experience of the Emergency when Vajpayee was in Ambala jail and unwell. Mishra, then a journalist, informed the PM of this. 'Do convey my good wishes to him for a quick recovery,' she responded. Mishra boldly suggested that sending her personal physician would be a better gesture; she agreed. When this was conveyed to the distinguished prisoner, tears rolled down his cheeks.

♦

After a few months in the MEA hostel on Kasturba Gandhi Marg, we finally moved into 11, Willingdon Crescent, where my predecessors as chiefs of protocol had resided. This was preceded by a bureaucratic stand-off. The paperwork in the Ministry of Works and Housing, under pressure to allot the house to political claimants, took the view that this was not in the category of earmarked houses. Thanks to the initiative of the then additional secretary in charge of administration, S.K. Singh (later Foreign Secretary and Governor of Rajasthan), a file surfaced dating back to 1974 showing a decision by PM Indira Gandhi to allot this house to the CoP 'for functional reasons'. Since this could be reviewed only by that high authority, a compromise at the official level was arrived at to show the living rooms section of the residence as 'required for official purposes' by the incumbent.

The house itself, small and with two bedrooms, had a spacious garden and was, in the original scheme of things, intended for the surgeon general to the Commander in Chief of India, who resided in what is now the Teen Murti Bhavan just across the road. Salma and our children, more than me personally, have very pleasant recollections of our stay there for almost five years.

◆

The change of government resulted in a very large number of senior-level visits from countries having a stake in their relationship with us. My colleagues in the division and particularly in the protocol section bore this burden cheerfully. Each head of state or government was for us *sui generis* and some a little more so, like President Ahmed Sékou Touré of Guinea, who made a 40-minute speech at the airport, holding up air traffic. His pilot did not carry a Yellow Fever certificate and locked himself in the aircraft to escape quarantine; tense negotiations and a very reluctant waiver delayed a state dinner by almost an hour. Not content with one aberration, the next morning, our guest insisted on including refuelling of his aircraft in local hospitality.

Visits by our dignitaries were not without episodes that stretched organizational arrangements and negotiating capabilities. President Sanjiva Reddy visited the Soviet Union in October 1980 and on the second day in Moscow, we accidentally discovered that the Soviet leader would not attend the return banquet being hosted by us as per the then prevailing practice. A belated Soviet excuse of this having been conveyed in a presidential conversation the previous evening did not wash, since the local protocol had communicated that day a full list of 71 Soviet participants to the banquet. (The original, in Russian, remains with me.) This caused much annoyance on our side and led to a communication that night from the president to the PM seeking advice if the visit should be called off. A very quick response from Delhi cited wider considerations. Next morning, and in a calibrated reaction, President Reddy called off an important official engagement. Foreign Minister Gromyko then came to see him to assuage our ruffled feelings and that afternoon Premier Leonid Brezhnev himself accompanied President Reddy to the airport to resume his visit to other cities in the itinerary. A full account of the incident has been penned by the then ambassador, I.K. Gujral.[38] There were a few other occasions on presidential visits abroad—in Sri Lanka, Nepal and Yugoslavia—when deft handling saved what could have resulted in protocol 'incidents'. Another instance of President Reddy's candid expression of views was when a special envoy from Saudi Arabia presented him a ceremonial Arabian sword with elaborate gold work on the hilt and the casing. Accepting the present, Reddy said that our leader Mahatma Gandhi taught us that 'the pen is mightier than the sword'.

Soviet President Brezhnev visited New Delhi two months later. Prior to it, a Soviet team came for protocol arrangements. Negotiations were difficult. The Soviet visitor insisted on a public reception at the Red Fort, as was done during his previous visit in 1973. Our security officials were equally adamant on account of the presence of a good number of Afghan refugees in Delhi. Finally, matters reached the PM, who asked the External Affairs Minister to visit the Red Fort and assess the situation. The final decision landed the function at Vigyan Bhavan and Delhi government officials were given a day off and buses to attend the function.

Happenings of lesser intensity during other state visits, particularly to Nepal and Yugoslavia, required deft handling; this also related to food preferences beyond the borders of India. In Kathmandu, the requirement of an additional bed in the guest suite led to tense negotiations neatly defused by MEA Secretary Romesh Bhandari. In Yugoslavia, a third dignitary in the rear seat of the limousine led to the expression of displeasure. These highlighted the relevance of the subjective in human affairs, particularly in the higher echelons. This was equally true of some of the visiting high-level dignitaries. The challenge in each case was to resolve the crisis without much fuss and without allowing it to overflow into the wider objective of the visit. My colleagues and I generally succeeded in doing so and the confidence of my superiors in our ability to do so remained unimpaired.

---

[38] I.K. Gujral, *Matters of Discretion: An Autobiography* (New Delhi, 2011) pp. 195–99.

President Zail Singh's visit to Argentina in April 1984 helped us discover a Sikh community deep inland, in a place called Salta. The president was keen on visiting them and so it was included in the programme. Sardar Tarlochan Singh, his press secretary, and I located the eldest in the group since all others were Spanish speaking. He told us a fascinating story. He and another person from Punjab were dock workers in Calcutta in 1939 and, on a whim, smuggled themselves onto a ship 'going to a distant land'. Because of the interruption of World War II, they were able to re-establish contacts with their families a few years later and bring them over to Argentina.

The presentation of credentials by a new ambassador or high commissioner was an elaborate affair, with the new arrival being taken to Rashtrapati Bhavan in an open car, where he is escorted from the main gate by the 'sawars' of the President's Bodyguard, presented a guard of honour and then taken up in procession on the open staircase to the Ashoka Hall. The recipients of this honour loved every bit of the affair, but, it was, in equal measure, considered archaic and a waste of time by senior officials of the MEA, who had to be dressed formally. In my five years, I participated in about 130 of these ceremonies. Over time, the procedures have been simplified and now, I understand, group presentations is the norm. Traditions, even elegant ones, do not survive in our new age of time constraints.

The dean of the diplomatic corps, Ambassador Issa Al Issa of Kuwait, brought to my notice grievances in certain sections of his tribe regarding our procedures and restrictions. After some discussion, we worked out an arrangement in which once a quarter or so, the dean would invite me for a cup of tea at his residence along with interested heads of missions (selected by him). This arrangement worked to the satisfaction of all concerned.

In a very large diplomatic community, incidents and problems *did* surface from time to time. Tensions from the Iran–Iraq War (1980–88) led to Iraqi diplomats using firearms against Iranian student demonstrators. This impunity and breach of security were viewed seriously by us. Iraq's ambassador to India, highly connected in his own network, took his own sweet time to come to the ministry and did not defend the outrage. We had no option but to expel three members of his team. A West European mission's insistence on bypassing the usual immigration procedures for the repatriation of a defaulting staff member caused a midnight reading of the Riot Act. In another case, a head of mission's insistence on not calling on a joint secretary required more subtle correctives. And, in a period when electronic scanning of diplomatic cargo was not the norm at our airports, problems did surface from time to time.

Developments in the Libyan Arab Republic led its resident mission to intimate formally in a note verbale[39] that the embassy would henceforth be designated a 'People's Bureau established on the debris of the traditional system of embassies' for contacts with foreign governments. I had to inform the head of mission that while he was free to act on his government's instructions, a change in nomenclature would, on our side, result in the withdrawal of immunities and facilities extended to him under our laws. This persuaded him to adhere to the status quo.

A matter of perennial concern to resident heads of mission (except those from the most important countries) was that of access at appropriate levels. Since the principle of reciprocity is often invoked in such matters, our wider interest would seem to lie in a balanced approach. However, this was not always appreciated sufficiently by many colleagues and this problem seems to have aggravated over time.

The big challenge to protocol and, in fact, to the totality of our facilities emerged in October 1982 when, in response to an appeal from senior members of NAM, the PM agreed to host the Seventh NAM Summit in New Delhi, in the first week of March 1983. In

---

[39] A diplomatic communication prepared in the third person and unsigned. It is less formal than a note but more formal than an aide-mémoire.

normal practice and on previous occasions, the notice period for such summits was three years. The decision for the Seventh Summit was taken at the time of the Sixth Summit in Havana in September 1979. The decision to change the venue from Baghdad to New Delhi was taken on account of the ongoing Iran–Iraq War, both NAM members. The practical implications of this political decision were enormous. The preparation time for the summit was thus reduced to just five months and our existing facilities and capabilities for hosting a conference of this magnitude were clearly inadequate.

The next few months were hectic, to say the least. Natwar Singh, secretary in the external affairs ministry, was appointed Secretary-General of the conference. He headed a core committee with representatives from all the departments concerned. Protocol's responsibility pertained to arrivals, departures, accommodation, transport and liaison with our security agencies. Satinder Lambah, who was heading the Pakistan division, was made Deputy Secretary-General, responsible for making arrangements at the conference venue in Vigyan Bhavan. The whole team, within the MEA and from other departments, worked harmoniously in the short time given to us. Major challenges on my desk related to the availability of appropriate hotel accommodation and transport for the heads of state or governments attending the conference, as well as arrangements at the Delhi airport, including the parking of VIP aircraft or their dispersal to nearby airports.

As the date of the conference drew closer, security issues of formidable dimensions cropped up. Security for the outgoing NAM chairman, President Fidel Castro of Cuba, was *sui generis* since the Cuban threat perception related, as they put it, to US security agencies. We were fully appreciative of this and the requisite cooperation and assistance was extended. The Cuban leader's place of stay was a very closely guarded secret and so was the schedule of his arrival and departure. Two aircrafts, a Cuban and a Soviet, landed and took off within minutes of each other and the visitor emerged and departed in one of them. No less difficult were the security requirements of the Iraqi, Libyan and a few other leaders. Fortunately, no mishaps happened and our security procedures, which were carried out under the able supervision of R.N. Kao, Research and Analysis Wing chief, and his colleagues survived the test.

Given the number of prima donnas attending the conference, there was no dearth of protocol and procedural surprises. On one occasion, four heads of state arrived on the same plane and some innovative thinking led us to play along with what Brig. Bhandari from the army headquarters called the General Salute. Then one night, Major Jalloud of Libya arrived without any intimation. The Iraqi delegation arrived with over a dozen or more security personnel carrying weapons; they were made to disarm as they deplaned, but my suspicion was that a few still got away.

Dietary requirements were another headache. President Robert Mugabe of Zimbabwe brought along his own supply of beef steaks, but the Ashok Hotel kitchen, under a standing union agreement, refused to do the needful. The presidential dinner then had to be prepared in the adjoining hotel, but it was not allowed to be taken to his suite without a security check-up and tasting, making it go stone cold in the process. Hampers of drinks were made available to all heads of delegations, but a senior Bangladeshi delegate wanted the Pakistani share too, invoking the latter's laws against consumption of alcohol.

The conference itself was a challenge at times, especially with regard to the mediatory role of the chairperson when confronted by divergent viewpoints. After a late-night session, Mrs Gandhi commented (to her foreign policy aide, Ambassador Chinmaya Gharekhan) on 'the habit of diplomats' to indulge in prolonged late-night discussions when decisions could be arrived at earlier in the day.

Despite being busy with weightier matters, the PM found time (as always) to scrutinize the menu for the conference banquet being hosted by her and emphatically deleted from it Cuban cigars that Natwar Singh and I had deemed appropriate for the occasion and, in fact, ordered and received them. After rejection, these became the property of the hospitality section and as the word spread, I noticed a marked improvement in attendance at routine official dinners.

After the NAM marathon, the Commonwealth Heads of Government Meeting (CHOGM) in October 1983 was organizationally a simpler exercise except for the retreat at Goa. A few questions relating to ceremonial practices did emanate from the British, who could not understand why the door-opening time of Her Majesty the Queen's aircraft could not be at 1200 hours instead of the 1205 suggested by us[40] and also why the guard of honour at the National Defence Academy (NDA), Khadakwasla, had to be inspected by the Queen only and not with her consort, the Duke. More ticklish was the Queen's desire to have an investiture ceremony for Mother Teresa in Rashtrapati Bhavan; the finesse in Mrs Gandhi's tactics has been written about by Natwar Singh in *One Life Is Not Enough*. An instance of the PM's attention to detail in matters of hospitality, perhaps slightly excessive, surfaced when she insisted on seeing the menu of the lunch being hosted by the then chief minister of Andhra Pradesh for a visitor to Hyderabad and, being unhappy with it, suggested that Begum Idris Lateef, spouse of the then governor of Maharashtra, fly down from Bombay to Hyderabad to supervise it.

My involvement in the arrangements for two conferences, very ably assisted by colleagues such as Muthu Venkatraman, O.P. Dawesar and many others, was professionally and personally a satisfying experience and the work done was acknowledged. The Padma Awards list of January 1984 indicated a Padma Bhushan for Natwar Singh and a Padma Shri for me.[41]

Natwar Singh also presented me a framed photograph of a grumpy boy with the following inscription:

---

[40] This was as per the then prevalent practice of Rashtrapati Bhavan not scheduling any programme at 1200 noon. This was shared with the Buckingham Palace advance party and led them to speculate with the British media about astrological advice given by Indians.

[41] The Ministry of Home Affairs (Public Section); Padma Awards Directory (1954–2013) p. 74, sl. no 14 and 18.

> *As soon as the rush is over, I am going to have*
> ***A Nervous Breakdown,***
> *I owe it to myself, I worked for it, and nobody is going*
> ***To Deprive Me of It***

The photo frame remains in my study, a reminder of interesting times.

Our protocol ritual of that period required the Vice President of India to attend the national day receptions of foreign diplomatic missions in New Delhi. In that context, I saw a good deal of the then vice president Mohammad Hidayatullah, who was genial, communicative and a stickler for rules. On one occasion when he was officiating as President during President Giani Zail Singh's absence abroad for medical treatment, I asked him about the controversial Indian Post Office (Amendment) Bill, which was pending presidential approval to become law and whether it would be placed before him (Hidayatullah) for signature. 'They dare not,' was the cryptic answer. The bill was destined to have a longer history since Zail Singh kept it pending till the end of his term in what Fali Sam Nariman later described as 'a calculated process of deliberate inaction'.[42]

The long-standing practice of according ceremonial honours to visiting heads of state and government at the airforce section at the Delhi airport was subjected to critical scrutiny on the commuting time taken and the traffic disruption that resulted. I was asked to undertake a study of the practice elsewhere in the developing and the developed world. On its basis, a report was submitted to the PM suggesting that a good alternative would be to conduct this ceremony in the forecourt of Rashtrapati Bhavan. Punctilious to details, she wished to see a dress rehearsal, which was scheduled for 1 November 1984. However, fate wished otherwise. The new system became operational sometime in 1985.

By the end of summer 1984, I had done protocol for over four years. So I was looking forward to greener pastures abroad, and

---

[42] Fali. S. Nariman, *Before Memory Fades: An Autobiography* (New Delhi, 2001) p. 434.

remarked to a visiting fellow professional that I had experienced and handled every ceremonial situation except a state funeral. I was to learn that I had anticipated fate.

A little earlier, on her return after attending the funeral of Marshal Tito of Yugoslavia, Mrs Gandhi had commented on the efficacy of the arrangements made there and enquired why our own on similar occasions could not be likewise. The query, addressed to the foreign secretary, landed on my desk for appropriate action. My response was that these arrangements were the allocated responsibility of the home ministry and were spelt out in an MHA book of instructions, whose copy was in my office drawer but never used. I did, however, point out that our traditions and practices of public expression of grief invariably transcended ceremonial procedures on such occasions.

In 1984, President Zail Singh was on a state visit to the Yemen Arab Republic and was scheduled to return home on the afternoon of 31 October. With no official engagements that morning, all members of the entourage went about their business casually. Around nine in the morning (IST–2hrs 30 min), the president received a call from Foreign Secretary Rasgotra informing him of the attempt on the PM's life. He ordered immediate departure and with some effort and assistance from the Yemeni authorities for deviation from air corridors, etc, the travel time was shortened and the presidential aircraft was able to reach Delhi by around sunset. At the Delhi airport, Rasgotra told me to proceed to the ministry and chair a meeting about funeral arrangements. Fortunately, most of the members of the NAM-CHOGM team were present in Delhi and we were able to identify the task ahead fairly quickly. The next three days, however, were to show a very different set of challenges.

In the days preceding the funeral, the situation in Delhi was anything but normal. Lawlessness seemed to prevail in parts of the city and killings of members of the Sikh community were rampant. Apathy and neglect at the official and political levels were evident. One of my protocol deputies, a Sikh lady, and her family, were rescued only when a senior Intelligence Bureau officer acted beyond the call of duty and was assisted by off-duty colleagues outside duty hours. In such a situation, orderly arrangements for the participation of a large number of high-level dignitaries from abroad in the funeral posed unanticipated challenges. Since a large number of motorcades could not be allowed near the cremation site and also due to the absence of tourist coaches whose drivers (mostly Sikhs) had disappeared, foreign dignitaries were transported part of the distance in Delhi Transport Corporation buses—a rare happening indeed! Their anxiety to embark and disembark from the buses was not very different from that of regular passengers. One foreign dignitary and two of our own senior people were actually transported in a police patrol car.

My tenure as CoP remains the longest in the history of independent India. It was stressful but enjoyable. By the end of the year, I was informed of my next assignment, Australia. Schooling for two of our children was a high priority and we looked forward to being in Australia with its obvious advantages of being an English-speaking, sports-loving land. Our departure for Canberra was unexpectedly delayed by a few weeks since Salma landed up in Holy Family Hospital for a gall-bladder surgery by our old friend and reputed surgeon, Dr Randhir Gupta. As soon as she recovered, we left for Canberra.

CANBERRA

Much has been written about the role played by camels and camel men from India in the opening up of inner Australia. Despite many affinities as being 'colonial cousins' and having ecclesiastical connections through the new bishop of Calcutta being the bishop for the whole of Australia on the one hand, and some less savoury connections of social behaviour on the other, as well as sporting ties and the English language, Canberra as a posting was not highly rated in our scheme of things then. My predecessor, a very senior colleague, had sought an early move since, as he put it in the customary handing-over brief, 'there is not much content, let alone liveliness, in Indo-Australian relations'. Trade was minimal;

the Australian definition of Asia tended to begin with Thailand; ties between the armed forces had all but stagnated; academic contacts were left to the initiatives of individual scholars and political contacts to the periodic Commonwealth conclaves.

Before departure from Delhi, I was told about the decision to undertake extensive repairs and renovation to the residence on Mugga Way. This prestigious property was acquired by the first high commissioner to Australia, Sir Raghunath Purushottam Paranjpe, in January 1945. My first task on arrival in Canberra was to move into a rented villa in the suburb of O'Malley, where a few other diplomatic missions had their residences. We discovered, much to our delight, that our next-door neighbour was the Jordanian ambassador and our old friend from Rabat, Sulaiman Dajani. He, his charming wife Huzaima and their three daughters made the settling down in a new city much easier. Sulaiman induced me to take up golf and join the Royal Canberra Golf Club, where I was to spend many mornings and afternoons over the next four years.

Preparing for an early call on the CoP, Tonia Shand, led to the distressing discovery that my credential papers had yet to be received in the mission from my old charge in the MEA. A candid confession of this, CoP to CoP, brought forth a solution: a blank envelope that would not be opened in the ceremony. Compared to the rituals at Rashtrapati Bhavan, the Presentation to the Governor General of Australia was a much simpler affair.

A newcomer to Australia discovers sooner than later the peculiarities of the Aussie dialect and its robust terminology. A case in point is the multiple meanings of the term 'bastard' and the offence it caused on the first encounter to generations of English cricketers. It is often used as a term of endearment in Australia, unless combined with a harsher adjective. 'Whatever kind of a bastard the boss might be, he usually rolls up his sleeves [and] looks like one of the boys.'[43] The story told is of a very senior Australian Labour Party

---

[43] Donald Horne, *The Lucky Country* (Penguin Books, Australia, 1964) p. 18.

(ALP) politician, Bill Hayden, complaining in the early 1980s to the leader of the Opposition in the Senate, John Button, about another senior member (Bob Hawke) addressing him so. Button's response was telling: 'to the best of my knowledge, calling someone a bastard has never been a disqualification in Australian politics'.

A couple of years before my arrival in Canberra, the ALP government of PM Hawke had undertaken a comprehensive reappraisal of Australia's foreign relations in the context of the end of bipolarity, the emergence of Japan and China as important trading partners and the potential of beneficial ties with the Association of Southeast Asian Nations (ASEAN) and others in the neighbourhood. This covered the strategic dimensions of increasing naval involvement including a review of ties with India; its outcome was candidly expressed by Foreign Minister Hayden: 'A failure to recognize the scale of India's performance and a serious misunderstanding of India's anxieties and objectives.' He stressed in conclusion that 'the relatively low level of priority we have given to our relationship with India has not been to our advantage'. Consequently, the Centre for the Indian Ocean Region at the Curtin University of Technology in Fremantle in Western Australia was established in 1980.

In accordance with this, and perhaps also anxious to undo the damage done by an unusually sharp exchange between Australian and Indian leaders in a CHOGM summit, the effort in Canberra was to breathe some vitality into a relationship that had stagnated. This took the shape of PM Rajiv Gandhi's visit to Australia in October 1986 and a return visit by PM Hawke in February 1989; both these, in Hawke's words, led to 'injection of new vitality' and rejuvenation of the relationship.

Within the framework of these efforts, differing perceptions between India and Australia on global issues did crop up from time to time. One of these was Fiji and, given our interest in it, the PM sent a special envoy to Australia to explain our viewpoint. Hawke was polite but his acting foreign minister, Gareth Evans, was sharp in asserting the Australian understanding of the matter. Another matter on which perceptions differed significantly was with regard to our efforts to develop the Indian navy and the leasing of INS Chakra from the Soviet Union and its journey from Vladivostok, in the Russian Far East, to Visakhapatnam. Faced with budgetary constraints and amidst a raging domestic controversy, the Australian government had earlier decommissioned its sole aircraft carrier and the Opposition therefore sought to use the journey of INS Chakra to ridicule the government's incapacity to safeguard Australian interests. In TV debates, I was asked why India needed a blue-water navy; in response, I drew attention to their own defence minister's earlier assertion that 'there is no such thing as a brown-water navy'! (There has since been a sea change in Australian thinking on these matters.)

Despite changing perceptions at the political level, the process of raising awareness was time consuming. In the initial period, Australia was averse to our suggestion of directly marketing Argyle diamonds in India instead of doing it through the Central Selling Organization in London; it sought a joint coal group for the marketing of coal instead of our suggestion for a joint business council to promote trade and investments. It saw no merit in an Australia-India Council on the pattern of the existing Australia-China Council. It did not respond positively to our suggestion of an exhibition of sculptures as part of the Australian Bicentennial. It cited budgetary constraints for the funding cuts for the locus of South Asian studies in the Australian National University (ANU) established decades earlier by the author of *The Wonder That Was India*, A.L. Basham. As a result, suggestion for intensifying academic exchanges remained confined to individual scholars in different universities.

Many of these shortfalls were acknowledged in a report of the Standing Committee on Foreign Affairs, Defence and Trade of the Senate in 1989 and correctives strongly urged. The Australia-India Council, I understand, was established in May 1992. The evolution in Australian strategic perceptions was reflected comprehensively in the 2012 White Paper on 'Australia in the Asian Century'. This included a mention of India, along with Japan and South Korea, as 'nations with which we share a widening range of security interests'. This was followed by the 2013 national security policy document 'Strong and Secure: A Strategy for Australia's National Interest'.

There were a great many joys of being in Australia and every member of the Ansari family has his/her own tales and recollections of it. I travelled extensively in the continent (a 60-hour train journey from Sydney to Perth being one of them), watched a good deal of cricket and had the opportunity of meeting famous Australian cricketing legends such as Keith Miller and Alan Davidson. On one occasion, in the press box at the Sydney cricket ground, I had an interesting conversation with the American journalist and author Bill O'Reilly, who tended to share my views on the Kerry Packer version of cricket. I corresponded with Sir Donald Bradman about a suggestion made by the president of the BCCI, N.K.P. Salve, and offered to visit him in Adelaide. His polite letter of regret remains a cherished memento.

I discovered and visited in the neighbourhood of Melbourne a bookshop that was exclusively devoted to cricket literature. There, I acquired a copy of a booklet (number 177 of a limited edition of 200) on *Cricket's Imperial Crisis of 1932–1933*, which was written by Brian Stoddart and published by the Australian Cricket Society. The book opened with the text of a telegram sent in January 1933 by the Australian Cricket Board of Control to the Marylebone Cricket Club (MCC) in London. It referred to a situation arising out of bodyline bowling, calling it 'unsportsmanlike', and asserted that 'unless stopped at once [it] is likely to upset friendly relations existing between Australia and England'. The MCC 'deplored' the message and 'deprecate[d] the opinion that there has been un-sportsmanlike play'. The situation was considered serious enough for the two governments to get involved. The British representative in Australia was asked to have the word 'unsportsmanlike' withdrawn or else face the cancellation of the tour with all its attendant implications for the imperial relationship. These interventions resulted in a statement by the Australian Board that 'we do not regard the sportsmanship of your team as being in question... We join heartily with you in hoping that the remaining Tests will be played in the traditional good feeling'.[44]

I met many people of Indian origin, including members of the Sikh community in Woolgoolga in New South Wales (subject of a 1984 Sydney University sociological study *Indians in White Australia*), many Anglo-Indians from Calcutta in the Perth region, professionals in Sydney and Melbourne and a smattering of academics in universities.

A particularly satisfying aspect of being in Australia was interacting with university scholars who had an interest in Indian studies. Many of them were students of Prof. Basham and had sustained their interest in India-related studies. These included Jordens in ANU, Jim Massilos in Sydney, Robin Jeffery in La Trobe, Peter Reeves and his team in Perth, Carl Bridge and S. Arasaratnam in New England. I was made a life member of the South Asian Studies Association of Australia and New Zealand.

A little over 8 per cent of Australians claim Scottish ancestry. I was invited twice to the St Andrew's Day dinner of the Melbourne Scots, a Scottish society in Melbourne formed in 1919 to 'foster Scottish sentiments and to maintain Scottish traditions'. As per convention, I had to be a speaker on the second occasion. I said my countrymen have a traditional reverence for trinities, in this case being Scotland, Australia and India. I also added that while in contemporary India, the term 'scotch' commands a wider recognition than the word 'scot', our historical memory of British rule indicated that the imperial system tended to have English administrators, Irish policemen and Scottish traders and educators and, for that reason, an Indian can be forgiven for remembering them with greater fondness than for the other two!

My group in the Royal Canberra Golf Club included, apart from Sulaiman Dajani, Tan Sri Zakaria of Malaysia, Admiral T.K. Khan of

---

[44] Harold Larwood eventually migrated to Australia in 1950 and was given a friendly reception.

Pakistan, Abol Hasan of Lebanon and Jaafar Abdollah of Brunei. The idyllic surroundings of the club, and its kangaroos, remain embedded in memory. The frequency with which Admiral Khan and I played golf together induced the head of the South Asian desk in the Ministry of Foreign Affairs to enquire if some quiet diplomacy was underway!

In January 1988, I inaugurated in Sydney the *Anjuman Taraqqi-e-Urdu* (Australia) and in my address said that even in distant Australia the poet Daagh Dehlvi's couplet remains valid.

Urdu hai jiska naam hamien jante hain Daagh
Saare jahan main dhoom hamari zubaan ki hai

(We do know, Daagh, that the name of our language,
Urdu, is renowned the world over.)

Salma divided her time between being a high commissioner's spouse, playing tennis at the court of the residence that had become a representational asset and dabbling in the mystical healing powers of crystals. Salma and I travelled a good deal in Australia. Apart from frequent visits to Sydney and Melbourne, visits to Perth, Darwin, Brisbane and Hobart were enjoyable. We also visited Alice Springs, where Salma climbed the Ayers Rock (Uluru); this is now forbidden in deference to local sentiments. Sulaiman entered ANU. Nuriya was active and happy in her school and young Osman had his first taste of schooling in a nursery. My nephew Rashid (Rooshi) spent a year with us in Canberra before returning home.

Late in the summer of 1988, I was informed by Delhi that my next assignment would be Afghanistan. On the informal net, it was whispered in my ear that some other options in the neighbourhood were also considered, but not pursued. The official communication also said that the precise time of the move would be indicated later, closer to the date of the proposed Soviet withdrawal pursuant to the Geneva Accords, then in its final stages of negotiations. This state of tentativeness continued for several months. Then, at the end of March, Foreign Secretary S.K. Singh called, instructing me to immediately proceed to Kabul since the Afghan government attached importance to the Indian envoy's presence there at that juncture.

We left Canberra on 7 April. Sulaiman stayed back to complete his studies in Comparative Religion in the ANU. By the time I departed the country, a joint business council was fully functional and so was a science and technology agreement and memorandums of understanding on space and meteorology. An Australian aid package for the Piparwar coal mine project was also initialled during the Hawke visit that year. Other identified areas of cooperation included railways, telecommunications and agricultural research. The Australian Parliamentary Friendship Group of India, with about 30 MPs, was functional and the House of Representatives proceedings of 6 April record an appreciation of the work done by the outgoing high commissioner to enhance bilateral ties.

KABUL

I had used the intervening period to catch up on my reading on Afghanistan. Foremost among these was Vartan Gregorian's classic, *The Emergence of Modern Afghanistan: Politics of Reform and Modernization*. Rosanne Klass's *Afghanistan: The Great Game Revisited* was useful on recent happenings. I was fortunate to find two important works from an antiquarian bookshop at Berrima on the highway from Canberra to Sydney. One was Dilip Kumar Ghose's *England and Afghanistan: A Phase in their Relations* and the other was G.P. Tripathi's *Indo-Afghan Relations 1882–1907*. The latter included the text of the aide-mémoire given by London to the foreign secretary in the Government of India, Sir Louis Dane, who was deputed as a special envoy to Kabul in 1905 to negotiate a new treaty with the Amir of Afghanistan. Its operative clauses were candid.

> You should proceed on the assumption that the objects, interests and the enemies of the two countries are identical, and that their policy should be one of harmonious cooperation... Our object

throughout is to bind the Amir to us by ties of self-interest in which a set of quid pro quos (control of foreign relations, abandonment of intrigues with frontier tribes, and be a barrier to the advance of Russia) were mentioned in return for subsidies and arms.[45]

Representing India in Afghanistan thus necessitated an awareness of recent happenings as well as ancient history. Much has to be overlooked, if not forgotten. Ever since our Independence, the two countries have grown closer to each other based on a mutuality of interests and yet remained cautious and avoided involvement in each other's disputes with other countries. We did not support Afghanistan on the Pashtunistan issue or on the question of the 1893 Durand Line Agreement. Afghanistan adopted a similar approach to Indo-Pak matters. Zahir Shah was not supportive of India in 1947–49, 1965 and 1971. He equivocated on the Kashmir issue. Despite these unstated reservations, bilateral relations developed vigorously with frequent high-level visits and our developmental assistance projects such as several agricultural research stations and irrigation projects. An industrial estate in Kabul and the 100-bed children's hospital gifted by PM Indira Gandhi during her visit, also in Kabul, were greatly appreciated.

An unstated objective of our policy in Afghanistan was (and remains) the effort to counter and contain Pakistan's influence in Kabul. It was understood that Pakistan would be wary of close relations between India and Afghanistan.[46] Writing many years later,

---

[45]G.P. Tripathi, *Indo-Afghan Relations, 1882–1907* (New Delhi, 1973) pp. 175–87.
[46]A former foreign secretary of Pakistan, Riaz Mohammad Khan, has spelt this out in his book, *Afghanistan and Pakistan: Conflict, Extremism and Resistance to Modernity* (Washington & New Delhi, 2011). He also asserts that the Durand Line 'is a non-issue' since:
> The Pakistanis must understand that there cannot be a conventional, firm border formally recognized by Afghanistan, because such a notion would defy the region's history, geography and demographic realities. For their part, the Afghans must appreciate the necessity for a line marking the juridical and legal boundaries between the two countries; and, as the colonial

journalist Jonathan Steele of *The Guardian* observed that:

> India is not a major element in the current Afghan equation. Its position on Afghanistan's future is mainly seen in terms of denial. The Indians do not want a government in Kabul that is a close ally of Pakistan. The same is true of Pakistan's desires, only in reverse. This zero-sum logic has not changed from the time of the Daoud Khan regime and the subsequent Soviet occupation to Obama's war today.[47]

Referring to India's polite relations with the mujahideen and contacts with the Northern Alliance, he opined that 'India will have an important role to play in any talks on a regional agreement, provided it does not allow its dispute with Pakistan over Kashmir to distort the agenda or delay a solution.'[48]

Despite our unhappiness with the Soviet intervention, and PM Charan Singh's categorical refusal to endorse the intervention[49], the return of Mrs Gandhi to power and the overall geopolitical situation put constraints on our ability to oppose it.[50] The result was a policy of temporization, articulating our support for a friendly, moderate and stable Afghanistan, giving such assistance as was possible under conditions of conflict and lack of connectivity, maintaining good working relations with the Afghan government and contacts with most segments of Afghan opinion within the country and in exile,

---

precedents dictate, there has to be the Durand Line. Improved operational and functional management of the border is in the interest of both countries. (p. 164) Also, p. 338.

[47] Jonathan Steele, *Ghosts of Afghanistan: The Haunted Battleground* (Berkeley, CA, 2001) pp. 384–85.

[48] ibid.

[49] J.N. Dixit, *Across Borders: Fifty Years of India's Foreign Policy* (New Delhi, 1998) p. 134.

[50] ibid., pp. 137–38. She adopted a policy stance in which (i) opposition to intervention to be conveyed bilaterally to the Soviet leadership, (ii) no one-sided criticism of USSR in multilateral fora but opposition of intervention by all and (iii) general support to the People's Democratic Party of Afghanistan (PDPA) government.

refusing to have a formal policy for Afghan refugees but nevertheless allowing them to enter India and even allowing an official of UNHCR[51] to function in New Delhi under the banner of UNDP[52]. This, and memories of older personal and cultural affiliations, did help to temper the unhappiness and sense of betrayal in various segments of Afghan society (except in the hardline mujahideen groups) over our policy in the aftermath of the Soviet intervention.

After a few days of official briefings in New Delhi and leaving Salma and the children in the IFS apartment in Kasturba Gandhi Marg, I arrived in Kabul while the battle of Jalalabad was in full swing. The battle, mercifully, ended soon after with the victory of the Afghan government forces and a setback to the mujahideen and their Inter-Services Intelligence-sponsored Afghan Interim Government (AIG). This has since been acknowledged by responsible Pakistani officials.[53] The situation, nevertheless, was tense and my instructions were to destroy papers and be prepared to leave at short notice. The only diplomats left in the mission were Minister S.K. Mathur, two service advisors, Col. Amar Singh and Group Captain Pandey, and Shyam Mehra and Badan Singh from the Cabinet Secretariat. The Indian community in Kabul, many of them long-time residents, continued their stay and commercial activities in the city throughout the turbulent period; so did Dinesh Oberoi, an engineer working in the electricity department on deputation from a UN agency.

Shortly after my arrival in Kabul, a colleague in Islamabad sent me a clipping from the Urdu newspaper *Nawaiwaqt* of 25 April that reported the posting of a new Indian envoy in Kabul. It added that 'he is reckoned among those Indian diplomats who are equipped with the capacity of deeply interfering in the internal affairs of the countries of their stay'. Separately, High Commissioner Mani Dixit

---

[51]United Nations High Commissioner for Refugees.
[52]United Nations Development Programme.
[53]Asad Durrani, *Pakistan Adrift: Navigating Troubled Waters* (New Delhi, 2018) pp. 15–16 and 133.

sent me a note with a teasing comment: 'Welcome to the ranks of wicked Bharti diplomats!'

The embassy residence, a palatial structure that was acquired at the time of General P.N. Thapar, and its rose garden, considerably improved upon by Ambassador S.K. Singh and Mrs Manju Singh, extended a warm but somewhat lonely welcome. The butler and majordomo Mohammad Khan, who had joined service when Gen. Thapar was Ambassador, put me through the paces and Col. Amar Singh briefed me about the perils of rocket attacks, on the technique of ducking under the desk on hearing the whistling sound of incoming rockets and on the need to sleep in a ground-floor bedroom made secure by sand bags. I followed his advice the first night, but I found the arrangement to be suffocating. I then decided to sleep in the master bedroom, come what may.

There were other aspects of security that needed attention. The UN personnel suggested that shatter-proof film be put on glass panes of windows to guard against rocket or bomb explosions in the vicinity. They gave me the address of the American company manufacturing it and I forwarded it post-haste to Delhi for purchase. The process, I was told, required an Indian source of supply and that would take a little time. Irritated at the delay, I sent off a telegram in cricketing terminology: 'If I have to field at forward short leg, I need protective gear.' The telegram arrived in Delhi on a Sunday and found its way, unscreened, to PM Rajiv Gandhi's table. What followed can only be described as a minor storm since none of the officials in the immediate circle could decipher the message. I was reminded of the need to use standard vocabulary; alongside, the supply of the item so desperately required was expedited.

I presented my credentials to President Mohammad Najibullah. As a Pashtun who grew up in Peshawar, he spoke fluent Urdu and, as our conversations developed, it became clear that India's support and assistance were high on his list of priorities. He felt India could help in this and, on one occasion, he asked me if in the event of elections being held, India could assist by sending Lata Mangeshkar and Amitabh Bachchan.

My first headache was the Afghan public's demand for Indian visas. An unforgettable sight was the long line of visa seekers and the disappointment on the faces of the applicants when our very limited staff could not attend to most of them. On my first visit to Delhi for consultations, I brought this to the notice of External Affairs Minister Narasimha Rao, who directed that a team of officials be sent on temporary duty to Kabul to clear the backlog. As this exercise progressed, Foreign Minister Wakil Ahmad Muttawakil called to complain that the mission was causing an exodus. My response was that only those with valid passports were attended to, and he reacted by citing political compulsions. I returned the compliment and after a fortnight, the queues disappeared.

PM Rajiv Gandhi took a good deal of interest in developments in Afghanistan and quizzed me closely on military developments. On one occasion, he asked me to leave behind an operational map that I had taken to better explain the ground situation. In these meetings, there was no mention of the role he is said to have played in the abortive US-USSR-Pakistan and Afghanistan discussion on Afghanistan in 1985–87.[54]

President Najibullah's determination at the time of the battle of Jalalabad demonstrated the capacity of the government forces to fight unassisted by the Soviet army and also gave him the confidence to pursue his policy of opening contacts at local levels with mujahideen groups. He also spoke about accelerating the process of political reconciliation. He seemed receptive to the idea of national reconciliation as an alternative to bloodshed and fratricide. In the process, he presided over the reversal of virtually every aspect

---

[54]Kallol Bhattacherjee, *The Great Game in Afghanistan: Rajiv Gandhi, General Zia and the Unending War* (New Delhi, 2017); chapters 4 and 5, especially pp. 150–53 and pp. 245–76, n. 46–48, referring to President Reagan's letter to PM Rajiv Gandhi on the eve of Soviet leader Mikhail Gorbachev's four-day official visit to India in November 1986. Bhattacherjee's account also refers to President Najibullah's visit to New Delhi in December 1987, to the developments in the US Congress relating to Pakistan and its impact on Indo-US relations.

of the revolutionary process, abandoned the plan of the People's Democratic Party of Afghanistan (PDPA) for social transformation of the countryside and sought to reconcile the ethnic-ideological factions in his own party; this latter move failed and led to the attempted coup d'état of 6 March 1990 by his own defence minister, Shahnawaz Tanai. He defected to Pakistan after the failed coup and was alleged to have been hosted by the Central Intelligence Agency.[55]

March 6 was a normal day. I came to the residence for lunch and then started browsing through a pile of newspapers that had come that morning by the weekly diplomatic bag. Suddenly, I heard the sound of explosions. I ignored them for a few minutes and then got up to enquire from my security, who thought they were caused by the normal rocket fire from the mujahideen in the vicinity. Unable to get across on telephone to my military advisors, and on an instinct, I rushed to the car and drove to the chancery, where telephone facilities were a little better. I then learnt from Ross Mountain, the head of the UNDP team, that the city was being bombed from the air.

About 10 minutes after I left for the chancery, one of these bombs landed in the garden of the residence and its impact blew away the façade and the first floor of the house—and the chair on which I had been sitting! It also blew up a massive portion of the wall separating us from the Italian residence. The crater in the garden was almost six feet deep. Next morning, Col. Singh opined that it was caused by a thousand-pound bomb. I spent the next few days and nights in my office till basic repairs could be carried out at the residence.

These lines would not have been written had I kept reading the newspapers a few minutes longer! It is certainly a case of 'Providence sitting up aloft'.

A few weeks later, Foreign Minister Wakil telephoned to invite me to witness the *Nauroz* festivities in the northern city of Mazar-i-

---

[55] A somewhat dramatized account of what preceded the coup was given later by Steve Coll in the *New Yorker* on 28 November 2012: 'In Afghanistan, Dinner and then a Coup,' https://www.newyorker.com/news/daily-comment/in-afghanistan-dinner-and-then-a-coup.

Sharif. According to local legend of a much later date, it is considered the burial place of the Fourth Caliph, Ali ibn Abi Talib. I accepted the invitation but later repented when he welcomed me and our interpreter Shamim Quraishi onboard a military plane. We reached our destination safely and only then discovered the reason for the invitation: to participate in celebrations being attended for the first time by President Najibullah.

The city owes its name and fame to the Blue Mosque, which is said to be the mausoleum of the Fourth Caliph, Ali ibn Abi Talib, who was assassinated around the year AD 658 and was buried in Kufa in Iraq. Legend has it that the body was brought to the vicinity of Balkh by a camel. The original structure was destroyed in the Mongol invasion and was rebuilt by one of the Seljuk sultans in the fifteenth century.[56]

Later in the day, and before returning to Kabul, we witnessed a buzkashi (goat dragging) match. The Blue Mosque and the mausoleum, striking in appearance, are the centrepieces in the city and are places of pilgrimage, particularly for the Hazaras. The town of Mazar-i-Sharif itself is in close proximity to the ruins of the ancient city of Balkh, the capital of many ancient and medieval kingdoms, famous for its earlier Zoroastrian and later Buddhist shrines and known as 'mother of cities' to the Arabs. I was keen to visit the ruins, but the security situation did not allow it.

There was one occasion when I had to face the Afghan president's fury over a bilateral matter. A rival of his for power in the PDPA, Asadullah Sarwari, was exiled from Kabul, first as ambassador to Mongolia and then to the People's Democratic Republic of Yemen. He managed to leave Aden unannounced and come to Delhi. He was about to board a flight from Delhi to Kabul when he was detected by Afghan security personnel at the airline counter. A scuffle ensued and all concerned were arrested by the Delhi police. President Najibullah, using his own channels to the Cabinet Secretariat, requested his

---

[56]Nancy Hatch Dupree, *The Road to Balkh* (Kabul, 1967) pp. 49–52.

release and immediate repatriation to Kabul. He even sent a special plane for the purpose. The home ministry, however, insisted on the legal process being followed. At a reception in the palace a few days later, the president asked me to stay back till others had departed. He then walked up to me and said in chaste Urdu: 'Do you know that if I were not here, the flag of Pakistan would be flying over this building?' When I nodded in agreement, he asked why then was the Indian government insisting on legal technicalities. The matter got resolved after I spoke to all concerned in Delhi.

Najib's policy of seeking national reconciliation and gradual opening up of the political process made limited headway. It was also an admission of failure and a desperate attempt at survival by offering to the opposition groups within the country (excluding those in Pakistan and Iran) ceasefire and 'the right to a considerable share in government', because they had suffered for years and remained in the country. It led to the appointment of some personalities to ministerial positions. One evening, at a quiet dinner at a businessman's house, I asked one of these ministers about the authority conceded to them. His response, sent the next morning, was enigmatic. It was in the shape of an old poem by Abdu Rahman 'Shafqi' of Bokhara depicting a dialogue on the sharing of assets and duties between a brother and sister on the morrow of their father's death. A couplet summed up the conversation beautifully.

Az roo-e-huli ta ba lab-e-baam azaan-e-man
Az pusht-e-baam ta ba surayya azan-e-tu

(From the gate to the roof of the house is to be mine
From the roof to the sky is to be yours.)

The US approach to changes in Afghanistan seemed to waver. The proposed mutually acceptable 'negative symmetry' agreement never took off and the expectation was that after Soviet withdrawal the resistance factions would make substantive headway. Knowledgeable American opinion accepted the fact that the PDPA of President

Najibullah cannot be wished away before a broad-based successor government has been chosen.[57] One manifestation of this approach was an invitation to the New York-based non-governmental organization Human Rights Watch to send a team to Kabul to assess the situation. It was led by the former US ambassador to India, Harry Barnes, whom I had known from my time as CoP. He and his team came for dinner. He said that an official programme of meetings had been scheduled by the Afghan government, but he needed help in meeting people in the bazaar and in the university who were not overtly committed to the government. I responded positively and offered to host another dinner. After the Afghan guests departed, we sat down for a quiet chat and I told Ambassador Barnes that in our assessment, President Najibullah was anxious to become a traditional Afghan ruler and is, therefore, inclined to make such adjustments as may be needed to achieve it. I opined that this would include reconciliation with Pakistan. In response, Barnes simply shook his head and said that Afghanistan is no longer a foreign-policy matter in the US, but is instead very much on the domestic agenda that demands a change of regime in Kabul.

On 23 June 1990 and as part of its earlier initiatives, the Najibullah government announced a peace plan expressing its willingness 'to relinquish our monopoly of power and share power, but we are not prepared to sacrifice power in favour of anarchy and chaos'. This approach was reflected in the US–Soviet Union talks in July, with the latter taking the position that the Afghan resistance could not obtain at the negotiating table what it failed to achieve in the battlefield.

During the PDPA period, the diplomatic representation in Kabul was singularly one-sided. The Soviet embassy, headed in my time by Deputy Foreign Minister Yuli Vorontsov, was a class in itself—in terms of its size and importance—a virtual political fortress. For most non-Eastern Bloc diplomats in Kabul, the UNDP club in Kabul

---

[57] Selig S. Harrison, 'What Next in Afghanistan?' Testimony prepared for a hearing of the Subcommittee on Asian and Pacific Affairs, Committee on Foreign Affairs, US House of Representatives, 14 June 1989.

was both a 'watering hole' and a place to collect and piece together snippets of information and gossip. All socializing, however, had to conclude before the curfew hour of 9 p.m. More interesting and closer to ground reality were occasional meetings with members of the Indian business community (dubbed in our consular jargon as 'Afghan Hindus and Sikhs'), who worked as moneylenders and businessmen in the Kabul bazaar and had their associates in other cities. Occasionally, a political heavyweight such as the poet-revolutionary and minister for tribal affairs with Mujaddedi family connections, Sulaiman Laiq, would drop by to imbibe what he called 'the king of drinks'. (When last heard a few years back, he was seen emerging from a mosque in Peshawar sporting a Taliban-like beard. Truly, the doors of repentance are never closed!)

Dinesh Oberoi, an Indian engineer working for the Afghan government in Kabul and my two service attachés managed to revive interest in the resurrection of the Kabul golf course built in earlier days. It was on the outskirts of the city and within the firing range of an occasional rocket from the mujahideen groups in the Paghman Valley. Hazards notwithstanding, we did manage a round over the weekend. One Friday morning, we discovered that a mujahideen rocket had landed on some ammunition stored near the seventh hole and created a very visible hole-in-one! Sometime earlier, when the Soviet personnel were more visible, the *Economist* managed to have some innocent fun at the expense of the game: 'The Kabul Golf and Country Club has a new local rule: "a ball confiscated by a Soviet soldier may be replaced, not nearer the hole without penalty—and if it was a mujahideen who took it? The best rule is to run!"'

There were interesting asides to the diplomatic parleys with Afghan officials. On one occasion, the contents of a critically relevant liftvan of commissary stores from Denmark that had reached the Soviet-Afghan border had to be transported by air from there to Kabul, since the road was prone to mujahideen attacks. Our air attaché successfully negotiated for assistance from the Afghan air force. The operation commenced one afternoon. It landed at the

Kabul airport at around sunset and was being offloaded and put in embassy vehicles when the lights went off. Darkness descended for about 10 minutes and, in that period, a few cases disappeared. Next morning, formal apologies at different levels of hierarchy were forthcoming.

Being a non-family station (except for short visits by Salma, Nuriya and Osman), socializing in Kabul developed in its own ways. Apart from entertaining friends at the residence, diplomats and other foreigners often met at the informal club within the premises of the UNDP. The few Kabul-based journalists also came there to gather news and gossip, and among them were Lyse Doucet and Deepak Tripathi of the BBC. The former is now BBC's chief international correspondent and the latter an academic and author of several books on the follies of the US and other Western powers on what has been labelled as the Global War on Terrorism.

Amidst these distractions, and some bilateral irritations regarding procedures for the repatriation of a prominent opponent of the regime, Indo-Afghan relations progressed fairly smoothly. Our political support to President Najibullah was firm and consistent and was reiterated during his visit to India in August 1990. We expressed our support for national reconciliation and a negotiated political settlement based on existing realities and legitimate interests of all. Immediately after the visit, we sent medicines and food supplies to Afghanistan. Given the remarkable success of the Children's Hospital in Kabul donated by PM Indira Gandhi in an earlier phase, we initiated, but without much progress, exploratory discussions for a women's hospital too. An informed judgment on our policy was made a few years later by a former foreign secretary: 'We failed in giving effective support to the Government of Najibullah, who seriously attempted to move away from his Soviet connections to emerge as a leader with an Afghan national identity. We gave him general political support but our material assistance to him was less than adequate.'[58]

---

[58]Dixit, op. cit., p. 364.

General Abdul Rashid Dostum, the Uzbek strongman and a pillar of support to President Najibullah, enquired about medical treatment in Delhi. This was readily offered. His security advisors, however, felt less than comfortable about our arrangements and preferred the Central Committee Hospital in Moscow. According to an Afghan source, while there, a leading Soviet expert on Afghanistan called on him and the conversation went as follows: 'Comrade Dostum, what would happen if we stopped supplying arms to you?' The reply was brutally candid: 'If you stop the supply of arms, we will stop fighting; but when we stop fighting, you will start fighting.'

Shortly before the Afghan president's visit, I was called to Delhi by External Affairs Minister I.K. Gujral and told to prepare to proceed to Tehran. My objections on professional and personal counts were of no avail. Gujral said relations with Iran had hit rock bottom and that they needed to be addressed urgently. By that time, the MEA had already sought an agrément from the Iranian government!

In a farewell call on President Najibullah, he conferred an Afghan award on me despite my pointing out that my government's rules do not permit acceptance of foreign awards. He said, 'Afghan-India relations are not governed by rules.' I reported the matter to Delhi and, to my surprise, was allowed to retain the award. Referring to my next destination, President Najibullah said, 'I am a Pashtun; I do not trust the Iranian.' He gave me an autographed photograph of his with the inscription *'Ba doost-e-roz – hai – dushwar'* (to friend of difficult days).

At that stage, I had no premonition of the impending collapse of the Soviet state and of its immediate implications for Afghanistan's PDPA-led government that continued to labour with its publicly proclaimed ideology of a democratic and national struggle in the interest of '95 per cent of the people'. What was evident was its flawed effort to bolster a revolution from above and transform a very traditional countryside. The process was also hampered by the fatal divide between the Khalq and Parcham factions of the PDPA, which was reflective of the much deeper ethnic gulf[59] that ideology could not bridge and, as subsequent events were to show, contributed to President Najibullah's end, aided by Dostum's defection in March 1992 and the failure of the UN's attempt at an orderly, peaceful, transfer of power to the interim government of mujahideen groups.

I cannot help recall an earlier assessment of the Afghan thought process. Around the year 1935, poet Muhammad Iqbal was invited by King Nadir Shah, along with two other eminent Indians, for advice on educational reforms. Nothing significant seems to have come out of it. Iqbal did, however, write and dedicate a few Urdu poems to Afghanistan; one of these had a telling couplet:

Teri dua hai ki ho teri arzoo poori
Meri dua hai teri arzoo badal jai

(You pray for the fulfilment of your desire,
I pray that your desire be changed.)

Years earlier, during my tenure in Jeddah in the late 1960s, I had met the then Afghan ambassador to Saudi Arabia, Ustad Khalilullah Khaleeli. He was a poet of great repute—pious and retiring. In Kabul, I came across a poem of his, *Wada-e-fardaa* (Promise of Tomorrow). A couplet in it was expressive of the agony of a whole people:

Shab raft wa shikwa hai dilam na shaneenda mand
Ein arzoo ba wada-e-farda guzaashteem

(The night has passed but my heart's wail remains unheard
I spend it in this promise for tomorrow.)

I left for Delhi (from Kabul) on 20 September 1990 as I had to attend to family matters relating to the move to Tehran. Nuriya, who was in the British School, had to be shifted to a boarding school in Kodaikanal. We journeyed down south to leave her there and on the way back stopped for a day in Madurai to see the magnificent

---

[59] Aptly depicted as *Two Party Communism* by Anthony Arnold in his 1983 study.

Meenakshi Temple. The head pujari (priest) for the day had a puja for us since, as he put it, I represented India abroad.

Salma, Osman and I then travelled to Tehran on 13 October.

TEHRAN

Both history and geography have impacted India's relations with Iran. Tomes have been penned by scholars on the political, commercial and cultural interaction between the two societies and their state systems through the ages. A historian has observed that 'before the advent of Mughals in India, there were next to no relations between India and Persia on the diplomatic level, though there was, of course, an active and living contact in the realm of culture, ideas and commerce'.[60] In a different ideological framework, Iran 'is nothing but the base of *Aryabhumi*'.[61]

Before leaving for Tehran, I familiarized myself with the current state of bilateral relations between the two countries (India and Iran), which seemed to have emanated from the outbreak of insurgency in the Kashmir valley in January 1990 and Iranian statements in support of what they perceived to be an 'Islamic' cause. Iranian authorities also signalled that the time was inappropriate for the visit of our

---

[60] Riazul Islam, *Indo-Persian Relations: A Study of the Political and Diplomatic Relations between the Mughal Empire and Iran* (Tehran, 1970):
   The Mughals were not involved so deeply with any other foreign power, whether in friendship or otherwise. Their intercourse with Persia presents, in fact, the most important facet of the foreign policy... These relations were generally of a peaceful nature and an invasion in force by either side during this period never occurred. Qandahar was, however, a constant bone of contention, and changed hands several times, but its possession was not a matter of life and death for either party. (pp. xxi–xxii)

A recent work of diligent research, *Intertwined Lives: P.N. Haksar and Indira Gandhi* by Jairam Ramesh (New Delhi, 2018) records (on p. 313) a critical Iranian concern being articulated when Haksar called on the Shah of Iran on 24 January 1973. 'Tell me, quite frankly, is India even remotely interested in the breakup of Pakistan?' was the Shah's opening remark.

[61] M.S. Golwalkar, *His Vision and Mission* (Kochi, 2008) p. 45.

foreign minister. As a result, suspicions about Iranian intentions were rife in New Delhi.

On arrival in Tehran, I discovered that the atmosphere was almost antipathetic. Initial calls on ministers, which had nothing to do with foreign policy, tended to drift towards questions on the Kashmir 'situation' and the rights of the 'people of Kashmir'. On one occasion, where the discussion was on the possibility of a gas pipeline to India, I had to end the call by observing that these matters are in the domain of the foreign ministry. Since each of these meetings was covered by a foreign office official, the message seemed to go home.

'So you have finally arrived,' was the opening sentence of Rajai Khorasani, secretary of the foreign affairs committee of the Majlis and former PR to the UN, when I called on him. Puzzled, I asked him to elucidate. He said, 'Yours was the third name for which agrément had been sought and we were beginning to wonder if India was serious about having an ambassador to Iran.' On checking, I found this to be correct since two colleagues in the foreign service fraternity, for a variety of reasons, had expressed an inability to accept the assignment.

While presenting the Letter of Credence to the Iranian president, Hashemi Rafsanjani, I recalled Nehru's depiction of the Indian-Iranian relationship as that of twins lost in childhood but reunited as grown-ups through a tune familiar to them as children. I underlined India's desire to develop ties and strengthen its relationship with Iran by citing two couplets of Hafiz:

Baya ta gul bar afshaneem wa mai dar saaghar andazeem
Falak ra saqf ba shgaafeem wa tarhe nau dar andaazeem

(Come, so we may scatter roses of pleasure into the cup of existence
Pierce the roof of the sky and cast a new way.)

Agar gham lashkar angezad ki khoon-e-aashqaan raizad

Man o saqi beham saazim wa bunyadish bar andaazeem
(If grief sheddeth blood of the beloved
The saqi and I shall together uproot its foundations.)

The post-Khomeini Islamic Republic and the constitutional changes after it (subject to a referendum in which 56 per cent voted and approved the amendments by an overwhelming majority of 97 per cent), in which the late Imam's authority was divided 'between a clerically selected leader and a popularly elected President'[62], had by this time settled down and Rafsanjani's pragmatic approach on reconstruction was in evidence.

A few days after my arrival, I received a call from London. The caller identified himself as Gopichand Hinduja and welcomed me to Tehran. I was generally familiar with the name and with his role in the facilitation of some aspects of the relationship in the Shah's period. As time passed, I was to discover that the Hinduja family, notwithstanding its ties to Princess Ashraf Pahlavi of Iran, had succeeded in demonstrating its relevance to the new rulers of Iran and had established contacts at senior levels of the government. It was some time later, during my stay in New York, that I got to meet Hinduja personally. The experience underlined the relevance of informal channels in interstate relations.

The visa problem surfaced here too and was brought to my notice very early. The embassy had developed, perhaps on the pattern of missions of Western powers represented in Tehran, a complex and difficult procedure for Iranian nationals seeking visas. I took this up with Foreign Secretary Muchkund Dubey during my first visit for consultations. He advised wider consultations and after this was undertaken, left it to my judgment. 'You are plenipotentiary, but if you make a mistake, I will ask for your head!' On my return to Tehran, I reverted to normal procedures and the news soon spread

---

[62]Said Amir Arjomand, *After Khomeini: Iran Under His Successors* (New York, 2009) p. 37. Asghar Schirazi's *The Constitution of Iran: Politics and the State in the Islamic Republic* (London, 1998) has analysed in depth the constitution-making process.

in the bazaar that Indians no longer treat Iranians as pariahs.

Prior to my period, the denial of visa to a senior functionary of the Leader's office, Hojjatul-Islam Ali Tashkiri, had caused some unhappiness in that high office. I argued with Delhi that the points of contact of such a visitor would be to known places and personalities within Shia circles and unlikely to cause concern to our authorities. This was eventually accepted and the visitor's impressions, as conveyed to me, were generally but not exclusively positive.

Housekeeping problems were much in evidence. The chancery, rented many years earlier, was dilapidated and shabby. Alternate accommodation was expensive. With some difficulty, we managed to find a place in a street named (consciously and deliberately) after Khaled Islambouli, the assassin of President Anwar el-Sadat of Egypt. After much thought, a decision was taken to move the offices to a four-storey building purchased a few years earlier for residences of junior staff. It required some structural modifications on the ground floor, but the requisite permission was not forthcoming from the Tehran municipality. It was here that the full range of non-official contacts (cultivated during his 13-year stint) of our invaluable interpreter, A.A. Usmani came to our assistance. He sought the assistance of a friend, the Mayor of Shiraz, and resolved the problem. Usmani sahib, who along with an Iranian scholar had translated into Persian Dr Tara Chand's classic *Influence of Islam on Indian Culture,* had a wide range of contacts in cultural circles that reached the higher echelons and were at times resented by the officialdom in the Iranian foreign ministry. Some years later, he was instrumental in inducing a rethink on the stature of Maulana Abul Kalam Azad by bringing to the notice of eminent religious scholars in Iran such as Allameh Tabataba'i and Makarem Makarem Shirazi, the Maulana's theory that the Quranic figure of Dhul-Qarnayn (Sura 18 verses 83-101) was none other than Cyrus the Great. (This resulted in a square being built in memory of Maulana Abul Kalam Azad.)

In the autumn of 1990, Tehran still bore the imprint of the revolutionary period. Walls were painted with revolutionary slogans and sayings of Imam Khomeini. *A Decade with Painters of the Islamic Revolution*, which was published by the Art Centre of the department of Islamic Propaganda on the decade of the revolution, was gifted to me by a friend. Its preface describes the Islamic Revolution 'as the dawn of a new age by bringing about a divine transformation in the hearts of men and by renewal of a forgotten covenant... This renewed covenant necessitates the birth of a new art, thought and politics...' At the other end of the spectrum, a counterpoint, expressive of an average person's experience, was our Iranian driver's remark: '*Rahbar khudai mi-kunam, mardum gadai mi-kunam*' (the Leader plays God and the public has a begging bowl).

The Constitution of the Islamic Republic proclaimed Islam and the Twelver J'afari School as 'eternally immutable' official religion with full respect being accorded to 'other Islamic schools (Hanafi, Shafi'i, Maliki, Hanbali, and Zaydi)'. Alongside, 'Zoroastrian, Jewish and Christian Iranian are the only recognized minorities.' An unstated nuance of the latter is the exclusion of Anglicans and Catholics from their 'imperialist' associations and Baha'is, who in Khomeini's words 'are political factions, they are harmful. They will not be accepted'.

Despite official perceptions on the situation in J&K, conscious efforts were evident in containing differences. On one occasion, when on instructions I argued in the foreign office on an Iranian statement, the response was highly nuanced: 'A situation in *your* country has pained us. We do not have a remedy to relieve this pain; we know you have it and urge you to use it, get rid of the pain and you shall not hear about it from us.'

On the occasion of the Prophet's birthday, an annual gathering of Muslim ambassadors to felicitate Leader Ayatollah Khamenei was widely reported. I had it conveyed through Professor Jaafar Shahidi, a reliable channel, that on similar occasions in the period of the *Taghut* (tyrant, meaning the Shah) a Muslim envoy was invariably invited. The response was quick and emphatic: the error shall be corrected. A similar nuance was noticeable whenever the Islamic Conference came up for discussions in the context of its anti-Indian activities;

my Iranian interlocutors generally conceded India's position in the world of Islam, but cited constraints of OIC procedures.

The Iraqi invasion of Kuwait in August 1990 eventually led to Desert Storm[63], the US-led military operation to evict Iraqi forces from Kuwait and to the ceasefire on 28 February 1991. Iran condemned Iraq's invasion of Kuwait, but 'Rafsanjani was determined (after the experience of the Iraq war) to keep Iran out of any new conflict.'[64] I happened to visit the Iranian foreign ministry on the day of the ceasefire and in the corridors came across Shaikhul Islam, the deputy foreign minister in-charge of the Persian Gulf region. When I felicitated him on the 'defeat of your enemy', he said: 'the real enemy is now sitting next door to us'. Shortly prior to it, Rajiv Gandhi visited Moscow and Tehran as President of the Indian National Congress in an effort to explore the possibility of warding off war clouds around Iraq. He was accompanied by Sonia Gandhi. The Iranian government accorded him the status of a head of government and he had fruitful meetings with Rafsanjani and Foreign Minister Ali Akbar Velayati. A few months later, in May 1991, the news of his assassination brought to the embassy a large number of people from different walks of life who came to offer their condolences. These included former PM, Mehdi Bazargan and former foreign minister, Ebrahim Yazdi. I asked Bazargan if I could call on him; he said he would let me know. A message came a few weeks later; to go to his residence, however, I had to travel by taxi.

Bilateral economic relations, with primacy for energy supplies, were sustained. However, progress on the introduction of Indian products in the Iranian market was tardy. Initial exploratory discussions about a natural gas pipeline were initiated with Dr Rajendra Pachauri of the Energy and Resources Institute. Over decades, this has pursued a zigzag course, with many obstacles and

---

[63] On 16 January 1991, President George H.W. Bush announced the start of what came to be known as Operation Desert Storm.

[64] Michael Axworthy, *Revolutionary Iran: A History of the Islamic Republic* (London, 2013) p. 311.

variants. Suggestions for cooperation in some areas of science and technology remained stillborn for extraneous reasons attributed to Western pressures. One area of forward movement was the initiation of cooperation in naval training and the procurement of Indian-made batteries for Soviet-origin Iranian submarines.

Step by step, the bilateral relationship between India and Iran, vacillating between convergence and drift, tended to revert to its diversity that was based on the mutuality of interests. After the contretemps in early January, Foreign Minister Velayati wrote to I.K. Gujral and later in the year had a meeting with him in New York. Deputy Foreign Minister Alauddin Boroujerdi visited Delhi for joint commission-related matters and this was followed by visits by Foreign Minister Madhav Singh Solanki and Foreign Secretary Muchkund Dubey. Because of scheduling problems, the latter's return journey was delayed and the Iranian authorities were generous enough to fly him from Tehran to Dubai by a small executive jet aircraft in which Joint Secretary Naresh Dayal and I had to accommodate ourselves in the space at the rear of the plane meant for baggage. Foreign Secretary Mani Dixit visited Tehran in July 1992 with a letter from PM Narasimha Rao to President Rafsanjani and was told that Iran reciprocated the importance that India attached to the multifaceted bilateral relationship, 'was opposed to India's territory or unity being challenged in any manner' and that Iran's stand on Kashmir essentially emanated from religious perception of the unity of the Islamic world and this should be appreciated by India.[65] This approach was evident in developments later in the year.

Around this time, I received a communication from P.K. Iyengar, Secretary, Department of Atomic Energy, intimating that conversations with his Iranian counterpart on the sidelines of meetings of the International Atomic Energy Agency (IAEA) in Vienna had resulted in an Iranian request for the design of an experimental reactor. The accompanying package, the communication indicated,

---

[65] J.N. Dixit, *My South Block Years* (New Delhi, 1996) pp. 142–46.

was to be handed over to his counterpart personally. I sought a meeting and was told that this would be possible only after a month since the person concerned was travelling. In the intervening period, other developments led to my being asked to return the package to the sender.

Cultural relations are self-sustaining; at one level, they are reflective of deeper sensitivities nurtured over centuries. The influence of Persian Belles Lettres was pervasive in Mughal India, where patronage and prosperity attracted great many poets. The historian Abd-ul-Qadir Bada'uni enumerated 170, and scholar Shibli Nomani, citing Abul Fazl, has named 51 such poets who reached the court of Jalaluddin Akbar. One couplet, by Ali-Quli Salim (perhaps during Shah Jahan's reign) was reflective of the prevailing sentiments in literary circles:

Neest dar Iran zamin samaan-e-tahseel-e-kamal
Ta niyamad su-e-Hindustan hina rangeen na shud

(There exists not in Persia the means of acquiring perfection
Henna does not develop its colour until it comes to India.)[66]

Professor Juan Cole has opined that at the peak of the Mughal-Safavid period, there were perhaps seven times more readers of Persian in India than in Iran! The *Qand-e Parsi* did indeed reach all parts of India and left its mark on many of our languages. Prof. T.N. Devare of Poona (now Pune), in a seminal work published in 1961(and reprinted last year thanks to the effort of his son, Ambassador Sudhir Devare) had traced the impact of Persian in the Bahmani, Adil Shahi and Qutb Shahi courts in the Deccan and of its influence on Marathi. The world's first newspaper in the Persian language was published in Calcutta in 1823 by Raja Ram Mohun Roy of the Brahmo Samaj.

---

[66]Edward G. Browne, *A Literary History of Persia* (London, 1924), Volume IV, pp. 165–66. Also, Shibli Nomani, *Shir-ul Ajam* (Azamgarh, 1916), Volume 3, p. 10.

At another level, however, cultural relations left much room for inputs. We did not match the work being done in New Delhi by the Iran Culture House, and our visa policy post-revolution disrupted in good measure the flow of Iranian students going to Indian universities. Those who were fortunate enough to be admitted, including some in the higher echelons of the system, looked back with some pride and nostalgia on the time spent here and even formed themselves into an 'Association of Islamic Graduates from Indian Universities.' My effort to seek an invitation to their annual function met with a polite response: 'not yet'.

I was invited by the Iran Research Institute of Philosophy to give a lecture on Maulana Abul Kalam Azad. In my speech, I focused on his 'successful synthesis of Islam and nationalism' and the manner in which he was able to motivate Indian Muslims to participate in the freedom struggle and to consider it as an essential expression of their religious beliefs. I referred to his assertion (in 1927) that 'the large-heartedness of Islam neither negates nationalism nor is it necessary for nationalism to limit Islamic perceptions' and to his emphatic view on the role of Muslims in the national movement—'Whether we like it or not, we have now become an Indian nation, united and indivisible. No false sense of separatism can break our oneness.' I added that Abul Kalam Azad sought to eradicate the minority complex by asserting that factors other than proportionate difference in numbers are also important and that by these criteria the Muslims were not a minority in the accepted meaning of the word. Thus, nationality is not synonymous with the religious community since the two are in the shape of concentric circles that do not collide.

Witnessing the creative genius down the ages of the people of Iran (earlier known as Persia) is considered one of the blessings of spending time in that land. I have to confess that I did it inadequately. Preoccupation with work that focused on restoring the bilateral relationship to an acceptable level can be attributed as one reason; another was a shorter-than-usual tenure (26 months). Despite that, I did manage to imbibe a bit of Shiraz (described by E.G. Browne as 'the home of Persian culture, the mother of Persian genius, the sanctuary of poetry and philosophy'), visit the ruins of Persepolis, where the grand staircase bears bas-reliefs of tributary nations (including Indians) bringing presents, and the tomb of Cyrus on a high plinth at Pasargadae. I also experienced that the majesty of Isfahan's Maidan-e-Shah is reflective of the Safavid world vision; equally significant are the blue mosque of Tabriz built in Timurid grandeur and the shrine of Imam Reza at Mashad, a city famous for its innumerable madrasas including one named after its founder, Fazil Khan who, according to James Fraser's account 'made his money in India' but left a tablet in the building excluding three classes of people from it: 'Hindoos, Mazunderanees and Arabs; the first because they are void of truth; the second because they are quarrelsome; and the third because they are very dirty.'[67]

In September 1992, I was called to Delhi and told to undertake a special mission to Afghanistan. The assignment was to take a consignment of medical supplies to Mazar-e-Sharif, and to hand them over to the Uzbek warlord General Abdul Rashid Dostum, who had, earlier in the year, prevented President Najibullah from leaving Kabul. From Delhi, I flew in an Indian Air Force transporter. Special permission to overfly Pakistan had been taken. At Mazar, I was joined by Vijay Nambiar, our ambassador in Kabul and the embassy interpreter Dr Quraishi. We were told that Gen. Dostum was some distance away in his fort and this involved a helicopter journey in an Afghan helicopter. It was, to say the least, hazardous. We survived, met Dostum, delivered the gift and came back in the same helicopter to Mazar. There, I asked my namesake, the governor, if I could go to the market to buy the famed watermelons (*sardas*). In response, he presented a few dozen! They were loaded onto the plane, which then developed an engine snag, forcing us to stay there overnight. Communications being what they were, this change of plans could

---

[67]James B. Fraser, *Narrative of a Journey into Khorasan in the Years 1821–1822* (Reprint of the 1825 edition, New Delhi, 1984) p. 457.

not be communicated to the air force headquarters and caused a near panic. On return to Delhi the next day, I sent the bulk of the watermelons to the air chief and the air force mess since they were the only people privy to the special mission.

One Friday morning in October 1992, on my return from a game of golf at Tehran's well-crafted course in an earlier era, I received a telephone call from Delhi informing me of my transfer to New York to succeed Ambassador Chinmaya Gharekhan as PR to the UN. It came as a very pleasant surprise, perhaps tinged with the thought of leaving Tehran with many things only partially done, and some trepidation about a responsibility of multilateral work, with which I was unfamiliar.

An India-Iran Joint Commission Meeting in Delhi had been scheduled for mid-November. The Iranian team was led by Foreign Minister Velayati and, in a separate one-on-one meeting with PM Narasimha Rao, the wider context and framework of bilateral relations were set. One afternoon after the meeting, I went to see some colleagues in the MEA and was invited to join a special briefing for our envoys in the neighbouring countries on the Babri Masjid question. It was taken by the special adviser in the PMO, Naresh Chandra. On its conclusion, I asked one of the invitees, ambassador to a neighbouring country, about his impression. He said, 'The message is clear: we do not like it, but will do nothing to prevent it.'

The destruction of the Babri Masjid in Ayodhya on 6 December 1992 caused a sharp official and public reaction in Iran. There were demonstrations outside the chancery premises and the media was acerbic. Velayati summoned me and remonstrated in strong language. I noticed that apart from his usual aides who covered the meeting, a new face (presumably from the Leader's office) was also present. I reported the meeting to Delhi and was informed the next day of the government's response; I was told to convey that 'the mosque shall be rebuilt'. I conveyed this to the foreign minister, who said, 'This is satisfactory; I shall convey it to the leadership.' A few days later, I told Deputy Foreign Minister Boroujerdi that I should be given a chance to explain our position. This was forthcoming in the press and the television.⁶⁸

The outrage subsided but not without one last high-level outburst. It came in my farewell call on the second person in the pecking order, Speaker of the Majlis, Hojjat-ul Islam Ali Akbar Nateq Noori. His onslaught was sharp and disconcerting. The farewell call on President Rafsanjani, the next day, was a study in contrast. He spoke about the progress of relations in recent months, made some laudatory remarks about my work and the progress of bilateral relations, and asked me to convey his greetings to PM Narasimha Rao: 'I am sure he will soon get over his present difficulties.' This calibrated message was reflected in Iran's somewhat restrained reaction to the happenings and bore fruit when Pakistan mounted pressure on us in the UN Commission on Human Rights (UNCHR) meeting in Geneva, in March 1994.

The new trend in relations was in evidence when PM Narasimha Rao visited Tehran a few months later, in September 1993 and initiated a series of high-level visits that continued for over a decade.

Amidst the hectic activity of my last month in Tehran, Sulaiman got married on 29 December to Sanaz Asadi, an Iranian girl whose Indian father had much earlier settled and married in Iran. Official permission for the marriage was not forthcoming and required the intervention of President Rafsanjani's daughter, Fatima, whom Salma had assisted in organizing a charity bazaar (in the diplomatic corps) for victims of the then ongoing conflict in Bosnia.

The small but well-knit Indian community in Tehran gave us a

---

⁶⁸The assessment of Narasimha Rao's biographer is noteworthy: 'There is no question that Rao made the wrong decision on Babri Masjid. He should have imposed President's rule between November 1 and November 24.' (Vinay Sitapati, *Half Lion: How P.V. Narasimha Rao Transformed India* (New Delhi, 2016, pp. 253 and 232, n. 33.) The then Union home secretary, Madhav Godbole, has recorded that 'a contingency plan for a takeover of the complex and imposition of President's rule was kept ready but there was no clear view within the government on whether the centre should get so involved.' The whole of Chapter 11 of his 1996 book *Unfinished Innings* (pp. 332–418) is revealing.

farewell on the first day of the New Year. Its numbers had dwindled after the revolution, but its two gurudwaras were well cared for and were of help to the embassy in taking care, and feeding, Indian workers who had crossed over from Iraq at the outbreak of the Kuwait War. Kailash Narwani and his family, with their Calcutta connection, became good friends and knowing them was good fun.

A fascinating aspect of Iran is the intellectual landscape. An 'Empire of the Mind', as Michael Axworthy aptly described it, has been a place of heresies since early times—Mazdak, Khorrum, Bab and many more—suggestive of an inquisitive and questioning mind lending credence, perhaps, to George Bernard Shaw's observation that 'all great truths begin as heresies'. The Islamic Revolution produced its own share of dissidents, lay and clerical, Grand Ayatollah Montazeri and his thesis on compatibility between Islamic and democratic government, Ali Shariati, Mohsen Kadivar, Jalal Al-e-Ahmad and his (almost Gandhian) elaboration of *Gharbzadegi* or Westoxification— 'we have been unable to preserve our own historiocultural character in the face of the machine and its fateful onslaught'—and Abdolkarim Soroush; the latter with his assertion of Iran being the inheritor of three cultures—national, religious and western origin—in which identity (including cultural identity) should be viewed as dynamic and evolving and where 'we must not deem our ethnic and Islamic culture as a terminus but as a point of departure.'[69] The locus of power varied and in practice, no one group had a monopoly over the exercise of power on all matters and at all times.[70]

My colleague Usmani sahib drew my attention to an unusual expression of opinion in Iran's religious landscape. An article, almost heretical, had appeared in the newspaper *Jomhouri Eslami* on 4 April 1989 (some two months before the passing away of Imam Khomeini)

---

[69] Abdolkarim Soroush, *Reason, Freedom and Democracy in Islam* (New York, 2000) pp. 163 and 170.
[70] German scholar Wilfried Buchta, whom I met on a later visit to Tehran, has written on this theme in his very informative book *Who Rules Iran? The Structure of Power in the Islamic Republic* (Washington, 2000).

titled 'Mistakes of Amir-ul-Momeneen'. It was directed at the fourth Khalifa, Ali ibn Abi Talib and was published on the anniversary of his martyrdom. Was it suggestive of incipient dissent?

'Where is Iran heading?' was a question in my mind as I completed my assignment in Tehran. I felt that while a categorical prediction would be imprudent, it could be said that: (i) the economic and social compulsions had assumed an imperative shape and would increasingly impact perceptions and policies that were still evolving; (ii) President Rafsanjani had suffered setbacks, but he would adhere to his approach of making tactical compromises and would be irreplaceable in the coming 1993 elections; (iii) in foreign policy, the search for a *modus vivendi* with the West and with his Arab neighbours would be continued but would be decisively influenced by perceptions in Washington; and (iv) in relations with India, the endeavour would be to engage in a serious dialogue on regional matters and give shape and content to bilateral relations in terms of the decisions taken by the joint commission. This would very much depend both on hard bargaining and on our ability to produce a politico-economic package in response to Iranian overtures.

A few years later, and in a private exchange with a former European colleague in the diplomatic corps, I characterized the Iranian approach as 'CHOKER': a mix of chess and poker, played competently by a skilful actor.

My concluding thoughts were that generalizations would be hazardous, given the complexities of the situation and the intricacies of the Persian thought process. Also that Iran, in more senses than one, would remain an enigma, difficult yet endearing, and could perhaps be summed up in Akbar Allahabadi's couplet:

Kuchh tarz-e-sitam bhī hai kuchh andāz-e-vafā bhī
Khulta nahin haal unki tabiat ka zara bhi

(There are postures of injustice and gestures of faithfulness
The inclination of her mind remains undiscerned.)

I left Tehran on 3 January 1993 and travelled to New York, via London, arriving at my destination early on the morning of 5 January. Salma and our family travelled separately to Delhi.

NEW YORK

I was new to multilateral work, and looking forward to it with mixed feelings. My team of colleagues, as per well-established MEA practice, included some of the best minds of the IFS destined for higher responsibilities later in their career.

The end of the Cold War had generated expectations of a less contentious global scenario. A special meeting of the UNSC, the first ever at head of government level, was held on 31 January 1992. UN Secretary-General Dr Boutros Boutros-Ghali had brought forth his report *An Agenda for Peace,* which focused on preventive diplomacy, peace-making and peacekeeping. The meeting concluded with a statement recognizing 'the new favourable international circumstances in which the Council can fulfil more effectively its primary responsibility for the maintenance of international peace and security. The members of the Council stress the importance of strengthening and improving the UN to increase its effectiveness'.

PM Narasimha Rao, who participated in this summit, welcomed the newly effective role of the Security Council, which he attributed to cohesion among permanent members of the Council. He stressed that the role of the Security Council 'must flow from the collective will, not from the views or predilections of a few' and that 'wider representation in the Council [is] essential to ensure its moral sanction and political effectiveness'. On nuclear proliferation, he said that it must be 'universal, comprehensive and non-discriminatory and linked to the goal of complete nuclear disarmament'. Our viewpoint on proliferation-related issues was amplified in bilateral discussions with the principal players and has been written about by J.N. Dixit[71].

---

[71] J.N. Dixit, *My South Block Years* (New Delhi, 1996) pp. 370–74.

At the end of 1992, India had finished its two-year term as a non-permanent member of the Council and had contributed substantially to the Council's work. Some useful light on the inner working of this august body has been shed by Ambassador Gharekhan in his book, *The Horseshoe Table: An Inside View of the UN Security Council*.

Within the broad framework of non-alignment as a positive concept of exercising independence and judgment of action, India after Independence pursued a policy of combining national interest with the broad objective of establishing a just and equitable global order. Our contribution to the formulation of some basic international covenants—on Elimination of All Forms of Racial Discrimination; Economic, Social and Cultural Rights; on Civil and Political Rights; on Elimination of All Forms of Intolerance and of Discrimination Based on Religion or Belief; on the Right to Development—was widely acknowledged and earned us respect in the UN circles. We took a continuing interest in all the six main committees of the UN General Assembly and were particularly active at all stages on issues of decolonization, apartheid, disarmament and development. On the other hand, from time to time, we also had to defend, on global forums, our core interests that covered both matters of global concern and those pertaining to the security and integrity of India.

The issues that assumed primacy in my period in the Permanent Mission of India (PMI) related to matters on the agenda of the Second and Third Committees. The first concerned the forthcoming World Social Summit for Social Development (in 1995) and India as a member of the Coordination Bureau; in the second, we had to face and reverse the continuous onslaught of Pakistan on J&K-related matters. This was continued on other global forums.

The General Assembly session of 1993 was, from our viewpoint, acrimonious with a Pakistani onslaught on all fronts. External Affairs Minister Dinesh Singh led our delegation, while Abdul Sattar led the Pakistani team. Since the external affairs minister was in indifferent health, Union Minister of State Salman Khurshid, who was on tour in South America, was asked to be in New York just in case the senior minister had any difficulty in completing a longish speech on 29 September. Sattar's intervention in the debate was acerbic and had to be responded in kind. I did that later in the day and said 'all the water in the East River cannot wash off the stains of falsehood, prejudice and perversion' and that 'his eloquence is matched only by his sophistry and the two together constitute an impressive exercise in high-pitched salesmanship of a product whose shelf life is ending if it has not ended'.

Pakistan's effort to somehow internationalize the J&K question manifested itself in seeking ways to bring it up in all committees. At its instance, the OIC countries formed a Contact Group to sponsor a draft resolution on 'Peace and Security in South Asia' in the expectation that such a resolution 'will serve to convince India to be more constructive in the dialogue with Pakistan' without deviating from the bilateral approach. I addressed two circular letters to the ambassadors of all the OIC member states, pointing out that such a move will encourage militancy and terrorism and will not be conducive to robust bilateral negotiations between India and Pakistan. Separately, bilateral efforts were made with friendly OIC members such as Oman and some others such as Turkey in a quieter vein. These efforts bore success and the proposed OIC resolution was not tabled. Our choice, as I put it in one of our messages to Delhi, was to choose between 'standing like an oak and bending like a reed'. This seems to have worked.

An interesting account of what he called 'this disagreeable episode' was later recorded by the late Ambassador Jamsheed Marker, Pakistan's PR to the UN, in his memoirs.[72]

The delegation of MPs at the time of the General Assembly was in my time headed by the Leader of the Opposition, Atal Bihari Vajpayee. He was impeccably correct and punctual and it was a pleasure to work with him. Ambassador Brajesh Mishra accompanied

---

[72]Jamsheed Marker, *Quiet Diplomacy: Memoirs of an Ambassador of Pakistan* (Karachi, 2010) pp. 413–14.

him on both occasions and his experience and advice were of considerable help to us. Vajpayee used to walk the short distance from the mission to the UN building. One morning, I asked him about the working of the newly introduced system of Department-related Standing Committees and opined that a lacuna in their functioning remained. '*Woh kya?*' (What is that?) he asked. I said they required the presence of senior officials but not of ministers. '*Woh aana nahin chahte hain*' (They do not want to come) was his laconic response! Many years later, I learnt more about the real reasons.

On a visit to New Delhi for consultations regarding the pressures in New York, I was instructed by PM Narasimha Rao to see the Chief Election Commissioner (CEC) and be briefed about the preparations for elections in J&K. I was accompanied by Foreign Secretary Kris Srinivasan and we were in for a surprise. The CEC launched into a tirade against the PM and certain branches of the government, who, he alleged, were hampering his work.

The ongoing disturbances in J&K provided enough ammunition to Pakistan to raise the question of alleged violation of human rights in the Second Committee in New York and in the meeting of the UNCHR in Geneva, in March 1994, where Pakistan had tabled a resolution against us. Assessing the gravity of the matter, the government decided to add a political component to our delegation. This included Vajpayee, Khurshid, Dr Farooq Abdullah and former PR to the UN in New York, Ambassador Brajesh Mishra. I joined the delegation from New York and so did Ambassador Prakash Shah (from Tokyo) and Madhukar Gupta (from the MHA). With the number of votes in the committee almost evenly matched, a close watch on the evolving perceptions was essential and, every night, Ambassador Satish Chandra would give his assessment of the day's tally. The situation was complicated by some African delegations who pleaded lack of instructions from their respective governments. One evening, in the plenary, it was decided to continue after dinner and at around 11 p.m., I came out to puff at my pipe. Just then a senior member of the Pakistani delegation emerged for the same purpose. I asked him what the purpose of the exercise was since 'lung power would be matched sooner rather than later'. He sought my view and I suggested talks as the only sane view out. He said, 'We know we cannot snatch Kashmir nor can we match the Indian capacity to assist craftsmen there in terms of financial assistance or outlets. India instead should accept that the face of the Kashmiris is turned towards Pakistan rather than India.' I suggested an amendment to the last aspect and said the Kashmiris' faces are turned towards themselves. The conversation remaining unfinished.

A tense stand-off in the meeting and even the drafting of a statement in the event of an adverse vote were avoided by a last-minute Iranian appeal to Pakistan to desist from putting the draft to vote. This reflected the bonhomie developed in Tehran.

The crisis over, a celebratory dinner was hosted by a Geneva-based friend in one of those restaurants for which Geneva is famous. It was attended by the Iranian PR. Our approach to this meeting and the role of our political leadership in it were much lauded by our media.

The suggestion in the Security Council summit of January 1992 was given a formal shape in the General Assembly Resolution 47/62, in December 1993, on the 'equitable representation on and increase in the membership of the Security Council'. India took an active part in the proceedings of the Working Group. The effort for selective expansion in the category of permanent members, confining it to Germany and Japan, was thwarted and most members agreed with our view that in order to ensure political support of the international community (i) any package for restructuring should be broad-based (ii) have adequate presence of developing countries and (iii) be based on an agreed criteria of transparent consultations rather than on pre-determined selection.

Our position was also stated in External Affairs Minister Pranab Mukherjee's statement in the General Assembly plenary on 3 October 1994, that developing countries must be included in the category of permanent membership to reflect the universal character of the world body and that 'on the basis of any criteria, population, size of economy, contribution to the maintenance of international peace and security and to peacekeeping or future potential, India deserves to be a permanent member of the Security Council.' Different variants of these and other approaches have been explored since, but without any concrete results.[73]

No less important were matters relating to UN peacekeeping operations, in which we were an active participant in different theatres of conflict and won high praise. The role of our brigade in Somalia was particularly noteworthy. At the same time, we were alone (in principle, if not in practice) in voicing the view that intrusive peacekeeping and Chapter VII operations be avoided and the host country's consent be taken.

The Indian delegation to the world conference on Human Rights in Vienna in June 1993 was led by Finance Minister Dr Manmohan Singh. He insisted on deviating from the standard cautiously worded text of an opening statement suggested by the MEA and instead spoke candidly on India's commitment to human rights issues. This was welcomed by many Western delegations.

Committee-wise results were broadly satisfactory. In the First, there was a break within NAM ranks on the question of a NAM resolution to seek an Advisory Opinion of the International Court of Justice on the legality of the threat or use of nuclear weapons. In the Second, our position was broadly in step with that of the Group of 77[74]. In the Third, our general effort was to avoid (with some exceptions) country-specific resolutions in the Fourth and on the question of the Middle East and Palestine, our position evolved in favour of Israel. In the Fifth, we were supportive of the US effort to rationalize budgetary allocations. The 'Declaration on Measures to Eliminate International Terrorism' was successfully piloted and from our viewpoint that was a significant development.

---

[73]The present state of discussions on this subject are summarized in UNGA A/55/47 of 2011, Report of the open-ended Working Group on UNSC matters.
[74]Group of 77 is the largest intergovernmental organization of developing countries in the UN.

Despite our success in warding off the Pakistani onslaught, in overall terms, 1994 was not a good year for the UN. Success stories were few, if any; instances of inadequate comprehension and response were many more. Despite that, expectations from the forthcoming fiftieth anniversary of the organization, in 1995, were high amidst continued efforts by a group of likeminded countries to use the UN to focus on the 'widest range of global concern', establish a *new* framework of international relations premised on the widest possible interpretation of the Preamble and Article 1 of the Charter, on the use of a host of 'dormant' Articles and on an increasingly restrictive interpretation of Article 2(7), which has hitherto protected the freedom of action of the member states in matters perceived by them as being 'essentially within the domestic jurisdiction'. It sought to evolve guidelines that would be applicable to conflicts which are increasingly within states rather than between them. The thrust to this end of the principal players was to create new supranational structures for implementation of this new agenda.

The non-aligned and developing countries, on the other hand, were confused in conceptual terms and disunited in their response. Our own response to this new trend was somewhat tentative and ad hoc, influenced in good measure by issues of domestic concern and the impact of the proposed global agenda on J&K.

The activism on UN peacekeeping that was displayed in the early and mid-1990s and the limitations that surfaced were candidly commented upon by a contemporary, the British PR David Hannay, whose country is a permanent member of the Security Council:

> Now, in the middle of 1995, the triumph of the Gulf War and the success of several other UN missions stand in the deep shadow cast by Bosnia and Somalia. The pendulum which swung too far towards euphoria after the Gulf War has swung too far towards despair. From being an organization which was wrongly thought capable of solving everything, the UN now tends, equally wrongly, to be regarded as incapable of solving anything... We will

need however to be a bit cautious and conservative about what we ask the UN to take on in future. It needs a higher success rate than it has recently achieved if it is not to be discredited. It cannot afford more Bosnias and Somalias. So enforcement should be limited, to be undertaken either by 'coalition of the willing,' if possible with UN authorization, or not at all.[75]

Around mid-October 1994, Foreign Secretary Srinivasan informed me that my next assignment would be in Riyadh as the ambassador to Saudi Arabia and that this would be on re-employment since my date of superannuation was approaching. He suggested that I should move as early as possible after the end of the General Assembly session in December. It was agreed that this would be in early January.

On one of my consultation visits to Delhi, I met Prof. John Kenneth Galbraith, former US ambassador to India and the UN, in the lobby of the India International Centre. In a short conversation, his parting words were 'convey my regards to Krishna Menon'. It was evident that despite the passage of time, the rancour in American minds had not subsided.[76]

An Aligarh connection of earlier vintage incidentally surfaced in the shape of Philip Talbot, who was Assistant Secretary of State in President Kennedy's administration. He said American interest in developments in India in the pre-World War II years induced the administration to send him and another young scholar to India, him to AMU to learn Urdu and the other person to Banaras Hindu University to learn Hindi. Neither could devote much time to their

---

[75]Parris and Bryson, op. cit., p. 293.

[76]A former CIA official and now director of Brookings Intelligence Project, Bruce Riedel has written about Krishna Menon's resignation in the wake of the Chinese aggression: 'Before the month was over he was gone, first demoted to a more junior cabinet job and then removed from government service altogether. Menon was the symbol of anti-Americanism in India, and his departure was welcomed in Washington.' (*JFK's Forgotten Crisis: Tibet, the CIA, and the Sino-Indian War*, Washington, 2015; New Delhi, 2016, pp. 117–18).

assigned languages once hostilities commenced and they became war correspondents instead! Some sections of his book[77] such as his letters from his AMU days (in the December 1939–April 1940 period) and the account of his meetings with Nehru, Jinnah and other political leaders and his attendance at the Ramgarh Congress session make for an interesting read. This remote Aligarh bond did, however, persuade Talbot to sponsor my guest membership to the prestigious Century Association on 43rd Street West, New York.

An address to the Asia Society gave me an opportunity to express some views on Indo-US cooperation on global matters. I referred to a remark of my American colleague Ambassador Madeleine Albright that the UN's agenda 'now bears a striking resemblance to America's agenda'. I said that the themes mentioned in a recent Carnegie report on 'Changing Our Ways: America and the New World'—namely promotion of democratic values and institutions, support for an open and growing global economy, building of a new system of collective security and assuring global habitability—can be subscribed to in principle, but the conceptual framework of each reveals areas of disagreement of varying proportions which, when translated into negotiating and implementing modalities, constitute challenges to be overcome. I pointed out that the US, more than most other countries, is 'somewhat prone to drastic U-turns on policies relating to the multilateral agenda' and this makes other nations hesitate on long-term commitments.

In the summer of 1995, I wrote two papers for edited collections published in New Delhi on the occasion of the fiftieth anniversary of the UN.[78] In the first, I argued that 'the need of the hour is to induce confidence through the removal of structural inequalities,

---

[77]Phillip Talbot, *An American Witness to India's Partition* (New Delhi, 2007) pp. 53–80.
[78]'Democratizing the Security Council,' in Satish Kumar (ed.) *United Nations at 50: An Indian View* (New Delhi, 1995) pp. 205–22 and 'Some Reflections on the Concepts of Intervention, Domestic Jurisdiction and International Obligation,' in M.S. Rajan (ed.) *United Nations at 50 and Beyond* (New Delhi, 1996) pp. 321–30.

through democratic functioning and through a genuinely common agenda' to make the UN, in the words of the Charter, a centre for harmonizing the actions of nations in the attainment of common ends. In the second, I opined that 'the time for defensive postures is long past' and 'what is needed is a proactive approach anchored on the one side in juridical correctness and, on the other, in normative commitment' to achieve both the *purposes* and the *principles* of the Charter, so that there is no gap between the principle of sovereign equality and unequal participation.

I had friendly relations with the UN Secretary-General. Dr Ghali was assisted by my predecessor, Gharekhan, who was his under-secretary-general. My mission and I had much to do with Kofi Annan, who was then the under-secretary-general for peacekeeping; his team included Shashi Tharoor. Amongst the diplomatic colleagues whom I had known earlier or developed good working relations with were ambassadors Ravan Farhâdi of Afghanistan, Richard Butler of Australia, Juan Somavía of Chile, Kamal Kharrazi of Iran, Gad Yaacobi of Israel, Paulo Fuchi of Italy, Abulhasan of Kuwait, Ahmed Snoussi of Morocco, Ahmad Razali of Malaysia, Biegman of the Netherlands, Graf Zu Rantzu of Germany, Ibrahim Gambari of Nigeria, Yuli Vorontsov of Russia, Inal Batu of Turkey, David Hannay of the UK and Madeleine Albright of the US. Many of them I had the occasion to meet later in my other responsibilities.

Salma did not really settle down to the pace of life in New York. Osman went to a private school on Park Avenue and liked it. Sulaiman spent some time with us in between jobs. His son, Sabir, was born there.

We left for Riyadh on 10 January 1995. My New York assignment of just two years was too short to allow me to savour the charms of the city in a meaningful way. The museums, bookshops and good restaurants were a saving grace. I had little leisure to go to the theatre.

RIYADH

We were back in Saudi Arabia after almost two decades. My earlier assignments had been in Jeddah on the west coast. Riyadh is almost in the middle of the Arabian Peninsula and was an unknown city to me despite occasional visits on previous assignments. The Saudi addiction to the insularity of its capital city was legendary; foreign embassies were kept away in Jeddah and norms of appearance and of public behaviour were different and draconic. The diplomatic corps was kept in Jeddah till the early 1980s; our own mission shifted in 1985. For those interested in the past, the process of change, as recorded for posterity by old-timers such as Philby, does tell its own story; that of a rigid social order collapsing under the weight of alien influences and of 'the wealth poured upon them by a bountiful Providence as a reward for the virtue of other days'. This process of change and of the official and public tussle between tradition and modernization continues to this day. 'A product of state control and modernity, Saudi religio-political discourse proliferated, fragmented and challenged state authority'; the response has been called 'the state's effort to domesticate religion and its interpreters'.[79]

In Riyadh, as in Canberra, but on a different and bigger scale, one of my assigned priorities was to supervise the construction of a new embassy complex, including a residence. Our residence on arrival was a rented house; it had several swimming pools, including one that was carefully shielded from any possibility of prying eyes. After some time, we shifted to the new residence designed like the rest of the complex by an eminent Indian architect, whose imagination ran riot with regard to privacy measures and ensured that there were no windows in the bedrooms!

My predecessor in Riyadh, Ambassador Ishrat Aziz, had left a year earlier and in the intervening period some administrative matters had cropped up that needed attention. I suggested a full-fledged enquiry,

---

[79] Madawi Al-Rasheed, *Contesting the Saudi State* (Cambridge, 2007) pp. 257 and 260.

but Delhi felt otherwise and allowed the concerned personnel to move out. Sujan Chinoy from the PMI joined me as number two. Also in the team was a young officer, P. Harish, who had finished his language examination in Cairo and, being an engineer by training, was assigned to Riyadh to supervise the construction of the new embassy complex. He had a good command over Arabic and a flair for political reporting.

Saudi Arabia in early 1995 was very different from the country I left two decades earlier, in June 1976. The change was both regional and local. Sequentially, the revolution in Iran came first in February 1979. It was followed by the attack on the mosque in Makkah in November and the Soviet intervention in Afghanistan in December.

The revolution in Iran and the fall of the Shah disturbed King Faisal's carefully crafted arrangement, including intelligence cooperation,[80] to contain the old suspicion of Iran through advocacy of conservative Muslim states as a corrective to Nasser's Arabism. It came as a rude shock to the Saudi leadership. The post-revolutionary pronouncements of Tehran were anti-monarchy and advocated revolutionary Islamism. One broadcast from Tehran cited the Qur'anic verse about Islam rejecting monarchy since kings despoil a country and promote meanness.[81] To this was added the advocacy of grievances of the Shia minority in the Eastern Province.

The attack in Makkah was an unprecedented domestic happening and shook the ruling establishment. On the morning of 20 November 1979, a group of about 400 young Saudis, with impeccable tribal affiliations and radical Islamist leanings, sneaked into the Grand Mosque in Makkah and defied the security forces for two weeks. They were led by Juhayman ibn Muhammad ibn Sayf al-Otaibi, who had served in the Saudi Arabian National Guard and studied in the Islamic University of Madina. He was also the author of a tract published a

---

[80] Saeed M. Badeeb, *Saudi-Iranian Relations 1932–1982* (London, 1993) pp. 131 and 155, n. 27.
[81] *Surat Al-Naml*, verse 34. Also William W. Quandt, *Saudi Arabia in the 1980s*, pp. 39–40.

year earlier titled *Rules of Allegiance and Obedience: The Misconduct of Rulers*, wherein he used the classic Islamic argument that Muslim rulers who do not follow the Qur'an and *Sunna* have no legitimacy and must be opposed along with the *ulema* who support them. He also recalled the age-old argument of a saviour, a *Mahdi*, to rescue the faithful. One such person was named among his followers. The government responded with force (including some foreign, non-Muslim, troops) to put down the rebels and execute them publicly in different cities.[82]

The Soviet intervention in Afghanistan in December 1979 gave an opportunity to assert the leadership of the Islamic world through the call for Islamic jihad and massive financial support for it. It evoked substantial response in terms of donations and volunteers; amongst them was Osama bin Laden. Its implications were to surface later.

An observer of the Saudi scene noted later that 'what the 1979 siege of the Holy Haram revealed, above all, was the existence of serious cleavages in Saudi Arabia'.[83] The Makkah episode highlighted the vulnerability of the Saudi establishment (and other Gulf sheikhdoms) to attacks emanating from religious elements and underscored its dilemma in accommodating traditionalists to new challenges. In a first step, the conservative elements were pacified by imposing greater restrictions on women and foreigners. A conference of Islamic scholars was called in June 1983 to explore ways of modernizing Islamic law through *Ijtihad* or independent judgment, in theological interpretation. In 1986, the title 'His Majesty' was dropped in favour of Khadim al Harmain (Servitor of the Two Noble Sanctuaries). It had been earlier used in the twelfth century by the Mamluk rulers of Egypt. Also dropped was the earlier title of Imam (Imam al-Muslemeen). Calibrated debates on Islam and modernity

---

[82]M.H. Ansari, *The Islamic Boomerang in Saudi Arabia: The Cost of Delayed Reforms* (ORF Studies of Contemporary Islamic Societies – 1, New Delhi, 2004);
Yaroslav Trofimov, *The Siege of Mecca: The Forgotten Uprising in Islam's Holiest Shrine and the Birth of al-Qaeda* (London, 2007).
[83]Joseph A. Kéchichian, *Legal and Political Reforms in Saudi Arabia* (Routledge, 2013) p. 167.

were encouraged in social groupings and universities. Some of this, however, went in a different direction, since the support for jihad in Afghanistan had motivated many Saudi youth to travel to Pakistan (with the knowledge and consent of their government).

These happenings brought forth the contradiction between religious conservatism at home and Islamic radicalism abroad, which became evident in the aftermath of the Iraqi invasion of Kuwait in August 1990 and the Saudi acceptance of the stationing of US forces on Saudi soil. It became a catalyst for social change. Hard questions were asked. Some wondered why Saudi Arabia, after spending $300 billion on defence, still lacked the capacity to defend itself. Others, particularly in religious circles, were highly suspicious of US motives. The more educated attributed the situation to the mismanagement of the affairs of the state, and sought reforms.

These viewpoints crystallized in two documents, from two very different quarters, which were given to the king in December 1990 and May 1991. Both opted for the classic and accepted methodology of tendering advice to the ruler. The first, *Letter of Demands,* emanated from a group of 43 intellectuals who described themselves as 'liberal conservatives' and as loyal citizens owing allegiance to 'the present system of government and to preserving the cherished royal family'. Stressing the need for reform so as 'to anticipate events rather than reacting to them', they suggested a 10-point programme of reforms in order to make Saudi Arabia 'a modern Islamic state'. They proposed a regulatory system for the issue of *fatwas,* an examination of the system of government 'in the light of statements and declarations pronounced by leaders at different times', the establishment of a Shura Council, a revival of municipal and district councils (with a suggestion of elections on the pattern of the chambers of commerce), a review of the judicial system and the observance of the due process of law, freedom of expression in the media, a comprehensive review of the working of the Committee for the Promotion of Virtue and the Prevention of Vice (the religious police), an opening up of areas of public life for women, and radical and comprehensive reform of the educational system. These proposals, in short, sought a curtailment of the system of absolute rule and the influence exercised on it by the religious establishment. By focusing on the issuance of *fatwas,* the religious police, the judicial system, education and the role of women, they sought to undermine one of the two pillars of the Saudi state.

The second document, *Memorandum of Advice,* was sent to the king under the signature of 51 religious and academic personalities including the Grand Mufti Sheikh Abdul Aziz Bin Baz. It reacted, in some measure, to the first petition and emphasized the role of religious scholars in directing the rulers to do what is obligatory in terms of religion. It stressed that 'during this critical period when all have conceived the necessity of change', reforms on a 12-point programme should be undertaken. These should include the creation of an independent consultative council with 'the actual power to determine domestic and foreign policies', social and economic justice, a cleaning of the state apparatus to eliminate corruption and introduce accountability for all officials, a unified system of justice and independent judiciary, building up of a strong army, reform of the media in consonance with Islamic policy and 'constructive criticism within the limits of the Sharia'. In foreign policy, the emphasis should be on Muslim causes and the avoidance of 'alliances that violate the Sharia'. Individual rights and human dignity, within the Sharia limits, should be guaranteed.

The government's initial response to these proposed changes was somewhat elliptical. Another group of *ulema* came into the picture to point out the procedural incorrectness of tendering advice publicly: 'the advice to Muslim leaders should be sincere and in a confidential manner, taking into account the dangers of dividing the ranks of the Muslims'. It stressed the need for obedience to rulers and cautioned against a repetition of the exercise. First steps were also taken to institute long-heralded reforms.

In March 1992, the Basic Law of Governance was promulgated 'to codify existing practices'. It forbade in Article 12 'all activities that may lead to division, disorder and partition', guaranteed protection of human rights 'in accordance with the Sharia'(Article 26) and asserted in Article 55 that the King 'shall rule the nation according to the Sharia' and 'shall also supervise the implementation of the Sharia'. Article 68 announced the establishment of a Consultative (*Shura*) Council and a separate royal decree spelt out the details, including the fact that the new law replaced the one made 65 years earlier (but not implemented). All this was of no avail; in September 1992, over 400 *ulema*, judges and scholars signed an Explanatory Memorandum of Advice. It ostensibly sought to explain and amplify the *Memorandum of Advice*. In the process, it boldly advanced a new set of demands: the removal of constraints on the *ulema*, an acknowledgement of their primacy, a thorough cleansing of the administrative system, a review of the existing 'secular' legislation, a thorough screening of foreign ideas and material in the educational system and the media, and the establishment of an army of half a million motivated by the spirit of jihad to 'protect this holy land, fight the Jews and help the Muslims'.

How representative of the Saudi society were those who signed the various Letters of Advice? An analysis showed that in regional terms, 72 per cent of the signatories were from Najd (in central Saudi Arabia) and only 4.7 per cent from Hejaz (in the west of Saudi Arabia). Profession-wise, 3.7 per cent were religious scholars and jurists, 59.8 per cent were university academics and 22.4 per cent were businessmen. In terms of positions held, 48 per cent were occupying religious positions, while 34.6 per cent were involved in secular disciplines. They clearly differed considerably from the 1979 group that had been involved in the attack on the Grand Mosque.[84]

Thus, in the aftermath of the Kuwait War and by late 1992, a challenge to the legitimacy of the status quo became evident and was perceived as such by the government. The response came in the form of an admonition from King Fahd personally. Using a broad brush and addressing himself to the *ulema*, the King cautioned against

---

[84]Hrair R. Dekmejian, 'The Rise of Political Islamism in Saudi Arabia,' in *Middle East Journal* 48(4), Autumn 1994, pp. 627–43.

'the irrational criticism being circulated in pamphlets and cassettes' and said that 'advice will not be accepted if it was made for secular purposes or received orientation from some foreign circles'.[85] As on similar occasions in the past, the government sought to divide the Opposition on the one hand and procrastinate on the other. It also sought to co-opt some elements into the system by naming them to the Shura Council, whose composition was finally announced, after considerable delay, in August 1993.

This did not curtail the tide of protest and several groups appeared in 1994, including bin Laden's London-based Advice and Reform Committee. In April that year, a telex was received in my office in Riyadh from 'The Islamic Movement for Change—the Jihad Wing in the Arabian Peninsula'; it read: 'It is now proved that the ruling regime in the so-called Kingdom of Saudi Arabia is a *kafir* regime which has no legitimacy.' In November, an explosion at the Riyadh headquarters of the US training mission for the National Guard killed four US nationals and injured 37. In June 1996, a building housing American military personnel in the eastern province of Al Khobar (adjacent to the oil city of Dhahran) was bombed, in which 19 US Air Force personnel were killed and 498 of various nationalities injured.

These pressures on the government were further aggravated by the drop in oil prices, the resultant budgetary pressures on social spending and a host of other problems related to social issues and a growing population. Despite being a heavyweight in the global oil market, most sectors of the Saudi economy remain opaque. A matter of concern flagged in the International Monetary Fund (IMF) reports was the burden of interest payment on public debt. The drop in oil prices aggravated the pressures; the resultant compulsion for fiscal discipline was articulated by the Crown Prince personally in December 1998: 'the boom period is gone and will never come back'.

All of this had an impact on the management of foreign policy that remained focused on regime security and geo-strategic

---

[85] Saudi Press Agency report from Madina in *Riyadh Daily*, 22 December 1992.

considerations. Having land borders with eight states in the Arabian Peninsula, in being a part of the West Asian and Persian Gulf subsystems, in having a certain centrality in the Islamic world because of the geographical accident of having the two holiest cities of Islam within its borders, and playing a crucial role in the world energy market, together required judicious management. The priorities for public purposes were elucidated in a well-publicized address to the council of ministers in September 1997. Saudi diplomacy, the Crown Prince said, functioned in four circles: Gulf, Arab, Islamic and international. In terms of hard statecraft, however, the priorities were different since the Saudi state did not have the physical capacity to defend itself and needed strong and powerful friends in times of need. These priorities had not changed over decades.

Experience at home and elsewhere compelled correctives to Islamic policy. The occasion to proclaim it was carefully chosen—Crown Prince Abdullah's address to the Islamic Summit in Tehran in December 1997: 'The Islamic house has to be put in order, focus should be on dialogue, on pursuing jihad by political means rather than violent ones and in depicting Islamic activism as misguided and even 'un-Islamic.' This was repeated in the annual messages on the occasion of the Hajj and was reflected in the approach of Saudi-based Islamic bodies and the media.

Contrary to Professor Galbraith's perception that an ambassador's job is 'a splendid example of disguised unemployment', the tasks entrusted to an Indian envoy in most stations in the world are many. Mine in Riyadh was even spelt out in a newspaper article on the eve of my arrival in the capital city. It listed three major tasks: bilateral relations, the OIC with its headquarters in Jeddah and affairs of the Indian community.[86]

There have been many ups and downs in Indo-Saudi bilateral relations. The bonhomie of earlier times, in the 1950s and early 1960s, was disrupted during the Yemeni Civil War. Relations improved after

---

[86]Mir Ayoob Ali Khan, *Saudi Gazette*, 9 January 1995.

the Six-Day War of 1967, but dipped again during the Bangladesh crisis. The Saudi approach was helpful during the oil crisis and the improving trend in relations was highlighted by PM Indira Gandhi's visit to Saudi Arabia in 1982 and the Saudi participation in the NAM summit in New Delhi in 1983. Thereafter, exchanges with varying intensity and occasional disruptions continued. A fresh start was sought to be made when Finance Minister Dr Singh visited Riyadh for the joint commission meeting and the point was made officially that the 'political will' for developing relations existed. This was a tacit acceptance of a new strategic situation embodied in the emergence of India as a new power—political and economic—in the immediate vicinity of the Persian Gulf.

Other indications of changing Saudi views surfaced in areas of oil supplies and investments. The significance of India as an important market for Saudi crude was publicly signalled by the oil minister, who also visited India in December 1996. A first public acknowledgement of this came in his speech that future markets for Saudi crude oil would be in Asia: Japan, China, Korea and India; so did SABIC's (ranked among the world's largest petrochemicals manufacturers) decision to have a product-research laboratory in Vadodara (Gujarat). A specific suggestion to explore investment in an existing refinery was not acceptable to us; we offered instead an upcoming refinery in Punjab 'with no restriction on destination of exports'. This did not seem to be in line with Saudi thinking. Prince Al-Waleed bin Talal explored investment in the hotel industry. In each of these exploratory ventures, the ground reality of our thinking was not fully appreciated. A little over two decades later, Saudi Arabia is now inclined to invest very substantially in a new refinery in India and also in a crude oil storage facility, both on our west coast.

When I presented my credentials to King Fahd, he talked at some length about the Iraqi invasion of Kuwait and his efforts for two days to establish personal contact with President Saddam Hussein. The sense of betrayal was evident in his remarks. As his health deteriorated, the occasions to see the Custodian got fewer. When Minister of State for

External Affairs Saleem Shervani visited in November 1997, he called on the King, who talked vaguely about a dream he had the previous night about a visitor from India. On the other hand, conversations on several occasions with the Crown Prince were substantive and his disposition towards India was very positive; this was evident a few years later when he visited India in 2006.

While there were no U-turns, improvement in relations was steady, more like the turning of a big ship. Nuances, therefore, had to be taken note of. A decision by the OIC to study the condition of Muslim minorities in non-OIC states was entrusted to a committee headed by a senior diplomat in the Saudi foreign office. When I enquired about the progress of its work, a senior functionary in the secretariat confided that a meeting of the committee had not been convened for several years!

The OIC Secretary-General did, however, submit to the 23rd Conference of Foreign Ministers held in Conakry (Guinea) in December 1995 a *Report on Muslim Communities and Minorities in non-OIC Member States*. It gave continent-wise and country-wise statistical details and percentages to the extent available; cautioned against exaggeration or underestimation of numbers and stated that 'the best dependable approach in this respect may probably be to strengthen ties with these Muslim communities and minorities and to seek the help of the different Islamic Centres, Societies and Federation'. It said in conclusion that 'we should not be oblivious of the conspiracies to which Muslim communities and minorities in Africa, Asia and Europe are exposed. A war against Muslims and Islam is being planned. Every day a new method is introduced'. It further added that:

> Our Muslim brothers should accord due attention to Muslim communities and minorities bearing in mind that they represent such a large part of the Islamic Ummah. This could be achieved by adopting the necessary means of promoting links with these Muslim minorities and communities so that their entities may be

strengthened in the face of the conspiracies designed to suppress and melt them away.[87]

Similarly, when the OIC Contact Group in New York endorsed an India-focused draft resolution for a forthcoming OIC meeting in Burkina Faso (West Africa), I urged Deputy Foreign Minister Al Shura to desist from supporting it. He said: 'Please understand this is not a choice between an enemy and a friend but between two friends. Let me see what I can do about it.' The Saudi effort, it transpired, did result in the proposed resolution not being pursued. On another occasion, I took adverse notice in his room of a map of the Indian subcontinent with boundary lines wrongly drawn. He sought to explain it away unconvincingly; my response was that in India, too, we have maps that show the provinces of Jizan and Najran in south-western Saudi Arabia as parts of Yemen. This hit the bull's eye and his immediate reaction was to accept the need for maps that are correctly drawn.

Quiet contacts between our respective intelligence organizations were initiated with occasional exchange of views about the evolving situation in Afghanistan. After bin Laden's move to Afghanistan, the Saudis had developed concerns about the Taliban regime in Kabul and an effort by the head of Saudi intelligence, Prince Turki Al-Faisal, to personally convince Mullah Omar to expel bin Laden met with no success and led to the downgrading of relations to the Charge d'Affaires (CDA) level. Sometime in the summer of 1999, the latter conveyed a specific request from his foreign minister for talks 'at a place of India's choosing', adding that his government had no hostility towards India. This was conveyed to Delhi.

Another instance of changing perceptions came in the wake of the nuclear tests in Pokhran in May 1998. A goodwill visit by one of our naval vessels was planned a few weeks later and, contrary to expectations in some quarters, it took place with due courtesies and honours. In the aftermath of the Chagai-I explosions conducted by

---
[87] ICFM/23-95/MM/D.1/Rev.1

Pakistan, the Saudis were suspected to have coordinated their efforts with the US to put discreet pressure on Pakistan. An emergency meeting of the OIC in Jeddah at the level of senior officials, convened at the request of Pakistan to consider assistance in the wake of economic sanctions, was underplayed by the Saudis and assistance was confined only to the deferred payment for oil supplies. There were other indications, too, of developing complexities in Saudi-Pak relations with views being expressed, albeit privately, about Pakistan's flawed 'Islamic posture'. Differences were also evident on a variety of issues, including Afghanistan, and while UN resolutions on J&K were formally endorsed, private advice was given to seek a bilateral solution with India. (More evidence of these positive nuances in Saudi perceptions came to the fore when External Affairs Minister Jaswant Singh visited Riyadh in January 2000, a few weeks after my departure.)

I maintained correct and cordial contacts with the OIC secretariat in Jeddah. The presence there of an old friend, Ambassador Mohammed Mohsin of Bangladesh, was helpful.

The dimensions of the Hajj exercise in relation to Indian pilgrims had undergone a substantive change from what I had experienced in my earlier assignments in Jeddah. Policy matters apart, it remains a comprehensive exercise in management. The figure for the 1999 Hajj stood at 98,072 and the decision to make it proportionate to the size of the Muslim population took into account this reality of rising numbers, besides sending a political signal.

In the 1997 Hajj, about a million foreign pilgrims and perhaps a similar number of domestic ones participated. During the stay of pilgrims in Mina, a fire broke out in one of the tents in which pilgrims were staying. With over a million pilgrims in the Muna Valley, the evacuation process and the journey to Makkah, which was 8 km away, was complex. Our friends from Washington, Mohsin and Shakila Ali Khan, were performing the Hajj with us and shared with Salma the experience of a hurried evacuation from the Mina camp. It took me some time to locate them. There were some fatal casualties among our pilgrims in a camp nearest to the one where the fire broke out.

Enquiries after the tragedy revealed that the Saudi government's decision to ban the use of canvas tents and replace them with fire-proof ones was not implemented because of the large stock of the former with the private-sector agencies concerned.

Having participated in the Hajj pilgrimage in an official capacity during different periods on nine occasions, I have no hesitation in recording my own impression of it—an unmatched and unique experience in human terms. The city of Makkah is unquestionably the most international of such cities where every language imaginable is spoken and understood. The congregation of pilgrims is truly international, bringing in devouts from all corners of the globe. The sense of brotherhood and the bond of religion are very real and etch themselves in the memory of the participants. These experiences, down the ages, have been written about, compiled most recently by F.E. Peters in his comprehensive volume *The Hajj: The Muslim Pilgrimage to Mecca and the Holy Places* (Princeton, 1996). Michael Pearson's *Pious Passengers* (New Delhi, 1994) laments the paucity of indigenous Indian sources but does draw upon Qazvini's Anis al-Hujjaj (1676–77). Also interesting in some aspects is the Nawab of Bhopal, Sultan Jahan Begum's late-nineteenth-century account of her pilgrimage. A relative of mine, Hakim Abdul Ghani Ansari, popularly known as Khusro Shah Nizami, performed the Hajj in 1945 and recorded his impressions that were published in Hyderabad.

Makkah, being the epicentre of the world of Islam and Muslims, has had its own history of effort to draw it into the political mechanics of different periods. Earlier accounts from an Indian perspective have been pieced together in an interesting essay by Prof. Sugata Bose[88]. The end of World War I brought to an end the notional sovereignty of the Ottomans exercised through the sheriff of Makkah following the conquest of the Hejaz by the Sultan of Nejd and the establishment

---

[88]Sugata Bose, 'Pilgrims' Progress Under Colonial Rule,' in *A Hundred Horizons: The Indian Ocean in the Age of Global Empire* (Harvard University Press, 2009), pp. 193–232. His account is based on the Hajj journey of Khwaja Hasan Nizami in 1911.

of the kingdom of Saudi Arabia. Alongside, on 28 April 1926, King Abdulaziz Ibn Saud sent telegraphic invitations to Muslim rulers and associations urging them to attend a Muslim congress in Makkah,

> ...for the service of the two holy sanctuaries and their inhabitants, to secure their future, to increase the means of comfort for pilgrims and visitors, to improve the holy lands in all respects which all the Muslims in general care for, to fulfil our promises we made and with a view to our wish to see the Muslims cooperating in servicing these holy lands.

The Indian delegation to the conference (representing the largest Muslim population and having four votes in a weighted system of a total of 50) was an active participant in the proceedings, much to the dislike of the Saudi king; its members pointedly referred to Ibn Saud as 'Sultan of Najd' rather than as King of Hejaz and contemporary accounts state that 'it became clear that the congress was moving towards the creation of an international body which would oversee the government of the Hejaz and hold it to account'. The conference ended abruptly.[89]

The relevance of Indian Muslim opinion was evident from the fact that on 27 September 1925, Ibn Saud wrote to Hakim Ajmal Khan as 'president of the All India Khilafat Committee':

> I swear by God I do not want dominance or control. Hijaz is in my hands only as trust till Hijazis select a ruler for their country who would be obedient to the Islamic world and subordinate to respected Islamic organization like yours in Hindustan...[90]

The Indian community in the Kingdom had grown over the years, particularly after 1991. It numbered at around one million in the mid-1990s and was the largest expatriate group. It was peaceful and dedicated to its calling. 'It is one community about which unlike some

---

[89]Martin Kramer, op. cit., n. 25.
[90]Khawar Hashmi, *Masih-ul-Mulk Hakim Ajmal Khan* (New Delhi, 2016) pp. 393–95.

others I have no worries' was the response of Intelligence Chief Prince Turki, to whom I posed a query on one occasion. The composition of the Indian community too had changed over the years and included many more professionals. This was concentrated in the Eastern Province around the new oil and petrochemical industrial units. According to World Bank data, remittances of the Indian workforce in the Kingdom in the year 1999–2000 amounted to $12.8 billion.

In our first assignment in Jeddah in the 1960s, Salma had established the Embassy school and the foundation stone of its building was laid by PM Indira Gandhi during her visit in 1982. That institution now has over 12,000 students. Similar community schools had come up in Riyadh, Dammam and Jubail. The question of management raised problems from time to time. My own view was that the embassy's involvement should be minimal and that this be handled by committees drawn from the community and parents.

Salma continued her community welfare activities. In Riyadh, she initiated the establishment of a Special Care Centre for children in the community in need of it. It continues to this day.

The religious police or *mutaween* was active, and on one occasion, tended to object to Salma's appearance—dressed in a saree—in a hotel lobby in Jeddah. Our effort to organize in Riyadh a reading of the play *Tumhari Amrita* by Shabana Azmi and Farooq Sheikh (on the lines of what we had done with much success in the UN auditorium in New York) was objected to as a matter of protocol on the unfounded ground that local practice did not encourage visits by film actresses.

An instance of Saudi rigidity with regard to other faiths came to notice in a ruling by a distinguished jurist, Shaykh Saalih Al-Uthaymeen, in response to a query about felicitating non-Muslims on Christmas and the New Year. It was said that 'it is not permissible to congratulate non-Muslims on such occasions as it would be evidence of acceptance and confession (of their faith)'.

There were visible signs of social change after the experience of the foreign forces during the Kuwait War, but the signals were often contradictory. A field study conducted by a well-connected Saudi academic (a lady) in the late 1990s found 'the new generation's desire for freedom from constraints [were] overtly political or more generally social'. It found that 'the issue of women's rights and behaviour has been placed at the centre of a potential power struggle between the *ulema* and the state'.[91] The authorities were also aware of a rising tide of orthodoxy among the youth and wanted to control and calibrate it on their own terms. A few years later, another Saudi scholar wrote about the 'effort to domesticate religion and its interpreters' by the government:

> A product of state control and modernity, Saudi religio-political discourse proliferated, fragmented, and challenged state authority. Unexpectedly, control under authoritarian rule produced the seeds of mutation. Wahhabiyya developed interpretations that challenged the discourse of control.[92]

In any society that is subject to rapid change, nostalgia is unavoidable. A new-generation Saudi poet, Nimah Ismail Nawwab, depicted this in a poem, *The Streets of Makkah,* in which she wrote of the old city:

> Hours of tea drinking, hours of tales,
> Brimming with told and untold stories,
> Of past generations, present generations,
> Held in the collective memory,
> A memory retaining the glorious past,
> Undeterred by the present.[93]

There was no let-up in the exploitation of the blue-collar workers and agricultural labour due to local rules and regulations and employer behaviour. The corrective available in law was very often not available

---

[91]Mai Yamani, *Changed Identities: The Challenge of the New Generation in Saudi Arabia* (Royal Institute of International Affairs, London, 2000) pp. 95, 148–49.
[92]Madawi Al-Rasheed, *Contesting the Saudi State: Islamic Voices from a New Generation* (Cambridge, 2009) pp. 257 and 260.
[93]Nimah Ismail Nawwab, *The Unfurling: Poems* (2004) p. 45.

in practice. Part of the blame for this lay with the laxity in our recruitment rules and in the practice of contracts being changed after arrival. A visit to some missions in the region by the concerned parliamentary committee, led by Vajpayee, gave me an opportunity (in Kuwait) to put across the dimensions of the problem to them. Our assessment, based on a random survey of our workforce that came to the Embassy for consular assistance, tended to highlight the gaps in our regulatory procedures and show that recruiting agencies in India were often complicit in misleading our workers about wage structures and working conditions offered to them.

In a community dispersed in all corners of a vast land, one came across instances of the oddity of Saudi laws and practices. A few members of the community, practising Muslims and professedly members of the Jamaat-e-Islami in India, were served with an exit notice for a weekly get-together. In another case that was taken up by the embassy as a consular matter, we were informed in writing that the Indian national concerned was subjected to six months of jail, 50 lashes and deportation for 'practicing magic, bewitching and casting a spell' on a neighbour's sister.[94]

Given the historical links, there are great many Indian connections and families of Indian origin in different parts of Saudi Arabia. One region of concentration is the holy cities of Makkah and Madina, where for generations, and reasons of piety, Indian pilgrims stayed back around the holy precincts and rulers of Muslim princely states endowed properties (known locally as *rubat* or hospice) as places of stay for pilgrims. Over time, their management was entrusted to Saudi managers and the unscrupulous among them usurped them in the period of uncertainty that followed the Partition. When the Saudi government initiated plans for the expansion of the two mosques, it offered compensation to owners of these houses who could establish their claims in terms of Saudi law. The embassy or consulate general

---

[94]The Ministry of Foreign Affairs, Riyadh, Consular Division, note verbale no. 94/74/9/2/494 of 3.3.1415 (6 November 1994).

assisted this process to the extent possible, but the Saudi insistence was on owners or their rightful successors staking their claim. Many of these properties belonging to Hyderabad, Bhopal, Bohra sultan and Tonk were retrieved and are still being used by pilgrims from these formerly princely states; many others however were lost.

According to a Saudi friend, there are families with Indian connections—a grandmother or great-grandmother—in the interior of the Qassim Province of Najd around the cities of Buraidah and Unaizah, from where people travelled to the coastal cities on the Persian Gulf and then by dhows to the coastal trading points in western India.[95] And of course, there were several generations of Indian-origin families in Makkah, Madina and Jeddah, which were well integrated in society, including some with surnames Al-Hindi and Dehlavi. The same held for some others. I recall one incident relating to a member of the Alireza family in Jeddah. Sometime in 1967, during my first assignment in Jeddah, Ambassador Kidwai was called one day by Minister of State for Foreign Affairs Sheikh Omar Saqqaf, and asked if the Indian government had decided to levy income tax on a member of the King's family. After a quick check with Delhi, the answer was a firm no. The minister then mentioned the name of Mohammad Ali Zainul Alireza, a long-time resident in Bombay whom the King 'called his uncle and was for all purposes a member of the royal family'. With this clarification, the income tax was waived off and the matter resolved!

In 1986, a departing British ambassador, in his valedictory, leaked to the media that the subject of a late-night litigation that went in his government's favour, described the Saudis as 'xenophobic': 'the Saudis love not, neither are they loved'.[96] By the late 1990s,

---

[95] An early-twentieth-century account of such a journey, undertaken in 1916 by the Danish traveller Barclay Raunkiær is *Through Wahabiland on Camelback* (translated and published by the Arab Bureau, Cairo, for official use only, Cairo, 1916).
[96] The full text of Sir James Craig's valedictory remains under a high court injunction. The portions, before the injunction, appeared on the front page of *The Glasgow Herald* on 9 October 1986.

knowledgeable observers of the Saudi scene opined that the Kingdom must redefine its 'social contract' with its citizens and 'must evolve if it is to preserve its internal stability'. It must also 'redefine its support to Islam to preserve its traditional religious character without tolerating domestic Islamist extremists or the funding of extremist movements overseas'.[97]

On instructions from Delhi, I approached the head of Saudi intelligence Prince Turki al Faisal with a suggestion that lines of communication be opened. His response left me nonplussed. He said a decision to this effect was taken in Cancún (Mexico) in the meeting between PM Indira Gandhi and Crown Prince Fahd in 1981 and that pursuant to it, his deputy had visited Delhi. This initiative, however, was not sustained after 1984. He welcomed the approach to renew contacts. In subsequent meetings, I got to know Turki fairly well as also his deputy, Saeed Badeeb, with whom we exchanged notes on Afghanistan fairly regularly.

A few eminent Saudis, unconnected to the government, to whom a set of questions were posed at a personal level about a 10-year prospect, declined to portend in clear terms. They felt that the time span was not enough to bring about meaningful change and cited socio-economic problems, but opined that the regime's ability 'to buy' support must not be underestimated. However, field research suggested that among the new generation of Saudis 'there is detectable change in attitudes towards the government' and 'the constant theme that runs through all the interviews is desire for freedom from constraints. Generally, members of the new generation, replete with a definite sense of national identity, want their country to thrive but in tandem with this, they want space within Saudi society to develop their own attitudes and opinions without the overbearing presence of the state and *ulema*'.[98]

The critical question, I felt, was the pace of change; the challenge

---

[97] Anthony H. Cordesman, *Saudi Arabia* (Boulder, Colorado, 1997) pp. 181–87.
[98] Mai Yamani, *Changed Identities: The Challenge of the New Generation in Saudi Arabia* (London, 2000) pp. 147–49.

to the Al Saud was to be ahead of the pressures for change in order to renew its legitimacy. The challenge to the reformers, liberal or conservative, is to make the process sufficiently critical, without making it disruptive, and that the time available for converting these tensions into new balances may not be unlimited.

I concluded my Riyadh assignment on 30 November 1999 and with it brought to an end an association of almost 38 years with the MEA. I could look back with much satisfaction over the time spent in a profession into which I drifted almost accidentally, and with the satisfaction of having shared many moments of joy 'with delicacy and without capitulation' with friends and colleagues.

Chapter 5

'And Wilderness is Paradise enow'

NEW DELHI: A NEW LIFE

The 'home shelter' for nomads of the diplomatic service is the hostel on Kasturba Gandhi Marg (old Curzon Road) built in the early 1960s at the initiative of the late Badruddin Tyabji. It is centrally located, has single rooms and two bedroom family apartments. This is where we landed on arrival in New Delhi and stayed there for about a month while getting our Mayur Vihar apartment organized and furnished. Salma did a lot of running around and saw to it that basic comforts, and more, were available for a new beginning. After a few weeks, our heavy baggage also arrived and the difficult task of segregating the essentials from the dispensable was undertaken on a priority basis. I was amazed at how work of this nature can be expedited under pressure!

A few months prior to leaving Riyadh, a friend of mine in JNU had enquired if I would be interested in taking up the position of Visiting Professor at the Centre for West Asian and African Studies there. The idea perhaps emanated from some book reviews that I had done for *Frontline* and a paper I had written on *Security in the Persian Gulf*, which was published in the monthly journal of the Institute for Defence Studies and Analysis. I fancied the offer and looked forward to a calling I had desired decades earlier! Accordingly, two weeks after arriving in Delhi, I called on the then head of the centre, Prof. Gulshan Dietl and enquired what I was expected to do. She said that I should share my knowledge and experience in West Asian lands with senior students, attend weekly seminars and guide a few MPhil and PhD students. Other members of the faculty whom I got to know well included Prof. Girijesh Pant, Prof. A.K. Pasha and Prof. P.R. Kumaraswamy; the latter had worked in Israeli archives on Indo-Israel relations, a subject that I had handled in the MEA many years earlier.

I wrote a paper on *Persian Gulf Security: Past Perspectives, Future Prospects,* in which I argued for a new approach premised on an inclusive minimum common threat perception and for the establishment of a forum to conduct a continuous dialogue. It was published as an Occasional Paper by the Gulf Studies Centre of JNU. Another paper, *Strategies of Group Mobilization: Militant Groups and the West Asian Peace Process* was published by the *Journal of the School of International Studies*, JNU (July–Sept 2001).

Apart from colleagues at the centre, I met many other scholars in disciplines such as international relations, political studies, Arabic and Persian. The overall ambiance of the campus was conducive to learning, to those who teach and those who learn, and was very much in step with the ideas of those who crafted JNU's purpose and curricula of studies. The general approach was to be liberal and encourage those who seek knowledge. The student body was drawn from all over the country, to be expressive of the diversity of the land. For over three decades, the alumni distinguished themselves in all walks of life, in the country and abroad.

Besides teaching, attending seminars and engaging in academic writing, I contributed several book reviews to *Frontline*. Slowly, a new pace of life took shape. Living in the IFS apartments, in the company of many colleagues with whom memories and experiences of a lifetime could be exchanged, was pleasant. This tranquillity, however, did not last.

Towards the end of April or the first week of May, Sayyid Hamid sahib and Syed Shahabuddin sahib approached me separately to suggest that I should allow them to explore my name being considered for the forthcoming selection of the vice chancellorship of AMU. Having had no contact with the university since leaving it in 1961, I pondered over the suggestion and got to know something about the politics and pitfalls of the microcosm that was AMU. I was told that the tenure of the outgoing VC (who was keen on a second term) had been contentious and marked by a certain degree of violence on the campus and closure *sine die* three times in three years.

According to a report in *The Hindu* of 26 May 2000, the appointment of the new VC 'witnessed some real high-voltage drama dividing the university into two virtually warring groups'. Eventually, the prescribed procedure of a panel of five by the Executive Council, out of which the University Court selected three, for consideration by the government was adhered to. An editorial writer opined that 'bringing the university back on track will be no easy task and Mr Ansari will need all his diplomatic skills as he addresses it'. I was told later by President K.R. Narayanan that the National Democratic Alliance (NDA) government had reservations about my name on account of a shortage of tenure (22 months) due to my age, but that he overruled it after legal consultation with two former chief justices of India. And so, in the last week of May, my appointment was announced. I joined the university on 28 May 2000.

ALIGARH MUSLIM UNIVERSITY

To go back to head an institution where I had spent five years of my youth was both emotional and exciting. Much on the campus was a reminder of the past; much had changed too. The University Tarana was as evocative as ever. The central plaza adjacent to Victoria Gate, Strachey Hall, Aasman Manzil, the University Mosque, the cricket ground and Willingdon Pavilion, Old Boys' lodge, Aftab Hostel and Shamshad market, all brought back old memories. Most of the contemporaries were around, in Aligarh or elsewhere in the world; a few no longer so. Among the latter was my cousin and friend, Ziaul Haq. A visit to 'Minto-E', as the university graveyard was popularly depicted, was saddening.

An institution so intrinsically linked to the modern history of India does have a burden of recollections, perhaps even of history. Much has been written about AMU in the context of the Partition and the events before and after 1947. Some of the ambiance of the times, and later years, were penned many years later by Prof. Naseem Ansari of the medical college in his very readable *Jawab-e-Dost*. It was 'a traumatic experience' with a good percentage of its teachers and the student body opting for Pakistan and was reflected in good measure in the display of prejudice in the local politics of UP.[99] It was Sarojini Naidu, Nehru and Maulana Azad who came to the rescue and their chosen instrument was Dr Zakir Husain, who invited Nehru and Azad to address the annual convocations. Nehru said,

> I invite you as free citizens of free India to play your role in the building up of this great country and to share in common with others the triumphs and setbacks alike that may come our way. The present with all its unhappiness and misery will pass. It is the future that counts, more specially to the young, and it is the future that belongs to you.

Azad urged his audience 'to forget the pains of the past and set our sights on the distant heights which we have to conquer. To scale these new heights, you have to search for a new vision which will bring glory to you and to this great country'. Dr Husain supplemented these when he himself addressed the Convocation in 1951 in expressions

---

[99] Paul R. Brass, *An Indian Political Life: Charan Singh and Congress Politics 1937 to 1961* (New Delhi, 2011) citing a communication from Charan Singh to Chief Minister Govind Ballabh Pant suggesting that 'losses suffered by Hindus in Aligarh district in March 1946 as a consequence of the riots to be paid for out of the yearly grants to the Aligarh Muslim University' (p. 55–56). Chapter 3 of the book (pp. 38–66) gives details of Hindu–Muslim relations in that period in UP.

that need to be recalled and reiterated by succeeding generations:

> The way Aligarh works, the way Aligarh thinks, the contribution Aligarh makes to Indian life in its manifold aspects will largely determine the place Musalmans will occupy in the pattern of Indian life. The way every Indian deals with (it) will largely determine the shape of things in the future national life of our motherland.[100]

The AMU of the year 2000 was much bigger in size than the university I had left in 1961. The difference was more than physical; the intellectually accommodating ambiance seemed to be wanting. There was much less of an all-India character in the student body and much more of UP and Bihar. I called on a senior retired professor, shared with him my nostalgia over the past and asked him the reason for change. 'I will send you the answer' was his laconic response. The next morning, it came in the shape of a piece of paper bearing an Urdu couplet of Allama Iqbal:

> *Waa-e-nakami mata-e-karwaan jata raha*
> *Karwaan ke dil se ehsas-e-ziyan jata raha*
>
> (It is regrettable that not only has the caravan lost its wealth but has also forsaken the sense to feel the loss.)

The student body of 5,500 of the late 1950s had reached 19,000 and the number of the teaching faculty had gone from 150 to well over a thousand. Earlier, almost all students were residents in halls of residence; these proportions had changed over the years. As a result, the pressure on facilities had increased unbearably. Hostel rooms meant for three or four were being given to six; as a result, there was room for beds but not for tables and chairs. The only place available for study was the reading room in the Maulana Azad Library which,

---

[100] Jawaharlal Nehru, Address to the Annual Convocation, 24 January 1948 and Tariq Hasan, *The Aligarh Movement and the Making of the Indian Muslim Mind 1857–2002* (New Delhi, 2006) pp. 244–52.

I was told on arrival, was kept open round the clock. Unwilling to believe it, I decided to visit the reading room one night after midnight and found veracity in the claim. Much more serious was the pressure on laboratories in the science faculty.

I adhered to etiquette by requesting for a call on the district magistrate and collector. Being much junior in the civil service, he responded by calling on me. This established the basis for close cooperation with the local authorities. As some subsequent events were to show, it was helpful.

There is much that is laudable in AMU's inherited traditions; by the same token and perhaps less laudable, is indulging in satire verging on malice that has been refined into a fine art. Awaiting my arrival was an unsigned two-page letter in chaste Urdu bearing the caption *Aligarh, Second Kufa and Hamid Ansari sahib.* (The reference to Kufa was an episode in early Islamic history and the martyrdom of the Prophet's grandson, Hussain, who was invited by the people of Kufa and then betrayed.) An opening paragraph began with the assertion that lines of courtiers of different ideological affiliations await to reassure the new ruler of their loyalty to shoulder any responsibility, except teaching. It went on to opine that the biggest challenge for the new incumbent is to steer clear of these factions.

I discovered very soon that the ancient divide between 'progressives' and 'conservatives' had aggravated with time. A pamphlet said to emanate from a 'senior student' accused me of having 'a communist face'; another by some teachers accused the VC of partiality in administrative appointments. It took me a little time to explore and negotiate space to conduct a non-partisan administration. There were a few problems in dire need of attention; all related to unduly harsh disciplinary action. I was able to convince the Executive Council that the ends of justice would be met by toning down the measures earlier decided upon. This sent the desired message of fairness but not without allegations of compromise from some quarters.

An early challenge was in the office of the Controller of Admission and Examination. A practice had developed about attendance shortage of students being condoned before examinations under pressure from various quarters on the campus. We overcame it by informing the defaulting students periodically and, after mid-year, informing their parents that unless corrective action was taken, the student concerned will not be allowed to take the examination and would thus lose a year. To demonstrate our seriousness, over 1,300 students in different faculties were held back at the end of the academic year; thereafter, the desired results were forthcoming. Two stern Controllers, Professors Aziz Khan and Mehdi Rizvi, handled this and other related matters very competently. Other colleagues who were particularly helpful in different ways were Prof. Hakim Zillur Rahman sahib of Tibbiya College and Prof. Jafari of zoology, who was a very effective Dean of Student Welfare. Prof. R.P. Singh of botany did a good job of supervising the public relations department.

A few personnel changes in the administrative set-up of the university had to be made. The need for a Registrar, who was competent in administrative matters for a university campus the size of a virtual city, was evident. I felt I could do with the assistance of Afzal Amanullah, IAS, who was for some time a colleague in Saudi Arabia as Consul General, Jeddah and accordingly sought his services from the GoI on deputation. Unknown to me, it became a matter of contention between the establishments in New Delhi and Patna, with the CM of Bihar taking the view that he will not allow the Centre to 'steal' yet another competent officer. I sought the intervention of the then Minister of State, Vasundhara Raje, who asked if I wanted to add another item to her list of disagreements and grievances with the state government! I then sought the help of the late Saiyid Hamid sahib, who suggested the name of S.M. Afzal, IPS and this sailed smoothly through the official circles of the Department of Personnel and Training in New Delhi.

The practice of a few student netas continuing their stay in hostels after passing out was found to be at the root of most of the indiscipline on the campus. Prof. Nafees Ahmad as Proctor handled this in close cooperation with the district administration.

I discovered early enough that an open channel of communication with students was always preferable to stern procedures, that a dharna was often resolved by joining it and that slamming the door in the face of an agitated student group was but an invitation to them to storm it. In such an approach, I had the benefit of knowing the temper and culture that characterized the etiquette of the AMU campus. Morning walks and occasional visits to sports grounds were particularly useful. I found that the university cricket ground was being used for purposes unconnected with the game and took steps to have it fenced. Similarly, some of the stones bearing names of donors had been thoughtlessly discarded during renovation exercises; I had them collected and used them in the fence in front of the Aftab hostel. A few years later, I was happy to receive a copy of a volume *History on Stones: Inscriptions of Aligarh Muslim University* (by Prof. Ali Athar of the department of history), which was a compilation of images of some of the benefactors of the institution.

The lack of regular teacher attendance in some departments was noticed and could only be corrected by surprise inspections. A motivation to teach, impart knowledge to students and learn from mutual interaction seemed to be lacking. The real ailment, I discovered, lay in a subculture that had developed in the university over time, a propensity for inbreeding and a disinclination to venture beyond the confines of the campus and put intellectual skills to the test in the wider world. As a result, the standards of attainment varied greatly, publications were few and far between. The career advancement scheme in vogue assured promotions almost routinely since a sophisticated but undesirable system of assessment through known assessors had settled in. There were, of course, excellent exceptions, but it could be said of many that the attractions of the staff club were often greater than those of the library or the lab!

There was a perceptible drop in the number of PhD candidates who completed their coursework on time. I found that the old practice of having one examiner from outside India had been dispensed with in most faculties, except science and engineering. Neither were satisfactory explanations forthcoming nor could I locate a formal decision to this effect by the Academic Council. My decision to revert to the earlier practice caused heartburn among those who had dispensed with quality standards. I found a similar reluctance to opt for the National Assessment and Accreditation Council assessments. The real problem in each of these related to a propensity among some teachers and research guides to refrain from adhering to the prescribed standards. It seemed to be a classic case of abuse of university autonomy.

A few months after my arrival, in September, an unusual happening threatened to disturb the peace of the campus and the functioning of the university. An incident of a bomb blast in a train compartment near Agra was being investigated by the UP police and in pursuit of it, a police party picked up a student from in front of a hostel one afternoon. He had graduated that year and was staying there as a guest with a friend. To the onlookers, the police action of physically lifting a person and dumping him in an unmarked car looked like kidnapping (not uncommon in parts of the state) and this gave rise to an agitation, which, by dinner time, was moving towards the VC's residence. I intercepted them on the road, heard their grievance and contacted the local administration, which seemed to be blissfully unaware of the happening. By around 10 p.m., I rang up Union Home Minister L.K. Advani to inform him of a developing threat to law and order. A few minutes later, Home Secretary Kamal Pande telephoned to say that the UP government had been asked to keep me informed of the facts, which happened the next morning when they confirmed that the lifting of the student had, in fact, been done by the Agra police without even informing the Aligarh police authorities.

The matter seemed to have settled there but for an 'enthusiastic' exercise of a local Intelligence Bureau (IB) inspector, who in the guise of a salesman, was detected in that very hostel the next day.

Upon being questioned by students, he revealed his identity and was detained in the hostel. This agitated the local police, who informed me that a raid on the hostel was imminent to release the inspector. I prevailed upon them to desist from violent action and, instead, deputed a few senior-most teachers and the Registrar to negotiate the release. This was done successfully on the condition that the inspector would inform the local press about his action. Thereafter, normalcy prevailed, but the incident alerted both the university administration and the students. This seemed to have settled the matter but for a misguided intervention by the Ministry of Human Resource Development, motivated perhaps by considerations of local or state politics, urging me to close the university for some time on the pretext of a disturbed law-and-order situation. I found this unconvincing and the Executive Council concurred in a late-night meeting. The handling of the incident tended to reassure the university community, students and teachers, about my ability to deal with a potentially dangerous situation.

An annual convocation, an important event in the calendar of any university and to which graduating students attach much importance, had not been held by the university since 1986 when the chief guest was President Giani Zail Singh. This departure from the usual practice was attributed to an air of disquiet, within the university and nationally, that prevailed in those years. To correct this, we decided to revert to normal functioning and held a convocation in February 2002 to which former PM I.K. Gujral was invited as the chief guest. He devoted his address to harmony in our land and in the world, to the need to acknowledge diversities and plurality of identities and described the 'Clash of Civilizations' as 'a myth fostered to ensure the dominance of a few over the others'. He further added that there is universal convergence on the need to exorcise terrorism and terrorist activities in all their forms and there is at the same time, considerable awareness around the world that the roots of widely spread resentments must be comprehended and the sources of the maladies must be addressed. One consequence and 'a highly unfortunate development', he added, was the trend towards constricting civil liberties and democratic rights. Shutting the door on dissent, he concluded, is foolhardy as it amounts to closing one of the main avenues of innovation and improvement. 'Heretics have made far larger contributions to the progress of the world than those who stuck to the comfortable grooves of narrow conformities.'

In the VC's customary report on the occasion, I mentioned the services (in their respective fields) of the recipients of three honorary degrees—Prof. C.N.R. Rao, Yusuf Khan 'Dilip Kumar' and Justice V.M. Tarkunde—and the university's 'debt of gratitude' to Justice Tarkunde, to whom for a silly technicality an honorary degree could not be awarded. I gave an overview of the university and its activities. It had 89 departments of studies spread over 12 faculties and over 19,000 students, including 6,356 girl students residing in 15 halls of residence having 64 hostels. About 5,000 students were non-resident (day-scholars). On the credit side, the 10 Departments for Special Assistance programmes of the UGC in geology, mathematics, Urdu, physics and history testified to the quality of work being done in them. I also thanked the UGC for agreeing to initiate new centres on Nehru Studies and Women's Studies and referred to the programmes initiated with the government's approval in collaboration with the Indian National Trust for Art and Cultural Heritage (INTACH) to give advice on the restoration of heritage sites.

I referred to the vision for the students of the institution prescribed by the founder, Sir Syed Ahmad Khan: 'Go forth throughout the length and breadth of the land to preach the gospel of free enquiry, of large-hearted toleration and of pure morality', and drew attention to how the alumni are now to be found in all corners of the globe and have brought laurels to themselves and glory to the alma mater. This, however, should not induce complacency and one must respond to the imperatives of change—as the founder had done—and to address his unfinished agenda of fostering liberal and modernist ideas in an emerging and vibrant India among its students and through them the Muslims of India.

In the midst of all this, I contributed a paper on *Militant Islam: Cause and Effect* to the Delhi Policy Group's seminar on 'War and Peace in Islam' in February 2002. The impulse for my contribution was the events of 9/11 in New York and 'the influence of Islam in the political space occupied by Muslim populations'. I argued that in recent times, Islamic militancy arose out of a genuine resentment emanating from alienation and deprivation and a quest for authenticity. The corrective for alienation, I added, is a reform of the Muslim mind and the corrective for deprivation, which is real and widespread, can emanate only from an alternate development model, which the Islamist radicals have failed to put forward so far.

Salma, herself an alumna and president of the Women's College Union in her time, busied herself in various activities in the campus. She joined the riding club, got the university swimming pool that she as a student had agitated to be open to girls also, heated, and caught up with her friends. Her riding club classes led her to locate children in jhuggis around the campus, who had never been anywhere close to the schooling system. She started a free school for them in an unused room of the botany department in the Qila, with the help of many benefactors in Aligarh city. Over time, with grit, persistence and the goodwill of many, we were able to enrol around 4,000 students from the most economically backward segments of all communities in the school, Madarsa Chacha Nehru.

My time in Aligarh was limited to 22 months, less than half of a normal term. I prioritized it to the best of my ability. A spirit of purpose and optimism in the university community took precedence. This included updating the curricula of studies, sports and extracurricular activities.

One last responsibility of an outgoing VC is to prepare with the Executive Council, in accordance with AMU Statutes, a panel of five names for his successor. This is then sent to the University Court and the latter, in turn, shortlists three of those names for forwarding to the government and the Visitor to name a successor. This process, in my judgment, gave wide scope for canvassing, and worse, within the

Executive Council, and could be avoided if that august body delegates its responsibility to a group of experts to suggest nationally eminent and eligible candidates (and Muslim, given AMU's background) and that such a panel could then be sent to the AMU Court for its deliberation and action. Such a course, I felt, would keep the overall process as originally intended but save the churning and politicking in the Executive Council. My suggestion made no headway, perhaps because it came towards the end of my own term and because of local interests. I subsequently learnt that at least one nominated member of the Executive Council, the late Syed Shahabuddin, did pursue the idea but could not elicit my successor's support.

Coinciding as it did with the post-Godhra riots, the AMU Court meeting took note of the situation. It resolved 'to condemn unconditionally the most barbaric incident that occurred at Godhra' and requested the GoI to set up a Commission of Enquiry 'to investigate the heinous crime with a view to bring to book the criminals and to mete out exemplary punishments to the perpetrators of such a barbaric act'. It condemned 'in equally strong terms the slaughter of innocent people by the organized mobs of terrorists in Ahmadabad, Vadodara, Bhavnagar, Surat, Mehsana and many other adjoining cities and rural areas, allegedly sponsored and protected by local administrations and the government' and said 'these inhuman acts can only be described as acts of terrorism and deserve thorough investigation and exemplary punishment to the culprits'.[101]

The court appealed to the central government 'to take strong possible steps against these terrorists, irrespective of their political affiliation' and also against 'all organizations that are vitiating the atmosphere in the country by the communal rhetoric which is a threat to the law and order and even to the judiciary and the Constitution of the country'. Members of the court offered their services to the

---

[101] www.amu.ac.in-minutes of meeting of University Court, Aligarh Muslim University-Agenda and minutes, pp.11–12 of AMU Court on 4 March 2002 (No. 113).

central and state governments as well as public organizations for the promotion of peace and harmony in the country.

A promise made to a student group, to hold student union elections, remained unfulfilled. The principal reason for it was the disruption of September 2000 and apprehensions relating to it as was expressed by most members of my team.

A few years later, a close observer of the AMU scene wrote that:

> It was left to Hamid Ansari to restore a sense of purpose to this historic institution, which seems to totally lose its moorings—like Indian Muslims as a whole. Ansari had a vision for the university but he was handicapped by the fact that his tenure was limited to just about two years because of an age limit for this post. He was also hampered by the fact that his administrative team lacked cohesion and was not capable enough to face the challenge. This chink in his armour thwarted all attempts for ensuring long-term reforms.[102]

Before leaving, I donated some of my own books to the Maulana Azad Library; these included a photo-image of *The Shahnama of Firdausi,* which was given to me as a farewell gift in Iran.

In February 2000, the NDA government set up a National Commission to Review the Working of the Constitution. It was headed by the former Chief Justice M.N. Venkatachaliah. Its advisory subgroups included one on 'administrative system and standards in public life' and I attended a few of its meetings at the invitation of the late Dr Abid Hussain, former ambassador to the

---

[102]Tariq Hasan, *The Aligarh Movement and the Making of the Indian Muslim* (New Delhi, 2006) pp. 270–71. The author concludes by saying that:
> Any attempt to resurrect the spirit of the Aligarh Movement today cannot succeed for the basic reason that the AMU, which was established for moulding the minds of the 'brightest and the best' now lacks the dynamism to lead from the front. The fact that it has become too large and unwieldy makes it very difficult for the institution to 'return' from the ashes... The AMU owes to the nation at large and the Muslim community in particular to reform basic education to Muslim children at a national level. (pp. 272–73).

US. Its report remained a dead letter since it was not accepted by President Narayanan on the valid ground that it was set up without an appropriate mandate and the consent of the President of India.

In a final message to the students of AMU, I said that it was my privilege to have witnessed at close quarters their admirable endeavour to belie the image of the university as being synonymous with disruption and chaos. I also lauded their efforts to project a truer picture of a normal campus that is inhabited by young men and women raring to go, eager to learn and anxious to position themselves for a meaningful start to life. This has injected a new vitality; the challenge in the future is to prevent a relapse, to consolidate the gains made and quicken the pace. I reminded them that a globalized world has no place for mediocrity and that although times were difficult, the road ahead is negotiable, that the power to influence their destiny is within them and that 'Verily, never will Allah change the condition of a people until they change what is in themselves'. I urged them to 'dedicate themselves to this change, and stand fast'.

I left AMU on 31 March 2002 on the eve of my sixty-fifth birthday. Salma and I were given a warm and affectionate send-off, in which the district administration also participated.

The VC's car drove us to our apartment in Mayur Vihar in New Delhi.

NEW DELHI AGAIN

I woke up the next morning with the disturbing realization that for the first time in four decades, I would have no stenographic assistance. I, therefore, decided to educate myself in the simple, newer technique of self-reliance as far as writing and typing were concerned. Our daughter Nuriya became my tutor; I responded fairly quickly and imbibed the lessons. A few weeks later, I could write an article for the press and celebrated my competence when, a few months later, I succeeded in putting footnotes for a paper I had written for a seminar.

The post-Godhra killings in Gujarat caused an intense public outcry in various sections of society. I was part of a group of concerned citizens who called on PM Vajpayee to remonstrate and urge the government to take action. The Editors Guild of India sent a fact-finding team to the state to report on the role of the media. It revealed the chilling details and observed that 'when we met Narendra Modi, he had no explanation to offer and showed no contrition'.[103] Separately, the National Human Rights Commission and its chairman, Justice J.S. Verma, took up the matter with Vajpayee in a letter dated 3 January 2003. In 2008, Justice Verma said in a media interview that he had suggested the use of Article 355 to deal with the situation.[104] A good many civil society and Muslim community organizations mobilized themselves to attend to the plight and suffering of the displaced people affected by the carnage; the immobility of the state government, however, was shocking.

An eminent sociologist, Prof. T.K. Oommen, analysed in some detail the work undertaken by one civil society group—the CARE India-sponsored Gujarat Harmony Project. He concluded that:

> The provincial government had abdicated its responsibility to mediate peace between estranged groups. In fact, it was widely perceived to have played a partisan role, a party in the perpetration of violence against the minority. Leave aside reconciliation, its reluctance in providing immediate relief and subsequent rehabilitation was quite explicit. The Union government at the Centre, which could have swiftly and effectively intervened, as per the provisions of the Constitution,

---

[103] B.J. Verghese, *First Draft: Witness to the Making of Modern India* (New Delhi, 2010) pp. 444–49. Verghese adds: 'The truth of Gujarat 2002 in the "Words of Men Who Did It" came out in a special issue of *Tehelka* magazine of November 2007. It is nothing short of a bombshell. It was too well documented to have been faked, as alleged.'

[104] *Outlook*, 13 October 2008: Interview to Saba Naqvi. The reference to Article 355 is not in the letter and, perhaps, formed part of the Proceedings referred to in the letter.

remained tactfully non-committal. A substantial section of the police and other law-enforcing agencies, as per accounts of the survivors and reports of the various fact-finding teams, were found to be hand in glove with the perpetrators of the violence. This is also borne out by the selective application of Prevention of Terrorism Act (POTA) 2002, exclusively against Muslims. All the 123 people booked under POTA, were Muslims, whereas those accused of executing the carnage of Muslims were charged under the ordinary sections of the Indian Penal Code (Human Rights Watch, 2003). In such a scenario, to expect a mediatory role from the state and its institutions of criminal justice system was futile... Further, the market and its various institutions remained distant observers despite the fact that more than two months of unabated violence created huge financial losses... The proliferation of civil society organizations did little to contain violence in the state; their reluctance to intervene even in post-conflict scenario was conspicuous.[105]

In October 2002, I was invited by the Bangladesh Institute of International and Security Studies to participate in a conference in Dhaka. I presented a paper on *Politics in South Asia: Salience of Religion and Culture*. I argued that today 'the imperative is to recognize pluralism and secularism as the normative principles of politics' along with 'an unflinching adherence to principles of equality and equal treatment'.[106] While there, I caught up with old friends, ambassadors Mohammad Mohsin and Farouk Chowdhary.

In February 2003, I was invited to Patna to deliver the Khuda Bakhsh Lecture at the renowned Khuda Bakhsh Oriental Public Library. The subject of my lecture was 'Islam and Governance', wherein I argued that although 'the debate in the twentieth

---

[105] T.K. Oommen, *Reconciliation in Post-Godhra Gujarat: The Role of Civil Society* (New Delhi, 2008) pp. 251–52.
[106] A.K.M. Abdus Sabur (ed.), *Politics and Security in South Asia* (Dhaka, 2004) pp. 131–50.

century (had) settled the question of incompatibility with regard to democracy and made some dent in the traditionalist perception concerning secularism, the discussion remained confined to matters pertaining to the ruler and little was said on the form and content of governance.' I argued that an infra-historical rhythm had impeded the 'moment of free choice' and that the categorical imperative of our times was 'a change of rhythm'.[107]

While in Aligarh, I had a chance encounter and an interesting discussion with Prof. Paolo Cotta-Ramusino, Secretary-General of Pugwash, an organization that brings together public figures to work towards reducing the danger of armed conflict and to seek solutions to global security threats. Pursuant to it, I was invited to Pugwash meetings in Tehran to talk on West Asia, and in Kathmandu to promote inter-Kashmiri dialogue. Both brought forth interesting new perceptions; both were lost in the sands of geopolitics.

In 2003, Amnesty International (London) invited me to join a mission to Kabul to make a representation to the Afghan government ensuring that women's rights were adequately reflected in the new Afghan constitution. The experience of going back to Kabul in a very different capacity was a ticklish one! At the end of the mission, I stayed a day with Ambassador Vivek Katju, who took me to the Panjshir valley (to which I had no access in my time in Kabul) and I paid my respects at the tomb of Ahmad Shah Massoud.

Apart from readings that were focused mostly on West Asia and occasional lectures on related themes, I had no clear idea on what to do next. Then out of the blue, my Aligarh contemporary and friend, Shahid Mehdi, who was the VC of Jamia Millia Islamia, offered me a visiting professorship in Jamia's Academy of Third World Studies (now known as MMAJ Academy of International Studies), which was headed by historian Prof. Mushirul Hasan. I found it a worthwhile exercise and, in 2003, wrote a paper on the *Problem of Palestine: Diplomacy and its Limitations*. It was published as a monograph

---

[107] *Journal of Khuda Bakhsh Library*, No. 131, January–March 2003, pp. 1–18.

by the Academy. Some of us in the Academy, together with JNU academics, focused on that region and thought of creating a platform for promoting an interest in the area. The end product of this effort was the Indian Association for Central and West Asian Studies. It took off well; its first series of lectures was initiated by Minister of External Affairs K. Natwar Singh and was followed by an erudite discourse on *Pluralism in Muslim Societies* by Prof. Aziz Al-Azmeh of the University of Exeter, UK. The same year, I contributed a paper titled *Afghanistan: A Neighbour with a Difference* for the volume *External Affairs* edited by the former foreign secretary, J.N. Dixit. In December 2003, I drafted an article for *The Hindu* on Afghanistan, suggesting an alternate approach of institutional neutrality. I sent the draft to Ambassador Chinmaya Gharekhan, my predecessor in New York and former UN special envoy, with the fond expectation that if two former PRs made a suggestion, it might be noticed. It was published on 24 December, but elicited no response! We made another effort to revive the proposal, in the changed context of more recent developments, in an op-ed in the same newspaper of 19 January 2019. We had the satisfaction of observing that the meeting in Moscow on 5–6 February 2019 and its outcome in a nine-point statement indicated agreement that (i) the cooperation of regional countries and major countries are essential to determine lasting and nationwide peace in Afghanistan and (ii) to achieve lasting peace, there should be complete withdrawal of foreign forces from the country, all countries should avoid interfering in Afghanistan's internal affairs and assurance should be given to the international community that Afghanistan will not be used against any other nation. There was also agreement on a spate of assurances for attracting international assistance for the reconstruction of Afghanistan's infrastructure. This, thus, could become the basis of institutional neutrality suggested by us.

In June 2005, I was named leader of the Indian team to a 'Track 1.5' Asia-Middle East Dialogue (AMED) in Singapore. The other members of the delegation were Ambassador Sudhir Devare and Dr Narendra Jadhav of the Reserve Bank of India. The objective of the exercise, initiated by the Government of Singapore, was twofold: politically, to provide a platform for moderate voices for the promotion of tolerance and inter-faith dialogue and, on the economic front, to project the role of Singapore (in competition to Malaysia) in the wealth management industry. The sharper political messages in the meeting came from Malaysia and China, who spoke about the need to strengthen the normative framework for interstate relations (Malaysia) and the need to support each another politically and for consultations on security issues on the basis of equality and mutual trust (China). Altogether, it was salesmanship at a high pitch.

In September 2003, I was invited by the Pugwash General Secretary, Prof. Paolo Cotta-Ramusino, to attend a Pugwash regional exercise in Tehran. This gave me an opportunity to renew acquaintances and perceptions. In an article in *The Hindu*, I opined that the internal and external pressures for change, in a system that is simultaneously revolutionary, religious, democratic and popular, are nuanced and intertwined and the challenge is to manage it. I also used the opportunity to meet some old friends. One of the participants in this gathering was Ambassador Hua Liming of China, who had been my colleague in Tehran a decade earlier. Another participant in the gathering was the German scholar Wilfried Buchta, author of *Who Rules Iran? The Structure of Power in the Islamic Republic*. In December 2004, I attended another Pugwash meeting in Kathmandu which focused on intra-Kashmiri dialogue. An interesting conclusion in this discussion was that the UN resolution on J&K 'is now obsolete'.

OBSERVER RESEARCH FOUNDATION

The late R.K. Mishra, veteran journalist and founder-head of the ORF, suggested to me over a series of lunches in 2003 that I should consider joining the Foundation and contribute to its research activities. I said that the only theme that interested me was the state of democracy in contemporary Muslim societies. He thought it was little explored but a relevant subject. The net outcome was that I joined the ORF as a Distinguished Fellow.

In November 2004, I participated in a seminar on 'Jawaharlal Nehru and Contemporary India' organized by the Nehru Memorial Museum and Library and contributed a paper on *Nehru's Vision of India as a Major Power*. I argued that a complex judgment on Nehru is unavoidable since while realizing India's potential, he was also aware of the difference between potential and its realization and sought to accommodate his approach to the imperatives of power politics: 'The end product was a visionary who also possessed the requisite traits of *Realpolitik*...and that in the business of statecraft neither principles nor recollections take precedence over considerations of national interest, whatever be its limitations.' I cited as an example Nehru's observation in the Constituent Assembly in 1948 that while the purpose of developing atomic energy is for peaceful purposes, 'if we are compelled as a nation to use it for other purposes, possibly no pious sentiment of any of us will stop the nation from using it that way'.[108]

My focus of work in the ORF was on initiating studies on Muslim societies. I wrote the first monograph on Saudi Arabia. It was titled *The Islamic Boomerang in Saudi Arabia: The Cost of Delayed Reforms*. It covered the initiatives taken by different civil society and clerical groups to petition the King in the 1991–2004 period, suggesting correctives to governance procedures and practices. All of these, except one, were carefully worded within the accepted phraseology of advice to the Ruler. The exception was 'Statement Number 1 from the Islamic Movement for Change: The Jihad Wing in the Arabian Peninsula'. It was faxed from London, denounced the Kingdom as a 'Kafir regime that has no legitimacy' and pronounced that its jihad operations shall target (i) Christian forces unless they are withdrawn from the peninsula (ii) influential members of the Saudi family who are the leaders of the Kafir regime and (iii) the armed forces

---

[108]*Contemporary India*, Volume 3, No. 4, October–December 2004, pp. 47–58.

and police that protect the regime. Together, they signalled a new boldness and a sense of urgency. In response, a process known as the Makkah Dialogue was initiated in 2003. The study concluded that 'the challenge to the Al Saud is to be ahead of the pressures for change in order to renew their legitimacy' and for the reformers to make the process sufficiently critical without making it disruptive: 'the time available for converting these tensions into balances may not be unlimited'.

The second study in the series, undertaken by two eminent scholars of Persian, Professors Azarmi Dukht Safavi and A.W. Azhar Dehlavi, was *Revolution and Creativity: A Survey of Iranian Literature, Films and Art in the Post-Revolutionary Era*. It dealt with the cultural catharsis that was attempted in the immediate aftermath of the Iranian Revolution and a second stage in which correctives and regeneration emerged and concurred with an Iranian scholar's observation that 'the balance sheet of the last twenty years is interestingly bewildering—unprecedented progress juxtaposed with regressive changes'.

The third study took the shape of an international conference on *Iran Today: Twenty-five Years after the Islamic Revolution*. Its purpose was to explore the perception that while the religious face of Iran will remain, given its unique character of being Iranian, Islamic and Western simultaneously, the narrative from religion must continue to change, and that it must ascertain its pace and direction. Well-known scholars from Iran, the US, the UK, France, Germany, the Russian Federation, Israel, Switzerland, China and India participated and contributed papers to the conference, which was addressed by Brajesh Mishra. I edited the collection of papers presented by the participants as *ORF Studies in Muslim Societies: III*. In my Introduction, I referred to Leon Trotsky's observation about the direct interference of masses in historic events as 'the most indubitable feature of a revolution' and wrote that the purpose of the conference was to take a broad spectrum view of the direction Iran was taking after a quarter of a century to ascertain the direction and pace of change. I referred to

Imam Khomeini's litmus test in his Testament on the policies of the system: 'We owe the victory of the Islamic Revolution to the support of the people. Bereft of their support you will be done away with and tyrants such as there were during the monarchy will occupy your offices.'

The fourth study in the series was devoted to the experience of democracy in non-Arab Asian societies. It was edited by Prof. Zoya Hasan of JNU and included essays by scholars in Bangladesh, Indonesia, Iran, Malaysia, Pakistan and Turkey. It was published in 2007 as *ORF Studies in Contemporary Muslim Societies IV: Democracy in Muslim Societies, the Asian Experience*. The impulse for the study, I said in my Foreword, was President Bush's observation on 'the war for the Muslim mind' and the need to test the compatibility argument in theoretical and empirical terms. I noted that 75 per cent of Muslims live outside the Arab world, that 70 per cent of the total are in non-Arab Asian countries and that World Value Surveys show that a clear majority agree that 'democracy may have problems, but it is better than other forms of government' and that the percentage of agreement was 98 for Bangladesh, 71 for Indonesia, 69 for Iran, 82 for Pakistan and 88 for Turkey. Prof. Hasan analysed the situation in each of these countries and concluded that 'there is no fundamental incompatibility between Islam and democracy in the Asian Muslim world and no systematic effort has been made to build an enduring Islamic political system to the exclusion of other alternatives'.

Given the almost hysterical dimensions of the discourse in the US in those years, I raised a number of questions in a Foreword I wrote to Prof. Chintamani Mahapatra's study on *The US Approach to the Islamic World in Post 9/11 Era*: 'Does the United States have a problem with Islam? Does it have a problem with people who call themselves Muslims? Is it a domestic or a foreign policy question with domestic ramifications? What has been the wider domestic and foreign policy discourse on these matters before and after the trauma induced by 9/11?' I referred to Douglas Little's 2002 study *American Orientalism* and to its concurrence with an earlier observation that 'whenever the people of the Middle East have challenged US interests, America has usually borne down on them with its greatness in an effort to crush them'. This, I wrote, also bore the impression of what another study, *American Theocracy* by Kevin Phillips, described as the impact of the religious right, with its doctrinal imperatives in which Islam has been substituted for the Soviet Union as the 'modern-day equivalent of the Evil Empire'.

The ORF gave me space, intellectually and organizationally, to pursue my work. Our stay in the Mayur Vihar apartment was pleasant more so because of the close proximity to so many friends and former colleagues with whom moments of the past and problems of the present could be candidly discussed during the morning walks. Salma remained busy with the school in Aligarh and made periodic trips there. After his studies in Monash University, Australia, Osman continued working there and came back to get married to his school friend Sanah Kazmi in January 2006.

At the request of the Integrated Defence Staff (Directorate of Net Assessment) of our Ministry of Defence, I supervised in 2005–06 a study on *Emerging Strategic Scenario in the Persian Gulf: Implications for India*. I was assisted by Vice Admiral (Retd) P.J. Jacob, Prof. Girijesh Pant of JNU, A.C. Patankar of the Confederation of Indian Industry, Mumbai and Gunmeen Singh of the ORF. The study opined that the Persian Gulf is an area of opportunity for India in strategic and economic terms, as also of problems, and concluded that:

(i) An interstate war is unlikely in the region but turbulence could persist;
(ii) Non-traditional threats emanating from political and economic mismanagement could arise and hamper shipping and export of oil and require corrective action by affected parties;
(iii) While US hegemony in military terms persists, its primacy is debatable and the smaller states, therefore, seek a role for the Western powers. Iran's focus, on the other hand, remains on

a cooperative security regime of the littoral states and some opinion makers have gingerly suggested a role for larger Asian states such as China and India, and

(iv) The focus of Indian interests would remain on regional peace and security, the desirability of friendly regimes, preventing the emergence of hostile powers or combinations in the region, avoiding involvement in regional or extra-regional military ventures against a littoral state of the Persian Gulf littoral. In addition, it would focus on access to oil and gas resources of the region, freedom of navigation in the Gulf and through the Straits of Hormuz, and continued access to Gulf markets for Indian trade, technology, investments and workforce.

The US-led allied invasion of Iraq in 2003 induced me to write regularly for *The Hindu* about West Asian developments. It also prompted me to join a group of like-minded friends, who sought and obtained an appointment with the chairperson of the Parliamentary Standing Committee on External Affairs, Krishna Bose, to flag Indian public opinion's opposition to an Indian contingent joining the allied forces in Iraq. I followed on Prof. Juan Cole's website the young Iraqi woman's regular blog under the name 'Riverbend Blogger'.[109] I was deeply distressed over the destruction of Baghdad and cited in one of my articles a couplet of the Iraqi poet Jamil Sidqi al-Zahawi (who died in 1936):

> When ruin overtakes the land upon whose soil
> You grew up, and sorrow not, you are a stone.[110]

I was named a member of the track-two India–UK Round Table in 2003 and after the change of government made the Indian Co-chair. The purpose of this and a few other similar groupings was to discuss the wide aspects of bilateral relations and give suggestions.

---

[109]Later published as *Baghdad Burning* by Riverbend (New Delhi, 2007).
[110]A. John Haywood, *Modern Arabic Literature: 1800–1970* (London, 1971) p. 108.

When Mani Shankar Aiyar became the petroleum minister, he constituted an Advisory Committee on Oil Diplomacy for Energy Security with Dr Arjun Sengupta as its chair. I succeeded him in November 2005. The group, consisting of former ambassadors and civil servants, divided its work in seven regional subgroups whose members, on the basis of their specialized knowledge of political and economic conditions, produced regional assessments. It completed its assignment in February 2006.

THE NATIONAL SECURITY ADVISORY BOARD

In 2004, I was named a member of the National Security Advisory Board (NSAB). Besides participation in its deliberations, I contributed a paper on *India and the Muslim States,* in which I argued that while their strategic perceptions, interests and capabilities differ, all of these states (and Muslim communities elsewhere, including India) subscribe to an emotional bond of 'Muslim-ness'. The sentiment is amorphous as well as real; it is usually taken for granted but gets evoked at times of stress when protection, physical or emotional, is perceived to be required. It is, therefore, essential to understand the reasons and processes by which aspects of community life or its interaction with the wider world become subject of conscious reflection, discussion and debate. Since Muslim states are not identical, a common policy towards them cannot be crafted. What can however be done is to identify, and address, those concerns in which Muslim-ness is evoked in relation to India. These concerns are identifiable and relate to situations and occasions in which the Muslims in India, or sections of Muslims, are seen to be under threat or pressure. The first step in improving the image and influence of India in Muslim countries is thus to be taken in the domestic realm. A tension-laden communal situation or incidents of serious violence focus only on aspects of physical security; a tension-free communal situation, on the other hand, allows all aspects of the Indian situation to be brought into play. Its net impact, therefore, would be positive.

In this context, certain perceptions, developed over time and etched, albeit unevenly, in popular imagery need to be carefully corrected: (i) the minorities are a burden or a nuisance (ii) the stereotype image of a Muslim (iii) the identification of a Muslim, somehow, with Pakistan or talking of Muslims in the context of Pakistan.

Once the question of physical security is attended to, a comprehensive picture of the Indian Muslim scene, in terms of rights and safeguards, can be developed to substantiate the point that the position of India in relation to the Muslim world is *sui generis* by virtue of (i) its secular-state framework that is the best guarantee of Muslim rights (ii) its plural ethos and its rejection of the clash-of-civilization or forced modernization thesis (iii) the contribution that it has made, and continues to make, to Islamic culture (iv) its understanding of and empathy with the developmental imperatives confronting most Muslim states (v) its fast-developing capacity to be a substantial trading partner that is also capable of extending assistance in new areas of technology.

I suggested that our external projection should be of 'the Indian face in all its diversity' rather than of an 'Indian Muslim face in select destinations' since the latter is perceived as special pleading. Similarly, questions relating to Pakistan are often a complicating factor in our dialogue with Muslim countries, with both sides using it as the litmus test. There is a need to develop alternate approaches in order to take away the focus from this matter. We need to stress instead on our wider interests. We can maximize the advantages accruing to us from our unique position only if we have the will to do so. This will has to be consciously developed.

In an op-ed in *The Asian Age*,[111] I commented on the developing tensions in the triangular relationship between India, the US and Iran in the context of our vote for the resolution against Iran in the IAEA. I was critical of the Indian vote, reportedly under overt US pressure, supportive of the matter being referred to the Security Council and its

---

[111] *The Asian Age*, 30 September 2005.

adverse impact on the developing Indo-Iranian relationship. I wrote elsewhere that India did not subscribe to the US agenda of regime change in Iran and its plans for externally induced democratization. I opined that 'one Iraq should be enough for a generation. It is important for the Indian public to digest its implications'.

INDIA AND THE OIC

On the eve of his state visit to India in January 2006, King Abdullah bin Abdulaziz Al Saud of Saudi Arabia suggested in an interview to one of our newspapers that 'India should have an Observer Status in the OIC similar to that held by Russia' adding that 'it would be beneficial' if India's entry was put forward 'by a nation like Pakistan'. I commented on this in an op-ed in *The Hindu*[112] and said in the context of earlier happenings that 'if the debate is to be reopened, it needs to go back to the beginning'. I also added that:

> If India was an original invitee, the question of offering it an observer status should not arise. Instead, it should be a simple matter of restoring the founder-membership that was taken away from India by a sleight of hand that did no credit to those who did it, or assisted it in any manner. In fact, the offer and acceptance of an alternate status would revalidate what was done in 1969. For this reason, it should be rejected.

I concluded that neither an ostrich-like posture of ignoring the OIC nor an avid embrace will serve India's purpose. Incremental interaction, and a quiet insistence on the restoration of the original membership, would be a better alternative.

Given this context, and unlike most people in official and public circles, I was less than elated when many years later, Foreign Minister Sushma Swaraj, at the invitation of the UAE, addressed the OIC Foreign Ministers meeting in Abu Dhabi as a 'guest of honour' in

---

[112] *The Hindu*, 30 January 2006.

March 2019. A few days later, the same meeting, in its Abu Dhabi Declaration, criticized us for 'intensified Indian barbarities since July 2016' and 'illegal detentions and disappearances'. The dialectics of the process could be praiseworthy.

THE NATIONAL COMMISSION FOR MINORITIES

In February 2006, the UPA chairperson, Sonia Gandhi, asked me to become the chairman of the National Commission for Minorities (NCM). She said that she wanted to invigorate the Commission. I said this depended on the team and the terms of reference. She sought suggestions about new members; a few of these were accepted. The final team comprised Harcharan Singh Josh, Dileep Padgaonkar, Zoya Hasan and Lama Chospel Jodpa, with Michael Pinto as Deputy Chairperson.

While the term 'minority' is used only in Articles 29 and 30 of the Constitution, their objective, as also that of Articles 25 to 28, is in the words of a 1974 Supreme Court judgment, 'to preserve the rights of religious and linguistic minorities, to place them on a secure pedestal and withdraw them from the vicissitudes of political controversy'. Pursuant to it, some state governments made efforts in earlier years to assess the problems of minority communities. A central Minorities Commission was first established through a Government Resolution in 1978 'to safeguard the interests of minorities whether based on religion or language' and to evaluate the working of safeguards as well as to look into specific complaints.

The National Commission for Minorities Act of 1992 gave it a statutory status and, in a notification in 1993, the religious minorities covered by it were notified as Muslims, Christians, Sikhs, Buddhists and Zoroastrians (Parsis). A few years later, Jains were added to the list.

In 2004, the Common Minimum Programme of the UPA government included six 'measures to be adopted for the welfare of minorities'; one of these was 'to examine the question of providing constitutional status' to the NCM. This also figured in the President's Address to Parliament. Pursuant to it, two bills were moved in the Lok Sabha; the first of these proposed a new clause, Article 340A in the Constitution to bestow Constitutional status on the statutory NCM 'to inspire greater confidence amongst the minorities'. The bill was referred to the Standing Committee attached to the Ministry of Social Justice and Empowerment, then headed by Sumitra Mahajan. Several clauses in its Report of January 2006 were critical of the manner in which the government dealt with matters relating to the Commission. Three of these were sufficiently candid:

> 1.20 The Committee note with concern that though the Ministry has time and again emphasized that the main reason for the proposed amendment was to instill greater confidence amongst the minorities, yet in the absence of vital powers of inquiring and investigation, the NCM, even with a Constitutional status, would be a toothless tiger and be hampered a great deal in carrying out its mandate. The Committee therefore strongly recommend that section (d) of clause 5 be suitably amended as to inquire into specific complaints with respect to deprivation of right[s] and safeguards of Minorities and to investigate and monitor all matters regarding safeguards provided for the Minorities under this constitution or under any law.
>
> 1.21 The Committee also urge the Ministry to add another section in clause 5, namely 'To participate and advise on the planning process of socioeconomic development of the Minorities and to evaluate the progress of their development under the Union and any State'. The Committee are of the firm opinion that by incorporating the above-mentioned clause, the NCM would play a far more effective role in accelerating the socio-economic development of the Minorities.
>
> 1.27 The Committee express their deep concern over the tardiness exhibited by the Government in tabling the Annual

Reports of the NCM in Parliament. The Committee are alarmed to be apprised that the last Annual Report tabled by the Government in Parliament pertains to the year 1995–96.

1.27 (iii) The Committee strongly view that such a step on the part of the Government would inspire a sense of confidence amongst the Minorities and would portray real commitment on the part of the Government to work for the welfare of the Minorities.[113]

Despite these positive recommendations, and the draft bill's stated intent of inspiring greater confidence among the minorities through the conferment of constitutional status and being a more effective safeguard, legislation to confer constitutional status on the Commission was not forthcoming. This could only be attributed to political hesitation within the Congress party and some of its allies on minority-related questions.

When I assumed office in March 2006, I found that the annual reports of the Commission had not been tabled in parliament for several years. I drew the attention of the then minister for minority affairs, A.R. Antulay, to this default. Corrective action was taken but no occasion arose or was sought to discuss these in either Houses.

During my tenure, the Commission focused on a series of complaints from minority groups. We dealt with them by doing on-the-spot investigations and making recommendations about correctives to the government. For this purpose, teams of members were sent to undertake on-the-spot surveys and suggest recommendations for correctives. These were published as NMC Special Reports and related to Gujarat, Aligarh, Malegaon (Maharashtra), Madhya Pradesh and Chhattisgarh. Each pertained to incidents involving Muslim minorities except the ones in Madhya Pradesh and Chhattisgarh, where the complaints emanated from Christian communities.

---

[113]Fourteenth Lok Sabha, Report of the Standing Committee on Social Justice and Empowerment, Constitution 103rd Amendment Bill, 2004 and National Minorities Commission (Repeal) Bill, 2004.

We also took necessary steps, through the appointment of a special counsel, to reactivate judicial proceedings in the Hashimpura massacre of 1987, in which 42 Muslim youth were alleged to have been killed by the UP Pradeshik Armed Constabulary. Despite it, legal proceedings dragged on for many years and a final decision, to sentence 16 persons to life imprisonment, was announced by the Delhi High Court in the last week of October 2018.

The national and international furore that followed the post-Godhra riots of February–March 2002 was and remains a matter of national shame. It was said by both NHRC Chairman Justice Verma, and the Attorney General Soli Sorabjee that international concerns over the violation of human rights cannot be brushed aside on grounds of domestic jurisdiction.[114] The Gujarat complaint to the NCM in 2006 related to the plight of more than 5,000 families displaced after the communal violence of 2002 and living in makeshift colonies in four districts of the state. None of these were on land allocated by the state government and were established on land purchased at commercial rates by NGOs and community organizations. They lacked basic civic amenities, and residents there lived in an environment of insecurity.

A three-member team led by Deputy Chairman Pinto visited 17 out of the 46 camps and their findings and observations were recorded in an official statement:

> In their discussions with state government officials, and in their meeting with the chief minister of Gujarat, the team was informed of the state government's view that the inmates were living in the camps voluntarily. In view of the overwhelming

---

[114]*The Hindu* and the *Times of India*, 14 May 2002: 'Human rights are everyone's concern and any such violation could be challenged by anyone from anywhere in the world' (Justice J.S. Verma). 'Old dogmas of state sovereignty have changed and the international community can now express legitimate concern' (Soli Sorabjee). Relevant in this context was the 30 June 2003 report of the Human Rights Watch, New York: *Compounding Injustice: The Government's Failure to Redress Massacres in Gujarat.*

evidence to the contrary, the Commission finds this viewpoint untenable and evasive of a government's basic responsibility. The Commission cannot avoid the feeling that the State government is not fulfilling its constitutional responsibility and that even four-and-a-half years after the riots, it has not been able to create an atmosphere in which those displaced by the riots can return to their homes.[115]

The NCM recommended to the GoI the need for a special package for internally displaced families in Gujarat as well as for the framing of a national policy on internal displacement due to violence.

The Madhya Pradesh and Chhattisgarh visits were motivated by complaints from Christian groups about harassment and public humiliation meted out by some extremist groups, in early 2006, on schools and churches in Jabalpur, Jashpur and Raipur districts on allegations of conversions, and inaction by the authorities on complaints made. The NCM team observed that the fundamental right of professing and practising one's religion should not be infringed upon and stringent action must be taken on the perpetrators of disharmony.

The Aligarh riot of 6 April 2006 emanated from an inter-community matter that could have been dealt with by the authorities through timely action and by the use of the locally available Rapid Action Force unit. The report suggested an enquiry by a high court judge to restore confidence of the minority community.

The grievance of the minority community on the Malegaon bomb blasts, in September 2006, on the occasion of a religious festival, was that despite the town's history of being communally sensitive and cautionary advice from community leaders, timely action was not taken by the authorities. It was also suggested that apart from giving compensation to the affected parties, the state government should make a meaningful gesture to the public at reviving a dying city and

---

[115]National Commission for Minorities (NCM), Press Note of 23 October 2006, para 6.

giving it the assurance of equal treatment in developmental matters.

The Mangalore riots of October 2006 were initiated by provocative behaviour of a mob outside a place of worship and grew into a riot in which shops of the minority community were looted. Here, too, the local administration was alleged to be tardy. The NCM report suggested an enquiry by a high court judge and adequate compensation as well as pre-emptive action by the administration to forestall such occurrences.

Separately, it was suggested by the government to enquire into the Nandigram incident in West Bengal in 2007 to ascertain if there were any communal overtones to it. Dileep Padgaonkar and I travelled to Kolkata and then to Nandigram village in Purba Medinipur district. Scheduled Castes (SCs), Scheduled Tribes (STs) and minorities constitute about 60 per cent of the population there and three of the five Bhoomi Bachao committees were Muslim. We were told that when the attack on the village was imminent, members of both communities gathered in the village square to pray for safety. Our discussions with local officials revealed that although three civil magistrates were asked to be on standby, the standard procedures did not appear to have been followed before resorting to use of force, in which around 40 persons lost their lives and that no magistrate was actually present when the police firing took place. Local accounts also spoke of the role of easily identifiable party cadres in the carnage. In his discussions with us, the CM acknowledged the mistake of the local MP and the Haldia Development Authority's failure to communicate more effectively with the public about the objective of the planned land acquisition. In a discussion with the minister for minority affairs of the state government, I enquired how a Left Front government having given satisfaction on weightier law-and-order issues, could overlook the fairly innocent demands of the substantial Muslim minority in West Bengal. His response was revealing of the approach: 'We think in class terms, not in terms of religious groups!'

From time to time, the NCM received communications and representations from members of the public and community organizations, expressing concern over reported efforts to abridge the Right to Freedom of Religion as expressed in Article 25(1) of the Constitution of India. These specifically referred to existing and recent pieces of legislation, imposing restrictions on religious conversions, in some states of the Indian Union. They expressed the view that while coercion is inadmissible in matters of faith, restrictions based on vague or unsubstantiated allegations of 'inducement' and 'allurement' have resulted in interference with the practice of religion and hampered the legitimate activity of propagation. These representations asserted that such practices violate the guarantee given in Article 25; they also disregarded India's commitments under the Universal Declaration of Human Rights and the International Covenant on Civil and Political Rights. They urged the state governments concerned to repeal such laws and urge all religious and political leaders to work together to find ways of 'addressing disputes through dialogue and through non-violent, non-legislative and non-discriminatory ways'.

The NCM, whenever the occasion arose, endorsed the view that the right to profess, practise and propagate religion is an essential ingredient of our country's multi-religious edifice and urged all concerned to resolve misgivings and misunderstandings through dialogue.

A few months after I demitted office as Chairman, a team from the NCM consisting of Zoya Hasan and Dileep Padgaonkar visited Orissa on 6–8 January 2008 to look into reports of tension and violence in the hill districts of the state on 24–27 December 2007. They visited the Kandhamal district, which has a majority tribal population and a Christian segment of 18–20 per cent, many of whom seek ST status. Amidst unsubstantiated allegations of forcible conversions, they were attacked during Christmas celebrations and 'were unable to celebrate their most important festival' and thus deprived of a constitutional right. In its report, the team also recommended that the authorities must show greater vigilance to prevent the outbreak of violence and that the government must address issues of social exclusion and structural inequalities.[116]

The annual conference of the NCM in November that year was attended by PM Dr Manmohan Singh. In my welcome address, I dwelt on the intention of the NCM Act 'to infuse confidence among the minorities' by reassuring them of their place in the polity. I also drew attention to the fact that every sixth Indian belongs to a religious minority and that credible data showed that considerable segments amongst them remained marginalized in terms of socio-economic development. Thus, this had an adverse impact on the all-round progress of the country. The minorities need assurance of physical security, of a life of dignity and of equality of treatment at the hands of the agents of the state as well as accelerated development and carefully calibrated affirmative action so that they can march shoulder to shoulder with other citizens. This is hampered by shortfalls in implementation of government programmes, aggravated by attitudes in segments of society. I said that the human and financial resources given to the Commission were inadequate for the responsibilities entrusted to it and that experience has shown that these cannot be discharged devoid of the instrumentality of the type given to the NHRC and the National Commission for Scheduled Castes. I expressed the hope that the proposal to give constitutional status to the NCM would fructify. No assurance on the latter point, however, was forthcoming.

In December that year, on the occasion of Minorities Rights Day, I drew attention to the 1992 UN Declaration on the Rights of Persons Belonging to National or Ethnic, Religious and Linguistic Minorities and enquired if the Indian practice has lived up to the commitments undertaken. The answer, I asserted, is not a resounding yes.

---

[116]In a subsequent report in September 2008 by the vice chairperson of the NCM, it was said that 'the entire Christian community had been completely traumatized and that the Christians are subjected to repeated threats that they will never be safe if they do not convert immediately to Hinduism'. (Vrinda Grover and Saumya Uma, *Kandhamal: Introspection of Initiative for Justice 2007–2015* [New Delhi, 2017] pp. 67–68.)

In March 2005, the UPA government instituted a Committee on the Social, Economic and Educational Status of the Muslim Community in India under the chairmanship of Justice Rajinder Sachar and its very substantive report was submitted to the government in November 2006. It laid to rest the allegations of 'appeasement' and, with the help of comprehensive data, showed that the average condition of the community was comparable to, or even worse than the acknowledged historically most backward disadvantaged communities, the SCs and the STs. Commenting on some of the findings and recommendations, the NCM felt that the highest priority should be given to economy and development, access to bank credit, government employment programmes and recruitment procedures.

Pursuant to its recommendations and with a view to work out methodologies for their recommendation, the Ministry of Minority Affairs set up an Expert Group under Prof. Amitabh Kundu to shed light on the domain of community-based disparity and discrimination through a Diversity Index. Its 2008 report dwelt on 'inequality traps' in the political system that prevent the marginalized and work in favour of the dominant groups in society. It also observed that 'unequal economic opportunities [lead] to unequal outcomes which in turn lead to unequal access to political power. This creates a vicious circle since unequal power structure determines the nature and functioning of the institutions and their policies. All these result in persistence of initial conditions'.

'Profoundly skilled in analytic,' as Samuel Butler put it, is generally true of expert reports. The challenge always is on modalities of implementation and this necessitates societal participation; there is a shortfall in both. Our society has a very long way to traverse to achieve it.

I had an occasion to dwell on some of the fundamental questions on minorities in modern states in an India-European Union (EU) seminar in New Delhi in March 2007. I said social diversity is a fact, while homogeneity is a limiting concept. In that context, I referred to assimilation and tolerance and said the latter is a noble virtue but insufficient because while it permits a practice or a profession and prohibits discrimination against it, it does not necessarily endorse it and thus places it in the category of the 'other', with all its attendant implications. The argument for assimilation, on the other hand, is premised on the unstated assumption that the identity (linguistic, cultural and/or religious) of the minority group is eventually to be absorbed in the larger whole, or dominant culture, through a process of consistent integration since the greater good of the larger number lies in such integration. The democratic theory, and the argument of majority rule in decision-making, is used to good purpose to drive home the point. Both these approaches, however, overlook the minority perspective. Its theoretical foundations, therefore, need to be enunciated carefully. This was done many decades earlier in two judgments of the Permanent Court of International Justice. The first of these defined a community not in terms of numbers but in terms of shared religious, racial and linguistic traditions—traditions that the group wishes to preserve and perpetuate through ritual, education and socialization of the young. The existence of such a community, ruled the Court, is not dependent upon recognition by law.

In a second case, the Court said that the objective of minority rights was twofold: to secure for minority groups the possibility of living peaceably alongside the rest of the population and cooperating amicably with them, while at the same time, preserving the characteristics which distinguish them from the majority and satisfying the ensuing special needs. It held that these two characteristics are indeed closely interlocked, for there would be no true equality between a majority and a minority if the latter were deprived of its own institutions and were consequently compelled to renounce that which constitutes the very essence of its being a minority. The Court, therefore, held that:

> Equality in law precludes discrimination of any kind, whereas equality in fact may involve the necessity of different treatments

in order to attain a result which establishes equilibrium between different situations. It is easy to imagine cases in which, equality of treatment of the majority and the minority, whose situations and requirements are different, would result in inequality.

This approach underlies the effort by a great many modern states to develop a framework of minority rights on the twin concepts of *protection* and *promotion*. India and the EU would fall in this category. Referring to the Indian experience, I said a fourfold analysis is undertaken on (i) identity, (ii) security and (iii) a share in fruits of national development and (iv) role in decision-making. I stated that despite constitutional safeguards, all segments of population have not benefited equally, as is evident from the Sachar Committee Report and that the civil society's task, therefore, is to ensure that this is done as also to assess its speed and extent.

Early in 2007, the Commission formally expressed its concern over reported incidents of communal violence and said that:

> The right to life is the foundation on which the structure of the fundamental right of citizens is built (and) the recurrence of communal violence, and its unavoidable consequences, can only be viewed as a failure of our society to honour its basic social compact.

It also urged that the draft bill on Communal Violence (Prevention, Control and Rehabilitation of Victims) be enacted into law at the earliest. I also conveyed our views to the chairperson of the UPA, who seemed to concur. After many years of discussion and debate, the bill was eventually dropped.

WORKING GROUP ON J&K

After the general elections of 2004, the UPA government sought to take up its predecessor's unfinished work of seeking reconciliation through dialogue with the various groups representing segments of opinion in J&K.[117] This was done through two round tables, in February and May 2006, to evolve a consensus among different groups and sections of society on issues related to J&K. Dr Manmohan Singh said that 'there are two dimensions to the problems of J&K—one being the relationship between Delhi and Srinagar and the other being the relationship between Delhi and Islamabad'. He dwelt on the peace process with Pakistan and said, 'I have a vision that the peace-making process must ultimately culminate in our two countries entering into a Treaty of Peace, Security and Friendship to give meaning and substance to our quest for shared goals'.

Dwelling on the need to establish a credible mechanism for carrying this dialogue forward and based on suggestions made, Dr Singh proposed the setting up of five Working Groups composed of nominees of parties and groups to look more closely at the issues and problems. Group I would deal with confidence-building measures across segments of society in the state, Group II on strengthening relations across the Line of Control, Group III on economic development, Group IV on ensuring good governance and Group V on strengthening relations between the state and the Centre.

As part of this process, I was requested to be the convener of Group I in July. Its terms of reference, as enunciated by the PM in his 25 May speech, were (i) measures to improve the condition of people affected by militancy (ii) schemes to rehabilitate all orphans and widows affected by militancy (iii) issues relating to relaxation of conditions for persons who have foresworn militancy (iv) an effective rehabilitation policy, including employment, for Kashmiri

---

[117]A.S. Dulat and Aditya Sinha, *Kashmir: The Vajpayee Years* (New Delhi, 2015). Dr Radha Kumar has revealed that 'Singh asked me if I could explore whether Vajpayee would consider carrying forward the peace process as a special envoy. I took the offer to Brajesh Mishra, who thought Vajpayee would be interested. Some days later, he told me regretfully that the BJP was not in favour and Vajpayee would have to decline.' (*Paradise at War* [New Delhi, 2018] pp. 236–37; also, pp. 229–35.)

Pandit migrants, and (v) an approach considering issues relating to the return of Kashmiri youth from areas controlled by Pakistan.

The Working Group, with a total of 17 members (including the Chair), held three meetings in 2006: in Srinagar on 27 July and in Jammu on 19 September and 24 November. Except for the Hurriyat, all interest groups were represented. In specific terms, its discussions covered:

(i) How militancy had affected the conditions of people and its details relating to normal life
(ii) Numbers of militancy-affected orphans and widows, age group-wise
(iii) Issues related to those who have forsaken militancy with details of affected persons and of issues
(iv) Rehabilitation of Pandits: details of numbers/areas/physical, psychological and political impediments and the resources required
(v) Number of Kashmiri youth in PoK and issues relating to them and a definition of 'approach'
(vi) Preservation and/or revival of cultural and religious heritage

Our discussions were structured and candid. After the second meeting, I put down on paper my own impressions of areas of agreement and presented these to the members in the last meeting. Different viewpoints were consolidated and recommendations were finalized. There were no dissenting notes. The report was sent to the PM on 10 January 2007 who, in a subsequent informal discussion, found much merit in its recommendations but demurred on their immediate implementation for 'political' reasons relating to forthcoming state elections.

In its recommendations, the Group expressed concern over incidents of human rights violation in J&K and underlined the need to raise awareness about it among civil and military functionaries. It also drew attention to special laws such as the Armed Forces Special Powers Act that impinge on the fundamental rights of citizens. It was stated that such laws should be reviewed and revoked and matters should be dealt with through normal laws to the extent possible.

We suggested that the question of relief to victims of militancy should be prioritized and norms developed for giving government jobs instead of a one-time compensation. A special cell should be set up for collection of data within three months on affected widows and orphans. Those who have forsworn militancy should be treated in a dignified manner, be given a rehabilitation package and conditions created for them to avoid reversion. Cases of all persons in jail should be reviewed and those under trial for minor offences should be given general amnesty. For 'youth who joined militancy for misguided ideological reasons, monetary consideration and forced circumstances', a time frame should be decided for their return, within the framework of the confidence-building measures enunciated by the Round Table. They should be treated with dignity and a rehabilitation package given to them.

For Kashmiri Pandit migrants, the Group recommended an effective rehabilitation policy, recognition of their right to return to the places of their original residence and that a relief package be devised in consultation with their representatives. Jobs for them should be identified in police and other civil services. The setting up of a Minority Commission for J&K was also recommended. Similarly, problems faced by refugees who came from West Pakistan in 1947 and their demand for State Subject Status should be settled once and for all. It was also recommended that a comprehensive policy be developed with the help of experts for the preservation of monuments, structures and landscapes considered significant in indigenous history.

The Group suggested that steps be taken 'to start an unconditional dialogue process with militant groups for finding sustainable solutions to the problem of militancy'. It also stressed on the need to examine the role of the media in generating an image of the people of the state so as to lessen the indignity and suspicion that the people face outside the state.

The reports of other working groups, except the one on Centre–

A family photograph at Kendal Lodge, Simla, 1947–48 (Standing from left to right): Khalid and Naseem (Seated on the chairs from left to right): Haris, Mohammad Abdul Aziz Ansari, Aasiya Farooqi and me (Sitting on the ground from left to right): Safia and Zakia

The beginning of a remarkable journey: With Salma at our engagement ceremony in Baghdad in August 1964

Portrait of Salma gifted by Cynthia Stewart on our wedding in Baghdad in August 1964

On board the HM Yacht Britannia for dinner with Queen Elizabeth II at Abu Dhabi in 1979

With PM Indira Gandhi at Hyderabad House, New Delhi in 1982

Receiving the Padma Shri from President Giani Zail Singh in New Delhi in 1984

A gift by a cartoonist at the Sydney Cricket Ground in Australia in August 1985

'Providence sitting up aloft': The study where I might have been at my residence in Kabul on the fateful day of 6 March 1990

'Our enemies have beaten us to the pit': With Ross Mountain of the United Nations, inspecting the massive crater in the garden after the blast of 6 March 1990

Presenting the Letter of Credence to Dr Boutros Boutros-Ghali, Secretary-General of the United Nations, in New York in January 1993

Addressing the 1993 session of the United Nations General Assembly

Addressing the AMU Convocation with former PM I.K. Gujral as Chief Guest in February 2002

In conversation with UPA Chairperson Sonia Gandhi, in 2007.
Source: © The Times of India

Being administered the Oath of Office by President Pratibha Devisingh Patil in New Delhi on 10 August 2007

Being administered the Oath of Office, for the second term, by President Pranab Mukherjee in New Delhi on 11 August 2012

A historic meeting with Fidel Castro in Cuba, in October 2013

Bidding adieu: PM Narendra Modi greets me at my farewell function in Parliament in August 2017. Also seen is Sumitra Mahajan, Speaker of the Lok Sabha.
Photo courtesy: PM India; Prime Minister's Office

The Family

Salma

Visiting the cave city of Cappadocia in Anatolia (Turkey) with Salma, in October 2011

Sulaiman

Nuriya

Osman

With our children: Sulaiman, Nuriya and Osman

state relations, were also given to the government in the following weeks. They were said to have been 'pigeonholed'. The report of the last group, which held five meetings between December 2006 and September 2007, was submitted on 18 December 2009. Its tentativeness has been commented upon by competent observers.[118]

HAJJ ARRANGEMENTS

The UPA government decided to review arrangements pertaining to the Hajj pilgrimage in the context of the rising size of the subsidy on airfares given to Air India. It constituted a Group of Ministers headed by Pranab Mukherjee which, in turn, sought the assistance of an Expert Group. I was made its chairperson; other members were Hajj Committee Chairman Tanveer Ahmad, Ambassador Talmiz Ahmad, Afzal Amanullah and Sanjay Singh from the MEA.

Our report said that while it is the right of the citizen to undertake pilgrimage in exercise of his/her fundamental right to practise religion, it is the duty of the state to make appropriate arrangements for it, and provide assistance and common facilities but not individual costs. In discharge of this duty, the state should explore the most economical travel arrangements. We found merit in the criticism of the air transportation arrangements and of the fare structure that had remained unchanged since 1992 and, thus, cumulatively resulting in disproportionate increases in government 'subsidies' to Air India. We recommended that the existing practice be abandoned and Air India and the Civil Aviation ministry should view Hajj operations as an essential duty and therefore develop a costing structure that would bring down the official fare to the level charged by private operators. This should be done through a calibrated exercise of modest fare increases every year.

---

[118] A.G. Noorani, 'A Cruel Hoax,' *Frontline*, Volume 27, Issue 3, 30 January–12 February 2010.

ASSORTED PURSUITS

In early 2006, I was approached by the Delhi Policy Group to consider taking up its Chair on Non-Traditional Security. I toyed with the idea of a monograph on the 'Community Dimensions of State and Insecurity: Aspects of the Indian Experience.' This, however, was overtaken by other matters.

In July 2006, I finalized with Pearson-Longman the publication of my collection of papers and occasional essays and writings titled *Travelling Through Conflict: Essays on the Politics of West Asia*. In the Introduction, I drew attention to the churning process in West Asia, to a palpable thirst for change, to the unwillingness of the ruling elites to yield power, to the breakdown of the social contract between the rulers and the ruled, and to the return of foreign military bases in numbers never seen before. The book was published in 2007 (formally released on 4 March 2008) and a second impression made its appearance in 2015. Its Urdu translation, *Shehr-e-Aashob,* by Prof. Akhtarul Wasey, was published in 2014.

In November 2006, I was invited to deliver the fourth Prof. Mohammad Mujeeb Memorial Lecture by the Dr Zakir Husain Institute of the Islamic Studies at Jamia. Prof. Mujeeb's book, *The Indian Muslims,* is a classic among the socio-intellectual histories of people of the Muslim faith in the Indian subcontinent. My theme was *An Intellectual's Locution of Dissent,* in which I examined Mujeeb's exploration of the debate among Indian Muslim scholars in different periods of medieval and recent history on the question of Taqlid and Ijtihad, or between Sharia as Law and Sharia as a system of Living, or orthodoxy and dissent. He leaned on the side of Sufism and the Sufis and was supportive of Maulana Azad and his advocacy of 'a new world of religious thought to redress the balance of the old'.

Chandra Chari's edited volume *War, Peace and Hegemony in a Globalised World* was published in late 2007. It included my paper 'West Asia: Is there an alternative to sole superpower hegemony?'

I surveyed the post-Cold War developments and concurred with an American scholar's observation that 'the marriage of military metaphysics with eschatological ambition is a misbegotten one'. This in turn invites 'endless war and ever deepening militarization of US policy' that alienates peoples and nations and will end in abject failure.[119]

I had an unusual experience around April–May 2007. At the request of a friend, I penned a review of Bob Woodward's *State of Denial: Bush at War, Part III* for one of our journals. It concluded with the observation that the book has contributed to the documentation of deceit summed up in its concluding sentence: 'With all Bush's upbeat talk and optimism, he has not told the American public the truth about what Iraq has become.' I cited Otto von Bismarck's observation that: 'Woe to the statesman whose reasons for entering a war do not appear so plausible at its end as at its beginning.' The editorial board of the journal however felt that these views were not appropriate for a sitting Vice President of the Republic! Much to my regret, the review remained unpublished.

Around this time, I came across an interesting paper on *The Indian Parliament as an Institution of Accountability* by Devesh Kapur and Pratap Bhanu Mehta. The authors contended that the 'Parliament has self-abdicated many of its functions' by fewer sittings, inadequate committee oversight, less effective fiscal management and that while 'unparliamentary' behaviour by individual MPs has undoubtedly robbed parliament of the mystique that often underpins authority, its weakness as an institution of accountability stems from many factors, both within and outside the institution.

I had no idea at that stage that I would get a ringside seat for a whole decade to observe and assess the validity of these observations.

---

[119]Andrew J. Bacevich, *The New American Militarism: How Americans Are Seduced by War* (New York, 2005) p. 7.

Chapter 6

*Vice President of India and
Chairman, Rajya Sabha*

Vice President Bhairon Singh Shekhawat was completing his term of office and around early July 2007, there was speculation in the media about his likely successor. My name was mentioned amongst others. One afternoon, I got a call from Sitaram Yechury of the Communist Party of India (Marxist) (CPI [M]) enquiring—in strict confidence—if I would be amenable to the idea. A few days later, while I was waiting for a friend at the India International Centre, a call came from the PMO. It was Dr Manmohan Singh. He said that he was with Sonia Gandhi and they sought my acceptance of the suggestion that I be the candidate of the UPA in the forthcoming Vice Presidential election. My response was in the affirmative and I thanked them for the offer and the honour. The media reports of 21 July suggested that the Left's initiative became the unanimous choice of the UPA 'after [the] CPM assuaged doubts about his ability to conduct Rajya Sabha proceedings'.[120] My nomination paper, which was signed by all UPA leaders and their MPs, was filed on 23 July but not without a last-minute hitch when around lunch time, it was discovered that the Election Commission desk

---

[120]TNN, 'UPA, Left Name Hamid for VP's Post,' *Times of India*, 21 July 2007, https://timesofindia.indiatimes.com/india/UPA-Left-name-Hamid-for-V-Ps-post/articleshow/2222253.cms.

accepting nominations required a certified copy of the electoral roll of the constituency where my name figured. A colleague in the Minorities Commission saved the day by rushing to the office in East Delhi, obtaining the document, and getting it to me minutes before the deadline of 3 p.m.!

After the nomination and prior to the election, a report in *The Telegraph* called me 'a Calcutta boy'.[121] A longer piece by Swapan Dasgupta in *The Pioneer*[122] bore the caption 'Ansari is left but still right'; it was critical of my interview to *Outlook*,[123] wherein I criticized the US invasion of Iraq and India's vote in the IAEA against Iran's nuclear programme, adding that 'per se there is nothing extraordinary or undignified in Ansari's position. His criticism of the US matches the liberal critique of the Bush Administration and his position on Iran is shared by a large number of Indians, including many in the BJP. Moreover, Ansari has every right to hold these views. What I find somewhat disconcerting is that Ansari chose to air these views after he was named as UPA's candidate for Vice President'; also that 'he must take exceptional care to not be compartmentalized as a Muslim Vice President, he must see himself as India's Vice President'. Some in the Congress party also felt that the *Outlook* interview was untimely. The parameters of political correctness were being carefully defined!

Given my limited familiarity with names and faces in New Delhi's political world, it was suggested by my political minders that I should call upon the leaders and be available to all voters of the UPA at a conveniently accessible place. Accordingly, I was told to shift to 11, South Avenue, which had been used a few days earlier by the successful presidential candidate, Pratibha Devisingh Patil and was considered auspicious! I said I would do so during working hours but go back to Mayur Vihar for the night. I was also told that an

---

[121]Bureau, '"Boy" from Calcutta in battle for VP,' *The Telegraph*, 21 July 2007.
[122]*The Pioneer*, 6 August 2007.
[123]'I believe India acted with great haste on the Iran vote.' (Interview to Saba Naqvi, *Outlook*, 8 August 2007.)

individual by the name of Gurdeep Singh Sappal would be available to help me identify the new faces. This became the beginning of a decade-long friendship that continues to this day.

The exposure to the political bigwigs was educative. Lalu Prasad Yadav linked me to my roots in Yusufpur, which he had visited some time back. Sharad Pawar enquired if I had ever fought an election; my answer was a candid 'no'. Dr P.C. Alexander of the BJP, whom I had known from my protocol days, said, 'You have my good wishes but not my vote.' Others were curious and tentative about the 'new face' but fell in line with the decision of their leaders. The other two candidates in the fray were Najma Heptulla of the BJP, whom I knew well from my previous incarnations and Rasheed Masood of the Samajwadi Party (SP). On 10 August, the polling day, the result was a foregone conclusion: 96.46 per cent of the total of 790 voters cast their votes. I secured 60.52 per cent of the votes and Heptulla and Masood 29.5 and 9.97 per cent votes, respectively. The result was declared the same day by the Returning Officer, Dr Yogendra Narain, Secretary-General of the Rajya Sabha. The Gazette of India Notification was issued the next day.

I assumed the office of the Vice President of India the same day after I had expressed indifference, in response to a query, about the preferred 'auspicious' time for oath-taking. The Oath of Office, in terms of Article 69 of the Constitution, was administered by President Patil in the Ashoka Hall of Rashtrapati Bhavan.

It was an unconventional journey to the second-highest public office of the Republic. Many years later, a former member wrote a laudatory essay beginning with an Urdu couplet:[124]

Nairangi-e-siyasat-e-dauran to dekhye
Manzil unhain mili jo sharik-e-safar na the

(Behold! Strange are the ways of politics. Those who did
not run the race were the first to reach the goal.)

---

[124]Mohammad Adeeb, *Zindagi Zara Aahista Chal* (Aligarh, 2019) pp. 324–30.

Salma and I, accompanied by our children (Sulaiman, Nuriya and Osman) and nephew Rashid visited the Gandhi Samadhi at the Raj Ghat to pay our respects to the Father of the Nation.

An interesting observation on my election came from the US embassy in a cable of 10 August and made public by WikiLeaks. It said (perhaps referring to my views on US–Iran relations) that 'we found Ansari to be...moderate in most but not all of his views', and described me 'as an intellectual with left-of-center leanings'. It added that 'while at the United Nations, Ansari led the Indian delegation's successful resistance to Pakistan's two-year effort to gain a UN resolution on Kashmir favourable to Pakistan'.

CHAIRMAN, RAJYA SABHA

The next two days being a weekend, I entered the portals of the august and stately Council of States of the Parliament of India, the Rajya Sabha, as its ex-officio chairman on the morning of Monday (13 August) to be greeted, as per tradition, by an hour of laudatory welcome speeches. Many of these were laced with customary barbs directed at political adversaries.

The Leader of the House expressed his distress over the disruption of proceedings and unwillingness to engage in a dialogue. The retort of the leader of the Opposition was that 'the government can only have its way if the Opposition has its say'. Another leader said that 'contesting infallibility should not be construed as contesting integrity'.

Yet another leader gave a piece of advice to the Chair that I found invaluable:

Kal ke baad aap ko bahut takleef hogi. Mujhe aap se hamdardi hai ki is takleef ko aap jhail jaaen, aur ek salah bhi hai ki hum log kitna bhi halla karain, aap apne chehre par gussa mut dekhaiye aur hamesha haste rahye ga...hum sab ke sab lok desh ke dushman nahin hain, lekin hum sab ek muskaan par fida ho jaate hain aur chup-chap baith jaate hain.

(After tomorrow, you will experience great distress. I have sympathy for you and hope you will bear this distress and suggest that no matter how much disruption emanates from us, you should show no anger and keep smiling. All of us are not enemies of the country, but all of us are mesmerized by a smile and quietly sit down!)

In response, I thanked the Hon'ble Members and said that the assigned duty of the Chair is to ensure that all play by the rules so that the referee does not have to use the coloured cards in his shirt pocket! I stressed the need for institutional efficacy and reminded them of Machiavelli's caution that 'excesses of people are directed against those whom they suspect of interfering with the public good'. I drew the attention of the members to the first Vice President of India, Dr Sarvepalli Radhakrishnan's observation that 'a democracy is distinguished by the protection it gives to minorities and is likely to degenerate into tyranny if it does not allow the opposition groups to criticize fairly, freely and frankly the policies of the government', adding that 'minorities also have their responsibilities' and their right to criticize 'should not degenerate into wilful hampering and obstruction of the work of Parliament'.

Article 63 of the Constitution provides that there shall be a Vice President of India. Under Articles 64 and 89(1), he is the ex-officio chairman of the Council of States. Article 65(1) prescribes that the vice president acts as the president during the vacancy caused by the death, resignation or removal of the president until a new president is elected and assumes office. Under Article 65(2), the vice president discharges the duties of the president when he/she is unable to act owing to absence, illness or any other cause until the president resumes duties. Apart from stating that the Vice President of India is the ex-officio chairman of the Rajya Sabha, the Constitution is silent on his/her other functions; nor was any light shed on it in the discussion in the Constituent Assembly on 28 December 1948 except in certain eventualities.

In 1961, a well-meaning senior member of the Rajya Sabha had opined that 'the Vice President should be a non-party man, a neutral man who...is above party considerations'.[125] The list of vice presidents since 1952 indicates that many of them emanated from outside the mainstream political system.

Besides presiding over the Council of States, the vice president, as the second-highest constitutional dignitary, has a great many official, representational and ceremonial responsibilities within the country and abroad on behalf of the government, resulting in a pretty full calendar of engagements the year round. To some extent, each incumbent crafted his own course; each also left his imprint in the public domain and on the manner of the conduct of the House and official and personal interaction with the members. I recalled to myself the advice given to cricket umpires many years back, since it had relevance to the work of the chairperson of this constitutional office:

> To any man who is about to embark on this job of umpiring, I cannot give any better advice than this: Study and learn the Laws and continually review them, for only by knowing each and every one is it possible to apply the correct decisions, particularly when an unusual point arises.[126]

There was and continues to be much debate about the need and relevance of a second chamber. The Constitutional Advisor to the Constituent Assembly, B.N. Rau, had recalled an American argument that has universal validity. When Thomas Jefferson returned from France, he protested to George Washington against the establishment of two Houses. The incident occurred at the breakfast table and Washington asked, 'Why do you pour coffee into your saucer?' 'To cool it,' replied Jefferson. 'Even so,' said Washington, 'we pour

---

[125] S. Gopal, *Radhakrishnan: A Biography* (Delhi, 1989) pp. 305–06. The suggestion was made by Bhupesh Gupta of the CPI in the Rajya Sabha on 12 December 1961.
[126] Frank S. Lee, *The Umpire's Decision* (London, 1955) p. 7.

legislation into the senatorial saucer to cool it.'[127]

This matter was discussed at some length in the Constituent Assembly and its Union and Provincial Constitution Committees.[128] One of the members described the upper house as a 'a sobering House, a reviewing House, a House standing for quality and the members will be exercising their right to be heard on the merits of what they say, for their sobriety and knowledge of special problems; quantity, that is, their number, is not much of the moment'. Some others described it as 'the cultural face of India par excellence'.[129] Despite its evident functional merits, efforts continue to be made to downplay and undermine them and the effort in recent years to mislabel normal legislative proposals as 'money bills' under Article 109, and notwithstanding earlier practice, simply to avoid scrutiny and overwhelm opposition to them, is hardly in consonance with the spirit of parliamentary practice.[130]

The Rajya Sabha has some unique features. At different places in the text of the Constitution, it is mentioned before the Lok Sabha. It is the only institution in our constitutional system that is indissoluble except with its own consent. It represents the principle of continuity as a perpetual House. It is not merely a revising Chamber. It represents the federal ethos of India. It has been called, at least in its

---

[127] B.N. Rau, *India's Constitution in the Making* ([ed.] B. Shiva Rao) (Calcutta, 1960) p. 255.

[128] Granville Austin, *The Indian Constitution: Cornerstone of a Nation* (New Delhi, 1966, 2017) pp. 195–203. He cites the observation of Prof. Morris-Jones that the Council of States is one of the weakest second chambers in the world, weaker than even the House of Lords.

[129] B.L. Shankar and Rodrigues Valerian, *The Indian Parliament: A Democracy at Work* (New Delhi, 2001) pp. 295–96.

[130] The absolute power of the Speaker, Lok Sabha in this matter, under Article 109 is somewhat at variance with the House of Commons practice, wherein the Speaker has a duty to '"consult, if practicable, two members to be appointed from the Chairmen's Panel": i.e. two senior backbenchers, usually one from either side of the House, appointed by the Committee of Selection from amongst those senior MPs who chair general committees.' (*Money Bills and the Commons Financial Privilege: A Report*, House of Lords, 3 February 2001, para 11, p. 5).

initial phases, as a 'Chamber of Ideas'. Other comments have been less charitable; an extreme example is the remark by a Lok Sabha member, N.C. Chatterjee, on 11 May 1954, depicting members of the Rajya Sabha as 'behaving irresponsibly like a pack of urchins'. In more recent times, a member described it 'as a constitutional caravan that goes on continuously and ceaselessly unlike the other House. It does fulfil a constitutional role'.[131]

For reasons of security, and while the official residence of the vice president at 6, Maulana Azad Road was being given the customary coat of paint, I was advised to shift to Haryana Bhawan (near India Gate) where the then CM Bhupinder Singh Hooda graciously made available his personal suite. It also facilitated my meetings with the large number of callers—political and personal—who came to see me in my new surroundings. A very early caller was Narendra Modi, then CM of Gujarat. After the usual polite exchanges, I said that I had questions in my mind that would have been asked had we met in my previous responsibility as Chairman of the NMC. I referred to the post-Godhra happenings in his state in 2002 and asked why he allowed it to happen. He said that people look at only one aspect of the matter and pay no attention to the good work he has initiated, particularly for the education of Muslim girls. I sought its details and suggested that he should publicize it; 'that does not suit me politically' was the revealingly candid response.[132]

A few days after the swearing-in, and during a function in the Balayogi Auditorium, Lok Sabha Speaker Somnath Chatterjee mentioned the matter of a parliament TV. He said that some time back he had felt the need to inform the public better, and on a

---

[131]S. Jaipal Reddy on 7 March 1996 (*Rajya Sabha at Work*, Third edition, p. 19).
[132]In April 2002, the Editors Guild of India had sent a fact-finding team to Gujarat. They also met the CM. One of its members was the late B.G. Verghese, who subsequently recorded his impression of the meeting: 'When we met Narendra Modi, he had no explanation to offer and showed no contrition.' (*First Draft: Witness to the Making of Modern India*, p. 445).

continuous basis, about the work and proceedings of the two Houses and had initiated the idea of a joint channel. The Rajya Sabha, however, was not agreeable to it and so his idea was restricted to a Lok Sabha channel. He suggested that I have a fresh look at the idea. I thought the suggestion was eminently sensible and explored the reasons for its non-acceptance. I was informed that different sections of the opposition benches were not receptive to the idea. I then initiated a process of quiet consultations; this took a few months and at the end of it, I reverted to Chatterjee with our concurrence to his suggestion. A committee of officials of the two Houses was then set up to process it further. That exercise ran into a series of what can only be described as details of supervision and control and resulted in an impasse. When I reported this to the General Purposes Committee of the Rajya Sabha, it felt that a separate channel would serve our purposes better. The net outcome was the Rajya Sabha TV, with a chief executive functioning under the guidance of an all-party advisory committee. The new channel was well received by the viewing public and our effort to model it on the lines of the PBS in the US and the SBS in Australia did help create an advertisement-free platform for informed discussions.

The learning process in this new responsibility was interesting and fairly exacting. Rules, procedures and precedents in the Rajya Sabha had to be imbibed quickly. V.S. Rama Devi's compendium *Rajya Sabha at Work* (Third Edition) and the handbook of precedents were invaluable as was the guidance from the Secretariat. Dr Yogendra Narain finished his term a month later and was replaced by another senior civil servant, V.K. Agnihotri. Gurdeep Sappal as Officer on Special Duty in the chairman's office was invaluable for quiet liaison work with political groups and leaders with their behind-the-scenes manoeuvrings and compromises in the atmospherics of the day, and for his familiarity with precedents and procedures. The senior aide in the vice president's secretariat as Secretary to Vice President was Shumsher Sheriff (of the IAS), who was encyclopaedic in his command over rules and procedures, having served in the same capacity earlier with Vice President Narayanan and later with him in the president's secretariat. He was assisted by P. Harish (of the IFS), who had been a part of my team at the embassy in Riyadh and by Ashok Dewan, who was totally at home with household, administrative, protocol and travel arrangements and attended to them with quiet efficiency. In my second term, Sheriff became Secretary-General in the Rajya Sabha and the new and equally competent faces in the vice president's secretariat were Ambassador Swashpawan Singh, Nagesh Singh and Anshuman Gaur successively of the IFS. There was thus a rare continuity that I found very helpful and satisfying.

When I went for a round of golf some weeks after my election, an elderly member of the Delhi Golf Club said, 'You are the first vice president after Gopal Swarup Pathak to play here.' He did not mention Vice President Hidayatullah, who normally played on the Rashtrapati Bhavan course.

I settled into these duties fairly easily, more so because the 211th session of the House was of a short duration (from 10 August to 11 September). The normal routine was to have an internal meeting with the officials at 10 a.m. on the day's programme, followed by the Chair's meeting with leaders of political parties and groups. It was useful in a social sense but less so in terms of specific decisions; these were often not adhered to and after some time, I designated it the Chairman's Tea Club! Despite its limitations, the morning get-together did help in reducing barriers of formality. One day, when the perennial 'black money' problem was being discussed, I enquired that since association of a particular colour with things undesirable does not seem to be in God's vocabulary pejoratively, was it a legacy of racism of the colonial era imbibed thoughtlessly by the political discourse and a gullible public? No response was forthcoming!

The Parliament of India, like elected legislatures elsewhere, is entrusted with representative and participatory governance. Unlike the British parliamentary practices that 'evolved by time, fashioned by chance and adapted by experience', ours is a consciously crafted institution that is both a legislative and a deliberative body and the latter function requires effective oversight on the work of the government through various instrumentalities—rules, procedures, customs and conventions—to ensure regular accountability of the executive and consideration of issues of public interest and concern. Its success as a legislature hinges to a good extent on the efficiency, expertise and dedication of its members, the time spent on scrutiny of legislative proposals, and of the administrative support system of its secretariat. The extent to which these functions are discharged is less a matter of opinion and more of facts. So is it with the Rajya Sabha. The ability of individual members and party leaders to know and utilize the procedural nuances enhances their effectiveness, just as a lack of these limits their ability in what is often a game of wits. The task of the Presiding Officer (Chairperson or the Deputy Chairperson) is to know these well enough to conduct the proceedings and endeavour to live up to the ideal enunciated by a first-generation member as being a person 'gifted with the kind of strength and fortitude tinctured with understanding and suavity which can purposefully direct the often turbulent and tumultuous legislatures of today'.[133]

The two deputy chairmen in my period in the Rajya Sabha, K. Rahman Khan and Dr P.J. Kurien, were both very experienced parliamentarians, fully *au fait* with rules, procedures and precedents and were at all times in command of the proceedings. They were generally in the Chair in the afternoons except on the occasion of statements by the PM or other senior ministers, during important debates and whenever a vote was being taken. Both in their own way were masters of management of contentious situations and were cheerful at all times; their assistance in the conduct of proceedings was invaluable.

This exercise, hour after hour, every day of the sittings, is very ably and critically assisted by the Secretary-General, who 'is the

---

[133]Hiren Mukerjee, *Portrait of Parliament: Reflections and Recollections, 1952–77* (New Delhi, 1978) p. 38.

Advisor to the Chairman and through him to the House' and his colleagues on the Table Office and other members of the secretariat established pursuant to Article 98 of the Constitution. Anonymity and amiability characterize the functioning of the Secretary-General and his team. Apart from the general rules of etiquette relating to the Chair, a set of Rulings given from time to time on specific or general questions assist the Chair and the secretariat in the orderly conduct of proceedings. These have been collected in a volume titled *Rulings and Observations from the Chair 1952–2008*.

The schedule of work on a normal day commenced with the Question Hour (described in an earlier generation as highlighting 'the power and value of the legislative rapier'), followed by the Laying of Papers by the government and then Zero Hour, during which members could raise (with the permission of the Chair) issues of immediate interest to them. Then, after lunch, the legislative agenda of the government and discussions on matters of public concern would be taken up. Details for these would be settled in the Business Advisory Committee of the House, over which I presided, as I did over the Rules Committee and the General Purposes Committee. I also appointed members of the various Standing Committees and the Department-related Parliamentary Standing Committees. 'It is the right of the Chairman to interpret the Constitution and the rules in so far as matters in or relating to the House are concerned and no one can enter into any argument or controversy over such interpretation. The Chair's rulings constitute precedents of a binding nature.'[134] My preference always was to avoid being dictatorial about it and if necessary even allow what the then leader of the Opposition said in his farewell remarks to me on 10 August 2017—'a democratic debate'—about an expression used by the Chair.[135]

In 2007, the UPA government was more than halfway through its first term and was firmly in the saddle with comfortable majorities

---

[134]*Rajya Sabha at Work* (Third Edition, 2017) p. 95.
[135]Rajya Sabha: Parliamentary Debates, Official Report, 10 August 2017, p. 2.

in both Houses. In the Rajya Sabha, the Congress had 72 members as against 48 of the BJP. Other major groups in the UPA were the SP at 16, the CPI (M) at 14, the All India Anna Dravida Munnetra Kazhagam (AIADMK) at 10, the Rashtriya Janata Dal (RJD) at seven and the Telugu Desam Party (TDP) at six. The Leader of the House was PM Manmohan Singh and Leader of the Opposition was Jaswant Singh of the BJP. With the change of government in May 2014 following the general election, with an NDA government in the saddle, the UPA became the Opposition. The numbers in the Rajya Sabha changed only marginally with the Indian National Congress (INC) at 69, the BJP at 42, the Bahujan Samaj Party (BSP) at 14, All India Trinamool Congress (AITC) and Janata Dal (United) (JD(U) at 12 each, AIADMK at 11, the SP at 10 and the CPI (M) at nine.

Given the practical implications of the Anti-Defection Law of 1985 resulting in the Tenth Amendment, its impact on party discipline and the role of the party leader and leadership became evident.[136] He is assisted by the institution of the whip, which is required to facilitate the smooth and efficient functioning of the legislature and optimize its output. As depicted in a study, it is the 'arm-twister, bully and Machiavelli rolled into one'.

On the occasion of the golden jubilee of our Independence in 1997, the two Houses of Parliament had unanimously adopted an 'Agenda for India' Resolution, committing themselves to maintaining the inviolability of the Question Hour, refraining from shouting

---

[136]Shankar and Rodrigues, op. cit., p. 159. This has 'enormously increased the authority of the party leadership and can curb inner-party democracy. It can be argued that the provision has become a major hurdle in fresh thinking within parties and have had a deleterious impact on debates in Parliament'. Also, Kaushiki Sanyal, 'The Anti-Defection Law: Intent and Outcome,' in Sudha Pai and Avinash Kumar (ed.), *The Indian Parliament: A Critical Appraisal* (New Delhi, 2014) pp. 46–62.

It is, of course, another matter that political ingenuity and overriding material impulses can find ways to circumvent the stringent provisions of even this piece of legislation, as happened in the Telegana Assembly in June 2019 and commented upon editorially by *The Hindu* on 8 June 2019: 'In an ideology-lite polity, the MLAs seem to see no benefit in meaningfully representing their constituents, and find it rewarding to align with the ruling party for purposes of patronage.'

slogans or transgressing into the 'official' area of the House, and desisting from interference or interruption of the Address of the President. These are often observed in the breach and reflect poorly on the efficacy of the system under which the whips are required to function.[137]

Given the paucity of academic literature on the functioning of our parliament and after consultations with a cross-section of members and academic personalities, I instituted, in 2009, in the name of the first chairman of the Rajya Sabha, the Dr S. Radhakrishnan Chair and two Rajya Sabha Fellowships with the objective of promoting research on different aspects of parliamentary democracy in India. For implementing the scheme, a search and advisory committee, headed by Dr Karan Singh, was established.

I had assumed office as Chairman in the Rajya Sabha's 212th session and demitted office in its 243rd session. This covered 33 sessions, a period of a full 10 years that also witnessed two general elections (2009 and 2014) and one change of government. The players changed sides in the Chamber, so did the political ideologies articulated, behaviour patterns and tactics, but not the book of rules and the approach of the referee to the need for the players to play by the rules. It is, therefore, difficult to condense or encapsulate the proceedings or happenings in the Rajya Sabha over this period. Like vagaries of weather, they changed constantly. Each session had its own political priorities and these in turn reflected in its dynamics and procedural manoeuvres. I will nevertheless attempt to highlight important debates, legislative enactments of significance, and moments of disruptions, high drama and contention.

As parliamentary sessions proceeded, I discovered a total lack of predictability in them. Predictions were foolhardy. Attendance levels in the House were indicative of the interest levels of the members. It is a common practice, regrettably so, to sign the register and then

---

[137] An instance of a whip 'abandoning ship' is now on record! On 5 August 2019, Rajya Sabha member and Congress party whip Bhubaneshwar Kalita resigned his membership on an issue on which a whip had been issued.

refrain from actual attendance. In a sense, the schedule appeared settled, in another it was its very reverse and unduly sensitive to the vagaries of political weather. The Chair usually got an inkling of it but not the intensity in the morning meeting. Its first and principal casualty was the first item, the Question Hour, whose principal objective was and remains the accountability of the Executive. The Chair's decision of having the names of members coming into the *Well of the House* published, as a deterrent, in Bulletin Part I was of no avail. The disruptor(s) objective, on the other hand, was immediate satisfaction of drawing attention to his/her grievance, and live TV coverage greatly assisted the impulse. The modality of intervention aimed at what has been called (in a similar context) 'deliberately coordinated bullying'[138] varied; at times, a senior party leader seeking 'a couple of minutes' and at others, a member from the middle or back benches using his/her vocal cords to the fullest extent possible. Sometimes, these disruptions took a more organized form, descended into virtual pandemonium[139] and were accompanied with procedural justifications. It seemed to develop into a refined technique, with its own rationale. In January 2011, the Leader of the Opposition in the Rajya Sabha justified 'Parliamentary obstructionism' as a tactic to prevent an issue from being 'talked out'. A sense of getting 'sadistic thrill' from such disruptions was also whispered. A similar position was taken by his counterpart in the Lok Sabha, who declared that 'not allowing Parliament to function is also a form of democracy, like any other form'.

This line of argument, as if by natural piety, was unabashedly revered by the individuals when the incumbency of the Treasury Benches changed!

In my valedictory remarks to the 226th session in September 2012, I observed that 'it is likely to be remembered for the work that was not done' and listed the principal shortfalls that accounted

---

[138]Chris Bryant, *Parliament: The Biography, Volume 2: Reform* (London, 2014) p. 370.
[139]Depicted by the poet John Milton as the 'High capital of Satan and his Peers'.

for 62 hours lost on account of disruptions. I reverted to this in my valedictory remarks to the 228th session on 8 May 2013 and observed that 'the experience of this session, and particularly of its second half, should induce cogitation on a number of matters arising out of the situations in which the House finds itself in its daily functioning'. I said that three questions in particular need to be addressed: (i) has the balance between deliberations, legislations and accountability been lost due to regular disruption of the proceedings? (ii) has the time not come to bridge the growing gap between the Rules of Procedures and the need felt by different sections of the House to voice opinions on matters of concern? This has to be done in an orderly manner to preserve the dignity of the House, and (iii) has the membership of this august body assessed the impact of disruptive behaviour on public opinion?

In a meeting of party leaders in the Rajya Sabha which was 'called in agony and distress', in April 2013, I said that:

> The sad, and deeply disturbing, truth is that such adjournments have been taken with disturbing frequency. If this practice goes unchecked, public esteem for parliament as the highest forum of our democracy will be adversely affected, leading, eventually, even to questions about its very relevance. As the chairman of the Rajya Sabha, I deem it my duty to express concern about this trend, and to articulate a cautionary note about its possible consequences. We have to correct our individual and collective behaviour. We have to learn to play by the rules that we have made for ourselves and restore decorum and dignity to the House. We have to remember at all times that the people of India, and particularly the youth, do look up to their elected representatives as role models. We cannot violate rules with impunity and then expect the citizen body to observe the laws we make for them. We must bring to an end this dichotomy in our thinking and behaviour.

I thought long and hard about possible correctives but, being conscious of the sanctity of rules and practices, was diffident of innovations. Article 118(1) of the Constitution empowers each House to make rules of procedure and conduct of business. These, in the case of the Rajya Sabha, were made by the Rules Committee in June 1964 and adopted by the House in July. Rule 255 allows the Chair to direct a member to withdraw for the day on account of grossly disorderly conduct, while Rule 256 allows the Chair to name a member through a motion of the House to withdraw for the duration of the session for disregarding the authority of the Chair or abuse of the rules by persistent and wilful obstruction of business. In all my time, I used Rule 255 very sparingly (actually twice, on 17 December 2014 and 2 May 2016) and in one case (on 24 April 2008) cautioned a member of 'skating very close to it', whereupon the member walked off. A principal difficulty related to disruptions by groups of members. I consulted widely but realized the limitations imposed by these rules. The rule was actually used only once, with support from the principal opposition party, for evicting a group obstructing the passing of the Women's Reservation Bill on which a consensus had developed.

After much thought, and wide-ranging consultations, I suggested to party leaders and senior members that the only way to save Question Hour as the first item of business, described by a first-generation parliamentarian as 'the power and value of the legislative rapier', is to shift it to 12 noon and replace it with Zero Hour. There was considerable resistance to the idea; firstly from the government since it would involve rescheduling the presence of ministers in the two Houses and secondly from the ranks of the 'disrupters', who felt that noise-making in the Question Hour brought them wider publicity! Most sections of the House, however, saw merit in it and agreed to go along. This was accordingly piloted through the Rules and General Purposes Committees and approved in November 2014. Alongside, matters in the Zero Hour were restricted to 15 with a time limit of three minutes per person by an electronic device of the microphone being switched off. The three-minute rule (despite the *alaap* habit presumably imbibed from the tradition of our classical music) was generally observed but rarely by party leaders and senior members!

Following the shifting of the Question Hour, Calling Attention was moved to 2 p.m. and Special Mentions to 5 p.m. I had observed at the end of the 235th session that the eager participation of the members in the four Calling Attention notices for executive accountability indicated that more time needed to be given for them. This, however, would be possible if the duration of sessions was longer, as used to be the practice many years back. Some other correctives, designed to help all concerned, were introduced based on actual experience over a number of sessions. These, concerning the Question Hour, related to (i) reducing the numbers in the List for Oral Answers from 20 to 15 and for written answers from 160 to 155, (ii) allowing one question per member, instead of two, for Oral Answer and (iii) taking up an admitted question even in the absence of the member asking the question. The Chair also urged, without much success, both the members and the ministers to be crisp and focused in their questions and answers.

Persuing the proceedings of the Rajya Sabha at different points of time in the past, I came across instances when attempts had been made with success, in regard to contentious legislative proposals being assented to what came to be depicted as *in the din,* on account of vocal and noisy opposition to them with the object of stalling them, since the Chair was unable to ensure observance of proper procedures. This generated bitterness, it did not accord with the decorum associated with a legislative body, more so with the resolve in the unanimous Golden Jubilee Resolution of 1997. I, therefore, informed all sections of the House that barring a consensus, no bills will be passed *in the din* and that normal procedures of obtaining consent will be observed. Procedures apart, I felt that it is the debate that sheds valuable light on the intent of legislation and its assessment by the public and interpretation by the judiciary. This observation was welcomed by the opposition parties and was scrupulously observed by the Chair.

A point of direct access to the House for redressal of grievances of individuals or associations is the Committee on Petitions through which matters of interest to the public and representations about it can be submitted within the framework of rules and procedures mentioned in Chapter X of the Rules of Procedure and Conduct of Business in the Council of States. It was brought to my notice that these were restrictive; I, therefore, directed that instead of the preliminary, largely procedural, scrutiny by the secretariat, the committee itself 'shall take up consideration of representations, letters and telegrams from various individuals, associations, etc, which are not covered by the rules relating to petitions'.[140]

My relations with all sections of the House were cordial and friendly and I made it a practice to be approachable at all hours. One nominated member described it as 'spreading undercurrents of fairness'. The sole aberration to this norm was when a matter of particular interest to a party was being discussed and its leader felt that the Chair was not giving enough of his personal time to it by not always being in the House in the afternoon; this comment was disapproved by all sections of the House and both the leaders of the House and of the Opposition spoke about and reiterated their trust in the Chair and in the established conventions relating to it. The next day, the 'critic' made suitable amends and the matter was closed. On one occasion, disruptions and their decibel levels compelled me to observe that the behaviour of the disruptors was that of 'a federation of anarchists' whereupon the Leader of the Opposition interjected to point out that anarchists by definition cannot be a federation. I responded in good humour that such groupings do actually exist in some European countries!

The legislative business of the House followed a set pattern and the Chair's role was generally formal, restricted to ensuring procedures for introduction and for time allocation in the Business Advisory Committee. Difficulties surfaced whenever the government,

---

[140]*Rajya Sabha at Work*, ibid., p. 856.

for a variety of reasons, sought to abridge the process by suggesting that the prescribed procedure for referring the bill to the concerned Department-Related Parliamentary Standing Committee or to a Select Committee of the Rajya Sabha be dispensed with. The Standing Committees were first introduced in March 1993 to enhance the effectiveness of the law-making responsibilities of parliament by scrutinizing drafting, possible implementation challenges and the unintended consequences by ascertaining views of subject-related experts and public feedback. Another purpose of these committees was to provide a round-the-year forum of debate and deliberation, something sadly lacking in time-restricted normal sessions of parliament. In that sense, they are or can be a link between parliament and the interested public. Their reports, however, were not to be binding.

I had the occasion to dwell on the benefits of the Standing Committee system in a seminar of the National Social Watch Media in November 2009 and drew attention to what an Australian parliamentary committee had observed about their functional utility being in (i) providing a viewpoint other than that of the minister (ii) a sounding board for a wider section of opinion in parliament (iii) a safeguard against hasty, ill-considered legislation (iv) unprejudiced discussion on the subject beyond party barriers (v) a place where interest groups may be heard by members, and (vi) familiarizing the Executive with areas of expertise of members.

The UPA government's legislative agenda in its first term (2004–09) was substantive, premised in good measure on the Common Minimum Programme and, given the numbers, received parliament's approval without difficulty. Some of the proposals, nevertheless, faced problems and required intricate political manoeuvring; some others fell by the wayside. The NDA, after its electoral victory in 2014, focused on the priorities in its election manifesto, to move from what it called 'Governance of Enactment' to that of 'Action' and to 'restore the credibility of, and trust in the Union Government'. The manifesto of 2019 pledged to make the next five years the foundation-laying period for India of 2047.

◆

Two interesting Short Duration Discussions in my early months (November and December 2007) in the House were on the creation of a special economic zone (SEZ) in Nandigram (West Bengal) and on the Indo-US nuclear deal. The former, and the violence that accompanied the following land acquisition, was criticized by most sections of the House with the CPM, as the ruling party in the state, being on the defensive. D. Raja of the CPI and several other members suggested a rethink of the whole scheme of creating SEZs.

On the latter, Yechury urged the government to rethink it since,

> What we are now entering into, in my opinion, [is] a deal which actually takes India closer to the US positions on global issues as well as on regional strategic concerns and what is being done is to drag India into or suck India into the vortex of being a subordinate ally of [the] United States of America and it is this subordinate ally status which we think is not in India's interest at the present moment.

Yashwant Sinha of the BJP called it 'a great mistake, being done under US pressure: I strongly oppose this Indo-US nuclear deal and when we will be back in power, we will re-negotiate it'.[141]

An animated Short Duration Discussion took place on 5 March 2008 on the incidents of the reported attacks on north Indians in different places in Maharashtra. One member cited 2001 census data indicating that 43.2 million people migrate from one state to another and 37.6 per cent are those who go seeking employment. Another member said that 'the conspiracy to divide the country in the name of North, South, language, religion and state should not be allowed to be successful'. Many speakers considered the

---

[141] A full account of the government's position in this controversy which damaged the cohesion of the UPA is given in Pranab Mukherjee's *The Coalition Years 1996–2012* (Rupa Publications, New Delhi, 2017) pp. 127–59.

incidents 'condemnable' and were critical of the state government for inaction. Another speaker said that the attacks on north Indians were preceded by earlier attacks on Tamils and South Indians. Another said that political opportunism is inducing divisive politics but interstate migration is in search of jobs and the government should implement purposefully the Inter-State Migrant Workmen (Regulation of Employment and Conditions of Service) Act, 1979. A senior Shiv Sena speaker said that the 'Marathi people should get jobs in Maharashtra' and the rights of Bhumi Putra should be respected. He was highly critical of the suggestion that Mumbai should be centrally ruled. In response, the minister of home affairs asked the members to exercise caution and not aggravate the situation and provide a healing touch.

◆

An important legislative proposal, the Right of Children to Free and Compulsory Education Bill was introduced in the House by the HRD minister on 20 July 2009. It was approved after some amendments. Twenty-seven members participated in the debate. In reply, the HRD minister clarified that the bill was intended to fulfil the *right* under Article 21(a) of the Constitution.

◆

The Judges (Declaration of Assets and Liabilities) Bill, 2009 was sought to be introduced in August 2009. It was vehemently opposed by the BJP, the Left parties and many other members including noted jurist, Ram Jethmalani. This caused some embarrassment to the government and its introduction was deferred.

◆

In February 2009, the Chair received notice of a motion given by CPM leader Yechury and 57 others seeking the removal of a Calcutta High Court judge under Article 217 read with Article 124(4) of the Constitution of India. It was accompanied with a copy of a letter from the Chief Justice of India to the PM. The notice was examined, found to be in order and was duly admitted under Section 3 of the Judges (Inquiry) Act, 1968. Thereafter, and pursuant to the provisions of the Act, I appointed a committee headed by a Supreme Court judge to investigate the grounds of removal.

This was the first instance of this provision being invoked in our parliamentary history. Earlier, in 1993, a motion for the removal of a Supreme Court judge had been moved in the Lok Sabha. It could not obtain the requisite two-third majority of votes cast (196 in favour, zero in opposition and 255 abstentions in a House of 401 present) and was defeated.

The committee, consisting of Justice B. Sudershan Reddy of the Supreme Court, Justice T.S. Thakur, Chief Justice of the Punjab and Haryana high court and jurist Fali S. Nariman presented its report in September 2010. It found Justice Soumitra Sen of the Calcutta High Court guilty of (i) misappropriation of a large sum of money received by him in his capacity as reviewer appointed by the High Court of Calcutta and (ii) misrepresentation of facts with regard to the matter, and therefore guilty of 'misbehaviour' under Article 124(4) read with proviso (b) to Article 217(1) of the Constitution. The report was laid on the table of the Rajya Sabha in November 2010 and debated on 17–18 August 2011.

Moving the motion, Yechury cited Edmund Burke's speech in the House of Lords during the proceedings against Warren Hastings urging their Lordships to 'stand as unimpeached in honour as in power...as an ornament and security for virtue...as a sacred temple for the perpetual residence of inviolable justice'.

Justice Sen was then called to the bar of the House. His comprehensive defence took a little more than 90 minutes. He contended, *inter alia*, that the matter relating to his alleged misappropriation is still *sub judice* in the Calcutta High Court and should not have therefore been considered by a non-judicial body such as the Judges Inquiry Committee. After his withdrawal, the motion and the address to the president were comprehensively debated for over four hours. Sixteen members, many of them legal luminaries, participated. Among senior members, Satish Mishra of the BSP opposed the motion, which was approved by 189 votes to 16 and thus met the requisite two-third majority requirement.

◆

In the budget session of 2010, an important matter on the government's legislative agenda was the Constitution (One Hundred and Eighth) Amendment Bill, 2008 relating to the reservation of one-third of seats in local, state and federal legislatures for women. The bill was introduced on the eve of International Women's Day (8 March 2010) and the chairperson of the UPA had put it high on the government's agenda on that day. While it had wide-ranging support, sections of political opinion were adamantly opposed to it despite some back-room efforts to seek a compromise on a lower percentage. This opposition manifested itself in the House and led to riotous obstructions. Given the number of protesters sitting in the well of the House, Rule 255 was of no avail and eventually consultations in the chairperson's chamber between the treasury and principal opposition leaders led to the use of Rule 256 through a motion that suspended seven members for the remaining part of the Budget session. In a display of defiance, they refrained from leaving the House and, in an ugly scene, had to be physically evicted by the marshals. Care, however, was taken that the eviction process was not televised.

In the debate that followed, some members raised questions about the effectiveness and reach of the proposed arrangement with regard to the poorer and less fortunate segments (Other Backward Classes, SCs, STs, minorities and the economically backward) and suggested that political parties should make special provisions for them. One member suggested that out of 33 per cent, 20 to 25 per cent should be reserved for Muslims, Backwards and Dalits. With regard to the proposed reservation of constituencies, one member felt that better results would emerge from proportional representation than from the party list system.

The Constitutional Amendment Bill was approved by the requisite majority. It was, however, not taken up by the 15th Lok Sabha and is yet to be taken up by its successors. This is despite the BJP's electoral commitment of giving women '33 per cent reservation in parliament and the state assemblies through a constitutional amendment'.

◆

Another legislative proposal of that year met a somewhat similar fate. The government introduced the Prevention of Torture Bill, 2010 to give effect to the UN Convention against Torture that India had signed in 1997 but not ratified. The bill was referred to the Rajya Sabha Select Committee in August and its report was tabled in the House on 7 December 2010. Further action on this in the MHA took time and the bill lapsed in 2014 with the dissolution of the Lok Sabha. This matter was then taken up by the Law Commission in its 273rd Report and on its basis the Prevention of Torture Bill, 2017 was tabled and circulated to the state governments and Union Territories (UTs) in February 2018 for their views since criminal laws are in the Concurrent List of the Constitution. The government, in response to a public interest litigation (PIL) in the Supreme Court in January 2019, intimated that only eight state governments/UTs had responded whereupon the Court directed that replies be obtained within three weeks. In September, the Court reserved its verdict after the government sought time on the plea that it was in the process of receiving objections and suggestions from the states.[142]

◆

Corruption has been called the 'inconvenient fact' of Indian democracy. The government was conscious of the public disquiet and had initiated steps to establish an ombudsman. This, however, was considered 'toothless' by civil society groups, whose perceptions underwent a quantitative change when Anna Hazare emerged on

---

[142] *Business Standard*, 18 September 2019.

the scene in April 2011. His fast, and the movement initiated by it, forced the government to agree to a joint government-civil society drafting exercise for bringing forth legislation for a Lokpal.[143] Hazare's announcement of an indefinite fast and the resulting impasse brought forth the PM's statement in the House on August 17 and candid expression of views by leaders of political parties generally critical of the government.

The draft legislation, after a brief debate in the two Houses, was referred by the Lok Sabha to the Department-Related Parliamentary Standing Committee on Personnel, Public Grievances, Law and Justice chaired by Rajya Sabha member Abhishek Manu Singhvi. Its report, running into 589 pages including 10 minutes of dissent, reflected the totality of views of its members.

The Lokpal and Lokayuktas Bill, 2011 came to the Rajya Sabha on the afternoon of 28 December after it had been approved in the Lok Sabha following a 10-hour debate. The suggestion to clear the Lokayuktas Bill on the 28th itself was not acceptable to the opposition parties and so the decision was to take both on the 29th, which was the last day of the extended session.

An occasion of high drama ensued. The government introduced it along with the Whistle Blowers Protection Bill, 2011. The Business Advisory Committee had allocated four hours for debating the latter and eight hours for the former. The debate started immediately after the Laying of Papers and the chairman's farewell to seven retiring members. After the minister concerned had briefed the House about the contents and objectives of the bill, the opposition parties noticed the absence of the Leader of the House and insisted that he be present. This led to an adjournment of 10 minutes. The debate then started at 11.47 hours and except for a lunch interval of 45 minutes, continued till midnight. Leaders of political parties and many of those who had legal acumen participated. As many as 187 amendments were tabled. As the day wore on, questions were raised about whether the duration of

---

[143]Pranab Mukherjee, ibid., pp. 194–203.

the session could be extended. The Leader of the Opposition took the view that the House itself should decide how long to sit. The minister for parliamentary affairs, however, contended that the duration of a parliamentary session is the prerogative of the executive. He, instead, offered to have the bill passed as it stood. The impasse went on, accompanied by adjournments, with pressure mounting on the Chair to give a ruling. I adjourned the House for 15 minutes at 11.28 p.m. and also had a word with Finance Minister Pranab Mukherjee. He was emphatic that the period of a session was determined by the government, can only be extended by it and it was not inclined to do so. Any other course, he added, would amount 'to a Long Parliament'. It was clear to me that no deviation from this was possible. I resumed the session at 11.43 p.m. with the Leader of the Opposition alleging that the 'government had choreographed the entire debate' to prevent a vote. In the noise, one member proposed that 'the Bill be taken up for consideration'. The Chair said it required orderly proceedings. With the clock touching the midnight hour, I called for the national song to be played and adjourned the House *sine die*.

There was some uninformed comment in the days that followed suggesting that the Chair had erred. The procedural position, however, was emphatically clear. A few weeks later when the Rajya Sabha met in the budget session, the Leader of the Opposition gave notice under a rule that allowed an unfinished discussion to be taken up again. In his intervention, he conceded that 'since it was the last day and we quite appreciate the fact that the House then had to be adjourned *sine die*, the debate must be deemed to continue when the House resumes proceedings in the next Session'. In response, the minister for parliamentary affairs clarified that adjournment *sine die* had led to the House being prorogued and with that all listed business had lapsed, adding however that the bill was listed for discussion in the first part of the session itself. On 21 May 2012, on the government's initiative, the Rajya Sabha referred it to a Select Committee. The amended bill was subsequently passed by the House on 13 December 2013 and by the Lok Sabha the next day. It became law in January 2014.

♦

An instance of conflicting interests between central and state governments and between public policy and private interests came to the fore with regard to the Mines and Minerals (Development and Regulation) Bill, 2011. The first National Mineral Policy was enunciated in 1993, which ushered in liberalization in the mining sector. It was, however, noted that the contribution of the mining sector to the GDP of the country was a mere 2.3 to 2.6 per cent as compared to Australia and South Africa, where it ranged from 7.5 to 7.7 per cent. Procedural delays and absence of adequate infrastructure accounted for this. The objective of the new National Mineral Policy, announced in March 2008, therefore was to usher in greater liberalization and private-sector involvement and simultaneously widen the scope of the regulatory framework of the government by factoring in socio-economic issues of tribal and remote communities, where a large proportion of mineral wealth is located, through the sharing of mining profits with the tribal and local communities. The latter suggestion was opposed by mining companies and FICCI[144]. A delegation of opposition leaders, led by Baijayant 'Jay' Panda of the BJD, met me in the Chamber. They made fervent arguments regarding the need to study the bill in detail, as it impacted upon the federal rights of state governments. I found merit in their arguments and referred the bill to the Parliamentary Standing Committee. Though the Standing Committee presented its report in February 2009, the bill never saw the light of day. After the 2009 general election and the return of the UPA to power, several attempts were made to revive the bill but for various reasons, primarily disruptions, the bill could not passed. Its non-passage ensured that the old policy of granting coal blocks without competitive bidding continued, which later became the basis of a damning Comptroller and Auditor General of India (CAG) report and a major reason for the loss of credibility of the then government.

---

[144] Federation of Indian Chambers of Commerce & Industry.

The Standing Committee to which the proposed bill was referred took the view that the grievances in the matter of the state governments and stakeholders be taken into account. The Standing Committee proposed a large number of amendments, most of which (including a dilution of the proposed profit-sharing with local communities) were not acceptable to the government. In the event, the bill was not tabled and lapsed at the end of the tenure of the 15th Lok Sabha. A diluted version of the bill was passed by the 16th Lok Sabha and then approved by the Rajya Sabha after being referred to a Select Committee.

♦

Yet another matter of contention related to the charges of corruption in the allocation of 2G spectrum to telecom companies during the UPA-I period. The allegations of corruption were first raised by an NGO, who filed a complaint with the Central Vigilance Commission (CVC) in May 2009. The CVC took cognizance of the complaint and in October, the same year, directed the Central Bureau of Investigation (CBI) to investigate the matter. Later, avoidable premature publicity to the contents of the draft report of the CAG before its submission and scrutiny by the Public Accounts Committee tended to derail matters, excite public and parliamentary opinion on the real distinction between 'notional' and actual loss, and resulted in much adverse publicity for the government and loss of more than one session of the House.[145]

♦

The question of food security was high on the government's agenda in the light of the Right to Food campaign initiated in April 2001 by the Rajasthan unit of the People's Union for Civil Liberties and its writ petition in the Supreme Court on the ambit of the Right to

---

[145]A. Raja has shed much light on this matter in his book *2G Saga Unfolds* (New Delhi, 2018).

Life guaranteed by Article 21 of the Constitution and the Court's decision of 23 July 2001. It sensitized opinion about the need for food security to the poor and deprived sections of the population. This was included by the Congress party in its election manifesto of 2009 and was mentioned in the president's address to both Houses of parliament. Pursuant to this, the National Food Security Bill was introduced in the Lok Sabha in December 2011 and was referred to the Standing Committee. It examined the matter in the context of Articles 21 and 47 as also India's obligations under international conventions and the Millennium Development Goals of the UN. In a comprehensive report (with one note of dissent) it opined that:

> The proposed legislation marks a paradigm shift in addressing the problem of food security—from the current welfare approach to [a] right-based approach. About two-thirds of the population would be entitled to receive subsidized foodgrain under the Targeted Public Distribution System. It will also confer legal rights on women and children and other Special Groups such as destitute, homeless, disaster- and emergency-affected persons and persons living in starvation, to receive meals free of charge or at an affordable price, as the case may be.[146]

The bill replacing the Ordinance was passed by the Lok Sabha and the Rajya Sabha on 7 and 26 August 2013, respectively. A hundred and seven members in the Lok Sabha and 39 in the Rajya Sabha participated in the debate. Speaking in the Lok Sabha, the UPA chairperson said that 'our goal for the foreseeable future must be to wipe out hunger and malnutrition from our country. This legislation is only the beginning'. Some of the opposition leaders criticized the government for taking four and a half years in bringing out the bill. Others felt the CMs should have been consulted. In the Rajya Sabha, the Leader of the Opposition criticized the resort to the Ordinance

---

[146]The National Food Security Act 2013: Compendium of Parliamentary Enactments (Rajya Sabha Secretariat, 2014) p. 75.

path under Article 123. He described the bill as 'a repackaging of all existing schemes and not an effective Right'. Replying to the debate, the minister assured members that 'all constructive and positive suggestions will be carefully followed'. The bill became law on 10 September 2013.

◆

A particularly contentious legislative proposal surfaced in the budget session of 2014 in the shape of the Andhra Pradesh Reorganisation Bill, 2014. Much was said and written about its pros and cons. It had a stormy passage through the Lok Sabha and reflected poorly on adherence to parliamentary practices. In the Rajya Sabha, there was some debate amidst disruptions before the bill was approved through a motion supported by the principal opposition and after some clauses were amended. Some parties walked out, protesting against the Chair's inability to allow a division on account of 'some members standing in the well'.

The debate on the bill indicated both cross-party support as well as opposition to it, suggestive of the evident electoral considerations involved on the eve of a general election. A candid admission of the failings on the side of the government was articulated many months later by a senior member.[147]

◆

Given the centrality of land in the economy and culture of the country, the question of possession, dispossession and state acquisition of land has always been a subject of contention and was reflected in the proceedings of the Rajya Sabha. The state's power of 'eminent

---

[147] Jairam Ramesh, 'Congress Created Telangana but Killed Itself,' *The Economic Times*, 20 June 2016. On Telangana: 'We failed in political management. Our political intelligence was weak. Our political communication was non-existent. And to compound our problems, our own chief minister was opposing the bifurcation,' adding that Congress got 'electorally, zero. Politically, suicidal. We faced cataclysm in Andhra, catastrophe in Telangana'.

domain', inherent in the exercise of its sovereignty, allows the state to compulsorily acquire property belonging to private persons for a public purpose and upon payment of just compensation, following procedure established by law. This, in the British period, was done through the Land Acquisition Act, 1894. The twin requirements of public purpose and just compensation are based on the rationale that no individual should have to disproportionately bear the burden of supporting the 'public good' which the government, as the representative of the people, legitimately executes.

The Land Acquisition, Rehabilitation and Resettlement (LARR) Bill was introduced in the Lok Sabha in September 2011 and was referred to the Standing Committee on Rural Development. The latter, headed by Sumitra Mahajan, undertook extensive consultations with all interested sections of the public and submitted its report in May 2012. The bill proposed a unified legislation for the acquisition of land and adequate rehabilitation mechanism and replaced the Act of 1894. It refers to forcible acquisition of land from an unwilling seller and exempts 16 specified categories. Its provisions were proposed to be applicable to where the appropriate government acquires land (i) for its own use and control, (ii) to transfer it for the use of private companies for public purpose, and (iii) on the request of private companies for immediate use for public purpose. It proposed that a maximum of 5 per cent of irrigated multi-crop land may be acquired in a district with certain conditions and that every acquisition would require a social impact assessment by an independent body.

The bill was passed by the Lok Sabha on 29 August 2013. It was approved by the Rajya Sabha after a full debate in which a senior member of the main Opposition party made the point that 'public interest' should be properly interpreted and that the government should have no role in land acquisition for public–private partnership (PPP) and private sectors. The bill was passed on 4 September by a vote of 134 to 10 and became law.

After the general election and the change of government, an

Ordinance to amend the Act was promulgated in December 2014. It sought to amend nine main sections (including five categories: defence, rural infrastructure, affordable housing, industrial corridors, and infrastructure including PPP where the government owns the land) from the requirement of social impact assessment, restriction on it and was referred to a Joint Committee of parliament. The proposed changes were strongly opposed not only by the Opposition but some of the government's alliance partners. The discussion that followed was inconclusive; it was extended till the last day of the 16th Lok Sabha and lapsed with it.

◆

Sometime towards the end of the budget session of parliament in April–May 2012, speculation had started in political circles and sections of the media about the July 2012 presidential elections for a successor to President Pratibha Patil. Given the political make-up of the electoral college (elected members of parliament and elected members of Legislative Assemblies as per Articles 54 and 55 of the Constitution), it was evident that an initiative would lie with the ruling UPA, which had 41 per cent of the votes and needed another 9 per cent to make up a majority.

Record showed that out of the 11 previous vice presidents, six went on to be elected as President of India and five did not; of the latter, one resigned, one died in office and one was elected for a second term before being elected the president after two terms as the vice president. An adherent of numerology might have surmised that every fourth incumbent did not make it!

Media speculation initially named former president Dr A.P.J Abdul Kalam as a possible candidate; he, however, denied it. One report quoted the Leader of the Opposition in the Lok Sabha saying that the BJP will not support anyone connected to the Congress.[148] A commentator in May said that 'almost no one is thinking of

---

[148]Sunetra Choudhury and Sunil Prabhu, 30 April 2012 on NDTV.

the other man in the race, who has done his work quietly for 10 years, always speaking his mind but never in a way that it causes controversy: Hamid Ansari'.[149] Another report on 13 June said that 'at this point one can only say that either Pranab Mukherjee or Vice President Hamid Ansari is likely to be the Congress candidate', but this has to be finalized after acceptance by Mulayam Singh Yadav and Mamata Banerjee, whose votes would be essential, adding that 'a deal on many political issues' with the former would be essential.[150] Another media report said that 'a series of bizarre developments... made this contest quite intriguing'.[151] On 15 June, *Reuters* reported that the 'Congress party named Finance Minister Pranab Mukherjee as its nominee for president on Friday, capping a week of political turmoil that exposed the fragility of a coalition government that has lurched between crises as the economy sputters'.[152] The political thinking behind the decision was delineated later by M.L. Fotedar, a Congress insider.[153] Pranab Mukherjee's memoirs give some details of the political background and the position and postures of some of the leaders involved.[154]

Having nothing to contribute to the Byzantine process, on the day a decision was expected (12 June), I decided to play golf on a

---

[149] Aditi Phadnis, 'It Will Be Difficult to Fill Hamid Ansari's Shoes,' Rediff.com, 12 May 2012.
[150] Sheela Bhatt, Rediff, 13 June 2012.
[151] Amol Sharma and Vibhuti Agarwal, *The Wall Street Journal*, 15 June 2012.
[152] Satarupa Bhattacharjya and Rajesh Kumar Singh, 'UPA Names Mukherjee for President in Econ Shakeup,' *Reuters*, 15 June 2012, https://in.reuters.com/article/india-president-pranab-mukherjee/upa-names-mukherjee-for-president-in-econ-shakeup-idINDEE85E08B20120615.
[153] 'Hamid Ansari should have been the presidential candidate by precedence... A view was also gaining ground that the election to the 16th Lok Sabha could throw up a hung Parliament. The President was expected to play a vital role in government formation in these circumstances. Pranab Mukherjee, with his vast political experience and understanding of national issues, was being thought of as the ideal choice for that scenario.' (M.L. Fotedar, *The Chinar Leaves* [New Delhi, 2015] pp. 317–18).
[154] Pranab Mukherjee, *The Coalition Years 1996–2012* (New Delhi, 2017) pp. 204–34.

very hot afternoon with two friends, Ambassadors Gharekhan and Naresh Dayal. Halfway through the game, a call from my office told me of the decision and the game continued. That evening, Pranab Mukherjee called on me and I felicitated him on his selection. Late in the evening the next day, I conveyed to a senior functionary of the Congress my unhappiness at being pulled into the process without being consulted; he, in turn, shared with me some of the happenings that went into the decision-making.

A couplet of Daagh Dehlvi could have described the situation:

Qismat ki khoobi dekhyei, tooti kahan kamand
Do char haath jab ke lab-e-baam rah gaya

(See the irony of Fate, the ladder has given away when the rooftop was just a few feet away.)

What followed was unanticipated. A few days later, PM Manmohan Singh called on me. He was somewhat apologetic about all that had happened and, suddenly, asked me if I would like to be considered for a second term. It was my turn to be surprised; my answer was that I would be honoured. I thus became the second person, after Dr Radhakrishnan in 1957, to assume the office of Vice President for a second term.[155]

The election itself, on 7 August, was a formality. I received 67.31 per cent of the votes cast against 32.69 per cent for my sole opponent, the highly respected Jaswant Singh. On 13 August, I was welcomed back in the Rajya Sabha with effusive compliments from all sides. The Leader of the House spoke about my 'qualities of head and heart'; the Leader of the Opposition about the practice of 'two Zero Hours, one in the House and the other which the members can avail of in your Chamber, because if somebody does not get an opportunity to express himself, he has access to your Chamber and can express himself very easily there'.

---

[155] Gopal, op. cit., pp. 287–94, records the somewhat similar circumstances which led to Radhakrishnan's second term.

In response, I thanked the members for their cooperation and said that 'the manner in which we attend to our business is [being] watched by the citizen body with a discerning eye'. Referring to the legislative and deliberative responsibilities of the House, I said that:

> Both unavoidably relate to public concerns in an era of rapidly changing expectations pertaining to good governance, probity in all aspects of public life, justice, inclusive growth, societal cohesion and social peace. The transition in public mood from passive receptivity to active quest in qualitative and quantitative terms is real and urgent. Our responses consequently have to encapsulate these emerging trends in public perceptions.

◆

After the 2014 general election and the installation of the NDA government, the question of successfully piloting government-sponsored legislation through the Rajya Sabha and obtaining for it the concurrence of the opposition parties became a matter of high priority. In that context, a suggestion emanated from the Leader of the House that an Indian equivalent of what is known as the Salisbury Doctrine in British parliamentary practice should be instituted. This emerged from the working arrangements reached during the Labour Government of 1945–51, when the fifth Marquess of Salisbury was the Leader of the Conservative Opposition in the Lords. The Convention ensures that major government bills can get through the Lords when the government of the day has no majority in the Lords. In practice, it meant that the House of Lords does not try to vote down a government bill mentioned in an election manifesto.

This was strongly opposed by different sections of the House. It was pointed out that unlike the House of Lords, the Rajya Sabha is an elected House, integral to the federal and basic structure of the Constitution. In the discussion on the suggestion, some members even felt that the suggestion constituted a Breach of Privilege. I examined the matter carefully and accepted Arun Jaitley's contention that his observation was 'purely academic in nature' and was not intended to show disrespect to the members. I concluded that since the Rajya Sabha is an *elected* House, the Salisbury Doctrine or any variant of it has no relevance to it.

During 2014–15, a demand was raised by the government floor managers that a bill may be allowed to be passed in the din in the Rajya Sabha. It was pointed out to them that while there were instances in the past when bills were indeed passed in the din, that happened with a necessary precondition that the government had a majority in the House. With a paper majority, the bills at times were cleared with voice vote, provided no one asked for the division of votes. However, in the current case, the ruling NDA did not have the majority. So, it was technically, procedurally and morally impossible to pass the bills in din, assuming the majority for the government.

Furthermore and during the UPA period, I had taken a position that no bills will be passed in the din. This was appreciated by the principal Opposition leaders. This principle of 'no bill to be passed in din' was steadfastly observed throughout my tenure. It did bring discomfiture to both the governments, but the UPA took cognizance of my principled stand and compensated it by floor management and adjustments with the Opposition. The NDA, on the other hand, felt that its majority in the Lok Sabha gave it the 'moral' right to prevail over procedural impediments in the Rajya Sabha. An expression of this was conveyed to me authoritatively, and somewhat unusually, when one day PM Modi walked into my Rajya Sabha office unscheduled. After I got over my surprise, I made the customary gestures of hospitality. He said that 'there are expectations of higher responsibilities for you but you are not helping me'. I said that my work in the Rajya Sabha, and outside, is public knowledge. 'Why are bills not being passed in the din?' he asked. I replied that the Leader of the House and his colleagues, when in Opposition, had appreciated the ruling that no bills will be passed in the din and that normal procedures of obtaining consent will be observed. He then said that the Rajya Sabha TV was not favourable to the government. My response was that while I had a role in the establishment of the channel, I had no control over the editorial content and that a committee of Rajya Sabha members, in which the BJP was represented, provided broad guidance to the channel, adding that from all accounts, the channel's programmes and discussions were appreciated by the viewers.

A variant of this view, more troublesome for the Rajya Sabha, was the emergence of a practice of using the provisions of Articles 109 and 110 of the Constitution relating to money bills and to designate legislation having incidental financial implications as money bills on the strength of the certification of the Speaker of the House of the People in terms of Article 110(3). Such proposals, in the view of many members, would be within the ambit of Article 110(2) but made no headway in view of the absolute authority bestowed on the Speaker's certification.[156] It came to the fore in the context of the Aadhaar (Targeted Delivery of Financial and other Subsidies, Benefits and Services) Act, 2016 and was even challenged, unsuccessfully, by a member in the Supreme Court of India. However, the majority bench agreed that the Speaker's discretion in declaring a bill as a money bill can, henceforth, be subject to judicial review. On 13 November 2019, the Court, however, decided to refer the matter to a larger constitutional bench.[157]

The use of this procedural detour became evident when in 2017 (up to 10 August) out of the 31 bills passed/returned/deemed to be returned by the Rajya Sabha, 16 were money bills.

◆

---

[156]This issue was raised in the House on 13 May 2015 in the context of the Black Money Bill (Undisclosed Foreign Income and Assets) and Imposition of Tax Bill, 2015 by Naresh Agarwal, Sitaram Yechury, Jairam Ramesh and a few other members. The Leader of the Opposition said that 'this Bill has been made a Money Bill just to undermine the position of the Rajya Sabha'.

[157]Special correspondent, 'Congress Welcomes SC Decision on Referring Money Bill Case,' *The Hindu*, 13 November 2019.

During the 2014 general election, the BJP had promised to grant citizenship to Hindus persecuted in neighbouring countries. In the party's election manifesto, it said that it would welcome Hindu refugees and give shelter to them. The Citizenship (Amendment) Bill, 2016 was introduced in the Lok Sabha in July 2016. It sought to amend the Citizenship Act, 1955 by changing the definition of 'illegal immigrant' by providing that the following groups of persons will not be treated as illegal immigrants: (i) Hindus, Sikhs, Buddhists, Jains, Parsis and Christians from Afghanistan, Bangladesh and Pakistan, (ii) who have been exempted from the provisions of the Passport (Entry into India) Act, 1920 and the Foreigners Act, 1946. The bill also creates an exemption for these categories for citizenship through naturalization by reducing the time period requirement for these groups from 11 to six years.

The bill was referred to the joint parliamentary committee. Its report was received in January 2019. It was passed by the Lok Sabha but lapsed with the dissolution of that House in May 2019 after the general election of 2019.

The primary reason for the opposition to the bill is concern over the demography of northeastern India given the influx of migrants from Bangladesh. The bill also goes against the ongoing update of the National Register of Citizens and discriminates based on religious lines.

The bill was reintroduced in the Lok Sabha on 19 July 2016. It was referred to the joint parliamentary committee on 12 August 2016. The committee submitted its report on 7 January 2019, but it lapsed on 3 June 2019 at the end of the term of the Lok Sabha. It was revived after the 2019 general election, was endorsed by both Houses and signed into law in December 2019.

The real-life story of apprehensions and its implications, as reflected in different segments of public opinion in the agitations that followed in the winter of 2019 tells us much about hasty law-making and the disconnect between the formal processes of law-making and its perceived impact on the people. This can be avoided by closer scrutiny and wider consultations.

An infrequent occurrence was recorded in the 238th session on 9 March 2016 at the end of the customary motion of thanks debate to the president's address to the joint session. After many members had spoken, the PM replied, thanked the members and requested them 'to pass the motion of thanks unanimously so that this good tradition continues'. He also appealed to the members 'to play their role in taking this country ahead by passing bills pending here and the bills passed by the other House. We need to work at a fast pace for that'. The Leader of the Opposition then proposed an amendment to the motion of thanks by suggesting that a paragraph be added to it. In the discussion that followed, the minister for parliamentary affairs said that such an amendment 'means practically that the Centre has failed' in regard to the mentioned matter. The Leader of the Opposition, however, did not agree to withdraw his amendment and the deputy chairman then put the matter to vote. In the voting that followed, Ayes were 94 and Noes 61. The question so decided read as follows:

> That an Address be presented to the President in the following terms:
> That the Members of the Rajya Sabha assembled in this Session are deeply grateful to the President for the Address which he has been pleased to deliver to both Houses of Parliament together on February 23, 2016, but regret that the Address does not mention that the Government is committed to securing the fundamental rights of all citizens to contest elections at all levels, including to Panchayats to further strengthen the foundations of democracy, which also forms part of the basic structure of the Constitution and is consistent with the spirit of the 73rd Amendment to the constitution, intended to expand and encourage democratic participation of the poor and the marginalized without imposing educational or any other limitations on the right to contest elections.
> The motion was adopted.

As per established practice, the motion of thanks is forwarded to the president through a covering letter from the chairman and is acknowledged with thanks. Record shows that on three occasions—in 1980, 1989 and 2001—when motions with amendments were conveyed, these, too, were acknowledged with thanks.[158] On this occasion, however, no letter of acknowledgment appears to have been received.

◆

An interesting Short Duration Discussion on electoral reforms took place on 22–23 March in the budget session of 2017. It emanated from complaints about the manipulation of Electronic Voting Machines (EVMs) in the UP assembly polls. Most of the debate was focused on it and the delay in the introduction of Voter Verifiable Paper Audit Trails (VVPATs) in the light of an earlier Supreme Court judgment. Two other matters were also raised: state funding of elections and corrections of distortions in the electoral system in which the prevalent first-past-the-post system and the possibility of a candidate winning with 20 per cent of the votes cast. One speaker from the Left put it as 'a partial proportional representation system' in which in every constituency, each voter would have two votes, one for the individual and one for the political party. He also advocated reservation of one-third of seats for women. The proposal of simultaneous elections was raised and strongly criticized on the ground that it was a surreptitious attempt to bring in a presidential form of government.

The law minister's response was largely focused on the EVMs and was dismissive of its alleged defects. He also referred to various corrective suggestions for reforms made by the Election Commission, the Law Commission and various parliamentary committees.

◆

---

[158]*Rajya Sabha at Work*, pp. 233–40 and 243, n. 75.

A comprehensive Short Duration Discussion, the last in my period, took place on 3 August on 'Indian foreign policy and engagement with strategic partners'. The first speaker, from the Opposition, said 'this is the first time, after the NDA government assumed office that the government has agreed to discuss this'. He questioned the government's claim of having 'isolated Pakistan' and enquired about the government's road map. Referring to the developments relating to the tri-junction question, he said that 'developments on our border with China definitely have an adverse and negative impact on the special relationship that has been cultivated by successive governments'. He also raised questions about the fulfilment of commitments given to other neighbours, about certain aspects of Indo–US relations and about the need for balance in the Indo–Israeli relationship with regard to 'our commitment and solidarity with the people of Palestine'. Speakers also spoke of 'serious rupture in policy orientation'.

In a strident reply, the external affairs minister asked the members not to cast aspersions on the government's foreign policy. She took exception to the Congress president's reported meeting with the Chinese ambassador, explained in some detail the Doklam crisis, said diplomacy is the key to resolving the situation and read a statement issued by the MEA. On Pakistan, she said that a road map for peace, amity and cooperation was created but 'terrorism and talks cannot go together'.

◆

FAREWELL TO THE RAJYA SABHA

No landing is complete till it is completed and the aircraft towed to the disembarkation point. I was to discover, later, that two happenings in my last week in office tended to cause offence in some quarters and were perceived to be teeming with hidden meanings! The first was an address to the 25th Convocation of the National Law School of India University, Bengaluru, where my theme was *Two Obligatory Isms: Why Pluralism and Secularism Are Essential for our Democracy*, wherein I had argued for an urgency of going beyond tolerance, to acceptance, through continuous dialogue for promoting harmony since the need for it is 'highlighted by enhanced apprehensions of insecurity among segments of our citizen body, particularly Dalits, Muslims and Christians'. The second was an unscripted interview to Karan Thapar on Rajya Sabha TV on 9 August 2017, which covered all aspects of the work of the vice president. It also included questions about 'illiberal nationalism' and perceptions on Muslims in Indian society and polity. Some questions were focused on my Bengaluru address as also on the earlier speech of August 2015 at the All-India Muslim Majlis-e-Mushawarat. In answer to them, I said that 'a feeling of unease, a sense of insecurity is creeping in' among Muslims. I said that affirmative action where needed should be taken and opined that Indian Muslims are *sui generis* and are not attracted to extremist ideologies.

10 August 2017 was the last day of my term of office and my last day as Chairman, Rajya Sabha. The day's proceedings[159] record the details of the morning session. The interventions from party leaders, front and backbenchers, and nominated personalities were full of compliments and complimentary references. Procedural correctives, the 'no legislation in the din' rule and dignified impartiality were specifically mentioned. One senior member on the back benches blessed me with a Sanskrit verse and wished me long life in Upanishadic terms!

The PM participated in this, and while fulsome in his compliments was somewhat selective in his reference to my work. Hardly any mention was made of my period as Chairman, Rajya Sabha and while my professional career as a diplomat was alluded to and lauded, it was sought to be pigeonholed in the 'atmosphere, thought process, debates amidst such people' (meaning Muslim countries) where I was

---

[159] Rajya Sabha Parliamentary Debates, Official Record, Vol. 243, No. 18, pp. 1–35.

assigned, supplemented by work in Muslim surroundings as VC of AMU and as Chairman of NMC. 'There may have been some struggle within (all these years) but from now onwards you won't have to face this dilemma. You will have a feeling of freedom and you will get an opportunity to work, think and talk according to your ideology.' The tilt in overlooking my work elsewhere as a representative of India and particularly in the UN in a critical period was fairly evident and so was the reference to 'your ideology' and can hardly be attributed to poor staff work; nor can the fact be evaded that a Representative of India, anywhere and at any level including the highest, works on the articulation of Indian views and promotion of Indian national interests uninfluenced by personal preferences or prejudices of host countries.

The intended message of the seemingly laudatory remarks was picked up by party functionaries and sections of the media,[160] as also by the 'faithful' in the social media, and by the listening public at large. The reaction so generated has been sustained in various manifestations. Its rationale is perhaps summed up in the Urdu couplet:

Bhari bazm main raaz ki baat keh di
Bara be-adab hoon saza chahta hoon

---

[160]Kumar Shakti Shekhar, 'How PM Modi Gave a Left-handed Compliment to Outgoing Vice President Hamid Ansari,' *India Today*, 10 August 2017 ('A minute of PM's farewell speech for Hamid Ansari was devoted to taunting the outgoing Vice President over his latest controversial remark'). Also, Saubhadra Chatterji, 'Prime Minister Narendra Modi Took Subtle Digs at the Outgoing VP,' *Hindustan Times*, 11 August 2017; Special correspondent, 'Diplomatic Skills Helped Ansari in Rajya Sabha: Modi,' *The Hindu*, 10 August 2017. Also, Ajoy Ashirwad Mahaprashasta, 'Stung by Ansari's Observations, Modi and BJP Take Potshots at Outgoing VP,' thewire.in, 11 August 2017 ('Mohammad Hamid Ansari will probably go down in the history books as the vice president who received the bitterest of farewells from a sitting government'). Aakar Patel, 'Hamid Ansari Said Nothing Wrong,' *Asian Age*, 13 August 2007. The article added that 'the response from the BJP was quite vicious and aggressively communal... I was disturbed and saddened by the words of Narendra Modi, who mocked Ansari on his last day in office.'

(I have divulged in public what was hidden
I am very insolent, chastisement I desire.)

On the other hand, editorial comments and a good many other writings considered the PM's remarks to be a departure from the accepted practice on such occasions.

My response that morning began with an Urdu couplet:

Mujh pe ilzaam itne lagaaye gaye
Begunahi ke andaaz jaate rahe

(So much have I been accused of
That proving my innocence has deserted me.)

I thanked the members in customary terms and reminded them of what Dr Radhakrishnan had said on a similar occasion and mentioned by me a decade earlier:

> A democracy is distinguished by the protection it gives to minorities. A democracy is likely to degenerate into tyranny if it does not allow the opposition groups to criticize fairly, freely and frankly the policies of the government. But at the same time, minorities also have their responsibilities. While they have every right to criticize, their right should not degenerate into wilful hampering and obstruction of the work of parliament. All groups, therefore, have their rights and their responsibilities.

I reminded the members that 'the manner in which we attend to our business is [being] watched by the citizen body with a discerning eye'.

As I walked out for the last time through Gate 9 of that iconic building escorted by the deputy chairman and many senior members of the House and my own team of officials, I wondered if this temple of noise and reconciliation would remain so amidst suggestions of physical and spiritual 'renovation'.

Later that day, there was a farewell function in the Balayogi Auditorium on behalf of the Rajya Sabha members, where a Scroll of Honour was presented to me. It was attended by the vice president designate, the PM, the Speaker (Lok Sabha), the minister for parliamentary affairs, leaders of the House and the Opposition, and Deputy Chairman (Rajya Sabha). The PM spoke there too; he referred to my family background and experience in public life, mentioned Brig. Mohammad Usman and his martyrdom in the 1948 conflict and said nothing adverse had come to his notice about my long spell in office.[161] He hoped that the insights gained during the tenure would be recorded for public benefit.

This speech, different in content and tone, was not picked up by the media. The photograph of the function, with the Lok Sabha Speaker in the background, was!

That evening, the very competent household staff at 6, Maulana Azad Road gave us a farewell dinner and then Salma and I were driven to our new residence—31, APJ Abdul Kalam Road. Thus ended what had become my longest innings.

Zindagi naam hai judai ka

(Parting is the name of life.)

---

[161]PM's speech in the Balayogi Auditorium on PIB's YouTube (https://www.youtube.com/watch?v=BrGSsPxDzbY).

Chapter 7

Vice Presidency

Roger Sherman, a founding father of the American Constitution, had observed that 'if the vice president were not to be President of the Senate, he would be without employment'. Record would show that most holders of the office crafted a role for themselves.

The ceremonial and functional duties of the vice president are considerable. The record of daily engagements testifies to it. Visits to states and discussions with governors and CMs, public-speaking engagements, foreign visits and calls by governors, ministers of the central government, senior-most officers of the government, foreign ambassadors and visiting foreign dignitaries on official visits to India—each had its own flavour. And of course, there were many friends and old colleagues who wished to see an otherwise normal human being in a ceremonial cage! I adjusted to it; less so Salma, who still continued to be herself, 'a bird in flight' as she once put it many years back.

I called on former president R. Venkataraman and PMs Gujral and Vajpayee. Some friends who came calling included Philip Talbot from New York, who presented me a copy of his book *An American Witness to India's Partition*, which has been described by B.R. Nanda as 'the best contemporary account of the critical decade', Prof. Robin Jeffrey from Melbourne and my Austrian colleague in New York,

Ambassador Herbert Traxl, who was as much an Austrian as an Indian!

Amongst callers from abroad in early months were German chancellor Angela Merkel, who enquired about the recipe for accommodation of diversity in India, the Head of Iran's Guardian Council, Grand Ayatollah Ahmad Jannati, whom I had met in Tehran and the Deputy PM of Oman, who attributed the lack of foreign investment in India to 'too much bureaucracy'. I asked him if he would say the same about other large-scale management systems, including that of the Almighty! Other callers from West Asia in later years included former foreign minister of Iran, Dr Ali Akbar Velayati and Prince Turki bin Faisal of Saudi Arabia. In July 2013, I had a very interesting discussion with US Vice President Joe Biden. Another interesting visitor was an old friend from Australia, former foreign minister Gareth Evans.

UNIVERSITIES AND RESEARCH INSTITUTIONS

The ex officio functions of the vice president include being the chancellor of the universities of Delhi, Punjab and Pondicherry (now Puducherry) and president of the Indian Council of World Affairs (ICWA). The duties of the chancellors of universities, under our present system, are purely formal and ceremonial, since substantive supervisory powers of central universities rest with the President of India. The chancellor is expected to be present on ceremonial occasions and his role therefore, as I described once to the VC of the University of Delhi is 'to be seen infrequently and heard even less'.

In November 2007, I was invited by the Academic Research Centre of the University of Delhi to inaugurate the Third International Congress of the Asian Political and International Studies Association. Its focus on Asia has helped to explore specific areas of Asian experience. The first Congress focused on development, democracy and security; the second on aspects of governance and the current one on Asian concepts of justice. I was enthused by the theme and intrigued by it. The concept of justice is integral to social well-being; for this reason, it must be reiterated at every possible opportunity. It is also in the category of universal values, rather than being location-specific. Talk of an Asian concept may, therefore, convey an impression that there is something specific by way of value addition or value subtraction. This, presumably, is not intended.

Surveying the concept of justice down the ages and in different societies, I opined that selective good and selective justice is a recipe for trouble. A conceptual framework for justice, therefore, has practical implications and can only be viable if it is inclusive—at the societal, national and international levels. Asian societies, drawing upon their extensive heritage, undoubtedly would come to this conclusion and conceptualize it appropriately. I concluded that the modern concept of justice received international recognition in the Universal Declaration of Human Rights of 1948. It proclaimed 'a common standard of achievement for all peoples and all nations', asserted equality before the law and equal protection of the law. These were amplified in other international covenants.

◆

I addressed the 61st Convocation of the Panjab University at Chandigarh in December 2011. The theme of my remarks was the *Challenge of Change* and it was focused on the duality of the academic purpose—knowledge and change—with emphasis on the latter since the young people leaving the portals of the university are viewed as agents of change. Questions about its cause, nature, dimensions and desirability therefore arise and need to be addressed. Globalization induces change but is also disruptive. Fear of the unknown is a psychological reality and, therefore, to conquer fear is the beginning of wisdom. This also involves an ability to deal with diversity and homogeneity. I drew attention to the sociologist Robert Merton's observation that effective equilibrium between *culturally defined aspirational goals* and *socially structured means to achieve them* is maintained only so long as those that conform to both the goals and the means achieve satisfaction. Where symbols of achievement across classes remain unchanged but are coupled with limited opportunity for segments of the population to achieve them, social anomie or cultural chaos prevails, with the disappearance of predictability or regularity of behaviour. The need for a balance between *process* and *product* therefore is critical and, hence, also the need to pay heed to Gandhi's dictum that means matter as much as the end. Achieving goals at any cost will, in the long run, impose unacceptable costs on the individual, the community and the nation.

◆

Much of the strength of the University of Delhi emanates from its colleges and the diversity of their student bodies. A good example is Lady Shri Ram College, whose stated mission is the empowerment of women to assume leadership. I attended its annual day function in March 2008 and used the occasion to think aloud on this objective in the context of a remark made by Nehru. I cited official data to support the International Labour Organization's contention that women continue to be the untapped potential of South Asia. In terms of law, the citizens of India, including its women citizens, should be a satisfied lot but ground reality shows that poverty in our land has a feminine profile. Gender justice remains unachieved. The task of attaining it remains formidable; it remains urgent. Success would open the hitherto untapped reservoirs of energy. It would transform Indian society. The more difficult aspect pertains to social perceptions woven in the interstices of the mind and sanctified by tradition. Government legislation, experience shows, is an inadequate deterrent. The lead in changing these perceptions and practices has to be taken by individuals and groups in different strata of society. Social reformers such as Mahatma Jyotiba Phule and sociologists such as M.N. Srinivas have dwelt on the root causes of the problem. The need of the hour is to go beyond ritual slogan-mongering.

I did not visit the central Pondicherry University, which seemed to be bogged down, perennially, in internecine disputes and allegations and counter allegations of governmental interference.

◆

The vice president is, ex officio, President of the ICWA. This prestigious institution for the study of international affairs was established in 1943 by a group of individuals amongst whom the most prominent were Sir Tej Bahadur Sapru and Nehru. Some organizational problems relating to it in the late 1990s compelled the government to bring in correctives; these took the shape of The Indian Council of World Affairs Act, 2001, which declared it to be 'an institution of national importance' having a governing council that is headed by the vice president and the minister of external affairs as one of its vice presidents. A director general (DG) is to be its executive head. The latter, in initial stages, was drawn from the serving senior officers of the MEA, whose tenures varied as they were often transferred to higher responsibilities. I therefore proposed, and the government accepted, that the DG should be a recently retired Grade I officer of the IFS and should have a term of three years. This arrangement has turned out to be satisfactory and the ICWA is slowly but surely emerging, on the pattern of similar bodies elsewhere, to be a government-funded institution offering, among its other functions, policy options on critical questions of foreign policy.

There is, in my view, scope for more candid expressions of policy alternatives in writings and in-house discussions about them. The need is for a strategic culture of informed dissent as is the practice in other open societies.

CONFERENCE OF GOVERNORS

An annual feature in the presidential calendar is the Conference of Governors and Lieutenant Governors. It serves the purpose of a coordinating mechanism, and gives the president, the PM and his senior colleagues an opportunity to share views on policies and hear first-hand from the governors assessments on some specific and common issues. It provides the participants with an occasion to raise common housekeeping questions with the central government. The vice president is a regular invitee to these conclaves, whose tone and the agenda is set by the president. The PM and the home minister make substantive contributions to the issues of the day. Efforts have been made from time to time to explore the possibility of discerning patterns, if any, in responses made by governors to specific situations. One such effort was the Bhagwan Sahay Committee Report of 1971. It opined that 'it would be unrealistic and unwise' to lay down any rigid guidelines. The governors, as President Venkataraman put it in 1987, are expected 'to remember the central fact that they are not only the constitutional heads but are also expected to be sagacious counsellors and advisors to the ministry who can pour oil on troubled waters' and can assist in the implementation of socio-economic schemes for the benefit of the less-privileged, population control, adult education and employment generation.[162]

The focus of my remarks in the 2008 conference was on (i) the non-functioning of the legislatures (ii) the role of governors as chancellors of state universities and (iii) the governor's responsibility when the well-being of a section of the people of the state is seriously jeopardized. With regard to the first, I said that the blunt truth is that state legislatures have virtually ceased to function in the sense in which the legislature is expected to function in a democracy, that is, to be both a legislative and a deliberative body. The deliberative aspect of its work is to question and debate the policy of the government. This is seriously jeopardized by the duration of sessions—rarely exceeding two weeks and at times as little as three days. In 1995, a conference of the presiding officers of the state legislatures had recommended that state assemblies should meet for at least 60 days in the case of small states and 100 days in the case of larger states. The recommendation was reiterated in 1998.

---

[162]R. Venkataraman, *My Presidential Years* (New Delhi, 1994) pp. 73–75.

The perils of this disuse are evident and in such a dismal situation, should the governor be a mere spectator and allow the Constitution he/she is charged to preserve and defend be violated in spirit if not in form? Instead, can the governor use the prestige of the office innovatively to initiate and develop a non-partisan debate about the longer-term damage it can do to democratic politics, and to seek a broad consensus on a more productive approach to the functioning of legislatures?

With regard to the universities and given the ground situation, I suggested that the pattern and practice followed in the case of the central universities, which have the President of India as Visitor, be emulated to strengthen the governor's role in making appointments of VCs and also shield the universities from the vicissitudes of the political debate.

On social peace, I said that the governor is required to devote effort for the well-being of *all* sections of the public. These include the weaker sections and the minorities. Recent and not-so-recent happenings bring out instances where the official machinery has defaulted in the discharge of its duties. Many of these have been identified by the Supreme Court. This has generated unease and insecurity among the minority segments of the citizen-body. Communalism of various hues is threatening the already fragile social fabric. Any selectivity in tackling it would be detrimental to the constitutional principles of equality and secularism.

The Constitution, I concluded, assigns responsibilities to governors. Secreted in the interstices of the constitutional text is the spirit and the purpose for which the institution was created. These need to be explored in the context of the changing requirements of our times.

In the Governors' Conference of 2013 and on the agenda item of internal security and the interventions of several speakers on communal tensions, ethnic violence and religious extremism, and to the dangers emanating from them, I said it is evident that our social fabric is under stress. Given the plurality of our society, secularism is not an option but a necessity. Nor is it a mantra; instead, it is the practice of dos and donts that unite the citizen body and prevent or minimize divisions. It is premised on justice, equality and fraternity, in law and in fact. It goes beyond tolerance and requires acceptance.

Furthermore and since conflicts develop in the mind of humans, we need to develop a methodology by which the normal intelligence inputs of the state are considered together with deeper analysis of the reasons for the alienation of social groups. Since the governor is required to devote effort for the well-being of *all* sections of the people, and because the institution is above the political fray, it is best placed to undertake this responsibility and discharge it in a harmonious manner. A substantive reflection of this in the governor's reports to the president could become a useful input in policy-making.

On state universities, I repeated my earlier observations about the selection of VCs and the chancellor's role in regard to them. I referred to the 12th Five-Year Plan's focus on quality besides access and equity and said that the corrective lies not in sermons but in prescribing and enforcing stringent standards for teaching, for research papers that are refereed, and for PhDs that are passed through qualified examiners, one of who should be from a foreign university or research institution.

I recalled my earlier remarks on the institutional role of the governor and to their Oath of Office, that is to preserve, protect and defend the Constitution and devote himself or herself to the service and well-being of the people of the state. To do this, the governor cannot be a mere spectator and allow the Constitution he/she is charged to preserve and defend be violated in spirit if not in form. Instead, can the governor use the prestige of the office innovatively to initiate and develop a non-partisan debate about the longer-term damage it can do to democratic politics, and to seek a broad consensus on a more productive approach to the functioning of legislatures?

In the Governors' Conference of 2016, I said that the governor should be a model to emulate, rather than eschew. On the question of higher education, I dwelt on the pre-higher education stage and on the quality of students emerging from our primary and secondary school system. I cited a few reasons for it:

(i) While progress has been made in making enrolment at the primary level almost universal, the dropout rate of 47 per cent in the Class I to X levels mentioned by the president the previous day is a matter of serious concern. The same has to be said of learning levels where data in the public domain shows that a good percentage of students in rural areas have failed to acquire the required learning skills at different stages of schooling. How then will the demographic dividend be reaped when school children are not learning the basics?

(ii) Teachers are poorly trained and this is reflected in their work. Teacher commitment, despite the new higher salary levels in government schools, is lacking. A mechanism for accountability does not seem to be operative.

(iii) As a result, the feedstock for higher education is often of indifferent quality and entrants to college-level courses often display insufficient capacity to understand and absorb college-level teaching.

The result of this is vividly reflected in employability surveys conducted by industry bodies from time to time. On the other hand, societal priorities in many sections of society do not propel the best minds at post-graduate levels to opt for research. This is reflected in the modest R&D scorecard in most, though not all, of our universities.

This state of affairs cannot be corrected merely by procedural changes in the administration pattern of our universities at senior levels. What is needed is a culture of motivation for excellence at all levels and inbuilt systems of accountability. Universities should not be viewed merely in terms of the job market to the detriment of intellectual excellence for its own sake.

Another matter in need of serious consideration is the shifting balance between public and private colleges and universities and its longer-term implications for the state's role in the field of education on the one hand and social cohesion on the other. A society dedicated to welfare and development of all cannot opt out of its responsibility to promote and sustain essential services in areas of public health and education.

VISITS TO STATES

Visits to states and UTs of the Union of India, in response to official or non-governmental invitations, were undertaken fairly regularly. Its benefits were evident: interaction with a very wide cross-section of people in all walks of life, as well as discussions with governors and CMs that shed much light on how the national scene was viewed from state capitals. In the nature of things, these were short visits and confined to speaking engagements in principal cities with only occasional forays beyond them.

Amidst routine engagements, a few do linger in my memory. In a conducted tour of a local museum on a visit to Mizoram, I was shown a lamp post bearing bullet marks of the IAF strafing of insurgents in the Mizo National Front uprising of March 1966. The very well-kept war cemetery in Kohima was a grim reminder of the tragedy and futility of warfare. The Naga system of village councils and their role in the modern electoral process are indicative of the role that tradition actually plays in more recent procedures of our republican process. The visit to the Rann of Kutch on a full moon night, at the suggestion of the then CM of Gujarat, Shri Narendra Modi, was a fascinating experience. Also in Gujarat and at the suggestion of an old friend, Hasmukh Shah, I attended in February 2012 the launch of a scholarly volume on *Gujarat and the Sea,* which was the proceedings of an international conference on the subject. Conversations with Shri Modi on each of these visits were substantive even when viewpoints did not converge.

I visited Kashmir on several occasions, the most enjoyable experience being a round of golf on the divinely picturesque course at Pahalgam. Conversations with N.N. Vohra on local issues and on a range of national and security-related questions were always educative. A visit to Dras was planned but abandoned since the IAF helicopters (essential as per security requirements) could not be used, though an Indian army one could be! On a visit to Srinagar sometime in 2013, I had a long talk with Mufti Mohammad Sayeed sahib. He was emphatic in his prognosis that the problem of J&K can be solved only in the context of a solution of the India–Pakistan problems.

Visits to Mumbai were many, one of them was in December 2016 for the launch of an unusual and perceptive book by Sudheendra Kulkarni suggesting a South Asian Union of the three South Asian lands in the shape of a 'spiritual and cultural confederation'. I welcomed the vision of the suggestion and said the practical approach would be to make haste slowly, to be accommodative rather than exclusionary so that negative perceptions are allowed to fade away. (Three years hence, I am less optimistic and more pessimistic about such prospects.)

I found three successive governors of Karnataka—Rameshwar Thakur, Hans Raj Bhardwaj and Vajubhai Vala—interesting company and enjoyed talking to them on my fairly regular visits to Bangalore. The same was the case with Gopal Gandhi and M.K. Narayanan in Kolkata, B.P. Singh in Sikkim and S.C. Jamir, K. Sankaranarayanan and Vidyasagar Rao in Maharashtra, Ram Naik in UP, E.S.L. Narasimhan in Andhra Pradesh and General S.F. Rodrigues and Shivraj Patil in Punjab.

A noticeable aspect of visits to the Northeast (as also to Kargil in J&K) is the practice of giving petitions; some of these were on substantive local matters and all very candidly expressive of public views.

FOREIGN VISITS

The vice president wears two hats in our system, but by established convention dons only one in his incarnations beyond the shores of

India. So all invitations to bilateral or multilateral parliamentary conclaves are dutifully passed on to the deputy chairperson, Rajya Sabha, and the chairman personally undertakes foreign travel, as the Vice President of the Republic is accorded appropriate honours only at the request of the government.

There are manifold motivations for such visits, carefully assessed and planned by the government: to initiate or further bilateral political, commercial or cultural relationships, to participate in ceremonial or politically significant occasions where high-level but not the highest-level participation is considered necessary, or return similar visits on similar occasions by counterparts in friendly countries.

I visited 17 countries in my first term and 30 in the second. The preparatory work for these visits was coordinated by Ashok Dewan in the vice president's office, supervised by the secretary to the vice president, and done by the protocol and concerned territorial division of the MEA and by our diplomatic missions abroad. Having done it in my earlier incarnations in the MEA, I was familiar with the minutiae involved. On all these visits (except the purely ceremonial ones), apart from senior MEA officials, I was accompanied by a designated minister of state of the government, a few MPs selected from different political parties on a rotational basis and a media contingent comprising official print and electronic media and journalists from news agencies and newspapers.

The general pattern of programmes consisted of meetings with counterparts, calls on heads of states, discussions with members of legislatures and business groups and at times, an address usually to an academic or parliamentary institution on bilateral relations or Indian perceptions of the global scene. The travel on Air India or Air Force aircrafts also provided occasions for in-depth discussions with the minister-accompanying and the MPs and exposed the latter to the general ambiance in which foreign relations are conducted.

For Salma and me personally, these travels had an added attraction of revisiting many of the places where we had lived many years earlier in our younger days, whose recollections resonate often in the memory.

An incidental benefit of travelling by Air India chartered aircrafts was that the airline's culinary skills could be tested and tasted. These were very much to the expected requirements, and so were the in-cabin service standards.

◆

The first set of visits in April 2008 was to the central Asian lands of Turkmenistan and Kazakhstan. Both were part of the former Soviet Union and became independent states in 1991. They are part of our extended neighbourhood and we consider them as natural allies and key partners. They are also part of an older geopolitical and cultural edifice of central Asia, which had historic relations with India. In this context, I referred to Bairam Khan and his son, Abdur Rahim Khan-e-Khanan in the reign of Emperor Akbar. As independent entities, both countries are well endowed with energy resources and are of interest to us. I referred to the success of our pharmaceutical industry in the Turkmen market and said that more can be done in this field. The other promising area of cooperation is the energy sector. (A relationship with Turkmenistan was to develop a few years later, in 2015, when we joined the proposed TAPI [Turkmenistan–Afghanistan–Pakistan–India] gas pipeline).

In Ashgabat, the official part of the visit included wreath-laying at the tomb of the founder-president and at the Independence monument and talks with the president. Besides that, a visit to a horse-breeding farm was of particular interest to see the world-famous Akhal-Teke stallions that are bred and trained. Salma had no difficulty familiarizing herself with them.

To me, of particular interest was the visit to the ruins of the ancient city of Marv, once located on the banks of the Amu Darya but now some distance away from it. Its origins as a centre of administration and trade on the ancient silk route dated back to Achaemenian times; it is said to be the place of origin of Zoroaster, was of significance in the Buddhist period and in later central Asian history and remained one of the largest cities of the world till its total destruction by the Mongols in the thirteenth century. Marv has the tomb of Buraydah ibn Al-Husayb, a companion of the Prophet.[163] The ruins of the Seljuq period (twelfth century) are more visible, the principal one being the mausoleum of Sultan Sanjar (AD 1157).

From Ashgabat, we flew to Astana (now Nur-Sultan), capital of Kazakhstan. My host there was the chairman of the Senate, Kassym-Jomart Tokayev (now President of the Republic). In talks with him, I congratulated him on his country's election as Chair of the CSCE and said that this is indicative of its importance in world affairs. I stressed the need for closer cooperation between our parliamentary institutions.

My discussions with President Nursultan Nazarbayev were wide-ranging and substantive. He spoke of his country's geographical location and about its 'Eurasian' concept of wide-ranging cooperation. His government's approach is for peace, collaboration and friendship with all neighbours and a policy motto of 'come, invest and work'. He expressed interest in pharma, textiles, IT and education. He was supportive of India's global role and its quest to be a permanent member of the UNSC. I conveyed our appreciation of Kazakhstan's role in the Organisation for Economic Co-operation and Development and the Shanghai Cooperation Organisation and also about the role that the country can play with regard to energy security and food production for export. Avenues of bilateral cooperation were explored. Given the size of the country and its sparse population, he suggested that Indian farmers could come and till the vast stretches of fallow land. I followed this up with a meeting with the minister of agriculture, who clarified that state land could be leased to foreigners for 50 years. When I conveyed this to PM Manmohan Singh on my return, he remarked that half of Punjab would be willing to respond to the offer!

---

[163]Tabari, *The History of Al-Tabari, Volume xxxix: Biographies of the Prophet's Companions and Their Successors* (New York, 1998) pp. 70–71.

I visited the Academy of Public Administration and in discussions with the faculty and students, drew attention to the connection between governance and development and said there is enough empirical evidence now that governance plays a central role in economic development and growth because of its crucial role in resource accumulation and allocation.

♦

I visited the Maldives on 11–12 November 2008 for the swearing-in of the opposition candidate President Mohamed Nasheed. It was a simple ceremony. I called on the new head of state as also on his predecessor, Maumoon Abdul Gayoom. The latter seemed relaxed and said that he had no intention of quitting politics.

♦

A three-day visit to Myanmar in April 2009 was substantive, given the criticality of the relationship with our eastern neighbour. Important issues were discussed at some length in a meeting with my host, Vice Senior General Maung Aye and with the chairman of the State Council, Senior General Than Shwe. In discussions with General Aye, and in delegation-level talks, the focus was on bilateral relations. It was emphasized by my interlocutors that the security of India cannot be separated from the security of Myanmar. General Aye said that his visit to India in the year 2000 'marked the beginning of a series of initiatives and was designed to bring our people together'. The question of the insurgent groups in our Northeast and of cross-border insurgency was discussed and Myanmar pledged not to cede its territory to them. No formal agreement about it, however, came to be signed.

Security matters were also discussed in my call on the chairman of the State Peace and Development Council of Myanmar, General Than Shwe. He reiterated that we should 'rest assured that Myanmar will never do anything negative towards India'. The terrain on our common border did impose constraints and required greater attention to improvement of roads in the border areas.

A number of agreements were signed during the visit. These covered a truck manufacturing unit being set up in Myanmar by Tata Motors and the establishment of an English language training centre and an industrial training centre. Also mentioned were the Kaladan multi-modal transit-cum-transport project that will connect Kolkata with the Sittwe Port in Myanmar, and then further to Mizoram by river and road and for which a framework agreement was signed by the foreign ministers in April 2008.

The new capital Nay Pyi Taw has all the signs of its youth. The real beauty of Myanmar, however, is in its exquisite pagodas in Yangon and Mandalay. A place of particular importance to most Indian visitors is the grave of Bahadur Shah Zafar in Rangoon, who died in exile there and was buried in a grave that remained unmarked in the belief that it might otherwise become a place of pilgrimage. It was rediscovered in December 1994 and is now a place of pilgrimage for local Muslims.

◆

A visit to Kuwait in April 2009 was altogether pleasant and gave an opportunity to renew ties with old acquaintances. Discussions with the Amir, Sheikh Sabah, whom I had met many times in the past, were focused on regional political matters. He was as always judicious, but expressed concerns over the rise of violence in Iraq. The defence minister, Sheikh Jaber, was 'cautiously optimistic' about the situation there. On Iran, the Amir's views were reflective of the balance that has characterized Kuwait's relationship. He referred in this context to 'some problems on the continental shelf'. He felt there should be 'frank and transparent relations particularly on the nuclear issue' and said he did not want Iran to possess nuclear weapons. Hence, there is need for a dialogue. Kuwait, too, would benefit from nuclear energy.

There were detailed discussions with the oil minister, Sheikh Ahmad Abdullah. India, he said, is an important customer for crude oil, but discussions with Indian companies since 1964 have made no progress on the refinery project. Discussions with the defence minister were focused on security issues and the threat of terrorism. He also spoke about the 'Peninsula Shield' arrangement of the Gulf Cooperation Council countries.

♦

The visit to South Africa a month later was to represent India at the inauguration of President Jacob Zuma. The swearing-in ceremony in Pretoria was in the open and light showers and a drop in temperature forced the invitees to seek blankets available in limited supply. Nelson Mandela and the then president of the African Union, Muammar Gaddafi, were among the prominent participants.

♦

The next set of visits, in January 2010, was to the southern African countries of Zambia, Malawi and Botswana. The stage for it was set by the India–Africa Forum Summit of 2008 (held in New Delhi), and the enunciation of a desire to 'infuse the close political relationship with greater economic content'. Bilateral trade had made progress in the decade and increased from $1 billion to $40 billion. Similarly, the cumulative Indian investment in Africa is said to have reached $54 billion.[164]

In Zambia, apart from meetings with Vice President George Kunda and President Rupiah Banda, a number of bilateral agreements were signed. These included an agreement between the Government of Zambia and our Exim Bank, under which the latter was to provide a loan of $50 million for the construction of a power project being executed as a joint venture between the Zambia Electricity Supply Corporation and Tata Africa Holdings. Besides that, we offered a two-year credit of $75 million and a grant of $5 million.

I also called on the former Zambian president Kenneth Kaunda,

---

[164]'Indian investments in Africa to increase because of unified market under AfCFTA: Goyal,' *The Hindu Business Line*, 23 September 2020, https://www.thehindubusinessline.com/economy/indian-investments-in-africa-to-increase-because-of-unified-market-under-afcfta-goyal/article32679939.ece.

whom I had met on several occasions earlier. He talked of the historic ties between our two countries. He said that he devotes his time in retirement to the fight against AIDS and urged India to join this effort.

The possibility of exploring cooperation in supply of minerals—coal and uranium from Malawi and uranium from Botswana—were explored in talks at official levels. Our assistance in agricultural development, vocational training and training of professionals in specialized fields were discussed. In Botswana, our assistance in defence training was recalled with gratitude. During the visit, agreements on the educational exchange programme and cooperation agreements in the field of agriculture were signed. The visit enhanced awareness about India. Apart from official engagements, we enjoyed exposure to Botswana's immensely rich diversity of wildlife.

The visit to Malawi was the first ever at a high level. We announced a new line of credit of $50 million to Malawi for its developmental projects. We also announced a relief fund of $1 million for an earthquake that had recently hit some parts of Malawi, and a grant of $4 million for projects in social sectors. Agreements were signed on cooperation in the field of agriculture and allied sectors and between the National Small Industries Corporation of India and One Village, One Product Programme of Malawi, for cooperation in the development of small-scale industries. A protocol on Consultations between the two foreign ministries was also signed.

◆

Later in the year, in June, I visited the Czech Republic and Croatia. In Prague, apart from official discussions, three agreements on social security and administrative arrangements, on economic cooperation and amendments to a 1996 agreement on promotion and protection of investments were signed.

I was invited to address the Prague Security Studies Institute. I spoke on 'Global Governance in the Twenty-First Century', on the need for a new global consensus and a new paradigm for assessing performance, and cited Václav Havel's 1992 call for a radically changed new definition of modernity appropriate for the requirements of the age.

In Croatia, agreements were signed on cooperation in the areas of health, medicine and culture. In the latter, and given Croatia's strong tradition of Indology, the cultural exchange programme included exhibitions on contemporary Indian art and on Indian miniatures. Given the excellent bilateral relations, both governments pledged their support for our bid for a permanent membership of the UNSC and were also supportive of our non-permanent membership in the UNSC for 2011–12.

♦

A short visit to Brussels in October 2010 to represent India in the Eighth ASEM Summit gave Salma and me the opportunity to go down memory lane and recollect memories of the very pleasant three years we had spent in that beautiful city, where our daughter Nuriya was born. Apart from the conference, I called on the King of the Belgians and had bilateral meetings with the president of the European Council, the President of Latvia and with the PMs of Belgium, Finland, Malaysia and Greece. I also visited 'A Passage to Asia' exhibition organized by the Centre for Fine Arts, Brussels, on behalf of the Government of Belgium on the occasion of the ASEM Summit under the Belgian presidency.

♦

My foreign visits in 2011 were to Bangladesh, Uganda, South Sudan, Turkey and Australia.

The visit to Bangladesh in May 2012 was to inaugurate and participate in the sesquicentenary celebrations of Rabindranath Tagore. This was pursuant to a decision of the two PMs to hold joint celebrations to honour that versatile genius who has a very important place in our common cultural heritage. It was preceded by the visit of Anand Sharma, our commerce minister and the occasion provided an opportunity to discuss bilateral relations, particularly in the area of trade. Apart from the formal function, my programme included visits to the Bangabandhu Memorial Museum, the Liberation War Museum, a call on President Zillur Rahman, meeting with PM Sheikh Hasina, who said both countries share common concerns and have a long uninterrupted journey of democracy; 'hence, we should have no delays and look forward to concluding things'. The requirements of infrastructure and power are being addressed through mutual connectivity and benefit as in the case of Tripura.

The leader of the Opposition, Begum Khaleda Zia, who also called on me, reiterated bilateral friendship but referred to 'some problems', for which dialogue is necessary. She cited these as water and border issues and said that Bangladesh has rivers but no water.

♦

After a long civil war and a referendum, the Republic of South Sudan came into existence in July 2011 on its secession from the post-colonial Republic of Sudan. The final process was orderly, with the participation of the international community in the ceremonies that included the lowering and hoisting of the two flags and the playing of the two national anthems. On my way to Juba, I made a transit stop at Entebbe and called on the long-serving president of Uganda, Yoweri Museveni, who along with others in the African Union had played a constructive role. A stopover on the return journey gave me the opportunity to meet some of the very influential Indian community members in Kampala, who hosted a reception in my honour.

♦

I had an enjoyable and productive visit to Turkey in October 2011. The wreath-laying ceremony at the Ataturk Mausoleum was particularly impressive. Historical ties and cultural relations were recalled and my interlocutors were aware of the humanitarian assistance rendered by the Indian Medical Mission, led by Dr M.A. Ansari (in which my own father was a junior member), to Ottoman Turkey in the Balkan

War of 1912. The Speaker of the National Assembly, Cemil Cicek, presented me a framed photograph of Dr Ansari and an album of photographs.

In discussions with President Abdullah Gul and PM Recep Tayyip Erdoğan, the focus of discussions was on the promotion of bilateral ties and on possible use by us of the Turkish expertise in the field of infrastructure. On political matters, the focus was on regional issues. Both the president and the PM spoke about the situation in Syria, with which Turkey has a 900-km border, and of the security and refugee problems. Erdoğan and later the foreign minister explained in detail the effort made by Turkey to defuse the crisis. They expressed their disappointment at the lack of Syrian response. On Libya, Erdoğan said that he had made several attempts to persuade Gaddafi to avoid a confrontation. On Afghanistan, I was given a briefing on the process initiated by Turkey. Both leaders appreciated India's role.

The journey from Ankara to Konya was by road, through the Anatolian plateau. The city of Konya conferred honorary citizenship on me and the Mevlana University an honorary doctorate in international relations. In my address on the occasion, I dwelt on the similarities and parallels in the spiritual traditions of Turkey and India with specific reference to Maulana Jalalu-'d-din Muhammad Rumi and Khwaja Moinuddin Chishti, who were virtual contemporaries and were important pillars of a seamless, borderless world of culture, art, spiritualism and philosophy that extended from Maghreb and Andalusia in the west to all corners of Asia in the east, enriched humanity for over a millennium, assimilated and synthesized many distinctive local, cultural and ethnic features and displayed much diversity within unity.

Two bits of pure tourism were very rewarding. The first was to the ancient remains of Cappadocia and the second to many historic palaces and mosques in Istanbul. The latter included the mausoleum of Abu Ayyub Al Ansari, a figure in early Islamic history who participated in the siege of Constantinople in the seventh century and from whom my own family traces its descent.

◆

Two weeks later, I represented India at the Commonwealth Heads of Government meeting in Perth, a city I was familiar with from my tenure in Australia a quarter of a century earlier. Apart from official engagements, our high commissioner Sujata Singh introduced me to Joyce Westrip and Peggy Holroyde, co-authors of *Colonial Cousins*, a very interesting book on the historical connections between India and Australia and their 'stop-start' relationship.

♦

In my second term, the pattern of visits abroad in the remaining period of the UPA government, till May 2014, was sustained. I made official visits to Vietnam, Tajikistan, Uzbekistan, Peru and Cuba, in addition to representing India on ceremonial occasions in Ethiopia, Iran and Afghanistan.

Vietnam is a critical part of our Look East Policy. The visit there in January 2013 was thus particularly significant, bringing to a close the 'Year of India–Vietnam Friendship'. This was preceded by a number of high-level visits from Vietnam, which focused on strategic cooperation aimed at deepening bilateral defence and strategic cooperation. In my banquet speech in Hanoi, I expressed our admiration for the indomitable spirit and tenacity of the people of Vietnam and for their rapid economic and social development. My discussions with the Vietnamese leaders, including the Secretary-General of the Communist Party were substantive and underlined convergence of views on bilateral and regional issues. I said that:

> We have set a target of $7 billion for bilateral trade by 2015. We are confident of achieving it. We need to generate greater awareness about mutually beneficial business opportunities. Indian companies have ventured into Vietnam in increasing numbers... Indian companies in the field of oil and gas exploration are actively engaged in several projects in Vietnam. India is also prepared to continue extending a line of credit on concessional terms, especially for infrastructure development.

The curious thing about the Vietnamese leadership's strategic approach is the apparent dichotomy in their very functional party-to-party relationship with China and their safeguarding of their strategic interests vis-à-vis China in the South China Sea, which they insist on calling the East Sea.

Our visit to Ho Chi Minh City (Hanoi) was equally productive and provided an opportunity to interact with the resident Indian business community in a reception hosted by my PMI colleague Ambassador Ranjit Rae. Given the potential for business, the need for a direct air link was emphasized by them. The programme included a visit to the War Remnants Museum (earlier named War Crimes Museum) and to the amazing subterranean network of the 200-km Cu Chi tunnels that were used with great effect in the war against the Americans. One member of my delegation, Rajya Sabha Member Bhagat Singh Koshyari (now Governor of Maharashtra) was courageous enough to enter the tunnel network!

◆

The visit to Tajikistan and Uzbekistan a few months later was a voyage of discovery.

With Tajikistan, besides historic ties and cultural affinities, the relationship was raised to 'strategic partnership' level during Tajik president Emomali Rahmon's 2012 visit to India. In a statement before the visit, I said that:

> One area of common interest between two of us and of high priority is the problem of terrorism emanating from the territory between us and them—which means Pakistan and Afghanistan. Tajikistan has enormous interest in the stability of Afghanistan. We have the same kind of interests, [the] same kind of concerns.

In my talks with President Rahmon, I emphasized India's commitment to our strategic partnership and we agreed to strengthen our relations further in the energy, IT, health and education sectors as well as the establishment of micro industries in Tajikistan. We discussed cooperation on security issues and on countering cross-border terrorism, as also regional security issues, particularly Afghanistan, and agreed that the international community should strengthen Afghanistan's capacity to maintain peace and stability and ensure prosperity of the Afghan people. The programme included visits to the Nurek Hydroelectric Station and the Tajik Technical University. I made a separate visit to the Ayni Air Base, where I met the Indian personnel stationed there.

♦

Equally fascinating and rewarding was the visit to Uzbekistan in May that year. My host was the chairman of the Senate. The substantive discussions were with the long-serving president, Islam Karimov, whose opening remarks were: 'We have known you for centuries and the Chinese for seven decades; yet, where are the Indians?' He spoke at some length about the regional situation and Afghanistan and, given the common border and ethnic ties, about the need for stability there, particularly in the wake of the US withdrawal from there. He recalled his last visit to India two years earlier and the affirmations in the Joint Statement on strategic partnership.

Two places of historic significance were included in the programme. The first was Samarkand and its Shah-i-Zinda complex, the mausoleum of Amir Timur (despite an Indian's memory of his carnage), the Registan Square and the Bibi Khanum Madrassa. Each is reflective of the grandeur of that age. The second was Bokhara and the monuments there: the Samani Mausoleum, the Pa-i-Kalan minaret and mosque complex, the Mir-i-Arab Madrasa and the Khwaja Bahauddin Naqshband khanqah and madrasa. The Naqshbandi Sufi order has many followers in the Indian subcontinent. Separately, and in Tashkent, Salma visited the SOS Children's Village of Uzbekistan and the Art Gallery.

♦

Later in the year, in October–November, I visited Peru and Cuba. In Lima, I had bilateral talks with the president of Peru and the vice president, inaugurated the Festival of India and the new Indian Chamber of Commerce (INCHAM). I also visited an archaeological site and museum. A number of agreements were signed. Much to our regret, a visit to the famous historical site of Machu Pichu of the Inca period could not be included in the programme due to shortage of time. The visit, to commemorate the fiftieth anniversary of the establishment of diplomatic relations, concluded with a Joint Statement covering all aspects of the relationship.

◆

The Cuban ambassador had called on me before our departure from Delhi and I had said to her that while I fully appreciated El Comandante Fidel Castro's decision to refrain from meetings with foreign visitors, the Indian tradition of paying respects to elders induces me to make a request for it. A response to this was given to me in an aside by my Cuban counterpart at the end of our formal meeting and before the official lunch he hosted for me and my delegation. Salma and I were accordingly driven in the afternoon to his villa for the 'social call' that lasted for 65 minutes. Mrs Castro and our ambassador to Cuba were present. The 87-year-old comandante appeared to be in good health and talked at some length, and with a good deal of nostalgia, about his visits to Delhi, including the one in 1983 for the NAM summit. He talked about gardening and horticulture. He expressed his concern over the direction of global politics, over the stockpiling of nuclear weapons and failure of nuclear disarmament, and the limitations confronting NAM. It was altogether an enjoyable and historic meeting. Later that afternoon, he sent a bunch of photographs taken during the meeting.

I opened the Cultural Festival of India and witnessed the Canon Ceremony of an earlier age. An MoU on cooperation between Prasar Bharati and the Cuban Radio and Television Institute was signed.

The delivery of passenger buses promised to Havana authorities—

an important ingredient in the bilateral programme—remained unfulfilled for reasons that, to me at least, remained inexplicable.

◆

On the way back to New Delhi, I stopped over in London for a day to fulfil a commitment. Dr Farhan Nizami of the Oxford Centre for Islamic Studies had invited me some time back to speak at the centre. I availed of it on this occasion. The theme of my lecture was *Identity and Citizenship: An Indian Perspective*.

◆

The 2014 general election and the installation of the NDA government under PM Modi witnessed a number of high-level visits to New Delhi. Among them was the foreign minister of China who, besides felicitating the new government, brought an invitation for the President of India to attend a Trilateral Summit of China, India and Myanmar to mark the sixtieth anniversary of Panchsheel in the last week of June. Since the president was unable to accommodate this in his programme, Foreign Minister Sushma Swaraj requested me to deputize. Since I already had a pending invitation from the Vice President of the People's Republic of China, I said I would undertake it provided the multilateral visit could be distinct from the normal bilateral one. Our Chinese hosts were agreeable to this.

The four-day visit was a comprehensive one and started with a day in the historic city of Xi'an, where the accompanying delegation and I visited the Great Mosque of Xi'an, the Big Wild Goose Pagoda and the Terracotta Museum. The latter was impressive, but it appeared that additional terracotta figurines were being made and added. I presented an *alfi* Qur'an (each line of the text beginning with the letter 'a') published in India to the Imam of the grand mosque and, in turn, received an exquisitely painted vase with a verse from the Holy Book. The next day, we visited the Great Wall of China before going to Beijing for the formal ceremonies of the Trilateral Summit.

In my speech at the Trilateral Summit Meeting, I said that Panchsheel emanated from the civilizational matrix of Asia and is Asia's contribution towards building a just and democratic international order. It has come to be accepted almost universally by countries and finally by the UN in the conduct of international relations. UN Secretary-General Dag Hammarskjöld described them as 'a reaffirmation of the obligations and aims of the UN'.

The Bandung Conference of Asian–African Nations in 1955 expanded Panchsheel into the Ten Principles of Bandung, whereas the Non-Aligned Nations accepted Panchsheel as the core principles of the NAM at the Belgrade Conference in 1961. During the visit of Chinese Premier Li Keqiang to India in May 2013, India and China decided to mark the sixtieth anniversary of the Five Principles of Peaceful Coexistence in 2014 by designating it as the 'Year of Friendly Exchanges' and it was my privilege to have formally launched the 'Year of India–China Friendly Exchanges' in New Delhi a few months earlier. I expressed my confidence that various programmes under the Year of Friendly Exchanges will help forge a closer and stronger relationship between India and China. I said that the pursuit of world peace is a fundamental tenet of India's foreign policy and it draws inspiration from our ancient civilizational value of considering the world as one family. This shapes and guides our actions in international relations.

I concluded by citing two lines from a poem by Tagore that set the stage for this common endeavour:

In front lies the Ocean
Into that ocean of peace, my friends, let us launch our boats.

The last and the most important engagement of the visit was the call on President Xi Jinping. Substantive policy issues were raised in the discussions. The candid exchange lasted longer than the scheduled 30 minutes.

◆

Two functional one-day visits, to Afghanistan and Saudi Arabia, were made in September 2014 and in January 2015, respectively. The first was to attend the swearing-in ceremony of Afghan President Ashraf Ghani and CEO Dr Abdullah Abdullah. The occasion gave me the opportunity to call on the former president Hamid Karzai and benefit from his reading of the local and regional situation. The visit to Riyadh was to offer condolences to King Salman on the passing away of his predecessor, King Abdullah bin Abdulaziz Al Saud.

◆

In September 2015, I visited the Kingdom of Cambodia and the Lao People's Democratic Republic. The objective was to reaffirm our partnership with these ASEAN countries as part of our Act East Policy. In Cambodia, we visited the famous Angkor Wat temple, where our experts are involved in the conservation and preservation. In Vientiane, we visited the Mekong-Ganga Textile Museum.

◆

My visit to Indonesia in November 2015 was substantive and fruitful in terms of discussions with President Joko Widodo and Vice President Jusuf Kalla on bilateral and regional issues, including regional maritime questions and the challenge of radicalization and terrorism. In this context, the extensive damage caused by the tsunami in northern Sumatra and the area of Aceh and the relief provided by the Gulf countries and its impact on radicalization were mentioned.

I had a separate meeting with Megawati Sukarnoputri, chairperson of PDI–P[165]. She recalled the long history of exchanges with India and suggested greater political interaction and more frequent exchanges with MPs.

At my request, our ambassador had arranged a separate meeting with a 'civil society' delegation consisting of senior leaders of a very influential Muslim organization. In demographic terms, Indonesia is

---

[165]Indonesian Democratic Party of Struggle (PDI-P), Indonesian Partai Demokrasi Indonesia-Perjuangan.

the largest Muslim society in the world, with India being second or third. I opined that Islam is not synonymous with Arabs since around 60 per cent of the Muslims of the world live in non-Arab Asia-Pacific countries and that Muslim perceptions on contemporary happenings assume an importance that cannot be ignored. The happenings in the Arab world have their own geopolitical background and impulses and that experience cannot be generalized. Speaking of India, I said that the Indian experience is *sui generis* and has left its imprint on all aspects of Indian history, culture and day-to-day life. This is equally true of the Indonesian experience. Both suggest that moderation and accommodation need to be projected, particularly to the younger generation, as a relevant response to radical ideologies.

The last day of the visit was to Bali and its unique cultural heritage. A volcanic eruption in a neighbouring island and the closure of the airport compelled us to extend our stay there by a day and put off a scheduled visit to Brunei Darussalam. I telephoned my host, Vice President Kalla, and told him to pray for an early end to our predicament. He said that he will proceed to the mosque straight away and do so!

◆

In December 2015, I visited Ashgabat to represent India at the ground-breaking ceremony in Tajikistan of the TAPI pipeline. At a well-organized function, the leaders present were asked to pour cement into the foundations and sign symbolically on one segment of the pipeline. Standing next to PM Nawaz Sharif, I said, 'This is historic,' upon which he said in Urdu, 'Does it mean we have become history?' Given the troubles in Afghanistan, the prospect of this project being realized remains remote.

◆

The deferred visit to Brunei Darussalam on account of the volcanic eruption around Bali took place in the first fortnight of February 2016 along with the visit to Thailand. My talks with the Sultan and the Crown Prince were focused on a reaffirmation of ties bilaterally and within the ASEAN framework.

In an address at the University of Brunei Darussalam, I said that India was among the first countries to welcome Brunei in the comity of nations when it gained full independence in 1984. Since then, we have shared warm and friendly relations. The visit of His Majesty to India in 1992 and 2008, and again in 2012 for the ASEAN–India Commemorative Summit held in New Delhi, helped strengthen our ties and my visit was a reaffirmation of the importance that India accords to its relations with Brunei and our keen desire to further deepen and intensify them.

India is grateful for the assistance and cooperation that has been extended by Brunei for India's space programmes through the Telemetry Tracking and Telecommand Station of the Indian Space Research Organisation in Brunei. The station was a crucial component in India's spectacular success in deploying Mangalyaan in orbit around Mars. We look forward to continuing our cooperation in this area. The 10,000 strong Indian community of professionals such as doctors, engineers, entrepreneurs, teachers and skilled personnel are contributing to the economy of Brunei.

◆

In Bangkok, I had interesting and substantive discussions with PM Prayuth Chan-ocha individually and at delegation level. Given the historical and cultural linkages, our relationship has been strong and multidimensional, with high-level exchange of visits at reasonably frequent intervals. Our Look East and Act East policies have added impetus to these exchanges.

The Bangkok programme included visits to the temples of the Reclining and Emerald Buddha and a meeting with Princess Maha Chakri Sirindhorn, renowned for her interest in Indian culture. Scholars of Indology, in a separate meeting, articulated with much justice the point that the Indian interest in Indology in Thailand is not reciprocated by similar studies in India of Thai culture.

In a lecture at Chulalongkorn University on *India, Thailand and ASEAN: Contours of a Rejuvenated Relationship*, I spoke of the need to synergize bilateral and regional commercial and economic ties. I also stressed on the need to encourage our private sectors to make investments in infrastructure and manufacturing sectors in each other's country and for this the two governments are willing to provide a predictable and comprehensive legal and taxation framework. There is also tremendous potential for enhancing our bilateral defence ties. India places ASEAN at the core of the Act East Policy and at the centre of our dream of an Asian century. There is a special emphasis on India–ASEAN cooperation in our domestic agenda on infrastructure, manufacturing, trade, skills, urban renewal, smart cities and Make in India programmes. Connectivity projects, cooperation in science and technology development and people-to-people exchanges are to be the springboard for regional integration and co-prosperity.

This trident of commerce, culture and connectivity defines the future focus areas of cooperation between ASEAN member states and India. Science, technology and innovation constitute a vital pillar of India–ASEAN cooperation. It is evident that a stronger ASEAN–India partnership would give us a stronger voice on global governance issues. The time is ripe for our common engagement to bring greater equity into the international order. ASEAN members and India have similar aspirations to have an open trading system through global organizations such as the World Trade Organization. We have also shown a strong commitment, based on the principle of common but differentiated responsibility, as we take up our own role to address issues related to climate change. We are also together in the efforts for reforming the UN, particularly its Security Council. The role and composition of the UNSC need to reflect the requirement of developing countries to have a greater say in decision-making. India has a shared vision for a peaceful region and the seas around us. We believe that all trade routes and sea lanes must be protected from traditional and non-traditional threats and all countries using these international waters must act with responsibility and restraint. As the countries in the ASEAN region strive for greater economic integration, the safety of sea lanes—critical for maritime trade and commerce, maritime security, and access to marine resources in accordance with accepted international norms, continue to assume greater significance.

The evolving situation in the South China Sea demands restraint from all parties. We support collective efforts by ASEAN member states and China to conclude the Code of Conduct to keep peace and stability in the region. Non-traditional threats such as piracy, smuggling, transnational crimes and drug-trafficking are on the rise and pose a challenge for our countries and require strong, determined and coordinated action to control. The spreading tide of extremism and terrorism is a threat we both face. Dealing with such threats successfully requires strong cooperation among like-minded partners. Thailand and India already have a robust cooperation in this area and I am glad that we have also taken steps to institutionalize such cooperation at the regional level.

Thus, the rationale for a strong ASEAN–India Strategic Partnership is clearer than ever. As in the distant past when countries in this region and India shared robust trade links for mutual benefit and prosperity, today they have again emerged as key drivers of economic growth for the Asia-Pacific, and, indeed, the world. Together, India and South East Asia constitute a community of 1.9 billion people, representing one-fourth of humanity and account for a combined GDP of $4.75 trillion; it is therefore only natural that they would work towards a qualitatively more substantive and invigorated relationship.

◆

My visit to Morocco and Tunisia in May 2016 was a follow-up to the government's initiative in the earlier India–Africa Summit. The first destination was also a journey down memory lane, having spent some time as a young diplomat in Rabat, where our first child was born. My host was PM Abdelilah Benkirane, and Mrs Benkirane took the trouble of identifying the nursing home of Salma's confinement, now headed by the daughter of the gynaecologist concerned.

My delegation was informed at a late stage that King Mohammad VI was unwell and in France for treatment. Official delegation-level talks took place with the PM and separate calls were made by the foreign minister, the speaker of the House of Representatives, and the president of the House of Councillors. The PM and I jointly launched the India–Morocco Chamber of Commerce. A separate meeting was arranged in an institution where Imams and intellectuals from Morocco and some neighbouring African countries are trained in what was termed 'moderate Islam'.

The Mohammed V University, Rabat, conferred a honoris causa on me. The subject of my address was *Accommodating Diversity in a Globalizing World: The Indian Experience.* Referring to cultural links dating back to Ibn Battuta, I observed that the terms 'Arab' and 'Islam' are not synonymous since out of a global Muslim population of 1.9 billion in 2010, about 60 per cent are in the Asia-Pacific region, 17.3 per cent in Sub-Saharan Africa and only 15 per cent in the Arab world. Consequently, efforts to ascertain Muslim perceptions on contemporary happenings cannot ignore the trends of thought in non-Arab segments. In this, India remains *sui generis* since Indian Muslim numbers and their long history of interaction with the majority of people of other faiths—at times as rulers, at others as subject, and now as citizens—bear the impact in varying degrees of local surroundings in manners and customs. In turn, the impact of Muslim influence on Indian thought and practices is evident and has been written about by travellers down the ages. I concluded by asserting that the challenge for the modern world is to accept diversity as an existential reality and to configure attitudes and methodologies for dealing with it. In developing such an approach, the traditional virtue of *tolerance* is desirable but insufficient and the effort, thinking and practice have to look beyond it and seek *acceptance* of diversity as a civic virtue. We in India are attempting it but cannot yet say that we have succeeded; we invite all right-minded people to join us in this endeavour.

The visit concluded with a day's visit to Marrakesh to see its mosques, gardens, marketplaces and Berber horsemen. It was an enjoyable and worthwhile distraction.

◆

Tunisia has been for long at the forefront of political perceptions in the Arab world and I looked forward to this visit to get some insight into it. An area of specific interest is the deepening of Indian investment in the phosphate sector in Tunisia. Apart from the call on President Beji Caid Essebsi and official meetings with PM Habib Essid, the signing of agreements and the meeting of the Tunis-India Parliamentary Group, the rewarding part of the visit was a meeting with Cheikh Rachid Ghannouchi, the leader of the Ennahda Party that espouses Islamist ideology. He had spent many years in exile in London, had done some thinking on basic issues and written in an essay two decades earlier that 'one of the great accomplishments of secularism is the space it provides for pluralism and a reasonable degree of coexistence... A democratic secular system of government is less evil than a despotic system of government that claims to be Islamic'.[166] Ghannouchi gave me a sober and candid assessment of the difficulties Tunisia faced and of the difficulties that lay ahead. He was critical of both Libya and Algeria for creating an untenable security situation by encouraging radical elements in their own societies to transit Tunisia on their way to southern Europe.

I was invited to address the Tunisian Institute for Strategic Studies. I spoke on *India and the World* and cited Kofi Annan's observation that human security can no longer be understood in purely military terms and must cover economic development, social justice, environmental protection, democratization, disarmament

---

[166]Rachid Al-Ghannouchi, 'Secularism in the Arab Maghrib,' in Azzam Tamimi and John L. Esposito (ed.), *Islam and Secularism in the Middle East* (London, 2000) p. 123.

and respect for human rights and the rule of law. I added that the traditional security architecture has been slow to respond to the new realities in the world that tend to undermine the nation state and create friction between neighbouring countries. India is not a rejectionist power that stands outside the global order; instead, its interests lie in working to change, reform and improve the global order. This demands external engagement within the ambit of a non-intrusive policy. Terrorism has emerged as a principal global challenge and can only be defeated by organized international action.

On bilateral relations, and given our long history of friendship and similarities of approach on many issues, India sees Tunisia as a locus for production of pharmaceuticals and generic medicines at affordable costs and as a hub for our trade with both Europe and Africa.

I was able to see my old friend Ambassador Ahmad Ounaies, whom I knew well when he represented his country in Delhi in the early 1980s.

We visited the ruins of Carthage. I could not help but recall my St Xavier's readings of ancient history, on how an imperial tussle resulted in the destruction of a civilization.

◆

A two-day visit to Mongolia to represent India in the Eleventh ASEM Summit gave me a glimpse into a land I had read much about but never visited. Apart from vast open spaces, the most visible entity everywhere is the legendry national hero, Genghis Khan. In the city of Ulaanbaatar, local tourism offers 'Genghis Khan Tours' to tourists.

The bilateral element consisted of calls on the president, the PM and Speaker of Parliament as also a visit to the Pethub Buddhist monastery, where I unveiled a statue of Mahatma Gandhi.

An ASEM Village had been created for the conference. Delegates were also taken to a Nomadic Festival, where traditional wrestling and horse-riding skills were displayed. At the end of the function, each leader of delegation was presented with a Mongolian pony and requested to name it. I named mine 'All-Done'—an expression used a few weeks earlier by our youngest grandson! I requested our ambassador to take care of the gift and on return to Delhi requested PM Modi to have the pony brought to India and added to the collection of breeds in the President's Bodyguard.

A useful addition to my collection of books was a gift received in Ulaanbaatar—a deluxe edition of *The Secret History of the Mongols*. It records towards the end and in a matter-of-fact way that 'having destroyed the Tangut people—maimed and tamed, they are no more because they gave their word but did not keep it—Cinggis Qa'an came back and in the Year of the Pig (1227) ascended to Heaven.' (The sequence of events of that carnage, historians now tell us, was somewhat different but made no difference to the gory end).

◆

A long way from home was the journey to Venezuela in September 2016 to represent India in the seventeenth summit of NAM countries. On account of the local security situation, the venue of the meeting was Margarita Island off the coast of Caracas. PM Modi's decision not to attend this meeting was the subject of some adverse commentary in our media and the view was expressed that 'India is slowly but surely veering away from the principles of non-alignment that defined its foreign policy for more than four decades after independence'.[167]

I found the Venezuelan president, Nicolás Maduro, an engaging personality and had an interesting discussion with him on the politics of the region. He seemed to be confident about containing the turmoil in his own country.

Our statement at the plenary was along standard lines except for the absence of the traditional paragraph on Palestine. On enquiry, I was told that this was on instructions and was without prejudice to bilateral commitments to the Palestinian Authority.

◆

---

[167] John Cherian, 'NAM Summit: Bye-bye Nam?' *Frontline*, 14 October 2016.

My visit to Nigeria and Mali in September was part of the government's Africa Initiative. Nigeria is our biggest trading partner in Africa and also a major source of energy. It has a large and prosperous Indian trading community and has, for decades, benefited from Indian experts in different fields, including teachers and medical personnel. In West Africa, over a hundred Indian companies have made Nigeria the base of their operations. Many new areas of bilateral cooperation have been identified and Nigeria has also shown interest in our space programme. Indian assistance was availed of by Nigeria in the establishment of its higher defence training institutions and many senior officers of its armed forces have attended courses in our National Defence College.

Apart from my meetings with President Muhammadu Buhari and other senior dignitaries, I addressed the National Defence College in Abuja and spoke on national security in any modern state, the changing nature of security threats in different segments of society and of the response patterns. This task of defining and implementing a security paradigm is far more challenging in democratic, pluralistic, developing societies with heterogeneous populations having diversity of religion, ethnicity and language, each having its own common denominator. The challenge then is to establish the credibility and legitimacy of the state and its institutions, with an ability to resolve aberrations in a transparent and just fashion.

In Lagos, I had a useful meeting with the Indian business community settled there. I was invited to address the University of Lagos and I spoke on the *Legacy of the Indian Freedom Movement*, which provides one of the few instances of a colonial, exploitative and tyrannical political system being successfully and peacefully replaced and transformed. It offers the only valid case where state power was not seized in a single historical movement of revolution but through prolonged popular struggle of a moral, political and ideological level; where reserve of counter hegemony was built up through progressive stages; where phases of struggle alternated with 'passive' phases. The Indian national movement provides one of the few instances of a colonial, exploitive and tyrannical political system being successfully and peacefully replaced and transformed. One of its lasting legacies was the rise of Indian nationalism and the creation of an Indian identity.

The visit to Mali was the first ever by a senior Indian personality. In an address to the National Assembly, I recalled President Ibrahim Boubacar Keïta's visit to India for participating in the third India–Africa Forum Summit. I said that the sense of political affinity and solidarity between India and Africa dates back to many decades when both were involved in a struggle to regain their freedom. The purpose of that day's talk however was not recounting the past but identifying a vision for the future that is peaceful and prosperous, a future where both would stand shoulder to shoulder claiming their rightful destinies and justice for our people. Ours is not a transactional relationship. Ours is a two-way street. India's development partnership is centred on human resource development and establishment of institutions that in turn are creating skills and capabilities in Africa including in areas such as agriculture, food processing, textiles and small industries to expand exports. We are confident that with its sagacious leadership, abundant natural resources and its talented youth, Africa is well on its way to realize the vision of *Agenda 2063: The Africa We Want*. In this journey, India will be there as a friend and privileged partner to share our experience and resources to support African nations in whatever manner they want.

As two countries that have demonstrated our commitment to democratic values, we share unique bonds of trust and mutual understanding. We see ourselves as partners in Mali's economic development and growth. The GoI has extended seven lines of credit worth $353 million to Mali and a large project of $150 million for power transmission connecting Bamako and Sikasso via Bougouni is being finalized. We are looking forward to enhancing our cooperation in cultural and educational sectors. We condemn the destruction of heritage sites and places of immense cultural value to entire humankind by extremists and are ready to support Mali's effort to revive and restore the rich glory of Timbuktu.

◆

In October, I travelled to Hungary and Algeria. In Budapest, discussions with PM Viktor Orbán focused on terrorism and we were in agreement that the setting up of a global legal framework was necessary for sustained action to eliminate this scourge. On the situation within the European community, my host expressed his disquiet and said that 'Brussels has been taken over by anarchists'. Referring to the events in his country in 1956, he lavished praise on the role of the then Indian Charge d'Affairs M.A. (Ishi) Rahman and said, 'Hungary cannot forget either him or Nehru, who advocated the Hungarian cause in the United Nations. It was a friendly gesture we can never forget.' I told him that as a young diplomat I had worked with Ambassador Rahman.

In a lecture at Corvinus University, I referred to the work of Hungarian Indologists and particularly of Alexander Cosma de Koros and of his association with the Asiatic Society, Kolkata, and of his tomb in Darjeeling. The bulk of my talk was on *The Achievement and Challenges of Indian Democracy* and the mechanics of its functioning. In conclusion, I mentioned a paradox confronting us: 'That while public participation in the electoral exercise has noticeably improved, public dissatisfaction from the functioning of elected bodies is breeding cynicism with the democratic process itself.'

I visited the nearby town of Balatonfüred, which honours and remembers its most famous visitor, Rabindranath Tagore and has a Tagore promenade in a lakeside public park. I laid a wreath at this monument.

◆

For a fleeting moment, I was torn between the past and the present when our plane touched down at Algiers International Airport, because in the original scheme of things, I should have touched the soil of Algiers late in the year 1962! Since then I had kept alive my interest in the developments in that land, in the struggle against French colonialism, the role of Algeria in NAM, and in the more recent domestic developments. The Algerian struggle was in many ways unique because it involved a whole people. This was reflected in the subsequent political tussles and the accompanying bloodshed.

After the wreath laying at the Cemetery of the Martyrs, I had useful meetings with the presidents of the National Assembly and the Council of Nations. The discussions with the PM were focused on bilateral cooperation. Mansukh L. Mandavia, the Accompanying MoS, was able to have some focused discussion with his Algerian counterpart on the setting up of a joint project using Algeria's vast reserves of phosphates for the manufacture of fertilizers.

I called on the ailing president Abdelaziz Bouteflika, who communicated in whispers through a special device and a special translator. I was advised to stay no longer than a few minutes; he however insisted on talking for over 20 minutes and recalled events in the long and very cordial Indo-Algerian relationship.

We visited a few Roman ruins in the vicinity of Algiers city but logistics came in the way of a visit to the historic city of Tlemcen. On her visit to an orphanage and other places, Salma was accompanied by Mrs Houda Feraoun, the minister of posts and information. She spoke a good deal about the role of women in the Algerian freedom movement and about the ongoing struggle with Islamist forces trying to bring in regulatory constraints.

◆

In February 2017, I visited Rwanda and Uganda, two landlocked East African countries with whom our relations at the levels of the African Union, the Regional Economic Communities and at the bilateral level have substance. Both our engagements are response based and focused on developing capabilities and human capital. Both are part of our government's Africa Initiative.

After independence, Rwanda had a tumultuous past with internecine civil war, resulting in ethnic cleansing on a massive scale. International intervention and the Arusha Accords helped resolve it to some extent, but the process of recovery and national reconciliation took some time. Our programme in Kigali included a visit to the Genocide Memorial.

Salma and I were keen to see the mountain gorillas in one of the national parks but time, logistics and security requirements came in the way. We were left to satisfy our curiosity with a small-scale replica available in the hotel.

In Kampala, where I had made a transit visit in July 2011 on the way to Juba, discussions with President Yoweri Museveni and his colleagues were useful. Bilateral political and commercial relations are now substantive and the fairly large Indian community there is now fully involved in developmental activities in different walks of life. The Speaker of Parliament, Rebecca A. Kadaga, gave us a detailed briefing on the role of women in Ugandan politics; separately, Salma had an interesting meeting with Mrs Janet Museveni about the work she is doing in social work and on the issue of HIV/AIDS in Uganda.

•

The last in the series of visits beyond the shores of India was in the last week of April 2017 to Armenia and Poland. The programme in Yerevan, apart from official discussions with the president and foreign minister, included a visit to the Genocide Memorial, a lecture in the university, a visit to the Institute of Saved Manuscripts and a meeting with the Patriarch and Catholicos of All Armenians. I mentioned to the latter my Calcutta connection and my recollection of Armenian churches, and the contribution of Armenians to our trade and commercial activities.

I had interesting discussions with Foreign Minister Edward Nalbantian, who accompanied me on my visits to different places. He conveyed some interesting perception on regional problems, including the long-standing one with Turkey.

My lecture at the Yerevan State University, apart from a passing reference to the work by Armenian scholars in and on India and the role of an Armenian by the name of Sarmad in medieval Indian Sufism, was focused on the theme of *The World of Tomorrow* in the context of the recent and pending challenges to human security emanating from what an observer has called 'systematic vulnerability to unregulated greed'. These are suggestive of failure of governance at national and global levels and to the need to rethink the parameter for the future. From this emerges the need to rethink the challenge of emerging imperatives at both technological and socio-political levels.

◆

From Yerevan to Warsaw was a short hop. The programme covered all the essential ingredients, including a visit to the Museum of the Warsaw Uprising and a meeting with the business community. A suggestion for a visit to Gdańsk and a meeting with Lech Wałęsa was not encouraged. I spoke at Warsaw University and had a Q&A with the audience. The subject of my talk was *Seven Decades of Indian Democracy*, focusing on our experience with its principles, the mechanisms and the challenges posed.

◆

Scheduling difficulties came in the way of what would have been my last foreign visit, to the UAE in May, at the personal invitation of the Crown Prince of Abu Dhabi, with whom I had shared, on his official visit to India in January 2017, my personal recollections of conversations as an ambassador with his father, Sheikh Zayed Bin Sultan Al Nahyan.

PUBLIC ADDRESSES

An observer of public debate had written that the Vice Presidency offers a formidable pulpit that can be made use of. I did so in good measure. University convocations, memorial lectures and anniversaries gave me, with a certain regularity, opportunities to think aloud on matters of public interest and communicate particularly with the younger generation that was leaving the portals of academia and stepping into life and its challenges. These numbered over 500, and ranged from polity, governance, rule of law, security, human rights, religious harmony and secularism, minority issues, foreign policy, culture and gender issues. In selecting the theme of a speech, my approach, most of the time, was to focus on challenges we as a society faced or are likely to face in the foreseeable future. I found a resonance of my approach in a remark of the late B.G. Verghese, that timeless India is being born anew and needs 'new instrumentalities of communication, education, institutions and policies to help negotiate the country's myriad diversities in the years ahead'.

At the risk of abruptness, I have sought to record the gist of some of these speeches in the succeeding paragraphs. Those made during foreign visits have been mentioned in that section.

♦

Jamia Millia Islamia, New Delhi, invited me (in October 2007) to address its convocation. I spoke of the twin challenges of conformity and dissent in the origins of Jamia Millia and of tradition and modernity in the lives of Muslims in India and said the model was embodied in Dr Abid Hussain's expression *insaan-e-kamil, sachcha Musalaman aur pucca Hindustani* (complete human being, true Muslim and confirmed Indian). This, while it settled the core of Indianness of Indian Muslims, kept alive the need to balance the imperatives of identity with the ability to conduct an authentic dialogue with fellow citizens in a secular society and to cope with the ever-changing pattern of life's requirements through the Islamic concepts of Ijtihad and Maslaha and the relevant experience of Muslim communities elsewhere. I said that despite the quantification of the extent of social backwardness, the community effort to ameliorate it has remained confused and inadequate. The way out, I suggested, is to reinvigorate the traditional practice of charity through focused philanthropy and impart a new dynamism to the management of the very considerable resources available in Awqaf (religious endowments).

◆

A few days later, while addressing the convocation of the Indian Law Institute, New Delhi, I dwelt on the imperatives of Rule of Law and on Prof. Upendra Baxi's view that our constitutional perception of it links the four core notions of rights, development, governance and justice, as also on the Supreme Court's 1996 ruling that it 'is a potent instrument of social justice to bring about equality in result'. This ideal, I opined, is falling short in practice due to what Attorney-General Goolam Vahanvati had termed 'cancerous development' in each of the principal institutions of the polity, giving substance to Ambedkar's apprehension about 'a life of contradictions' and its threat to the structure of democracy. This unravelling of the social consensus anticipated by Ambedkar has come about on account of the inequalities of the growth process and a balkanization of the mind. I recalled John Adam's premonition about the propensity of democracies to 'commit suicide'. The corrective would, therefore, lie in developing a new consensus on the imperatives of entitlement and empowerment, translating each into state policies and developing the resolve to implement them and a commitment from the media and the civil society to uphold the Rule of Law.

◆

My effort in the IDSA Foundation Day Lecture (October 2007) was to shift the focus from the traditional, state-centric concept to that of comprehensive human security, where protection of individuals from all forms of violence, hunger and disease, is critical if the discourse in a globalizing world is to evolve and progress. We need to constantly remind ourselves that the primary purpose of conducting foreign policy, and of the effort to 'promote international peace and security' and 'maintain just and honourable relations between nations', is to do it in the interest of the People of India. The umbilical cord linking domestic and foreign policy and conditioning all aspects of the security perspective is the complexity of the Indian reality, particularly in its economic, sociological and human dimensions. The sources of strength and weakness of this reality need to be kept in mind by scholars devoting themselves to national security studies.

◆

In the P.N. Haksar Memorial Lecture in Chandigarh (November 2007), I dwelt on Haksar's theme of 'holding aloft the banner of the moral universe' since this along with ecological balance 'are conditions precedent to survival and growth not only of India, but of this entire earth'. The challenge for India, according to Haksar, is:

> To use its material, intellectual and cultural resources to regenerate itself into a true, free, just and humane society and simultaneously to strive for a similar world society. The two are different aspects of the same objective, for a humane and peaceable India is not possible if it lives in an aggressive world atmosphere.

I drew attention of the audience to Gandhi's depiction of the Seven Social Sins inscribed on the tablet at Rajghat and said that there is need for a unified concept applicable to individuals and institutions and also for states within their domestic jurisdiction and in their dealings with other states. In actual practice, however, moral and legal deterrence is almost non-existent.

I referred to successive reports of the Ethics Committee of the Rajya Sabha and to their disappointing conclusion that 'ethical questions are mainly matters of one's conscience' and therefore cannot be dealt entirely by legislation. It should, nevertheless, be the duty of the state and the civil society to be proactive in jostling public behaviour because only then would the moral realm in public life become meaningful and make the India of the future truly free, just and humane.

◆

The Fourteenth All India Whips Conference in Mumbai (February 2008) gave me the opportunity to dwell on the effectiveness of the functioning of our parliamentary institutions, cite data on the declining number of sittings, on the bills passed, on the time spent on their scrutiny and the time lost in disruptions. I opined that 'the instrumentalities at the disposal of our legislatures have either been blunted or become dysfunctional'. The single most important issue of concern today is the decreasing credibility of legislatures as an effective institution capable of delivering public good and contributing to the effective formulation of laws and public policy. I referred to Ambedkar's caution that:

> The working of the Constitution does not depend wholly upon the nature of the Constitution (since) the factors on which the working of those organs of the State depends are the people and the political parties they will set up as their instruments to carry out their wishes and their politics. Who can say how the people of India and their parties will behave?

◆

The pursuit of the ideal of world peace in an otherwise conflict-ridden world of our times was taken up in the D.D. Kosambi Memorial Lecture in Goa (February 2008). I cited Robert Fisk's observation that governments 'want their people to see war as a drama of opposites, good and evil, "them" and "us", victory or defeat. But war is primarily not about victory or defeat but about death and the infliction of death. It represents the total failure of the human spirit'. The challenge then is to see if a war can be waged against war and can be addressed only by admitting the impracticability of war in the nuclear age in which, as per the IAEA chief Dr Mohamed ElBaradei's prediction, 'soon there could be 30 nuclear weapon states on the horizon'. Humankind therefore has to demonstrate that peace is good in both value and practical terms as a pre-requisite for development as also for equality, justice and democracy. The strategic paradigm, as hitherto understood, offers no escape from the possibility of states resorting to war. This necessitates a qualitatively different approach if perpetual peace is to be made a human objective.

Experience indicates that competitive security results in confrontation and conflict. The new paradigm of human existence has to be premised on comprehensive and cooperative security, covering both conventional and non-conventional security. The intensity of conflicts can be controlled and lessened through a globally applicable scheme of disarmament beginning with nuclear disarmament.

The requisite accommodation would require a point of reference, a principle that can help reconcile differences and disagreements and impede their aggravation. Such a principle can only be based on the concept of justice. A global society based on justice has no place for war since both greed and aggression would be curtailed by its operative principle. The actualization of such an objective cannot be left solely to state action and must involve active participation of 'other stakeholders' in civil society.

Such an approach, far from being utopian, must be shown to be good in value terms as also in practical terms since war can be demonstrated to be genuinely harmful. Thus Kosambi's vision that peace was a pre-requisite for development and that true peace required true democracy where all human beings are equal. The struggle for world peace must therefore be a quest for equality, justice and democracy. The modalities of furthering it would inevitably be conditioned by public awareness and public action.

♦

The D.P. Kohli Memorial Lecture of the CBI (April 2008) was focused on 'The Enemy Within: Corruption, Development and Governance' and dwelt on governance as an aspect of non-military security and the adverse impact of endemic corruption. The question then is whether we consider challenges to governance to be equally threatening to our chosen way of life, as enunciated in the Constitution.

The interaction between polity and economy reflects on governance in its totality. In public perception, one major factor of debility in governance is corruption, defined as 'behaviour by a public servant, whether elected or appointed, which involves a deviation from his or her formal duties because of reasons of personal gain to himself or herself or to other private persons with whom the public person is associated'. Independent studies undertaken by Transparency International India and other civil society or professional groups support this perception.

Corruption is pervasive, cancerous and multidimensional. In its moral dimension, it impacts the foundations of the social and political fabric of society and increases injustice; in its legal implications, it results in disregard for the rule of law; in its developmental aspect, it tends to distort the decision-making processes on investment projects and other commercial transactions and is wasteful of resources. It is more than an irritant or growth retardant; it has emerged as a significant national security threat. The creeping assault of corruption on the national fabric has shaken the legitimacy of the Indian state.

In a democracy, political corruption becomes the most lethal and damaging form of corruption. The quality and integrity of the political representative, therefore, becomes a matter of critical relevance for its functioning.

The conclusion that corruption hampers governance and development and that it constrains the progress of Indian society is unavoidable. Since it impacts all aspects of state activity, it becomes the most important threat to the state, more so because it is less visible than the external enemy.

The imperative for correctives is evident. A 2008 UNDP report has estimated that if corruption levels are reduced to those of Scandinavian countries, investment in India would increase by 10 per cent and the GDP growth by 1.5 per cent. The bar of integrity has to be raised. Beyond the framework of law enforcement, civil society, NGOs and community-based organizations must be harnessed in raising awareness. The Right to Information Act, PIL and a few steps taken by the CVC has helped the process. So has the use of IT and e-governance.

In the political realm, the question goes beyond the individual legislator and relates to the functioning of the political system, the money flows to political parties and individuals, the funding of elections, the phenomenon of 'vote buying', and the practices through which private and corporate interests extract illicit gains from the system in its totality.

In the final analysis, national institutions for governance and for fighting crimes against it sustain their legitimacy by responding meaningfully to the public's desire for clear, effective and transparent governance. Failure to do so in adequate measure would corrode public confidence, breed cynicism and would be altogether harmful to the Republic and its democratic principles. This is the challenge that a premier institution such as the CBI has to address.

♦

In the Foundation Day Lecture at the Rajiv Gandhi Centre for Contemporary Studies in Mumbai University (March 2008), I referred to Prof. Sunil Khilnani's assertion that 'conflict is written in the idea of India' and despite political unity and unity of the market, the imperatives of ethnicity bring forth a 'balkanization of the mind'. Hence, it becomes the duty of the state to retain its legitimacy by protecting society from multiple threats—physical, internal, ideological, and of resources—and to synchronize multiple impulses.

♦

I chose to speak on the subject of 'Diversity' at the University of Kota Convocation Address (May 2008). I said that the plurality of our society is a fact of life. Democracy and secularism are the result of conscious decisions whose objective is a structure of equality and justice for all so that plurality is allowed to flourish within it. Three questions do pose themselves: how far have we succeeded? What remains to be done? How can others benefit from our experience? Each of the core values of pluralism, democracy and secularism are perceived to be under siege and need to be rejuvenated. Four aspects of pluralism stand out: (i) pluralism involves energetic engagement with diversity; (ii) pluralism is not just tolerance but the active seeking of understanding across lines of difference; (iii) pluralism is not relativism but the encounter of commitments, of holding our deepest difference not in isolation but in relationship to one another; and (iv) pluralism is based on dialogue, on speaking and listening in a process that reveals both common understanding and real difference.

♦

Sir Syed Day is celebrated the world over by the alumni of AMU in memory of the founder and, hopefully, do some introspection and some accountability. This institution came into existence in 1875 in response to a specific need and on the basis of a vision. The centrality of education and of the spirit of rational thinking and scientific enquiry were central to it. The mission succeeded to a point but failed to go beyond it and did not participate in the exciting venture of relevant education in modern India. Reasons for this lie in its (i) failure to appreciate the need for universal education particularly at the primary stage (ii) delay in/failure to appreciate the need for women's education and its relevance for educating new generations (iii) failure to adopt creative ventures in education of other communities independent of government agencies and (iv) failure to appreciate the need for organized philanthropy.

The World Summit of AMU Alumni (October 2008) can become the catalyst for a corrective beginning at the grassroot level. The Aligarh fraternity should propagate the need to inculcate a spirit of competiveness so that maximum benefit is drawn from government scholarship schemes, seek equity (not concessions) from the government and mobilize opinion for channelling income from religious endowments (Awqaf) for educational and professional institutions whose focus at all times should be on quality and relevance.

♦

I was invited to address The Indian Ocean Naval Symposium (February 2008). It was a voluntary initiative that brought together navies of littoral states of the region with the aim of increasing maritime cooperation and enhancing regional security. It has since increased its membership and activities. Earth is a planet of oceans. They constitute 71 per cent of its total area. The Indian Ocean is the third-largest ocean in terms of area but unquestionably the first in terms of its impact on human civilization. It was the mastery of the sea lines of communications that allowed the colonial European powers to dominate the world for several centuries. Today, 95 per cent of the world's trade is conducted through sea and their vulnerability and choke points become a matter of global concern. Apart from the security paradigm, questions of disaster management, oceanic resources and environmental questions become a matter of common concern. Thus, measures to create transparency, confidence-building and security become matters of legitimate concern. The totality of objectives sought to be achieved in the Indian Ocean by the littoral, hinterland and user states can only be achieved through a methodology of cooperation.

India is and will remain a maritime nation, having a coastline of 7,516 km, 27 islands in the Lakshadweep chain and 572 in the Andaman and Nicobar chain, 13 major and 185 minor ports, a merchant shipping fleet and an exclusive economic zone of 2.54 million sq. km. Its security imperatives are thus compelling. It is a UN-recognized pioneer investor in deep-sea mining and participates in bilateral and multilateral disaster management. It is thus well placed to be part of bilateral, non-discriminatory and inclusive regional and multilateral arrangements for maritime security in consonance with international law, respecting the sovereignty of littoral states.

♦

The same month (February 2008), a seminar organized by the Association of Indian Diplomats (AID) gave me the opportunity to spell out my perceptions on India's approach to the Persian Gulf and its littoral states that are in our proximate neighbourhood, within our security parameter, within the operational radius of our navy, being the principal source of hydrocarbon energy and investments, being a principal destination of manpower exports and a major source of their remittances, a major trading partner, a destination for projects and IT services and having Indian-friendly regimes desirous of enhancing bilateral relationship.

The focus on the Indian interest therefore is to develop a policy framework that would sustain and enhance these. It demands a Look West Policy to complement the existing Look East Policy.

◆

Two memorial lectures gave me the opportunity to dwell on some other aspects of national security and intelligence. In the Field Marshal KM Cariappa Memorial Lecture (October 2009), I probed the concept of insecurity to understand it clearly in all its dimensions since without it, our endeavour to craft a comprehensive national security for the world of tomorrow would remain elusive. This is because the emerging dimensions of insecurity and the threat of explosion and implosion induce the imperative of redefining security in terms of the state, the market and civil society. The need for a new approach to comprehensive security is underlined by a survey of both the traditional and non-traditional threats faced by us in the past three decades. The data is in the public domain. It presents a complex picture; it is also indicative of a certain imbalance in our allocation of resources and in the efficacy of their utilization. This suggests a need for correctives directed at capacity-building in societal structures and, in the security framework, a rationalization based on qualitative upgradation and quantitative resizing.

The same challenge, of redefining the objective and the methodology of intelligence, was the theme of the R.N. Kao

Memorial Lecture (January 2010), since the future is unlikely to be like the past and one in which, in Philip Bobbitt's words 'the three certainties about national security—that it is national (not international), that it is public (not private) and that it seeks victory (not stalemate) are about to be turned upside down by the new age of indeterminacy into which we are plunging'. This involves a conceptual shift from threat-based to vulnerability-based strategies and to the ability to assess changes in public consciousness and would in good measure necessitate comprehensive reorientation of the work of the intelligence apparatus.

A particular problem relates to the misuse of intelligence. The intelligence apparatus are not the monopoly of one nation or a set of nations and have led to follies and catastrophes. These together propel thinking in the direction of accountability and necessitate oversight. I urged the need for parliamentary oversight, through a Standing Committee, of intelligence agencies to ensure better accountability, as is the practice in other democracies. Such a body would also function as a surrogate for public opinion and thus facilitate wider acceptance of the imperatives of a situation.

♦

The Indian Institute of Advanced Study, Shimla, invited me to deliver the thirteenth Radhakrishnan Memorial Lecture (November 2009). I devoted it to the role and responsibility of the intellectual in society and to the intellectual's role in creating social consciousness and a sense of responsibility that transcends the limits of the political community. I recalled Radhakrishnan's lecture in 1942, where he said that:

> The final ends of political action are to be considered by the thinker and the writer. In them, society becomes conscious and critical of itself. They are the character of a society. Their business is to educate us to a consciousness of the real self of society and to save guardians of the values of a society, the

values which are the real life and us from spiritual callousness and mental vulgarity.

He had added that:

> The intellectual need not take an active part in politics or in the actual affairs of administration. It is their primary function to serve society with intellectual integrity. They must create social consciousness and [a] sense of responsibility which transcend the limits of the political community. Those who can serve society in this way have a duty not to engage in politics. For every society, there will be a few for whom participation in political activity would be a perversion of genius, a disloyalty to themselves... If the intellectuals abandon the interests of culture, and repudiate the primacy of spiritual values, we cannot blame the politicians who are responsible for the safety of the state.

Where then do we locate the role and responsibility of the intellectual in contemporary India? This is integral to the healthy functioning of a society and as observed by Rajni Kothari, political theorist and writer, the challenge before the intellectual 'is to keep alive the flame of hope and resurgence and to continue offering ideological alternatives to the struggling segments of the mass public'. I amplified this with reference to the role intellectuals have played in the furtherance of this objective with regard to institutions, economic amelioration, corruption, rights and environment. In addition, I drew attention to Edward Said's caution about 'habits of mind' that 'are corrupting': If anything can denature, neutralize, and finally kill a passionate intellectual life, it is the internalization of such habit;' hence the need 'to speak truth to power' and do so by advocating the correct alternative. In doing so, awareness and analysis of the major and minor premises of proposed approaches become unavoidable.

◆

My Khuda Bakhsh Memorial Lecture in Patna (December 2009) focused on the uniqueness of Indian Islam, on the diverse variety of Indian Islamic traditions and on the need to be cautious of generalizations about Indian Muslims. The Indian Muslim community has a long history of interaction both with the external world of Islam as with the larger Indian community. Two questions arise with regard to the latter: are the parameters of interaction frozen in time? Has the community been sufficiently critical and felt the need for newer impulses to respond to the new situation?

The contemporary Indian reality, in the perception of its Muslim citizens, is perceived on the one hand with the benefits of a pluralistic society, a secular polity and a state structure based on the Rule of Law and, on the other, with the shortfalls delineated in the Sachar Committee Report of 2006 and the identified 'inequality traps', resulting in insecurity, frustration and uncertainty emanating from grievances focused on five core issues: security, employment and reservations, Urdu, AMU and Muslim Personal Law.

The correctives, to ensure the national objective of equitable growth, lay partly in action by the state apparatus and also with invigorated inter-community dialogue and a good measure of self-correction, whose shortfalls have tended to freeze the boundaries of diversities, thus resulting in people living together separately. There is, therefore, an urgent need to correct the image, go beyond identity issues, project a more holistic view of Muslims as normal and fellow citizens with the same rights and responsibilities as other citizens, resulting in a genuine dialogue that leads to Gandhi's 'union of hearts'.

◆

I was invited to give the Foundation Day Lecture of the University of Calcutta (December 2010). It was the first of our modern universities; its foundations were laid in January 1857 and were unambiguously linked to a colonial purpose. After Independence, the need to revisit the framework of higher education was acutely felt and several focused efforts were made for this purpose. The most recent of these was the National Knowledge Commission of 2008 that concluded that 'the emerging knowledge society and associated opportunities present a set of new imperatives and new challenges for our economy, polity and society. If we fail to capitalize on the opportunities now, our demographic dividend could well become a liability'.

I said that there are five questions that need to be addressed urgently:

(i) Whether the existing means of instituting new universities are desirable and sustainable;

(ii) Higher education cannot improve in India unless state universities, which are the backbones and represent the bulk of enrolment, are able to obtain greater funds, create new infrastructure and enrich their existing academic programmes. Anecdotal evidence suggests that the budget of one central university is almost the same or more than that of all state universities in some states;

(iii) A significant focus of reform should be the college system, numbering around 26,000 colleges, where most of the enrolment in higher education occurs;

(iv) We need to liberate education from the strict and fragmented disciplinary confines of our formal higher education structures; and

(v) Higher education in our country must be an arena of choice, not of elimination. Increasingly, one notices that entrance and admission criteria and procedures are designed to screen out and eliminate, due to the adverse ratio of demand and availability, especially in disciplines with job potential or where the college or university reputation is likely to be a determining factor in employment. We must create avenues for skills training and vocational education so that entering universities does not become a default choice for the sake of employment, particularly for those who might not have interest in the subject or desire for higher education.

Thus, the entire gamut of issues dealing with the rejuvenation and restructuring of higher education in India is in the public domain for an open policy debate. This is a positive development and must be pursued to its logical conclusion.

◆

I addressed the ninety-third Convocation of the Banaras Hindu University in March 2011 and spoke on 'Nationalism and Internationalism in the World of Tomorrow'. Globalization and interconnectedness, I said, have brought forth a new consciousness that impacts the notion of nationalism, which emerged as a motivating force in the early nineteenth century, expressed itself through the organs of the sovereign state, exalted national interest, provided the glue that made possible the modern state and modern industry, assumed aggressive dimensions and flowed into imperial channels and colonialism. These heightened rivalries and shaped history.

Indian nationalism, however, took shape as the political articulation of anti-colonial consciousness. It was accommodative of diversities and synthesizing, premised on the existential reality of a plural society and manifesting itself in a democratic and secular polity. Our Constitution, therefore, recognizes and amplifies multiple identities—as many as 13—and consciously accommodates them as a distinctive feature of the Indian state and eschews a standardized image of an Indian. So while we subscribe to the political, economic and cultural imperatives of globalization, we contend uneasily with the counter trends (at home and abroad) with homogenizing nationalism that flattens diversities.

◆

'Challenges to a Homeless Language' was the theme of my Nizam Lecture at the University of Delhi in January 2012. It focused on the paradox of the sixth largest language group in the country, with a very rich cultural repertoire, and having 51.5 million speakers, amounting to 5.01 per cent of the population.[168] The census data also showed that this percentage had been 5.25 and 5.18 in 1981 and 1991, respectively. I enquired if this suggested a pattern of language abandonment, particularly in some parts of the country. The reason, I said, was candidly spelt out in PM Nehru's letter of 16 July 1953 to the CMs, wherein he spoke of 'a pettiness in mind, narrowness in outlook and an immaturity' that characterized 'a deliberate attempt to push out Urdu, which is spoken and written by a large number of people'. The net result of such policies was to deny primary stage education in the mother tongue and go against the ethos of linguistic diversity of the Constitution, thus resulting in what Gopi Chand Narang has depicted as 'a patient on oxygen at the fag end of his life'. The question eventually pertains to our perception of Indian pluralism and to the ambit of Indian culture. Is it to be inclusive or exclusive?

The dire need to correct the shortfalls in governmental efforts is one aspect of the matter; another is the individual and community efforts of Urdu speakers and Urdu lovers. Urdu is now an international language and the use of modern technology by bodies such as the Rekhta Foundation is bringing forth very encouraging results.

◆

The theme of my Sardar Patel Memorial Lecture (November 2012) was 'Physical Integration and Emotional Inconsonance'. I premised it on Sardar Patel's remark (recorded by V.P. Menon) that while integration of states has brought about an integrated administrative system, 'the real integration has to take place in the minds of the people' and that would take time. The challenge for the Constitution-makers therefore was to address 'the layered Indianness'; prevent Balkanization; promote emotional unity and the integration of minds and hearts; and suppress the feeling of separatism. This, as a political scientist put it, 'is not a process of conversion of diversities

---

[168] According to the Census of India 2001.

into uniformity but a congruence of diversities leading to a unity in which both the varieties and similarities are maintained'. Some of this was achieved through constitutional arrangements, but the objective of 'fraternity' remains elusive. This has been aggravated by the emergence of what has been called 'multitudinous but hitherto dormant diversities'.

The conclusion that the process of emotional integration is in dire need of reinvigoration is thus unavoidable. A corrective is imperative and would lie in reaffirmation of the democratic process bequeathed to us by the founding fathers, adherence to the letter and spirit of the Constitution, rejuvenation of institutions, beginning with parliament and the state legislatures, and reaffirmation of the sanctity of dialogue. These principles need to be imbibed and implemented at all levels of the polity and particularly in educational policy, in the workshops of the mind that mould the thought process of the citizens of tomorrow.

♦

'Prudence and the Moral Imperative' was my subject for the first G. Parthasarathi Memorial Lecture at JNU (March 2013) in honour of its founding VC, whom one of his successors, President Narayanan, described as 'an undeclared social rebel'. Parthasarathi also contributed in good measure to diplomacy and statecraft. He subscribed to the quest for a cooperative, egalitarian and just world order in which concepts such as 'national interest' should eventually get defined by the conjoint concern of the state, market and civil society. The typology of threat perceptions should accordingly delineate threats emanating from domestic and external origins as also from ideological, territorial and ecological sources. He was a negotiator par excellence, subscribed to the view that negotiations must be conducted without illusions and that in the contemporary world, the challenge is to define options that would enhance our strategic autonomy and maximize our choices. This necessitates the need for the maintenance of domestic power and legitimacy through good governance and accountability.

◆

I spoke on 'Virtue in Public Life' in my Bhimsen Sachar Memorial Lecture (December 2012) and the need for it in public perception. I drew attention to the 2003 UN Convention against Corruption and its somewhat belated ratification by India in 2011. This covenant urges states 'to foster a culture of rejection of corruption'. Its three aspects—propensity, opportunity and scope—have been analysed threadbare in official and civil society reports. The correctives lie in a fourfold approach of (i) training in norms incorporated in legally enforceable Code of Ethics, (ii) comprehensive protection of human rights, (iii) a legal framework and regulatory practices that enforce clash of interest rules, and (iv) laws and procedures that forbid nepotism in all its manifestations.

◆

The 'Scorecard of our Democracy' was the subject of my Ambedkar Memorial Lecture (December 2012). Six decades later, we have to concede that the glass of democracy remains half full. We have practised electoral democracy mechanically, without making it fully representative. Our electoral procedures and practices have accentuated rather than diminished social cleavages. We have yet to succeed in eradicating electoral malpractices. We have allowed money power, in all its manifestations, to distort electoral outcomes. Our political process depicts ideological decadence and a declining observance of constitutional morality. Our society exhibits a disturbing disregard for moral order and public conscience and, in the words of an eminent academic, 'the lines between legality and illegality, order and disorder, state and criminality, have come to be increasingly porous'. Are we then on a slippery slope? There is, clearly an imperative need to rejuvenate our commitment to the values, objectives and the judicious balance of the Constitution.

◆

'Citizen and State Conduct' was the theme of my V.M. Tarkunde Memorial Lecture (November 2014). He was the founder of the Centre for Public Interest Litigation, and a strong advocate of secularism and the philosophy of radical humanism. He highlighted the fragility of individual liberty in the modern state. He kept alive 'the hope of the dawn of a new day' with the 'recognition of the inherent dignity and of the equal and unalterable rights of all the members of the human family as the foundation of freedom, justice and peace in the world' and above all, for his persistent efforts to highlight the fragility of individual liberty in the modern state and in specific cases of injustice. He was a passionate believer in the core values of our Constitution.

The Nandini Sunder case in the Supreme Court (2011) highlighted the imperative of ensuring 'conditions of human dignity within the ambit of fraternity'. Thus, the operative concepts are dignity and equal and unalterable rights to all. Thus Rule of Law becomes a potent instrument of social justice to bring about equality in results. Consequently, a prerequisite of participatory governance is a commitment of the State to its own laws and to their uniform application. As a jurist has put it, 'The Indian constitutional conception of the Rule of Law links its four core notions: rights, development, governance and justice.' This approach has been upheld in judicial pronouncements, with the Supreme Court describing the Rule of Law as 'a potent instrument of social justice to bring about equality in results'.

The obligations of the Republic of India towards its citizens have been stated in the Constitution, particularly in the sections on Fundamental Rights and Directive Principles of State Policy and the Fundamental Duties of Citizens. Together, they amplify the vision and the principles enunciated in the Preamble, namely, to secure to all citizens social, economic and political justice; liberty of thought, expression, belief, faith and worship; equality of status and opportunity; and furthermore to promote among them fraternity, assuring the dignity of the individual and the unity and integrity of the nation.

As against these, the record of the Indian state is to be judged through the annual reports of the MHA and the relevant documentation of the human rights bodies of the UN. The latter, in its 2012 report, noted that despite government initiatives, 'the continued prevalence of human rights violations across the country poses manifold challenges' and 'the ever-growing trend of atrocities against religious minorities, women, children, SCs & STs, apathy towards the disabled and other disadvantaged people, constitute a scar on the face of Indian democracy' and need 'a radical shift in economic, social and security policies both at the central and state level'.

◆

A set of lectures on West Asia allowed me to think aloud about past and more recent happenings in the Arab world. The Maulana Azad Memorial Lecture of the Indian Council for Cultural Relations (November 2014) was focused on a century of pitfalls of Arab nationalism since the Arab Revolt of 1916, the Sykes-Picot Agreement of that year and its commitment to bring into being 'an independent Arab state or a Confederation of Arab States' in the conquered territory of the Ottoman empire and subsequent declarations including the fatal Balfour Declaration, which was described by Arnold Toynbee as 'the winning card' in seeking the support of the Jews and Jabotinsky's depiction of Zionism as 'a colonizing adventure', whose success depended on armed force. These, together, led to the creation of Israel, the wars of 1948, 1956 and 1967, and to the resulting philosophical, political and social critique in Arab societies and the conclusion of nationalist attitudes trapped in the infra-historical rhythm of a dream palace, a romantic and lost past.

◆

The erosion of the legitimacy of the secular nation state bought forth a quest for alternatives. This was the subject of the Asia Centre Lecture, Bangalore, a few months earlier (February 2013).

The despondency of two lost generations, arising from the deficits of freedom, empowerment of women and knowledge, generated a public mood of an imagined past, an ideal of authenticity and an instrument of mobilization rooted in the consciousness of the masses. This brought forth Islamism in various manifestations. Added to this was the military and political turmoil in different countries and concerns about a new sectarian balance. The resulting turmoil took different shapes. In Tunisia, al-Nahda sought to establish institutions that safeguard public debate and electoral choice; it succeeded in good measure. In Egypt, it was the very reverse; the regime of Hosni Mubarak was toppled by a leaderless crowd that reflected the aspirations of all segments of society. The Muslim Brotherhood succeeded in the elections but could not bring the Salafists and the liberal-secularists into the political process. The resultant violence destabilized the Muslim Brotherhood and allowed the military to overthrow it. The counter-revolutionary forces within the region and turmoil in Libya, Yemen and Syria added to the chaos in the whole region.

A third lecture, at an IDSA Conference (January 2016) examined the obstacles to participatory governance in West Asia. The conflicting claims of pan-Arabism on the one hand and local patriotism in essentially tribal societies on the other, created conflicting loyalties in states with fragile institutions that were essentially patriarchal, authoritarian and hegemonic and were characterized by lack of transparency, information scarcity, nepotism, political irresponsibility and absence of Rule of Law. These evoked fear of the state rather than a commitment to its objectives and ideals. Thus, the domestic impulse for social cohesion was insufficiently anchored, did not accommodate diversity in sufficient measure and was susceptible to external pressures. It found reflection in all aspects of governance, which remained essentially non-participatory. The shortfalls in identified human development indices and rapid growth of population, added to these in good measure. The resulting picture at the end of 2015 was one of total disarray.

At the Pune Security conference (December 2015), I focused on the role of the Persian Gulf region in global security and reiterated my February 2008 remarks that inclusive rather than exclusive security is necessary. I also stated that the Indian requirement is fivefold: (i) friendly regimes and stability in the littoral states, (ii) access to the region's oil and gas resources, (iii) freedom of navigation in the Persian Gulf and through the Straits of Hormuz, (iv) security of the sea lanes and (v) continued access to the markets of the littoral states for Indian trade, technology, workforce and two-way investments. At the same time and keeping eventualities in mind, prudence suggests that the creation and reinforcement of an autonomous interdiction capacity geared to India's requirements of free movement of tankers from the region to India, eschew a marginal role in Western security arrangements and lend support, in principle, to inclusive security arrangements that may be proposed.

◆

I was invited to address the fiftieth anniversary of the All India Muslim Majlis-e-Mushawarat. It was formed in 1964 to respond to a perceived need to defend and protect the identity and dignity of the Muslim community in India in terms of the rights bestowed by the Constitution on Indian citizens. I devoted my speech to an assessment of the recent past and to the challenges ahead.

The events of August 1947 had cast a shadow of physical and psychological insecurity on Indian Muslims. They were made to carry, unfairly, the burden of political events and compromises that resulted in the Partition. The process of recovery from that trauma has been gradual and uneven and, at times, painful. Success has been achieved in some measure; much more, however, needs to be done. The Sachar Committee Report delineated the contours of the problem. It laid to rest the political untruth in some quarters about the Muslim condition and demonstrated that on most socio-economic indicators, they were on the margins of structures of political, economic and social relevance and their average condition was comparable to or even worse than the country's acknowledged historically most backward communities, the SCs and STs. It specified the development deficits of the majority of Muslims in regard to education, livelihood and access to public services and the employment market across states. The follow-up assessments of 2008 and 2014 opined that 'a start has been made, yet serious bottlenecks remain'. It became clear from these reports that the problems confronting India's Muslims relate to (i) identity and security, (ii) education and empowerment, (iii) equitable share in the largesse of the state, and (iv) a fair share in decision-making. Each of these is a right of the citizen. The challenge, therefore, is to develop strategies and methodologies to address them.

The default by the state or its agents in terms of deprivation, exclusion and discrimination (including failure to provide security) is to be corrected by the state. Experience shows that the corrective has to be both at the policy and the implementation level; the latter, in particular, necessitates mechanisms to ensure active cooperation of the state governments.

The official objective of *Sab Ka Saath, Sab Ka Vikas* (Together, for everyone's growth, with everyone's trust) is commendable; a prerequisite for this is affirmative action to ensure a common starting point and an ability in all to walk at the required pace. This ability has to be developed through individual, social and governmental initiatives that fructify on the ground. Programmes have been made in abundance; the challenge is their implementation. Equally relevant is the autonomous effort by the community itself in regard to its identified shortcomings. Corrective strategies, therefore, have to be sought on category-differentiation admissible in Indian state practice and hitherto denied to Muslims (SC status) or inadequately admitted (segments of OBC status). Available data makes it clear that a high percentage of Muslims fall into these two broad categories.

It is evident that significant sections of the community remain trapped in a vicious circle and in a culturally defensive posture that hinders self-advancement. Tradition is made sacrosanct, but the rationale of tradition is all but forgotten. It is here that the role of the Mushawarat becomes critical. It should go beyond looking at questions of identity and dignity in a defensive mode and explore how both can be furthered in a changing India and a changing world. It should widen its ambit to hitherto unexplored or inadequately explored requirements of all segments of the community, particularly women, youth and non-elite sections, who together constitute the overwhelming majority. The task in the foreseeable future is a threefold one: to sustain the struggle for the actualization in full measure of legal and constitutional rights, to do so without being isolated from the wider community, and to endeavour, at the same time, to adapt to the thinking and practices of a fast-changing world. This effort has to be made in the context of Indian conditions and the uniqueness of its three dimensions: plural, secular and democratic. This would necessitate sustained and candid interaction with fellow citizens without a syndrome of superiority or inferiority and can be fruitful only in the actual implementation of the principles of justice, equality and fraternity inscribed in the Preamble of the Constitution and the totality of the Fundamental Rights. The failure to communicate with the wider community in sufficient measure has tended to freeze the boundaries of diversities that characterize Indian society. Efforts may be made to isolate the community; such an approach should be resisted.

◆

I focused on the modalities of the actual functioning of legislatures in my address to the 135th anniversary of the Kerala Legislative Assembly (September 2013). Do they function well enough at central and state levels? Do they spend sufficient time on deliberation, legislation and accountability of executives? Is their functioning in keeping with established norms and in line with public expectations? Do they, by their functioning, set a model or a pattern of behaviour for the public, especially the youth, to emulate? Are correctives possible, or has the system irretrievably lost its way? Record shows that the notional time allocation is different from time actually utilized for conduct of business. A uniquely Indian contribution to parliamentary practice, known as 'disruption', has contributed to it.

I recalled Ambedkar's speech of 25 November 1949 and urged the legislative bodies in the land to follow his advice:

> If we wish to maintain democracy not only in form, but also in fact, what must we do? The first thing in my judgment we must do is to hold fast to constitutional methods of achieving our social and economic objectives. It means we must abandon the bloody methods of revolution. It means we must abandon the method of civil disobedience, non-cooperation and Satyagraha. When there was no way left for constitutional methods for achieving social and economic objectives, there was a great deal of justification for unconstitutional methods. But where constitutional methods are open, there can be no justification for these unconstitutional methods. These methods are nothing but the Grammar of Anarchy and the sooner they are abandoned, the better for us.

◆

The same day and in the same city, I unveiled a statue of Swami Vivekananda in Thiruvananthapuram and dwelt on his social agenda. He had used the Hindu idiom to be understood. However, his objective was not to sanctify but to change it. He was a man of religion and felt that the proof of one religion was the proof of the rest and that if one religion is true, all others must be too. This led him to preach the need to harmonize the essence of all religions. It was this advocacy of religious pluralism that led Vivekananda to his vision of India being the junction of two great systems—Hinduism and Islam—and to his observation in the letter of 10 June 1898 about 'Vedanta brain and Islamic body'.

Vivekananda was against exploitation and privilege and saw socialism as a possible remedy to India's problems. 'I am a socialist,' he said, 'not because it is a perfect system, but because I believe that half a loaf is better than no bread.' The inner core of his message to his own country was unambiguous: India needs development and social cohesion. The two complement each other. The absence of one is inherently disruptive to the other. The attainment of both paves the way for that higher humanity, which is the essence of all religions.

◆

Human Rights Day, 2013, gave me the opportunity to speak about 'Human Rights and Human Wrongs'. Having put in place the requisite intellectual, legal and institutional framework for the protection and promotion of human rights, we need to assess their realization in actual implementation and of their violations by state agencies, individuals and groups. The Annual Reports of the NHRC provide details of these and of the corrective action taken. The nature and extent of violations are a cause of concern. There is a gap between what the official agencies project and what is perceived to be the situation on the ground.

In this context of partial successes and noticeable failures, I raised a few questions. The beneficiaries of human rights are individuals who live in sovereign states that together constitute the community of nations. This is not a community of equals and it exists with more than one disjuncture pertaining to their capacity to influence matters. The interests of individuals therefore often get subordinated to the interests of nations. The intent of the Charter and of the Universal Declaration is thus subsumed in the structural framework of the international community. It does not stand alone.

The dilemma is a real one and while improvements and correctives to the existing mechanism continue to take place, perhaps the question needs to be addressed differently, conjointly from the perspectives of justice and human wrong, the latter term being any act by a human agency that transgresses on the right or dignity of a human being. The resulting situation was summed up succinctly by Rousseau, who described right-less human beings as those 'whose first gifts are fetters' and whose 'first treatment is torture' and yet whose 'voice alone is free'.

The challenge, as a distinguished scholar put it, is 'how to ground the pursuit of global security upon a terrain of moral principles' because 'morality and human rights are reciprocally related, and both bear on an unfolding debate about the changing character of security of states and peoples in an ever more integrated world order'.

This unavoidably takes the discourse to the question of the role of morality, justice and human wrong in national and global politics. This is not idealistic since justice figures as the first objective delineated in the Preamble of the Constitution of India. The term also figures amongst the purposes and principles outlined in the Charter of the UN.

Thus, notwithstanding the considerations of convenience or statecraft, human conscience and societal practice are conditioned by the dichotomy of expressions such as good-bad, right-wrong, just-unjust and moral-immoral. Human beings cannot avoid the impulse to invoke morality and justice in support of acts undertaken.

The challenge before humanity collectively and in all its segments therefore is to seek answers to two questions: do human rights as perceived today address human wrongs? Can a human wrong be considered virtuous? The victims of human wrongs operate between the polarities of suffering and the desire for relief and justice. It is the voice of the victims that needs articulation. But between the suffering and enunciation of human rights falls the shadow of state sovereignty. This necessitates a relook at the traditional approach.

Justice is the first principle of social institutions. It focuses on a sense of fairness. It necessitates the creation of institutions and environment that provide relief and begin the process of healing. As Amartya Sen put it, the principles of justice that the victims seek should be determined more by 'nyaya' rather than 'niti'. Providing justice itself constitutes partial relief from suffering. This requirement of justice cannot be subject to political bargaining or the calculus of social interests.

What follows, therefore, is that normative principles relating to human rights have to be related to human wrongs and, unavoidably, to a sense of morality. It has been argued down the ages that notwithstanding the virtues of private morality, public morality must be conditioned by realism, which needs to prevail over idealistic considerations. The challenge now is to reimagine the two in a construct that brings about a convergence between morality of means and of ends, a universal humanitarian morality that underpins and moulds considerations of security—national and global.

Such an approach may be dubbed utopian. The counterargument is that, as the political scientist Ken Booth put it many years back: 'We have barely begun to grasp the political, social and economic implications and possibilities of this most radical change in the world's material circumstances.' He went on to dismiss the permanency of the present global scenario and, instead, offered a fascinating alternative of skilled cosmopolitanism.

Thus optimism of the will for correctives has to take precedence over pessimism induced by depressing realities and it becomes our duty to give voice to those who continue to suffer and strive to seek for them both relief and justice. That is when human rights will begin to address human wrongs.

◆

The focus of the Conference of the Konkan Muslim Education Society in Thane (November 2013) was on Urdu language, which has suffered a decline after 1947 and has been subjected to a sense of alienation. In spite of that, it has the strength, power and passion to survive and has done so in the Deccan, Delhi and, especially, in Bombay because of the role played by the film industry in keeping it alive.

Urdu has two traits that are not noticeable at first sight. It is the language of rebellion and also a language of love and culture. It has seen these traits in different phases and often seen them together. This has become its temperament and by virtue of it, Urdu has resurrected itself in every period.

Today, Urdu has more than five crore speakers in the country and it occupies the sixth position in our language groups. Despite it, the number of Urdu speakers is declining primarily because the teaching of Urdu is going down at the school level in certain regions.

How can we rectify this situation? As citizens, we have to put our demands before the government and that is what we have been doing. The Constitution guarantees that every child will be given basic education in his/her mother tongue. But this is not happening. Why? A number of institutional excuses are put forward, but the truth is that we have to demand our rights and demand them vehemently. This is above all an individual responsibility.

I recalled what Maulana Abul Kalam Azad said a few weeks after Independence: 'Go with the times, do not say that we were not ready for the change.' Urdu as a language is no longer confined to our households, to specific regions, or to India and Pakistan; it is now an international language. The Internet testifies to it. Without doubt, we can say *'sarey jahan mein dhoom hamari zaban ki hai'* (Our language is celebrated the world over).

◆

In my address to the AMU convocation (May 2014), my theme was Mohammad Iqbal's couplet. It goes like this:

Is dour main taleem hai amraz-i-millat ki dawa
Hai khoon-e-fasid ke liyetaleem misl-e-naishtar

(In this age, education is the cure for ailments of the community
It is the surgical knife that drains the corrupting blood.)

I spoke about the uniqueness of the institution as reflected in it being a place of higher learning, located in India, and the inheritor of the totality of knowledge of the civilization of Islam. Thus, the challenges emanating from them were at all times notionally posited on a tripod and have today acquired greater intensity. Is the AMU prepared and equipped to respond to them meaningfully, in thought and in deed?

The historian Paul Kennedy in his book *Preparing for the Twenty-First Century* had concluded that three elements would be critical to the effort: the role of education, the place of women and the need for political leadership. Each of these is relevant to this campus and to us as a nation.

The shortfalls in education are evident. Data shows that mediocrity prevails, with both the teachers and the taught wallowing in it; its impact is reflected in employability assessments as also in research outputs. Correctives are thus imperative.

The Muslims of India, in their self-perception, prioritize their problems: physical security, education and employment. Each is within the ambit of affirmative action; some positive steps have been taken, more needs to be done. A younger generation, confident and assertive, seeks the right to equality and its share in decision-making.

The dead weight of tradition, poverty and communal politics has resulted in Muslim women facing handicaps relating to literacy, economic power resulting from work and income, and autonomy in decision-making. The net result is a pattern of structural disempowerment. Yet, social customs are neither sacred nor immutable and experience of other traditional societies shows that practical correctives can be introduced without transgression of values. Aligarh as a pioneer in the past must now help realize gender parity.

The same holds for political leadership. The deepening of the democratic process within our polity, and the emergence or crystallization of local, regional or sectional demands, compel both a wider understanding and a conscious development of the capacity to reconcile and accommodate competing requirements within the ambit of the Constitution. The civic training of young citizens should be facilitated in educational institutions and AMU's own record in this is credible.

An important aspect of AMU's ethos is its assertion of identity within the framework of diversity that characterizes modern India. Both are critical ingredients; both are cherished; both bestow a uniqueness that encapsulates a thousand years of history of the Indian subcontinent; both require careful navigation through treacherous rapids characterized by assimilative urges on the one hand and isolationist pressures on the other.

Any discourse on identity needs to begin with the ground reality. Ours is a plural society, a secular polity and a state structure that is democratic and based on Rule of Law. Plurality is thus an existential reality. Each ingredient of the mix is important. We steer clear of notions of assimilation and adaptation, philosophically and in practice. Instead, the management of diversity to ensure the integration of minds and hearts is accepted as an ongoing national priority. By the same token, every citizen has to contribute to it. Segregation, seclusion or self-imposed isolation is un-civic and a transgression of the spirit of a plural society. The objective is, and should be, to go beyond tolerance of the other and move towards acceptance of those who may be different. It would bring forth, in the words of Will Kymlicka, '[the] three interconnected ideas: repudiating the idea of the state as belonging to the dominant group; replacing assimilationist and exclusionary nation-building policies with policies of recognition and accommodation; and acknowledging historic injustice and offering amends for it'. This imposes obligations on the state to promote equal treatment. This is enshrined in our Constitution; the challenge is to universalize and deepen its implementation. The duty of the citizen is to be a participant in the process, assist it and actively seek his/her rights.

It is in this landscape that I go back to my earlier question: of AMU's preparedness in thought and deed to the emerging challenges of the twenty-first century. I have touched upon some aspects of the challenge. The answer is not with me; I do know that it is with the youthful segment of the audience before me. Will they rise to the occasion? Will they eschew mediocrity for excellence and pursue it in curricular and extracurricular fields? Will they help promote gender parity? Will they become active participants and builders in a new, changing India that is taking shape before us?

There are times in the lives of individuals when the imperative is to go beyond stale logic and pessimism of the intellect and lean instead on the optimism of the will. Such an occasion beckons the youth today. I repeat what I had said on an earlier occasion here:

> *Agar aflak ke tare torne hain to perwaaz ki taaqat paida karni ho gi; sirf guftaar kaafi nahin hai.*
> *Dekh zindaan se pare, rang-e-chaman, shour-e-bahaar*
> *Raqs karna hai to phir paaon ki zanjeer na dekh*

(If stars in the sky have to be plucked, the power to fly has to be developed, only talking will not suffice. Look beyond the prison to the colours of the garden and the gaiety of spring. Do not be constrained by the shackles on your feet.)

◆

The Twenty-second Justice Sunanda Bhandare Memorial Lecture (November 2016) provided me the opportunity to examine the question of gender equality and gender justice in our society. The comprehensive 2015 Report of the High Level Committee on the Status of Women had assessed that 'through a combination of family, caste, community and religion, among others, patriarchal values and ideas are constantly reinforced and legitimized'. It opined that India is a male-dominated society and that the progressive legislative initiatives 'are not accompanied by commensurate changes in the culture of institutions' charged with the responsibility of implementing them and that 'the process of empowerment must permeate institutions that hold the key to massive transformation including religious practices, family, marriage, education, law and order, judiciary and media'. It stated that in 2015, India had one of the worst gender gaps in the world when it comes to labour force participation.

Pursuant to a question in parliament, the government came forth with a National Policy document aimed at creating 'an effective framework and conducive socio-cultural, economic, and political environment to enable women to enjoy de jure and de facto fundamental rights to realize their full potential'.

Interestingly enough, the document does not mention the term 'patriarchy' and that the changes advocated are quantitative rather than qualitative and that the current efforts by the government are at best aimed to produce equity of varying intensity rather than substantive equality. The challenge of moving from the former to the latter is thus imperative. Without it, questions would remain on the sustainability of gender equality. The conclusion, that the process of dismantling patriarchy may have been initiated but is yet to deliver a finished product, is unavoidable.

◆

'Patriotism, Nationalism and Social Peace' was the subject of my speech at the 150th Birth Anniversary of Lala Lajpat Rai (May 2015). He ranked among the first three leaders of our nationalist movement prior to the advent of Gandhi in the 1920s, the other two being Bal Gangadhar Tilak and Bipin Chandra Pal. Reform of the Hindu society remained his abiding mission along with the question of social harmony. He was the first signatory in October 1923 on an Appeal for Inter-Communal Harmony signed by 100 public figures of all faiths. Its approach to the question was unique: that in religious terms, indulging in communal misdeeds is a sin and it is 'the duty of co-religionists of such offenders' to resist it.

Two months later, he devoted his address to the Punjab Provincial Political Conference to the problem of communal harmony and said that:

> The first article of our future constitution of India must provide absolute religious liberty to all religious denominations, subject only to such restrictions as are inevitable for the general maintenance of law and order. To this must be added the absolute religious neutrality of the future state... According to our idea, the future Swarajya government should not be at liberty

to use public funds for any religious or denominational purpose whatsoever. In a land of many religions and many cults this, in my view, is the best safeguard against religious or denominational partisanship. With this provision, the risks of the majority rule are very much lessened.

No progress, however, was made in this endeavour and instead, different perceptions crystallized. These were reflected in a set of articles he wrote in 1924, the last of which included a suggestion for proportional representation in legislature but not separate electorates, as also a suggestion to 'divide the Punjab into two Provinces to make majority rule effective'. He persisted in his plea for mutual co-operation:

> Let us live and struggle for freedom as brothers whose interests are one and indivisible. Let us live and die for each other, so that India may live and prosper as a Nation. India is neither Hindu nor Muslim. It is not even both. It is one. It is India.

He presided over the annual session of the Hindu Mahasabha in Calcutta in April 1925 and the programme of action adopted there has been called by a credible scholar as 'the single document that had the most enduring influence on subsequent programmes and strategies' of some of the successor organizations of that persuasion. This change of direction, or absence of consistency in the thought process and practical commitment, brings to the fore competing versions of nationalism that characterized the Indian scene in that period.

◆

A scholar who studied Indian secularism had observed that 'religion is most threatening to liberal democracy where it informs national identity or permeates everyday life'. In this context, I dwelt on the 'Role of the Judiciary' in my Jammu University Convocation Address (April 2016) and on the constitutional objectives of fraternity, unity and dignity through a secular republic characterized by its plurality and having a composite culture as spelt out in the Preamble of the Constitution and in Article 51A(f), respectively. The question is to ascertain how the Indian state has, in principle and in practice, given shape to the essential ingredients of the secular principle and composite culture.

The Basic Structure doctrine relating to our Constitution is now settled law and secularism is one of its ingredients. It is more than a passive attitude of religious tolerance and is, instead, a positive concept of equal treatment. This was authoritatively commented upon by the Supreme Court in its set of judgments in the Bommai case. It settled the principle but different judgments in the case tended to suggest that 'there is no real consensus within the Court on what secularism entails' leading to a comment that 'what the Court said is different from what it did'. It was then noted that subsequent pronouncements of the Supreme Court 'effectively vindicated the profoundly anti-secular vision of secularism' in some quarters.

The 'way of life' argument in philosophical texts and some judicial pronouncements does not help the process of identifying common principles of equity in a multi-religious society since the same could be said of other faiths because a wall of separation is not possible under Indian conditions. The challenge, therefore, is to develop a formula of equidistance and minimum involvement. For this purpose, principles of faith need to be segregated from contours of culture since a conflation of the two obfuscates the boundaries of both and creates space for equivocalness. Furthermore, such an argument could be availed of by other faiths in the land since all claim a cultural sphere and a historical justification for it.

Within the same ambit but distinct from it, the constitutional principle of equality of status and opportunity has to be substantive rather than merely formal and has to be given shape through requisite measures of affirmative action to eliminate 'inequality traps' that result in unequal access to political power. Another aspect of Bommai touches upon the cultural heritage of people of all faiths in the country and thus makes secularism and composite culture two sides of the same coin.

For all these reasons, it is incumbent on the Supreme Court to clarify the contours within which the principles of secularism and composite culture should operate with a view to strengthen their functional modality and remove the ambiguities that have crept in.

◆

I was invited by the Asiatic Society, Kolkata, to address the Indira Gandhi Memorial Lecture (October 2016). My theme was the tension between 'Cohesion and Fragility'. I cited Sardar Patel's remark that the superstructure of the modern state has been transplanted from above and has to take healthy roots, as otherwise it will run into chaos and V.P. Menon's citation that 'the real integration has to take place in the minds of the people' and go beyond regional loyalties. The reason for this was the presence of human diversities that are both hierarchical and spatial; hence, the necessity of building the political structure, keeping in mind the need to accommodate linguistic, religious and caste sentiments that together account for the 4,635 communities, 78 per cent of whom are not only linguistic and cultural but also social categories, including religious minorities amounting to 19.4 per cent of the population. Thus, the agenda for political, economic and social democracy remains unfinished and the *de jure* 'We the sovereign people' in the first line of the Preamble are in reality a fragmented 'we' divided by yawning gaps that remain to be bridged.

The Constituent Assembly sought to attain justice, liberty, equality and promotion of fraternity in all their manifestations. Ambedkar summed it up in his Conditions Precedent for the Successful Working of Democracy speech, wherein he defined democracy 'as a form and method of government whereby revolutionary changes in the economic and social life of the people are brought about without bloodshed'. He listed the essential ingredients of a working democracy: (i) absence of glaring inequalities; (ii) presence of an opposition; (iii) equality in law and administration; (iv) observance of constitutional morality; (v) avoidance of tyranny of majority over minority; (vi) a functioning of moral order in society; and (vii) public conscience.

These fissures nevertheless persist and the challenge today is to assess the balance between factors of cohesion and fragility in the polity so as to avoid what Ambedkar called a 'life of contradictions'. To avoid it and to seek justice in the sense suggested by the Constitution, we need to assess the efficacy of our institutions of representative government. Here, the problems of the FPTP system in elections are supplemented by unequal presence of the weaker sections of the electorate, especially women and minorities, in the power structure in most states, to deny or delay financial empowerment of local bodies under the 73rd and 74th Amendments.

It has been noted that the 'trajectories of federalism and democracy in India have thus frequently intersected, with more federalism containing the potential for greater democratization and both projects have yet to realize their fullest potential'. It has been argued that 'the metaphors with which we like to think of the federal arrangement are outdated'. It has also been argued that 'the idea of centre and periphery creates the sense of the marginality of the outer, instead of the diversity of the whole' and that 'the current politics can create an empty or indifferent Centre, enacting a form of federalism where the whole is less than the sum of the parts'.

In technical parlance, the Indian Union is an 'asymmetrical federation'. This suggests the need for a wider, reinvigorated perspective on the shape of the Union of India. Such an exercise would challenge the maturity and creative capacity of the polity and should be welcomed.

As Ambedkar put it, liberty, equality and fraternity form a trinity and divorcing one from the other is to defeat the very purpose of democracy. Liberty necessitates the accommodation and acceptance of the 'other'; this generates fraternity. The critical link in this chain is provided by equality—substantive and not merely formal. It is here that performance is lacking and the ingredients that would help promote equality remain undelivered in many cases and unevenly distributed in others. These have shifted the political discourse from mere growth-centric to vociferous demands for affirmative action and militant protest politics. Urban middle-class activism, often taking the form of violence, is being increasingly witnessed; Maoism is an extreme manifestation of it. Both tend to exercise a new hegemony over civil society; both are also inviting a strong response from the state apparatus which is alleged by its proponents as being 'endemic, extra-judicial and unaccounted violence'. One consequence of it is reflected in allegations of constraints on freedom of expression; another in dilution of efforts at promoting fraternity by constricting the accepted norms of pluralism in our society.

Do we then, as citizens of the Republic, stand at a crossroads undecided on how to proceed?

We have to acknowledge that the representation system in Indian democracy has fissures that need attendance; that claims of inclusiveness are only partially valid; that the objective of bestowing equality of opportunity to all citizens remains a promise, particularly to the weakest segment; that demands and pressures generated by the non-fulfilment of commitments emanating from the Constitution are propelling the state apparatus to resort to violent suppression at times, accompanied by curtailment of some fundamental freedoms; that the inherent plurality of Indian society can be endangered by suggestions of uniformity; and that sufficient effort remains to be made to promote tolerance and acceptance as civic virtues essential for the achievement of fraternity.

Neither is immobility an option; nor is certitude bordering on smugness, or panic on an impending doom. A saner course may be to be receptive to the complexities of the Indian reality and its contradictions, respond to it in all its diversity and refrain from a priori solutions not embedded in ground realities.

◆

Addressing the *Hindu* Huddle in February 2017 in Bengaluru, I raised the question of equity in the development discourse and said that viewing rising inequity as merely an inconvenient truth in the saga of India's shining future is a folly. Without equality, there is unlikely to be much of a future, let alone a shining one. There is a need to revisit our commitment to investing in social goods. We have to move beyond seeing corporate social activity and government welfare schemes as merely minimum relief for the misery of the masses, aimed mostly at neutralizing the more aggressive antagonism of those who have lost income and wealth, or those whose upward mobility seems permanently blocked.

We need to ask ourselves some uncomfortable questions: can we ignore the great inequity as merely a by-product of progress? Has the trickle-down model of growth failed us? Have we paid too high a price in terms of environmental damage for our material progress? Are conflicts and human suffering the new normal? To what extent are they induced by failed ventures in quest for unrealizable utopias? Can we simply accept the growing insularity, intolerance and discrimination? Have we made sufficient investments in improving our human capital and public goods, such as education and healthcare?

Faced with growing global violence, poverty and injustice, it may be difficult to retain hope for an equitable future. Yet, if the reality of global inequality inspires what Antonio Gramsci called 'pessimism of the intellect', work must nevertheless begin with what he termed 'optimism of the will'—the undaunted commitment that drives radical change.

◆

'The Regional Legacy of a Rich History' was the theme of my Mohammad Quli Qutub Shah Lecture at the Maulana Azad National Urdu University, Hyderabad (April 2017). I dwelt on two aspects of the geopolitics of the subcontinent in the medieval period: (i) the preponderance of a central power based in north India seeking to expand to the south and (ii) the independent or quasi-independent entities in the south who survived the imperial onslaught for varying periods by acknowledging some form of suzerainty. While the Deccan has no master narrative of its own, it did have intense interaction with the peoples, cultures and states of northern India that became a sort of their alter-ego. Individuals, communities and whole states defined their identity with respect to this colossus of the north, sometimes in opposition to it and sometimes in imitation. In the process, these states developed their own style of governance. They 'detached religion from statecraft' and culture from territorial boundaries and thereby gave themselves 'an enormously elastic and transnational character'. The first produced a pragmatic philosophy of governance, while the second pertained to the geopolitical considerations that confronted them in relation to the north.

The Qutub Shahis were of Iranian origin and had strong religious affiliations arising from their relationship with Iran, particularly after the year 1501 when Shah Ismail I resorted to strident sectarianism. Notwithstanding this, their approach to governance was pragmatic and secular and did not differentiate between Hindus and the Muslims so far as the affairs of the state were concerned. The period of Muḥammad Quli Qutb Shah was characterized by 'a spirit of camaraderie which existed between the Hindu and the Muslim sections of the population' and 'the whole policy of the Government seems to have been that of equality of opportunity for both the Hindus and the Muslims for practically all the offices of the state' and 'while he seems prejudiced in his enunciation of the inferiority of the non-Shi'a sects of the Muslims, he is culturally at one with the Hindus and the Parsis as well as the man in the street so far as his appreciation of their way of life is concerned'.

An aspect of this catholicity of approach was the Sultan's outlook to Telugu. To him, it was 'like a mother tongue' and he made 'a deliberate attempt to synthesize cultures in the Deccan, imbibing in the people of Hyderabad a relish of tolerance, love of spectacle and mildness of nature'.

An aspect of the region in that period was the quickening pace of its commercial and cultural interaction with the Iranian plateau. It 'had the effect of drawing the whole Deccan into the orbit of Persian culture'. This included sectarian affiliation. The regional state system of the Deccan also developed its own rules of interstate conduct and in view of Mughal incursions into Berar and Ahmednagar, Bijapur and Golkonda 'stood like one in the face of invaders and forgot their quarrels'.

Thus, the Mughal designs on the Deccan entities, and the latter's close affinity to Persia, resulted in a clash of interests and perceptions. A study of the bilateral relations of that period concluded that 'the distance between Persia and the Deccan, and the fact that the former was not a naval power, precluded the possibility of her providing material assistance to the latter, though a powerful ruler like Shah Abbas I could offer diplomatic support'. The diplomatic relations between Persia and the Deccan kingdoms and the recitation of the Shah's name in the Khutba in Golkonda were irritating to the Mughals, especially to a strong emperor such as Shah Jahan. Despite this, or on account of it, Mughal attempts at dominance persisted. Thus, in the reign of Shah Jahan, the Deccan entities were forced to sign Inqiyad Namas or Deeds of Submission. The document, in the case of Golkonda, stipulated acceptance to be designated as 'hereditary disciple' of the Mughal Emperor and undertook to (i) replace the names of the 12 Imams and of the Shah of Persia and replace them with those of the four Caliphs and the Mughal Emperor (ii) gold and silver coins to be struck with the formula passed by the Emperor (iii) specified amounts of annual tributes to be sent (iv) consider the Emperor's friends as friends and his enemies as enemies (v) swear on the Quran that the ruler would abide by each of these commitments and that 'if he were to stray from the right path, then the Emperor would be justified in ordering his servants to conquer the kingdom' and (vi) if a neighbour committed aggression and occupied Golkonda territory, necessary assistance would be provided and the loss compensated. The formal transition from 'sultan' to 'hereditary disciple' thus made clear the vassal status. Despite this, the wider diplomatic game between the Safavids and the Mughals, of seeking and restricting influence, continued.

In the War of Succession following Shah Jahan's death, there was clear evidence of Safavid intervention on the side of Dara Shikoh. In a countermove, Aurangzeb contemplated but did not pursue an invasion of Persia in alliance with the Uzbeks. In the meantime, the final incorporation into the empire of Golkonda and other Deccan entities, and a succession of weak successors of Shah Abbas II in Persia, did away with the necessity of diplomatic and military pressures emanating from Delhi.

The period of Muhammad Quli Qutb Shah and his successors raises two questions: 'what kind of political and socio-economic culture did the successor states of Hyderabad inherit and was there in this inheritance anything of value left to contribute to the Indian polity?' Can its inherited tradition of tolerance, coexistence, inclusiveness and cultural effervescence continue to signal its uniqueness and remain an example for the country?

◆

My last speaking engagement as Vice President was the convocation address to the National Law School of India University, Bengaluru (2017). I devoted it to the essential principles of Indian polity and to examining 'Why Pluralism and Secularism are Essential for Our Democracy'.

Our founding fathers took cognizance of an existential reality. Ours is a plural society and a culture imbued with considerable doses of syncretism. Our population of 1.3 billion comprises over 4,635 communities, 78 per cent of whom are not only linguistic and cultural but social categories. Religious minorities constitute 19.4 per cent of the total. The human diversities are both hierarchical and spatial. It is this plurality that the Constitution endowed with a democratic polity and a secular state structure.

Pluralism as a moral value seeks to 'transpose social plurality to the level of politics, and to suggest arrangements which articulate plurality with a single political order in which all duly constituted groups and all individuals are actors on an equal footing, reflected in the uniformity of legal capacity. Pluralism in this modern sense presupposes citizenship'. Citizenship as the basic unit is conceptualized as 'national-civic' rather than 'national-ethnic', 'even as national identity remained a rather fragile construct, a complex and increasingly fraught "national-civic-plural-ethnic combinations"'. In the same vein, Indianness came to be defined not as a singular or exhaustive identity but as embodying the idea of layered Indianness, an accretion of identities.

Modern democracy offers the prospect of the most inclusive politics of human history. It 'has to be judged not just by the institutions that formally exist but by the extent to which different voices from diverse sections of the people can actually be heard'. Its *raison d'être* is the recognition of the other. By the same logic, there is a thrust for exclusion that is a by-product of the need for cohesion in democratic societies; hence the need for dealing with exclusion 'creatively' through the sharing of identity space by 'negotiating a commonly acceptable political identity between the different personal and group identities which want to/have to live in the polity'.

An assessment of the functioning of our democracy has to be both procedural and substantive. On the procedural count, the system has developed roots with regularity of elections, efficacy of the electoral machinery, an ever-increasing percentage of voter participation in the electoral process and the formal functioning of legislatures thus elected. The record is commendable in formal terms, less so in substantive aspects. Five of these bear closer scrutiny: (i) the gap between 'equality before the law' and 'equal protection of the law' (ii) representativeness of the elected representative, (iii) functioning of the legislatures, (iv) gender and diversity imbalance, and (v) secularism in practice.

A definitive pronouncement on secularism for purposes of statecraft in India was made by the Supreme Court in the Bommai case. It stressed that religious tolerance and fraternity are basic features and postulates of the Constitution, as a scheme for national integration and sectional or religious unity. So, programmes or principles evolved by political parties based on religion amount to recognizing religion as a part of the political governance, which the Constitution expressly prohibits. It violates the basic features of the Constitution. Positive secularism negates such a policy and any action in furtherance thereof would be to violate the basic features of the Constitution.

Despite its clarity, its import was diluted by subsequent judgments. Credible critics such as Justice V.M. Tarkunde have opined that the 11 December 1995 judgment of a Supreme Court Bench 'is highly derogatory of the principle of secular democracy' and that a larger Bench should reconsider them 'and undo the great harm caused by them'. This remains to be done; 'instead, a regression of consciousness (has) set in' and 'the slide is now sought to be accelerated and is threatening to wipe out even the gains of the national movement summed up in Sarva Dharma Sambhav[169].'

It has been observed, with much justice, that 'the relationship between identity and inequality lies at the heart of secularism and democracy in India'. The challenge today then is to reiterate and rejuvenate secularism's basic principles: equality, freedom of religion and tolerance, and to emphasize that equality has to be substantive, that freedom of religion be reinfused with its collectivist dimensions and that toleration should be reflective of the realities of Indian society and lead to acceptance.

Our democratic polity is pluralist because it recognizes and endorses this plurality in (i) its federal structure, (ii) linguistic and religious rights to minorities, and (iii) a set of individual rights. The first has sought to contain, with varying degrees of success, regional pressures. The second has ensured space for religious and linguistic minorities, and the third protects freedom of opinion and the right

---

[169] Equal respect for all religions or peaceful coexistence of all religions.

to dissent. In this context, national integration is to be seen not as the conversion of diversities into uniformity but as a congruence of diversities leading to a unity in which both the varieties and similarities are maintained. Similarly, while majority in electoral terms does not have permanence and is time specific, it is indicative of settled situations in socio-political and demographic terminology. Any effort to use these expressions interchangeably has negative implications for the concept of citizenship in the Constitution and its explicit injunctions on rights and duties; it gives rise to value-loaded terms such as 'majoritarian' and 'majoritianism', which detract from the principle of fraternity inscribed in the Preamble of the Constitution.

Thus, a more comprehensive realization of the objectives of pluralism and secularism necessitate (i) the negation of impediments to the accommodation of diversity institutionally and amongst citizens and, (ii) the rejuvenation of the institutions and practices through which they [pluralism and secularism] cease to be sites for politico-legal contestation in the functioning of the Indian democracy. This would include a more diligent promotion in the practice of fraternity, the preservation of the heritage of our composite culture and going beyond tolerance to the principle and practice of acceptance of the Other in terms of what Swami Vivekananda had advocated. The urgency of giving this a practical shape at the national, state and local levels is highlighted by enhanced apprehensions of insecurity among segments of our citizen body, particularly Dalits, Muslims and Christians.

While pluralism and secularism are sought to be diluted as the core principles of the polity, a third 'ism'—nationalism—has been grafted in an exaggerated manifestation.

For many decades after Independence, a pluralist view of nationalism and Indianness, reflective of the widest possible circle of inclusiveness and a 'salad bowl' approach, characterized our thinking. More recently, a version of nationalism that places cultural commitments at its core and promotes intolerance and arrogant patriotism has tended to intrude into and take over the political and cultural landscape. One manifestation of it is 'an increasingly fragile national ego' that threatens to rule out any dissent however innocent. Hyper-nationalism and the closing of the mind is also 'a manifestation of insecurity about one's place in the world'.

The alternative to it is liberal nationalism that requires a state of mind characterized by tolerance and respect of diversity for members of one's own group and for others; it is 'polycentric by definition' and 'celebrates the particularity of culture with the universality of human rights, the social and cultural embeddedness of individuals together with their personal autonomy.' It focuses on the Preamble of the Constitution and ensures that citizenship—irrespective of caste, creed or ideological affiliation—is the sole determinant of Indianness. By implication, the 'other' is to be none other than the 'self' and any derogation from it would be detrimental to the core values of our plural secular democracy.

CONTROVERSIES

It has been said that a man of controversy is looked upon as a disturbing influence since the holder of a constitutional office is expected to be above it. Yet, public office and public statements in a free society cannot be restricted to bland repetition of the *ex-cathedra* pronouncements. I, therefore, ensured to be correct in terms of public norms of language and conduct, and be non-partisan with regard to political controversies. Yet, I held views on matters of public interest and concern and expressed them appropriately on relevant occasions and platforms, since the office I held provided opportunities of doing so. Some in the public domain commended it; a good instance being the editorial in *The Statesman* (Kolkata) of 4 October 2015, which observed that 'the Vice President is emerging as a rare national figure bold enough to swim against the current though it is evident that he is being targeted by the "saffron" tribe'.[170]

In July 2010, two newspapers caused some sensation with a report that a right-wing extremist organization was involved in 'an alleged plot to assassinate India's Vice President Shri Mohammad Hamid Ansari'.[171] The report was not denied and no intimation of it was given to me by any official agency.

A few of the happenings that excited media curiosity can be mentioned. US President Barack Obama was our chief guest for the 2015 Republic Day celebrations and was on the saluting dais on Rajpath along with national dignitaries when the military parade commenced. As per standard practice, President Pranab Mukherjee took the salute by raising his right hand. Others, including the US president, were expected to stand to attention. Since it was the first occasion with a military ceremony for the PM and the defence minister and perhaps due to inadequate briefing, both also raised their hands in salute. The visuals showed me doing otherwise and the 'faithful' took it upon themselves to fault me for disrespecting the national flag. It took some time, and diligent explaining, to put across the correct procedure for such occasions. One enthusiastic TV channel was reprimanded by the concerned authorities and banned for three days![172]

The first International Yoga Day was celebrated on 21 June 2015 and the PM personally participated in it. A ranking member of the ruling party commented adversely on my absence from the function. My office clarified that I had not been invited and this was confirmed by the minister concerned. The 'faithful' nevertheless persisted in lambasting me. After a few days, the dignitary concerned called on

---

[170] Editorial, 'Voice of Sanity,' *The Statesman*, https://www.thestatesman.com/opinion/voice-of-sanity-94831.html.

[171] Ashish Khetan, *India Today,* 15 July, the *Daily News & Analysis (DNA)*, 17 July, and *Mail Today* 16 July 2010.

[172] A few days before I demitted office, a media report opined that 'Ansari was surely trolled for not following the prime minister and the defence minister.' (Kumar Shakti Shekhar, '3 Controversies Ansari Will Be Remembered For. His Second Term Ends on August 10,' *Daily O*, 4 July 2017).

me to express his regret!¹⁷³

My speech on the occasion of the golden jubilee of the All India Muslim Majlis-E-Mushawarat in August 2015 was targeted out of context for some of the references to the grievances of the Muslim community while ignoring its message of the need for change: 'To sustain the struggle for the actualization in full measure of legal and constitutional rights and to do so without being isolated from the wider community and to endeavour at the same to adapt thinking and practices to a fast-changing world.'¹⁷⁴

Subjectivity in the assessment of subsequent events, as also of misplaced grievances associated with the norms of the functioning of the Rajya Sabha, are best left to the judgment of the readers.

∽

---

¹⁷³A report by the Express News Service (23 June 2015) said that 'it is the second instance in less than five months where an attempt has been made by supporters of the Narendra Modi government to cast aspersions on Ansari's patriotism', adding that 'all too often, when it comes to assertions of crude majoritarianism, in the ruling establishment, there is no separating the mainstream from the fringe'.

¹⁷⁴Describing it as problem-solving, creative, plural and democratic, Shiv Visvanathan wrote in *The Hindu* on 4 September 2015 ('Invigorating Islam in India') that the message of the speech is 'the Muslim is, here, easy with her identity, comfortable in her Indian citizenship and confident that she can solve problems within the framework of Indian democracy. This is cultural confidence, citizenship and constitutionalism at its creative best. The VHP and BJP must be tone-deaf to democracy to have missed the sheer creativity in Mr Ansari's speech'.

Chapter 8

Away from Routine

> *Freedom has a thousand charms to show*
> *That slaves, however contended, never know.*

Twice I came close to the pitfalls of routine: after Riyadh and again after Aligarh; neither however persisted and on both occasions a sufficiently interesting alternative came forth. It was made easier because in the recesses of the mind there was perhaps a quest for it. After the 10th August ritual, however, the inclination to explore new pastures seemed to slacken. The retreat nevertheless could only be partial as invitations for memorial lectures and book releases kept pouring in.

The temptation to go back to writing on West Asia did surface but did not last. I had, a few years earlier, spoken on the turbulence in the West Asian state system, the failure of the democratic impulses and the complications arising out of the regional and extra-regional inputs as also of the failure of political Arabism. These trends continue; in one sense, they highlight the relevance of Abdallah Laroui's thesis of 'infra-historical rhythm' and of Fouad Ajami's critique of the 'Dream Palace of the Arabs' and his urging to look at the 'Arab reality'. In the recent past, the revolutionary impulses of the Arab Spring have compelled more focused local assessments rather than regional ones.

Yet, there was no realization of the expectation to fade away. Apart from memorial lectures, many less formal occasions arose to express my views on a range of matters of contemporary interest. This took the shape of what in Delhi's parlance is called a 'book release'.

◆

In the last week of September 2017, I was invited by Dr Mohammad Manzoor Alam of the Institute of Objective Studies, New Delhi, to open a conference in Kozhikode on the *Role of Women in Making a Humane Society*. Given that the sponsor and the audience were both principally Muslim, I focused on the impact of patriarchy on gender issues in the Indian Muslim society and the resultant socio-educational backwardness of Muslim women and its very evident negative impact on workplace representation.

After the lecture, a controversy was sought to be created about my visit being associated with some local 'Islamic' body that had also participated in the function. It was clarified by my office that I had been invited by the Institute in New Delhi, had nothing to do with any local organization, was the guest of the state government as per standard GoI procedures and was accorded appropriate courtesies.

◆

Contemporary Challenges in the Realm of Culture was the theme of my inaugural address to a conference on 'Nationalism and Culture', which was organized by the Progressive Writers' Association, Chandigarh, in October 2017. The social responsibility of writers, I said, is to help shape public perceptions and to answer questions about our national identity. This has to be based on the ground reality of immense diversity, heterogeneity and complexity. It is this plurality that constitutes the Indian identity, expressed in the Constitution through the principles of democracy and secularism. It is not a melting pot, because each ingredient retains its identity. It is perhaps a salad bowl.

Nehru said that it is a palimpsest on which the imprint of succeeding generations has unrecognizably merged. For the same reason, Indian culture is not to be conceived as a static phenomenon tracing its identity to a single unchanging source; instead, it is dynamic and interrogates critically and creatively all that is new. This then is the reality. Can this reality be homogenized? Can we initiate a process of assimilation? In a democratic polity, how is any ingredient to be subsumed in another? Can we visualize an India that is non-democratic, non-plural and non-secular?

Why then is an effort underway to subsume diversity in a notional identity? Is its purpose to erase, subjugate or dominate this diversity and replace it with an imagined uniformity based on a version of history that correspond neither to the authentic record of India's past nor to the rich diversity of her present?

The alternative is to have an approach based on the principles of pluralism and secularism, whose ingredients are energetic engagement with diversity, going beyond mere tolerance to acceptance of those who appear to be 'the other', and having a continuous inter-community, inter-faith and cross-cultural dialogue, of speaking and listening in a process that reveals both common understanding and real differences.

History has thus itself become a site for struggle; it draws within its ambit all those who register and interpret human experience, particularly the writers. As citizens, they cannot remain oblivious to what happens in the polity. While remaining committed to their chosen art, their social responsibility requires that they use their art to guide the public and lead them out of the poisonous haze of ignorance, superstition and unreasoned prejudice and to ensure that our secular culture and liberal democracy are preserved.

At a time when the hitherto accepted norms of Indian culture are being repackaged and distorted, and the values of liberal nationalism are sought to be substituted by illiberal doctrines and practices that adversely impact individual freedoms guaranteed by the Constitution of India, all citizens, particularly those who mould public perceptions through their work, need to respond to this challenge.

♦

A pending invitation from Prof. Amin Saikal of the Australian National University (ANU), Canberra, was persuasive enough to make me undertake the journey to Australia in March 2018 and give a lecture on *India and Islamic Civilization: Contributions and Challenges*. Adaptability, accommodation and attendant creativity, I said, characterized seven centuries of Muslim (not Islamic) rule in many parts of India. I explored the topic in the context of four areas—statecraft, social life, creative arts and spirituality—and concurred with the assessment that Indian Islam has been remarkable for its identification with India, without ceasing to be Islamic and that while Partition has battered it, its size, past tradition and involvement in the transcending complex of India has helped recovery to some measure. At the same time, this model of accommodating diversity also confronts and resists the imperatives of ultranationalism and intolerance.

Being in Canberra gave me time to catch up with the local scene. Gareth Evans, the Chancellor of ANU, hosted a dinner in my honour, where I was able to meet some interesting academics. I also met some senior figures in the Opposition ALP, who sought India's views on regional issues.

♦

The Students Union of the AMU invited me to confer its Honorary Life Membership on me. The function, and an address by me, were scheduled for 2 May; it was however disrupted by a violent agitation by a non-student group said to belong to an extremist right-wing gang and purportedly incited by a local MP on the specious plea of taking down the portrait of M.A. Jinnah from the gallery of previous recipients of this honour, beginning with Gandhi in 1920. Media writings on the happening made clear the design behind the disruption.[175]

A few days later, I wrote to the president of the AMU Students Union, thanking the union for the gesture. I also praised the students for their peaceful protest, adding that:

> The disruption, its precise timing, and the excuse manufactured for justifying it, raise questions. The programme of the day, including an address by me in the Kennedy Auditorium, was publicly known. The authorities concerned had been intimated officially and were cognizant of the standard arrangements including security for such occasions. In view of it, the access of the intruders to close proximity of the university guest house where I was staying remains unexplained.

I added that the union's request for action against the intruders 'after a judicial inquiry' is justified. This, in turn, elicited a protest from a Rashtriya Swayamsevak Sangh-affiliated organization, Dharam Jagran Samanvay.[176]

◆

In August 2018, I delivered the Twenty-third Prem Bhatia Memorial Lecture on the theme of *Religion, Religiosity and World Order*. I enquired if religiosity or religious zeal is integral to faith per se. If it is desirable and conducive to it, what impulses propel it and what has been its impact on the world order. I surveyed the various global ideologies and practices of fundamentalism and the harm done by them—Evangelical, Zionist, Islamic, Hindu and Buddhist. I suggested

---

[175] Ali Khan Mahmudabad, 'Why AMU Violence is About Hamid Ansari and Not Jinnah,' *Outlook*, 14 May 2018, https://www.outlookindia.com/website/story/why-amu-violence-is-about-hamid-ansari-and-not-jinnah/311935. Also, Tariq Hasan, 'Was the Former VP Hamid Ansari the Real Target of Attack on AMU?' *The Citizen*, 3 May 2018, https://www.thecitizen.in/index.php/en/NewsDetail/index/2/%20 13707/Was-Former-VP-Hamid-Ansari-The-Real-Target-of-Attack-on-AMU.

[176] TNN, 'RSS Affiliate Demands a "Ban" on Hamid Ansari in AMU Campus,' *Times of India*, 13 May 2018, https://timesofindia.indiatimes.com/city/agra/rss-affiliate-demands-ban-on-hamid-ansari-in-amu-campus/articleshow/64150835.cms.

a new triad: that religion is not politics, that religiosity is not religion and that global order is to be premised on global interests and not on an exclusively national one, even if it involves going beyond the traditional paradigm of faith and national interest, since the alternative may be a modern-day version of Milton's Pandemonium, the High Capital of Satan and his Peers, built by little demons.

◆

I contributed an essay on 'Citizenship' to the Annual Publication (January 2018) of the journal *Seminar* and, in the context of the Citizenship (Amendment) Bill under consideration, argued that while religious persecution could be a principle for differentiation, it cannot be articulated in a manner that dilutes the secular foundation of citizenship in India and goes against constitutional morality. Also that 'the nobility of intent underlying the bill is belied by its selectivity in terms of [the] neighbouring countries and religious minorities confronting difficulties; thus the rationale for leaving out Ahmadis in Pakistan, Rohingyas in Myanmar and Uighur Muslims in China is unclear'. Thus, 'behind and beyond these legal tweaking, the question of their impact on the core values of the Constitution and of the idea of India envisaged therein remains a disturbing one'. Referring to the argument that 'India shall remain a natural home for persecuted Hindus and they shall be welcome to seek refuge here', I said that 'this seems to reflect in some measure Israel's Law of Return for the Jewish people and its opening proclamation that "every Jew has the right to come to this country as *Oleh* (an immigrant)"'.

◆

The travails of the media in our times were the subject of my B.G. Verghese Memorial Lecture in March 2019. I focused it on *Journalism in Times of Strident Nationalism*. The role of the press in a democracy, in contrast to what it becomes in a dictatorship, was spelt out several decades earlier by another eminent member of the Fourth Estate and I recalled his words:

The role of the press in a democracy is different from that in a totalitarian state. Democracy is government by law; totalitarian state is government by authority; in the former, decisions are arrived at by discussion, and in the latter by dictation; in the former, the press acts as a check on authority, in the latter, it is the handmaid of authority; in the former, the press makes the people think, in the latter, obey without question; in the former, the press is necessarily to be free, as without free press there is no free discussion; in the latter, the press supports authority.

The qualitative decline in the functioning of the press is reflected in the World Press Freedom Index. This, in recent times, has been heavily influenced by the national mood of strident nationalism reflected through Hindutva and the concepts of cultural revitalization and political mobilization that seek to subjugate and homogenize our ethnic pluralities by establishing the hegemony of an imagined cultural mainstream and the social violence generated by it. One consequence of this approach is ineptitude and bias in governance and departures from the Rule of Law; another is stridency in advocacy of this brand of nationalism accompanied by intolerance of dissent; both find their reflection in journalism. Violence against journalists is one aspect of it, with the state being complicit in acts of omission and commission. This is combined by pressures of job security on the journalists and economic pressures on the owners. The Editors Guild of India has taken note of the deteriorating situation 'on the increasingly challenging environ on freedom of the press'.

The casualty in the process is credibility and a failure to live up to the requirements of accuracy, independence, impartiality, humanity and accountability. One credible study has observed that 'a part-communal, part-pseudo-nationalist poison has seeped deep into India's collective thinking' and poses 'a very real threat to Indian democracy'.[177]

---

[177] Hamid Ansari, 'Journalism and the Media's Crisis of Credibility in an Age of

◆

Sins and Sinners: Where Did It Go Wrong? was the subject of my Fakhruddin Ali Ahmed Memorial Lecture in the Ghalib Institute (July 2019). I focused on the erosion of empathy as a public value and cited an academic's observation that 'in a short space of four years, India has made a very long journey. It has travelled from its founding vision of civic nationalism to a new political imagery of cultural nationalism that appears to be firmly embedded in the public realm'.

'Why has this happened?' was the question I posed. I cited another study that attributed its causes to populism, authoritarianism, nationalism and majoritarianism, and opined that the guilt lay with all those who soft-peddled the quiet impulses in society that worked to subvert the egalitarian principles so candidly spelt out by Dr Ambedkar in the closing stages of the Constituent Assembly, and by those who allowed the Rule of Law and the institutions of the state to be subverted by acts of commission and omission. The corrective, I concluded, lies in a meaningful alternative; in a reversion to the foundational principles of the Indian polity and their diligent implementation.

◆

The Centre for Research in Rural and Industrial Development, Chandigarh, organized an international seminar on the occasion of the 550th anniversary of the birth of Guru Nanak Devji. In my presentation, I thought aloud about *Some Dichotomies of Our Times* in relation to the emotive power of faiths and the propensity of faith-based systems to succumb to arrogant assertions of total righteousness and imagined Utopia, which has resulted in a period of 'organized insanity and deaths on a massive scale'. Two pandemics seem to generate this: religiosity and strident nationalism. Since these trends are at variance with the core of the teachings of all faiths, the need of our times is to bring forth a corrective by making

---

Strident Nationalism,' *The Wire*, 10 March 2019, https://thewire.in/media/india-media-nationalism.

humanity overcome this crisis of the spirit. This can be achieved by proclaiming a new triad that (i) religion is not politics, (ii) religiosity is not religion and (iii) peace, harmony and happiness can emanate only from adherence to principles of justice in human dealings with each other, at the individual and group levels—local, national and international. Similarly, a world full of sovereign state entities espousing strident nationalism cannot but propel them to violence or threat of violence and result in a fragile framework, which would not be in consonance with the global order we are seeking to build on agreed principles of cooperation and mutual benefit for humankind. This necessitates effective dialogue based on tolerance and going beyond to acceptance of the Other.

◆

In July 2019, I addressed the National Defence College on security and regional cooperation and focused on human security in the context of the depletion of land and fresh water resources and the warning about it in a 2018 UNDP Report. I referred to the present arrangements for interstate management of water resources and its limitations and stated that a longer-term holistic approach remains to be implemented. This requires regional cooperation in greater measure since the present arrangement is unlikely to be sustained in perpetuity, given the rising populations and the pressures on land and water resources. It is thus inevitable that renewable resources will be depleted and that the prospects of new battle lines over transboundary water resources may not be far-fetched and require imaginative thinking about the future. Thus river basin management on a regional basis becomes imperative.

◆

In book release functions, I found some works of particular interest. These included recent works by Sumantra Bose, Neera Chandhoke, Zorawar Daulet Singh, Niraja Gopal Jayal, Mujibur Rehman and A.G. Noorani.

Sumantra Bose has conducted an interesting comparative study of Turkish and Indian secularisms titled *Secular States, Religious Politics*. Both premised not on any 'wall of separation' doctrine, but one in which the state is legally and constitutionally empowered to have a regulatory presence, but with different trajectories. He bases his argument on Subhas Chandra Bose's belief that Indian national identity should not be grounded in a creed of interfaith solidarity or a narrative of religious syncretism: 'If you use religion to unite yourself today, you leave the door open for someone to attempt later to divide you using the same sentiments.' The challenge before advocates of secularism as a constitutional value is to focus on its contradictions and frailties and improve its framework. It is doable but not painless. The alternative of a non-secular state would impinge on both equality and fraternity and thereby on the very idea of justice as a primary social virtue.

Neera Chandhoke's study *Rethinking Pluralism, Secularism and Tolerance,* for which I wrote a foreword, makes the essential point that secularism is not a standalone concept and is intrinsically linked to democracy, since a secular deficit in a plural society results in a denial of democratic rights to equality and equal share in its benefits. Hence, the linkage of the four ideas constitutes its core. She argues that the debate be shifted from secularism per se to the antecedent moral principles from which secularism derives its specific meaning. She concedes that coexistence between religious identity and democratic politics is not easy and that it is in the nature of democratic, political life that 'irresolvable dilemmas' can only be negotiated through deployment of imagination and creativity in thinking and in practice.

Zorawar Daulet Singh's well-researched study, *Power and Diplomacy* on India's foreign policies in the Cold War era contrasts two phases, depicted as *peace makers* and *security seekers;* Nehru's preference 'for ethical statecraft relying on persuasion rather than coercion', with Indira Gandhi's realpolitik. Its use of new archival material shows how a demand for regional autonomy and its reflection in electoral verdict was turned by a neighbour into tactical gain and wider strategic benefit.

The 32 essays edited by Niraja Gopal Jayal in a substantive volume, *Re-forming India: The Nation Today* draw attention to the philosophy underlying the agenda of change in the past five years, premising it on Hindutva and 'cultural nationalism' instead of 'civic nationalism', which was the basis of the freedom movement and of the Constitution that was enacted in 1950. This negates the principles of the Constitution, abrogates fraternity, nullifies equality, differentiates between citizens on the basis of faith and, in effect, does away with the Rule of Law and its realization in terms of rights, development, governance and justice. Together they impact on the very meaning of democracy and the idea of majority, diversity and the nature of social interaction and bring into being a new political culture to which one of the essays draws attention and summarizes it in three crucial aspects: 'a shift away from expansion of democracy to a narrow formalization of democracy, a shift away from openness, and a shift away from diversity and mutual respect for each other's way of life and thinking'.

In the same vein, Mujibur Rehman's collection of papers on the *Rise of Saffron Power* analysed the results of the 2014 general election, in which a political party with a little over 31 per cent of the votes cast won a decisive victory. It shows that 'saffron power' is an ideology and not merely an election banner, that communal mobilization and the interlocking of the socio-religious with the political does work in our society and is premised on a strategy of denigration seeking to submerge our polity's democratic values of diversity and inclusiveness in an alternate paradigm of exclusion and homogenization, empowered by the limitations and failures of its immediate predecessor. However, the expectation of the euphoria of this phenomenon fading away nationally was belied in the 2019 general election.

A.G. Noorani's comprehensive study *The RSS* puts together documents on the origins of the movement, draws attention to Nehru's letter of 10 November 1948 to M.S. Golwalkar, in which he asserted that the real objectives of the organization 'appear to be completely opposed to the decisions of the Indian Parliament and the provisions of the proposed Constitution of India'. He recalls Nehru's prognosis a few years later that 'the danger to India is not communism. It is Hindu right-wing communalism'. Noorani's conclusion that the RSS has, over the years, developed public policy orientations and influence through the large number of its affiliates and by grafting and promoting Hindutva as a concept of cultural revitalization and political mobilization, which 'seeks to subjugate and homogenize the ethnic pluralities by establishing the hegemony of an imagined cultural mainstream', is irrefutable. The same can be said of the observation that 'this has also generated social violence by some of its adherents'.

Chapter 9

The Family

The bond of 56 years with Salma, considered improbable by sceptics, remains remarkably resilient. It was neither a lottery nor a match made in heaven nor altogether free of hiccups. It had to be worked on, propensities accommodated, even tolerated, till a median was reached. The strength of her personality, evident in youth, matured with years and so did her determination to pursue the course she considered correct. Her educational ventures in different lands testify to it. In the words of Ambassador K.B. Lall in Brussels, she kept a good table and from being someone who possessed virtually no culinary skills at the time of our marriage, she evolved into a fine cook and an even better judge of the skills of a succession of professional chefs in different lands. Above all, she remains a good and understanding mother to our three children and in a relationship that has matured into friendship. The intricate problems of schooling our children, from one land to another, were single-handedly taken care of by her. For these and innumerable other reasons, the family is Ammi-centric and is happy to keep it so!

Sulaiman, born in Rabat-Sale in a nursing home overlooking the coast that was once notorious for its pirates, moved with us when three months old from Rabat via Allahabad to Jeddah, where facilities were basic. When he was three, Salma initiated the nursery for him and a few other community children in a room in the chancery; it is now a full-fledged higher secondary school, with a student body of around 12,000. In New Delhi, he went to Elisabeth Gauba's school on Hailey road, in Brussels to a local French Catholic primary communal school (since the English-language ones were beyond our pay packet) where he took to French so well that the school principal recommended Sulaiman remaining in Belgium for the duration of his education. Our next destination, Abu Dhabi, confronted us with the same problem and so he was sent off to Lawrence School, Sanawar, only to be shifted again to Air Force Bal Bharti School on Lodhi Road once we returned to Delhi. In Canberra, he took a degree in sociology from the ANU. He then wandered around in the job market before settling down in business development with Unilever, where he has done well for himself, moving from Dubai to Singapore to New York, and in the process, familiarizing himself with most of the Pacific and Central-South American lands. His son, Sabir, studied in King's College London and is now based in Singapore while his daughter, Yasmin, after finishing her school in New York, is in the University of Toronto in Canada.

Nuriya, born in Brussels, became the first student in Salma's school in Abu Dhabi and then went to Air Force Bal Bharti School in New Delhi and to a school in Canberra, then to the British School in New Delhi and on to the Indian School in Tehran. Despite these disruptions and attendant traumas, she discovered herself in Jesus and Mary College and the University of Delhi. Hers is now an acknowledged name in the field of teacher training and school education in the country and some international institutions. She is very much a Delhi girl and takes a lot of interest in social and charitable work.

Like our other children, Osman, born in Abu Dhabi, suffered from our peripatetic life, though interspersed with a couple of years of good schooling at Loyola School in New York. He developed a fancy for mathematics and obtained a first-class honours degree in it from St Stephen's College in Delhi. He followed it up with a master's degree from Monash University in Melbourne. He is now well settled in the US, and he and Sanah have two lovely children, Zain and Zaydan.

While all the children grew up with distinct interests, they shared an interest in martial arts, the credit for which goes to my nephew Rashid, who lived with us for many years and teaches these arts.

Chapter 10

In Lieu of a Conclusion

An autobiographical effort generally has a brief beginning and an introspective culmination. At times, it remains an exercise of drawing partial conclusions from inadequate premises. A couplet premised on hard realism is often considered expressive:

> *Fikr-e-maash, ishq-e-butaan, yaad-e-raftagaan*
> *Do din ki zindagi main ab koi kya kya kiya kare?*

> (Concerns of life, claims of love, remembering friends bygone,
> How many things can one do in a two-day life span?)

An approach tinged with idealism however tends to bring forth a different prescription:

> *Tu ic-e paimaana-e-imroz-o-farda se na naap*
> *Jaawedaan, paiham rawaan, har-dum jawaan hai zindagi*

> (Do not measure life on a diurnal scale
> Never-ending is this life, ever young and hale.)

Looking back, I confess that the poles evaded me. My life has been a happy mix, work-wise and on the family front. I should therefore have no reason to dispute the end process.

I cannot help recalling an old lyric from the days when cricket was still a village game in England. It was penned around 1839 and described a universal process:

> Old cricketer your innings has been long,
> Your stumps must rattle when you are anon,
> Time takes the wicket, death begins to bowl
> It is vain to block, your score of runs is full.[178]

Till that stage is reached, life has to go on as the human being (exceptions apart) is a social creature that lives in societies, contributes to them, and at times, cogitates on the human condition and all experience, as Alfred Tennyson put it, is an arch through which 'gleams that untravelled world whose margin fades when I move'.

I could be no different. Coming into this world a decade before the freedom of India, I grew up and worked in post-Independence India, struggling with modernity and change. My university disciplines, professional career and experience in other public responsibilities defined my creed. My years of travel around the world led me to conclude that open, liberal and accommodative surroundings do bring about an atmosphere in which individual and group preferences find space for expression. By the same logic, its denial induces unfreedom in various shapes and forms and puts restrictions on physical and spiritual choices.

This was evident in post-Independence India, in which both plurality and diversity were evident as existential realities. Building on this, our founding fathers crafted a democratic and secular polity with a secular state structure. This was in tune with public perceptions. It became a durable basis for democratic institutions and endowed them with an aura of legitimacy.

In my last public address as Vice President, I had the occasion to think aloud about the state of the Republic in terms of its institutions. I focused scrutiny on five aspects: (i) the gap between 'equality before

---

[178] Neville Cardus, *English Cricket* (London, MCMXXXV [1935]) facing p. 33.

the law' and 'equal protection of the law', (ii) the representativeness of the elected representative (iii) the functioning of legislatures, (iv) the gender and diversity imbalance and, (v) secularism in practice.

I opined that the induction of ideological innovations into the core values of the Constitution was bringing forth dilution of principles and apprehensions of insecurity among segments of the citizen body. It gives rise to the suggestion that we are a polity at war with itself, in which the process of emotional integration has faltered and is in dire need of reinvigoration. On one plane, our commitment to the Rule of Law seems to be under serious threat, arising out of the noticeable decline in the efficacy of the institutions of the state, lapses into arbitrary decision-making and even 'ochlocracy' or mob rule, and the resultant public disillusionment; on another, are questions of fragility and cohesion, emanating from impulses that have shifted the political discourse from mere growth-centric to vociferous demands for affirmative action and militant protest politics. 'A culture of silence has yielded to protests.'[179] The vocal distress in the farming sector in different states, the persistence of Naxalite insurgencies, the re-emergence of language-related identity questions, seeming indifference to excesses pertaining to weaker sections of society, and the as-yet-unsettled claims of local nationalisms can no longer be ignored or brushed under the carpet. The political immobility in relation to J&K is disconcerting. Alongside are questions about the functioning of what has been called our 'asymmetrical federation' and 'the felt need for a wider, reinvigorated perspective on the shape of the Union of India' to overcome the crisis of 'moral legitimacy' in its different manifestations.

Two years later, each of these trends stood enhanced. The success of populism (rightly depicted not as an ideology but rather a strategy to obtain and retain power, and thriving on conspiracy, criminalization of all opposition, playing up external threats) proved itself in the 2019 general election. It was assisted by authoritarianism,

---

[179]Speech at the National Law School.

nationalism and majoritarianism. This ideological potion, premised simplistically on the desirability of oneness of language, ethnicity, religion, territory and culture was administered successfully to a little over a third of the electorate.

It is evident that a subversion of core values is now underway, an exercise that touches every citizen and leaves none untouched. Its impact is compounded by the abdication or failure of other social and political forces to comprehend its true nature and the urgency to counter it. I had the occasion to dilate on this regrettable phenomenon in my Fakhruddin Ali Ahmad Memorial Lecture in July 2019.

The impingement of these on pluralism and secularism has become evident in public discourse and political practice. It has been rightly observed that 'in the short space of four years, India has made a very long journey. It has travelled from its founding vision of civic nationalism to a new political imagery of cultural nationalism that appears to be firmly embedded in the public domain'.[180] Alongside, constitutional values such as fraternity, composite culture and promotion of scientific temper seem to disappear from our official and public discourse, to be replaced by promotion of beliefs and practices suggestive of the contrary.

The promised goal of all-round socio-economic development remains to be attained and progress towards it has been dilatory. Recent reports of our placement in global indices of progress—be they on GDP growth, the Democracy Index, the Corruption Index, health indicators and other determinants that figure in UNDP's annual Human Development Report—give little cause for satisfaction. Our progress towards becoming an inclusive society remains tardy since, as Prof. T.K. Oommen has pointed out, nine categories of people in our society who are deemed socially and/or politically and/or economically marginalized, remain excluded. These are: Dalits, Adivasis, OBCs, cultural minorities—both religious and linguistic,

---

[180] Niraja Gopal Jayal (ed.), *Re-forming India: The Nation Today* (New Delhi, 2019) p. xxxiv.

women, refugees-foreigners-outsiders, people from Northeast India, the poor and the disabled.[181] Thus, the fault lines in our society are visible; even official economists speak of 'two Indias—the urban rich India and the rural poor Bharat'. This continues to hurt and the numbers of the excluded add up to a high percentage of the citizen body. Ours is rated as the twelfth most inequitable economy in the world, with 45 per cent of the wealth controlled by millionaires. Almost half of India's total wealth was in the hands of the richest 1 per cent, while the top 10 per cent controlled about 74 per cent of it. The poorest 30 per cent have just 1.4 per cent of the total wealth.

It is evident that while democratic mobilization has produced an intense struggle for power, it has not delivered millions of citizens from abject dictates of poverty. Thus, the *de jure* 'WE, the People' in the first line of the Preamble is in reality a fragmented 'we', divided by yawning gaps that remain to be bridged. These 'dormant diversities' in multiple shapes and forms are coming to life and asserting their place in the sun. The politico-ideological effort now to superimpose on them the primacy of a religious majority in the guise of a transitory electoral majority, subject to periodic review in a democratic system, is the antithesis of equality and justice enshrined in Article 14.

The result of the 2019 general election has selectively generated a new momentum in the government's ideological agenda. Specific items in the *Sankalp Patra* of the ruling party (to which, admittedly insufficient attention was paid by many in the electorate) focused on 'securing the country against internal and external aggression' and to build a technologically modern $5-trillion economy, which would be the world's third largest. Specific political targets mentioned included abrogation of Article 370, which 'came in the way of development of the state of J&K' and annulment of Article 35A, which was 'discriminatory against non-permanent residents and women of J&K'. Alongside is the Citizenship

---

[181] T.K. Oommen, *Social Inclusion in Independent India: Dimensions and Approaches* (New Delhi, 2014) pp. 284–87.

Amendment Bill 'for the protection of individuals of religious minority communities from neighbouring countries escaping persecution' and giving them citizenship of India. These steps were placed high on the agenda of parliament and the procedural requirement of scrutiny by the Standing Committee or a Select Committee was dispensed with. Hence, the apprehension that parliament, instead of being a deliberative institution, becomes one for mere endorsement of majority vote since this would portray democratic deficit.

The steps taken in regard to the state of J&K and the sleight-of-hand tactics adopted do little credit to the regime of Rule of Law and the principles of democracy professed by the Republic. They amount to what has been called 'a show of brute majoritarianism'.[182] Similarly, the approach of the superior judiciary in opting for considerations of statecraft of the day, influencing the administration of justice does little credit to an iconic institution and damages public confidence. 'The result is the creation of an image of a nation-state whose security and prosperity depends on a strong Centre under the firm command of a single supreme leader.'[183]

The adverse international reaction to these moves has been expressed in official pronouncements from different governments and summed up by the *Economist*.[184] Alongside are credible scholarly assessments of its wider impact.[185] It is evident that the credibility of our discourse has been dented and is in dire need of qualitative correctives.

Since this coincides with 'a period of single party dominance on the national level, and as concern grows with the implications

---

[182] Pratap Bhanu Mehta, 'Winning Kashmir and Losing India,' *Foreign Affairs*, 20 September 2019.

[183] Partha Chatterjee, 'True Federalism Is the Counter-Narrative India Needs Right Now,' *The Wire*, 18 January 2020, https://thewire.in/politics/india-federalism-protests.

[184] The US State Department statements of 26 September 2019 and 12 January 2020. Also, *The Economist*, 23 January 2020.

[185] Sumit Ganguly, 'An Illiberal India?' *Journal of Democracy*, Volume 31(1), January 2020, pp. 195–202.

of majoritarian nationalism, federalism remains a critical area within which political and institutional checks and balances'[186] can come into play. A first manifestation of this has emerged in the shape of Kerala's current challenge in the Supreme Court to the Citizenship (Amendment) Act, 2019 and resolutions on similar lines in some other state legislatures. These suggest tensions in the federal system that need to be addressed before they get aggravated. The Sarkaria Commission's observation that 'a federation is not a static paradigm (but) a changing notion' remains relevant and so does its caution about the need to retain, protect and honour its core values.

The assaults on constitutional values have bewildered the citizen, who may well recall the situation depicted by a Persian poet:

Der ein shab-e-siyahum gum gushta rah-e-maqsood
Az gosha-e-barun aa ai kaukab-e-hidayat

(In this dark night I have lost the desired path
O star of guidance come forth and show me the way.)

The lodestar of our times is public opinion and the silver lining is the emergence of a vibrant debate in civil society and participation in it of the youth and women of all ages. India is undergoing a transformation and the younger generation has its own vocabulary for seeking dignity in the structuring of their future. The protests in the winter of 2019–20 'have exemplified the worth of constitutional and democratic methods of popular resistance'. We need to understand and accommodate it, but evidence of it is yet to emerge and portends civic tensions.

The civil society debate about the Constitution and its core values has been called constitutional patriotism. These values are enshrined in the Preamble and in the sections on Fundamental Rights and Fundamental Duties. Critical to all of these is the principle of equality and of fraternity, 'assuring the dignity of the individual and the Unity and Integrity of the nation'. It is to be noted that in the

---

[186]Louise Tillin, 'The Federalist Compromise,' ibid., Volume 28(3), July 2017, p. 74.

sequencing of values, liberty is anchored between justice and equality and these precede and are essential for fraternity. Thus, only a free and equal people can practice fraternity and derogation from any would derogate others. This is the ideology that 'We the People' gave ourselves and must pursue. Deviations from it in the shape of any version of strident nationalism premised on uniformity of faith and language have to be viewed is this context.

For both ideological and practical reasons, the debate about democracy and secularism has come to occupy a central place in the national discourse. The term 'secularism' itself has almost disappeared from the government's official vocabulary; while the 2014 Programme[187] had a section on equal opportunity for 'Minorities', the need for it was dispensed with in the 2019 *Sankalp Patra*. This gives credence to an eminent scholar's observation a few years back that India is on the path of making the transition from a liberal to an 'ethnic democracy'[188] making it a far cry from the concord delineated in the Bommai judgment's emphatic delineation of secularism for purposes of statecraft.

A perceptive observer has commented on the effort to impose religious majoritarianism on the functioning of our democracy of immense diversity and has aptly cited George Kennan's observation on the similarity between a democracy and the prehistoric dinosaur that is slow to wrath but destructful of its own habitat once disturbed: 'We, in India, must not let the dinosaur destroy our habitat.'[189]

The prognosis about our future as a society can fluctuate sharply. There is no dearth of models or of forecasts; they range from demographic to economic to geopolitical and to their overlapping. To be realistic, we have to admit that the consensus of yore no longer exists and the model of the type of society we visualize ourselves to be has to be reimagined and implemented.

The option may lie in choosing between making it inclusive

---

[187]BJP Manifesto 2014, p. 17.
[188]Christophe Jaffrelot, ibid. pp. 52–74.
[189]Fali S. Nariman, op. cit., pp. 442–45.

or exclusive, between social peace and social strife, between a secular society accommodative of all faiths and a theocratic one premised on the primacy of one faith. Each is a way of life and has a social cost reflected in the totality of all social activities. Record shows that a homogenous society is a rarity; the sheer diversity of the Indian scene rules it out and contrived religiosity may bring forth momentary electoral gains, but cannot be a substitute for the imperatives of sustained socio-economic progress. Strident nationalism and its illusory gains premised on falsehoods can also not be long-lasting.

What then is the alternative? My preference would be to revert in letter and spirit to 'We the People' and craft developmental programmes essential for attaining them. We need to commit ourselves to observance in letter and practice to the Rule of Law and ensure that government agencies, particularly the police, adhere to it and forsake the propensity of being above the law.

The institutions of the state are in dire need of reinvigoration. Democratically elected legislatures at all levels must revert to being deliberative and ensure an in-depth analysis of legislative proposals, executive accountability and discussions on matters of public interest and public concern. The present practice of pro forma observance of these must end. Electoral reforms and Law Commission Recommendations should see the light of day. Executive accountability must include restoration of the morale of the civil service and its professionalism.

Similarly, it has to be ensured that cooperative federalism is actualized and the Republic is not transformed into a de facto unitary state in pursuance of a majoritarian and ideological formula. Only this would ensure that the model committed to protecting cultural and religious difference, rather than imposing a uniform Indianness, is retained. None of these require innovation; each is achievable within the existing framework of laws and will prevent dissent and discord.

We should also not succumb to the temptation of the enforced homogenization being attempted in a social milieu traditionally enriched by its diversity between communities and within them. A simplistic or motivated reading of our history, suggesting that India is to be seen only in terms of religion, and of dividing its history in three religiously defined units of time, needs to be re-examined and, as shown in a recent study, the earlier periods and their socio-cultural landscapes were seen in terms of their own 'conceptual categories'; these compel a rethink of 'the proper place of religion' in India's past and the binary perceptions emanating from it.[190]

It would be prudent not to ignore the experience in our own times of other plural, non-homogenous societies and the limitations they confronted with regard to accommodation of diversities. It would be well to recall Ambedkar's caution of November 1949 about 'the life of contradictions' ahead and the three perils he foresaw. Each of these and all together beckon meaningful responses from us in thought and action.

In response to a query from an Iranian visitor a few months back, I depicted my life now as that of a *Darvish*. He reminded me of a couplet of Hafez that I found very appropriate:

Dar ein bazaar agar soodast ba darwesh khursand ast
Khudaya munemim gardaan ba darweshi o khursandi

(In the market of the world if profit there be, it is with the happy darvish
O God! Make me happy with darvishness and with happiness.)

---

[190]Richard M. Eaton, *India in the Persianate Age 1000–1765* (New Delhi, 2019) p. 10.

Acknowledgements

An autobiographical essay spanning over seven decades is essentially a journey in loneliness taken with ever-changing associates, family and friends. Each contributed in some measure to the shaping of my personality and its response to challenges. Naming them all would be ponderous; selectively would suggest partiality to time and place. Suffice it to say that the actual writing was undertaken last year and finished in the early months of 2020. I was not diligent enough to have the benefit of dairies and notebooks and, therefore, had to resort to memory and, at times, to publicly available sources. Salma's recollections were often invaluable.

I have to thank Rupa Publications for encouraging me to embark on this endeavour. My colleague, Shri Anil Kaushik, helped in the preparation of the manuscript for publication.

Index

Aadhaar (Targeted Delivery of Financial and other Subsidies, Benefits and Services) Act, 2016, 219
Aashufta Bayani Meri, 13
Aasman Manzil, 15, 139
Abdulaziz, Khalid bin, 49
Abdulaziz, Talal bin, 34, 41
Abdullah, Farooq, 110
Abdullah, Sheikh Ahmad, 243
Abdullah, T.T.P., 39
Abhyankar, Rajan, 46
Abu Dhabi, 52–58
  arrival in, 54
  fancy of, 55
  Indian Ladies Association, 58
  special care centre, 58
Abu Dhabi National Oil Company, 56
Accommodating Diversity in a Globalizing World, 260
The Achievement and Challenges of Indian Democracy, 266
activism, 49, 114, 124, 307
Adam, John, 271
Aden, 33, 86
Adil Shahi, 100
Advani, L.K., 55, 145
Afghan Interim Government (AIG), 82
Afghan refugees in Delhi, 64

Afghan–India relations, 91
Afghanistan
  bin Laden's move, 127
  internal affairs, 155
  no longer a foreign-policy matter in the US, 88
  objective of Indian policy in Afghanistan, 80
  Soviet intervention in, 118–19
  US approach, 87
  See also Kabul
Afghanistan: A Neighbour with a Difference for the volume *External Affairs*, 155
Afghanistan: The Great Game Revisited, 79
Afzal, S.M., 143
Agenda 2063: The Africa We Want, 265
'Agenda for India' Resolution, 194
An Agenda for Peace, 107
Agnihotri, V.K., 190
Ahmad, Barakat, 38
Ahmad, Habib, 9, 16
Ahmad, Islam, 16
Ahmad, Maqbool, 13
Ahmad, Nafees, 143
Ahmad, Talmiz, 179
Ahmad, Tanveer, 179

Ahmed, Fakhruddin Ali, 54, 325
Ahmedabad riots (September 1969), 40
Aiyar, Mani Shankar, 46, 162
Ajmani, Jagdish, 23
Akbar, Jalaluddin, 100
Akhtar, Begum, 38
al Faisal, Turki, 127, 135
Al Madina, 41
Al Saud, King Abdullah bin Abdulaziz, 15, 130, 164, 255
Al Shura, 127
Alam, Hakim Mahboob, 9
Al-Azmeh, Aziz, 155
al-Bakr, Ahmad Hasan, 26
Albright, Madeleine, 115–16
Al-e-Ahmad, Jalal, 105
Alexander, P.C., 184
Algerian national movement, 23
Al-Hitti, Shakir, 25
al-Hujjaj, Qazvini's Anis, 129
Ali, Maulana Mohammad, 4
Ali, Mushtaq, 18
Ali, Syed Mushtaq, 17
Aligarh Muslim University (AMU), 9, 12, 15–17, 114–15, 139–51, 225, 277, 282, 298–300, 321–22
   annual convocation, 146
   attendance shortage of students, 143
   career advancement scheme, 144
   churning and politicking in the Executive Council, 149
   customary report of VC, 147–48
   disturbed law-and-order situation, 146
   drop in the number of PhD candidates, 144–45
   early challenge, 142–43
   Giani Zail Singh as chief guest (1986), 146
   Honorary Life Membersip from Students Union, 321
   I.K. Gujral as chief guest (2002), 146–47
   incident of a bomb blast in a train near Agra, 145
   inherited traditions, 142
   lack of regular teacher attendance, 144
   morning walks and occasional visits to sports grounds, 144
   National Assessment and Accreditation Council assessments, 145
   negotiate space to conduct a non-partisan administration, 142
   visit to 'Minto-E', 140
Aligarh Se Aligarh Tak, 14
Alireza, Mohammad Ali Zainul, 134
All India Anna Dravida Munnetra Kazhagam (AIADMK), 194
All India Trinamool Congress (AITC), 194
Allahabadi, Akbar, 106
Al-Mansoori, Sheikh Abdul Rahman, 35
al-Muslemeen, Imam, 119
Alvi, Sharfuddin, 16
Al-Wardi, Ali, 30
al-Zahawi, Jamil Sidqi, 161
Amanullah, Afzal, 143, 179
Ambedkar's speech of 25 November 1949, 294
American Orientalism, 159
American Theocracy, 160
An American Witness to India's Partition, 228
Amnesty International, 154
Andhra cuisine, first exposure to, 22
Andhra Pradesh Reorganisation Bill, 2014, 212
Anjuman Taraqqi-e-Urdu, 78
Annan, Kofi, 116, 262
Ansari, Dr Islamul Haq, 9
Ansari, Hakim Abdul Ghani, 129
Ansari, Mohammad Abdul Aziz, 1
Ansari, Mukhtar Ahmad, 2, 4–5, 13
Ansari, Naseem, 7, 10, 18, 140

Anti-Defection Law of 1985, 194
Antonius, George, 26
Antulay, A.R., 50, 167
The Arab Awakening, 26
Arab-Israeli War of 1973, 47, 49
Arab nationalism, 34, 41, 49, 55, 289
Arab Revolt of 1916, 289
Arab Sheikhdoms, 42
Arab world, internecine conflict in, 41
Arasaratnam, S., 77
Arif, Abdul Salam, 26
Aristotle, 14, 18
Armed Forces Special Powers Act, 177
Aryabhumi, 93
Aryamehr, Shahanshah, 15
ASEAN-India Commemorative Summit, 257
ASEAN-India Strategic Partnership, 259
The Asian Age, 163
Asiatic Society, Kolkata, 266, 305
Association of Southeast Asian Nations, 74
asymmetrical federation, 306, 335
Athar, Ali, 144
Australia-India Council, 75
Australian Cricket Society, 76
Australian Labour Party (ALP), 73, 74, 321
Australian National University (ANU), 75, 77–79, 321, 331
Australian Parliamentary Friendship Group of India, 79
authoritarianism, 325, 335
Azad, Abul Kalam, 4, 7, 67, 101, 140, 142, 150, 180, 298
Aziz, Ishrat, 117
Azmi, Shabana, 131

B.G. Verghese Memorial Lecture, 323
Ba'ath Party, 25–26, 32
Babri Masjid, destruction of, 103
Bachchan, Amitabh, 84

Bada'uni, Abd-ul-Qadir, 100
Baghdad Pact, 25
Baghdad, 23–30
   1958 revolution, 27
   centrality of the river Tigris, 29
   charms of, 29
   deal of military activity, 24
   ethnic and sectarian terms, 30
   gregariousness and generosity, 29
   interesting aspect of consular work, 26
   Iraq's dissociation from the Baghdad Pact, 25
   Iraq's railways system, 29
   izdiwaj (split personality) of a value system, 30
   Kurdish insurgency in the north, 30
   land and social reforms, 24
   misadventure of reigniting Iraq's claims on Kuwait, 25
   pleasant memory, 29
   polygamy, 24
   women's rights, 24
Bahuguna, H.N., 55
Bahujan Samaj Party (BSP), 194
Bains, K.S., 20
Bakshi, Kamal, 20
Balfour Declaration, 289
Balkan War, 2–3, 247–48
Ballabh, Govind, 13
Banda, Rupiah, 244
Bandar Abbas, 56
Bandung Conference, 254
Banerjee, Mamata, 215
Bangladesh crisis of 1971, 44
Banya community, 54
Barka, Mehdi Ben, 50
Barker, Sir Ernest, 15
Barzani, Mulla Mustafa, 24
Basham, A.L., 75, 77
Basic Structure doctrine, 304
Battuta, Ibn, 29, 260
Batu, Inal, 116

Baxi, Upendra, 271
Bazargan, Mehdi, 98
Beg, Anwar Ali, 9
Beg, Gali Ali, 29
Belgrade Conference (1961), 254
Bhagat, Arun, 20
Bhagat, Usha, 60
Bhagwan Sahay Committee Report (1971), 233
Bhalla, Usha, 48
Bhandari, Romesh, 57, 64
Bhardwaj, Hans Raj, 238
Bhargava, Kant Kishore, 46
Biden, Joe, 229
bin Faisal, Turki, 229
bin Laden, Osama, 119, 123, 127
BJP, 176, 184, 194, 202–3, 206, 214, 219–20
Black Money Bill (Undisclosed Foreign Income and Assets) and Imposition of Tax Bill, 2015, 219n156
Blue Mosque, 86
Board of Control for Cricket in India (BCCI), 16, 76
book release functions, 326–27
Booth, Ken, 297
Boroujerdi, Alauddin, 99, 103
Bose, Krishna, 161
Bose, Subhas Chandra, 4, 327
Bose, Sugata, 129
Bose, Sumantra, 326–27
Bouteflika, Abdelaziz, 267
Boutros-Ghali, Boutros, 107
Bradman, Donald, 76
Brahmo Samaj, 100
British Broadcasting Corporation (BBC), 9, 90
British East India Company, 25
British Indian government a Sword of Honour, 2
British paramountcy, 53
Brookings Intelligence Project, 114n76

Browne, E.G., 101
Brussels, 45–48
    Cooperation Agreement, 46
    cultural and press relations, 47
    culturally rich, 45
    political hub of a new Europe, 46
    statue of Mahatma Gandhi, 46
Buhari, Muhammadu, 264
burden of political events. *See* Partition (1947)
Burke, Edmund, 204
Burton, Sir Richard, 34
Butler, Richard, 116
Butler, Samuel, 173
Button, John, 74
Bygone Heat: Travels of an Idealist in the Middle East, 27

'a Calcutta boy', 183
calling attention, 199
Canberra, 72–79
    life member of the South Asian Studies Association, 77
    St Andrew's Day dinner of the Melbourne Scots, 77
'cancerous development', 271
CARE India-sponsored Gujarat Harmony Project, 152
Castro, Fidel, 67, 252
Caudwell, Christopher, 9
Central Bureau of Investigation (CBI), 210, 274, 276
Central Selling Organization, 75
Central Vigilance Commission (CVC), 210, 276
Chagai-I explosions by Pakistan, 127
Chandhoke, Neera, 326–27
Chandra, Satish, 110
Charge d'Affaires (CDA), 127
Chari, Chandra, 180
Chatterjee, N.C., 189
Chatterjee, Somnath, 189

Chaudhuri, Nirad C., 11
Chavan, Y.B., 48
Chief Election Commissioner (CEC), 110
Chief of Protocol (CoP), 59
China, emergence as important trading partners, 74
Chinese revolution, 15
Chinoy, Sujan, 118
Choudhury, Humayun Rashid, 45
Chowdhary, Farouk, 153
Citizenship, 253, 312, 323, 337
Citizenship (Amendment) Act, 2019, 339
Citizenship (Amendment) Bill, 2016, 220, 323, 337–38
Citizenship Act, 1955, 220
Cold War, 24, 107, 327
Cole, Juan, 101, 161
College life, 10
  preference for geology, 10
  St Xavier, 10–11
  switchover to Intermediate (Arts), 11
'colonial cousins', 72, 249
Committee for the Promotion of Virtue and the Prevention of Vice, 39, 120
Commonwealth conclaves, 73
Commonwealth Heads of Government Meeting (CHOGM), 69, 74
communal violence, 5, 168, 175
line of argument against, 5
Communal Violence (Prevention, Control and Rehabilitation of Victims), 175
communalism, 5, 234, 329
Communist Party of India (CPI), 22, 194, 202
Communist Party of India (Marxist) (CPI [M]), 182, 194
Comptroller and Auditor General of India (CAG) report, 209
conceptual categories, 342
Confederation of Indian Industry, 160

Conference of Governors, 232–37
Conservation of Foreign Exchange and Prevention of Smuggling Activities Act (COFEPOSA), 1974, 54, 56
Constitution of India, 171, 203, 320, 329
  Article 25(1), 171
  Article 63, 186
  Article 35A, annulment of, 337
  Article 370, abrogation of, 337
  civil society debate, 339
  fundamental duties of citizens, 288
  fundamental rights and directive principles of state policy, 288
  fundamental rights, 293
  One Hundred and Eighth Amendment Bill, 2008, 205
  preamble of, 293, 296, 304, 314–15, 337
  principles of, 328
Constitution of the Islamic Republic, 97
Constitutional patriotism, 339
Contemporary Challenges in the Realm of Culture, 319
Controversies, 315–17
Cooperative federalism, 341
Corruption, 206, 274–75, 336
  hampers governance and development, 275
  'inconvenient fact' of Indian democracy, 206
  pervasive, cancerous and multidimensional, 275
Corruption Index, 336
Council of States, 185–87, 200
counter-revolutionary forces, 290
Cricket's Imperial Crisis of 1932–1933, 76
cross-cultural dialogue, 320
Crown Prince, 43, 55, 57, 61, 123–24, 126, 135, 257, 269
Cuban threat perception, 67
cultural revitalization, 324, 329
Current, 16

Dajani, Sulaiman, 32, 73, 77. *See also* Rabat
Dane, Louis, 79
Das, C.R., 4
Davignon report (1970), 46
Dawesar, O.P., 69
Dayal, Naresh, 99, 216
A Decade with Painters of the Islamic Revolution, 97
'Declaration on Measures to Eliminate International Terrorism', 112
Dehlavi, A.W. Azhar, 158
Dehlvi, Daagh, 78, 216
Democracy Index, 336
democratic polity, 311, 313, 320
Deutscher, Isaac, 26
Devare, Sudhir, 100, 155
Devare, T.N., 100
Dewan, Ashok, 191, 239
Dhul-Qarnayn, 96
Dietary requirements, 68
Dietl, Gulshan, 138
diplomatic corps, dean of, 65
'disagreeable episode', 109
district attachment period, 22
District Gazetteer, 1
Diversity Index, 173
Dixit, J.N., 107, 155
Dixit, Mani, 82, 99
Doddamani, J.N., 20
Dostum, Abdul Rashid, 91–92, 102
Doucet, Lyse, 90
Dubey, Muchkund, 95, 99
Durand Line Agreement (1893), 80
Duty Society, 14

earliest impressions and recollections of father, 6
Economist, 89, 338
Editors Guild of India, 152, 324
educational exchange programme, 245
e-governance, 276
ElBaradei, Mohamed, 273

Election Commission, 182, 222
electoral reforms, 341
Electronic Voting Machines (EVMs), manipulation of, 222
Elimination of All Forms of Racial Discrimination, 108
Elizabeth II, Queen, 57
The Emergence of Modern Afghanistan: Politics of Reform and Modernization, 79
employability surveys, 236
Energy and Resources Institute, 98
energy policy, 46
England and Afghanistan: A Phase in their Relations, 79
Erdoğan, Recep Tayyip, 248
Essebsi, Beji Caid, 261
Essid, Habib, 261
ethnic democracy, 340
European Economic Community (EEC), 45–46
Evangelical, 322
Evans, Gareth, 74, 229, 321
Exclusive Agreement of 1892, 52
'extraordinary leave', 21

Fahd, King, 122, 125
Faisal, King, 34, 36–37, 39–40, 42, 45, 49, 118
  annual banquet during the Hajj, 37
faith-based systems, 325
Family history, 1
Farewell to the Rajya Sabha, 223–27
  farewell function, 226
  interview to Karan Thapar on Rajya Sabha, 224
  last day of my term of office, 224
  PM's remarks to be a departure, 226
  procedural correctives, 224
Farhâdi, Ravan, 116
Farooqi, Aasiya, 2
Farooqi, Iqbal, 19

Fatima, 1, 58, 104
Fazl, Abul, 100
festival of India, 252–53
Fida, Maqbool, 38
first-past-the-post system (FPTP system), 222, 306
Five Principles of Peaceful Coexistence, 254. *See also* Panchsheel
foreign policy, 46, 68, 94, 106, 121, 123, 159, 223, 232, 254, 263, 270–72
Foreigners Act, 1946, 220
formative years, 13–19
　Aftab Hostel, 16
　applied for University Grants Commission (UGC) Fellowship, 18
　Cafe de Phoos, 16
　'introduction' ceremony in the hostel, 16
　preparing for the UPSC examination, 18
　Sir William Marris medal, 18
　university cricket ground, 17
Forty Years in the Wilderness and the Empty Quarter, 34
Fotedar, M.L., 215
Four Centuries of Modern Iraq, 26
Fraser, James, 102
fraternity, principle of, 314, 339
freedom movement, 4, 13, 15
Frontline, 137–38
Fuchi, Paulo, 116
Fundamental Rights and Directive Principles of State Policy, 288
Fundamental Rights and Fundamental Duties, 339

Galbraith, John Kenneth, 114, 124
Gambari, Ibrahim, 116
Gandhi, Gopal, 238
Gandhi, Indira, 39, 55, 59–62, 68–69, 71, 80–81, 90, 125, 131, 135, 327
Gandhi, Kasturba, 4

Gandhi, Mahatma, 46, 64, 262
　depiction of seven social sins, 272
Gandhi, Rajiv, 59, 74, 83–84, 98, 276
Gandhi, Sonia, 60, 98, 165, 182
Gaur, Anshuman, 191
Gavan, S.S., 27
Gazetteer of the Persian Gulf, Oman and Central Arabia, 43
GDP growth, 275, 336
genealogical tables, 1
General Assembly Resolution, 111
general election (2014), 175, 217, 220, 253, 328
general election (2019), 220, 328, 335, 337
General Maritime Treaty of 1820, 52
Geneva Accords, 78
'Genghis Khan Tours', 262
Ghali, Dr, 116
Ghani, Ashraf, 255
Ghannouchi, Cheikh Rachid, 261
Gharbzadegi or Westoxification, 105
Gharekhan, Chinmaya, 68, 103, 108, 116, 155, 216
Ghazi, Abidullah, 16
Ghose, Dilip Kumar, 79
global war on terrorism, 90
Gopal, S., 43
governance of enactment, 201
Governors' Conference of 2013, 234
Governors' Conference of 2016, 235
Govindarajan, R., 46
A Grammar of Politics, 14
Gramsci, Antonio, 308
Green, T.H., 14
Gregorian, Vartan, 79
Gromyko, Andrei, 60
Group of 77, 112
Grover, Vinod, 20
The Guardian, 81
A Guide to Diplomatic Practice, 59
Gujarat and the Sea, 237

Gujral, I.K., 64, 91, 99, 146, 228
Gul, Abdullah, 248
Gupta, Madhukar, 110
Gupta, Randhir, 72

Habib, Mohammad, 12–14, 19
habit of diplomats, 68
Haider, Ehsan, 9
Hajj pilgrimage, 33, 36–37, 129, 179
  arrangements, 36, 179
  fire broke out (1997), 129
  Indian delegation to the conference, 130
  multiple dimensions, 37
  relevance of Indian Muslim opinion, 130
The Hajj: The Muslim Pilgrimage to Mecca and the Holy Places, 129
Hamid, Sayyid, 139
Hannay, David, 113, 116
happenings of lesser intensity, 64
Haq, Ziaul, 9, 140
hard realism, 333
Haris, 1–2, 6, 8, 10, 12, 16, 18
Harish, P., 118, 191
Harmain, Khadim al, 119
Hasan, Abol, 78
Hasan, Hadi, 13
Hasan, Noorul, 13
Hasan, Ziaul, 9
Hasan, Zoya, 159, 165, 171
Hawke, Bob, 74
Hayden, Bill, 74
Hazare, Anna, 206
health indicators, 336
Hidayatullah, Mohammad, 70, 191
Hindu Mahasabha, 303
The Hindu, 139, 155–56, 161
Hindu right-wing communalism, 329
Hinduism, 294
Hinduja, Gopichand, 95
A History of Political Theory, 14

The History of the Russian Revolution, 26
History on Stones: Inscriptions of Aligarh Muslim University, 144
Hobbes, Thomas, 14
Holroyde, Peggy, 249
'home shelter' for nomads, 137
Hooda, Bhupinder Singh, 189
The Horseshoe Table: An Inside View of the UN Security Council, 108
House of Lords, 204, 217
Human Rights Day, 295
Human Rights Watch, 88, 153
Husain, Dr Zakir, 12, 140, 180
Hussain, Abid, 150, 270
Hussain, Azim, 42
Hussain, Syed Nazir, 38
Hussein, Saddam, 32, 125
hyper-nationalism, 315

Ibrahim, Ezzeddin, 55
idealism, 333
ideological innovations, induction of, 335
Ijtihad, 119, 180, 270
Independence Agreement of 2 December 1971, 52
India and Islamic Civilization: Contributions and Challenges, 321
India, Thailand and ASEAN: Contours of a Rejuvenated Relationship, 258
India–European Union (EU), 173
India-Iran Joint Commission Meeting, 103
India–Morocco Chamber of Commerce, 260
Indian Association for Central and West Asian Studies, 155
Indian Chamber of Commerce (INCHAM), 252
Indian Civil Services (ICS), 20–21, 31, 46
Indian Council of World Affairs (ICWA), 229
Indian Council of World Affairs Act, 2001, 232

Indian Foreign Affairs Journal, 41
Indian Foreign Service (IFS), 20–23, 31, 33, 82, 107, 138, 191, 232
The Indian Muslims, 180
Indian National Army, 44
Indian National Congress (INC), 5, 98, 194, 98
Indian National Trust for Art and Cultural Heritage (INTACH), 147
The Indian Parliament as an Institution of Accountability, 181
Indian Penal Code, 153
Indian Post Office (Amendment) Bill, 70
Indian Space Research Organisation, 257
Indians in White Australia, 77
Indo-Afghan Relations 1882–1907, 79
Indo-Iran relations, 44n31, 164
Indo-Pak conflict (1965), 49
Indo-Saudi bilateral relations, 36, 124
Indo-UAE relations, 58
Indo-US nuclear deal, 202
Indo–US relations, 223
Influence of Islam on Indian Culture, 96
infra-historical rhythm, 154, 289, 318
injection of new vitality, 74
INS Chakra, 75
Institute for Defence Studies and Analysis, 137
institutional role of the governor, 235
Insurance Regulatory and Development Authority (IRDA), 19
An Intellectual's Locution of Dissent, 180
inter-communal harmony, appeal for, 4, 302
International Atomic Energy Agency (IAEA), 99, 163, 183, 273
International Court of Justice, 37, 112
International Labour Organization, 231
International Monetary Fund (IMF), 123
International Yoga Day, 316
Inter-Services Intelligence, 82
Inter-State Migrant Workmen (Regulation of Employment and Conditions of Service) Act, 203
intra-Kashmiri dialogue, 156
An Introduction to Politics, 10, 18
Iqbal, Allama, 141
Iqbal, Mohammad, 92, 298
Iranian Majlis, 61
Iranian Revolution, 56, 158
aftermath of, 158
Iran–Iraq war (1980–88), 65–67, 98
Iraq Petroleum Company (IPC), 25
Iraq, US invasion of, 183
Iraqi invasion of Kuwait, 98, 120, 125
Iraqi National Guard, 26
Islam, 3, 12, 16, 35, 97–98, 101, 118–19, 124, 126, 129, 135, 148, 153, 159–60, 251, 256, 260, 282, 294, 298, 321
Islamic jihad, 119
Islamic law, 119
Islamic militancy, 148
'Islamic posture', 128
Islamic propaganda, 97
Islamic radicalism, 120
Islamic Revolution, 97, 105, 158–59
Islamic schools (Hanafi, Shafi'i, Maliki, Hanbali, and Zaydi)', 97
'Islamic' television channels, 51
Istiqlal Party, 32
Iyengar, P.K., 99

Jacob, P.J., 160
Jadhav, Narendra, 155
Jaitley, Arun, 217
Jamaat-e-Islami, 14, 133
St James's School for Boys, 10
Jamia Millia, dissent in the origins of, 270
Jamia's Academy of Third World Studies, 154
Jamir, S.C., 238
Janata Dal (United), 194
Janata Party government, installation of the, 54–55

Jannati, Ayatollah Ahmad, 229
Japan, emergence as important trading partners, 74
Jashanmal, Atma, 26
Jashanmal, Mohan, 57
Jawab-e-Dost, 140
Jayal, Niraja Gopal, 326–28, 336
Jeddah, 33–41, 48–51
  absence of schooling for our children, 39
  Arbitration Agreement of 1954, 35
  ban on visas to Sikhs, 36
  constitutional monarchy, 34
  difficulties of political reporting, 35
  Indian-origin families in, 134
  modest-sized city, 34
  politically motivated uproar, 40
  posting, 33
  productive and rewarding stint, 41
  Saudi style of communication, 49
  Shahabuddin's 'activism', 49
  social mores, 35
Jefferson, Thomas, 187
Jeffrey, Robin, 228
Jha, A.N., 20
Jilani, Sheikh Abdul Qadir, 28
Jiluwi, Abdullah bin, 39
Jinnah, M.A., 6, 115, 321
Jinping, Xi, 254
Jodpa, Lama Chospel, 165
St John Philby, 34
Jomhouri Eslami, 105
Josh, Harcharan Singh, 165
Journalism in Times of Strident Nationalism, 323
Jubayr, Ibn, 29
Judges (Declaration of Assets and Liabilities) Bill, 2009, 203
Judges (Inquiry) Act, 1968, 204
Judges Inquiry Committee, 204
Jyotiba, Mahatma, 231

Kabul, 79–93
  battle of Jalalabad, 82
  children's hospital, 90
  Indo-Afghan relations, 90
  interim government of mujahideen groups, 92
  objective of our policy in Afghanistan, 80
  Pakistan's influence, 80
  socializing in, 90
Kadivar, Mohsen, 105
Kairanvi, Maulana Mohammad Saleem Usmani, 38
Kalam, A.P.J. Abdul, 214
Kalla, Jusuf, 255
Kao, R.N., 68, 280
Kapadia, Farouk, 46
Kapur, Devesh, 181
Karim, Moulavi Abdul, 2
Karimov, Islam, 251
Kashmir issue, 80
Kashmir 'situation', 94
Kashmir valley, insurgency in January 1990, 93
Kashmir, rights of 'people of Kashmir', 94
Katju, Vivek, 154
Kaul, T.N., 44
Kaunda, Kenneth, 244
Kazmi, Asadullah, 27
Kazmi, Salma, 18
Kazmi, Sanah, 160
Kazmi, Yedullah, 16, 27
Keïta, Ibrahim Boubacar, 265
Kennan, George, 340
Kennedy, Paul, 299
Kerala Muslim League, 43
Khaimah, Ras Al, 55
Khaleeli, Akbar, 23
Khaleeli, Ustad Khalilullah, 92
Khalid (elder brother), 1, 6, 8, 10, 12, 19, 28

Khalifa, Sheikh, 55, 57
Khaliquzzaman, Chaudhry, 2
Khamenei, Ayatollah, 97
Khan, Abrar Mustafa, 14
Khan, Admiral, 78
Khan, Arshad Sami, 41
Khan, Asjad Husain, 16
Khan, Aziz, 143
Khan, Bairam, 240
Khan, Begum Sakeena, 23
Khan, Bismillah, 38
Khan-e-Khanan, Abdur Rahim, 240
Khan, Fazil, 102
Khan, Hakim Ajmal, 130
Khan, Hamiduddin, 13
Khan, K. Rahman, 192
Khan, Kunwar Ammar Ahmad, 12
Khan, Mansoor Ali, 18
Khan, Mohammad, 83
Khan, Muhammad Zafarullah, 37
Khan, Rafaqat Ali, 16
Khan, Rifaqat Ali, 9
Khan, Sadat Ali, 23
Khan, Shah Nawaz, 44
Khan, Shakila Ali, 128
Khan, Syed Ahmad, 147
Khan, T.K., 77
Khan, Yahya, 40–41
Khan, Yusuf 'Dilip Kumar', 147
Khandaria, Brajesh, 48
Kharrazi, Kamal, 116
Khilafat movement, 3–4
Khomeini, Imam, 97, 105, 159
Khorasani, Rajai, 94
Khurshid, Salman, 108, 110
Kidwai, Hasan, 19
Kidwai, Hashim, 15
Kidwai, Midhat, 36
Kidwai, Rafi Ahmed, 7
Kifayatullah, Mufti, 4
'the king of drinks', 89
'Kiswah', 50

Klass, Rosanne, 79
Kohli, Sunita, 60
Koshyari, Bhagat Singh, 250
Kothari, Rajni, 281
Krishna, V.K., 47
Krishnamurti Foundation, 19
Krishnaswamy, K.R., 26
Kulkarni, Sudheendra, 238
Kumar, Naresh, 46
Kumar, Shiv, 31
Kumar, Sushil, 22
Kumaraswamy, P.R., 138
Kunda, George, 244
Kundu, Amitabh, 173
Kurdistan: Divided Nation of the Middle East, 27
Kurien, P.J., 192
Kuwait war (1990–91), 32, 105, 122, 131
Kwatra, D.R., 31
Kymlicka, Will, 300

Labour Government, 217
Lady Brabourne College, 10
Lady Shri Ram College, 231
Laiq, Sulaiman, 89
Lal Bahadur Shastri National Academy of Administration, 19
Lal, K.M., 20–21
Lall, K.B., 46, 330
Land Acquisition Act, 1894, 213
Land Acquisition, Rehabilitation and Resettlement (LARR) Bill, 213
Laroui, Abdallah, 31–32, 318
Laski, Harold, 10, 14
Latif, Niazul, 17
Law Commission Recommendations, 341
Lawlessness, 71
Leanart, Rik, 47
Legacy of the Indian Freedom Movement, 264
Letter of Demands, 120

Libyan Arab Republic, 66
life of contradictions, 271, 306, 342
Little, Douglas, 159
Locke, John, 14
Lokpal, 207
Long, Richard, 27
Longrigg, Stephen, 26
Look East and Act East policies, 257
Look West Policy, 279
Lord Curzon's edict of 1903, 42
Lorimer, John Gordon, 43

Machiavelli, 14, 186, 194
Madina, 3, 30, 36, 38, 49, 133–34
Madrasa Saulatiya, 38
Madrassa, Bibi Khanum, 251
Maduro, Nicolás, 263
Mahajan, Sumitra, 166, 213
Mahapatra, Chintamani, 159
Mahapatra, Sitakant, 20
Mahdi, 119
majoritarianism, 325, 336, 338, 340
Makkah, 33, 35–38, 50, 118, 129–30, 133–34
   attack in, 118
   Indian-origin families in, 134
   Muslim congress in, 130
   region of concentration, 134
Makkah Dialogue (2003), 158
Malankara Catholicos, 56
Malaviya, Pandit Madan Mohan, 4
Malhotra, Moni, 20
Malik, Abdul, 2
Mandavia, Mansukh L., 267
Mangalmurti, Madhav, 20
Mangeshkar, Lata, 83
mango-eating competitions, 8
Marker, Jamsheed, 109
Marx, Karl, 14
Marylebone Cricket Club (MCC), 76
Masjid-e-Aqsa, attack on, 39
Masood, Rasheed, 184

Masood, Sheikh Ibrahim, 44
Massilos, Jim, 77
Mathur, S.K., 82
Mathur, S.N., 20
Maulana Azad Library, 15, 141–42, 150
Mazar-e-Sharif, 102
Mazar-i-Sharif, 86
Meenakshi Temple, 93
Mehdi, Shahid, 16, 154
Mehra, Shyam, 82
Mehta, Ashok Nandlal, 43
Mehta, Pratap Bhanu, 181
Memorandum of Advice, 121–22
Menon, Krishna, 114
Menon, V.P., 285, 305
   symbol of anti-Americanism in India, 114n76
Merkel, Angela, 229
Mianwali jail (now in Pakistan), 4
Militant Islam: Cause and Effect, 148
Millennium Development Goals, 211
Miller, Keith, 76
Mines and Minerals (Development and Regulation) Bill, 2011, 209
mining, liberalization in, 209
mini-refugee camp, 7
Ministry of External Affairs (MEA), desk attachment, 22
Mirza, Baber, 14
Mishat, Mohammad, 32
Mishra, Brajesh, 109–10, 158
Mishra, R.K., 62, 156
MMAJ Academy of International Studies, 154
mob rule, 335
'moderate Islam', 260
modern democracy, 312
Modern Review, 5
Modi, Narendra, 152, 189, 237
Mohammed, Sheikh Tahnoun bin, 56
Mohammedan Anglo-Oriental (M.A.O.) College, 2

Mohammedan Sporting Club, 10
Mohsin, Mohammad, 128, 153
Moinuddin, 19, 248
Money Bill, 219n156
Montazeri, Grand Ayatollah, 105
moral legitimacy, crisis of, 335
'mother of cities' to the Arabs, 86
Mother Teresa, investiture ceremony in Rashtrapati Bhavan, 69
Mubarak, Hosni, 290
Mugabe, Robert, 68
Mukerji, D.P., 13
Mukherjee, Pranab, 111, 179, 208, 215–16, 316
Mukhtar Ahmad Ansari School, 13
Murtada, Saaduddin, 36
Muslim Brotherhood, 41, 55, 290
Muslim Chamber of Commerce, 8
Muslim Institute, 8
Muslim Personal Law, 282
Muslim Salvation Army (Al Junood-ul-Rabbaniya), 3
Muslim women, socio-educational backwardness of, 319
Muslim World League (Rabitat al-Alam al-Islami), 35
'Muslim-ness', 162
Mutawa, 39
Muttawakil, Wakil Ahmad, 84

Nadwi, Abul Hasan Ali, 35
Naga system of village councils, 237
Naidu, Sarojini, 4, 140
Naik, Narendra, 20
Naik, Ram, 238
Najibullah, Mohammad, 83–92, 102
  policy of seeking national reconciliation, 87
  peace plan, 88
  Indian political support to, 90
Nambiar, Vijay, 102
NAM-CHOGM team, 71

Nanda, B.R., 228
Nandini Sunder case (2011), 288
Narain, Yogendra, 184, 190
Narasimhan, E.S.L., 238
Narayanan, K.R., 139, 151, 286
Narayanan, M.K., 238
Nariman, Fali S., 70, 204
Narwani, Kailash, 105
Naseem (Sister), 1, 7, 10, 19, 140
Nasser, Gamal Abdel, 41
Nath, Syam Sunder, 31
National Assembly and the Council of Nations, 267
National Commission for Minorities Act of 1992, 165, 172
National Commission for Minorities (NCM), 165–75
  Aligarh riot of 6 April 2006, 169
  annual conference of, 172
  complaints from Christian groups, 169
  corrective action, 167
  framework of minority rights, 175
  grievance of the minority community, 169
  'inducement' and 'allurement' allegations of, 171
  'inequality traps' in the political system, 173
  Mangalore riots of October 2006, 170
  Minorities Rights Day, 172
  Nandigram incident (2007), 170
  on-the-spot investigations, 167
  special package for internally displaced families in Gujarat, 169
  Sachar Committee Report, 175
National Democratic Alliance (NDA), 69, 139, 150, 194, 201, 217–18, 223, 253
National Food Security Act 2013, 211n146
National Food Security Bill, 211
National Human Rights Commission, 152

National Knowledge Commission, 283
National Mineral Policy (1993), 209
  objective of the new, announced in March 2008, 209
National Security Advisory Board (NSAB), 162–63
National Small Industries Corporation of India, 245
National Social Watch Media, 201
nationalism, 101, 224, 265, 284, 303, 314–15, 320, 324–26, 328, 336, 339–41
Nawaiwaqt, 82
Nawwab, Nimah Ismail, 132
Nayyar, Vineet, 20
Nazarbayev, Nursultan, 241
'negative symmetry' agreement, 87
Nehru, B.K., 61
Nehru, Motilal, 4
Nehru, Jawaharlal, 4, 13, 23, 26–27, 35, 285
Nehru's depiction of the Indian-Iranian relationship, 94
Nehru's Vision of India as a Major Power, 157
New Delhi posting, 41–45
  area of work as Deputy Secretary, 43
  crass interference by a foreign mission, 44
  desk dealing, 45
  meagre salary, 43
  my first stint at the headquarters, 41
  no prospect of government accommodation, 43
  tiger shoot safari, 43
New York, 107–16
  broad framework of non-alignment, 108
  Indo-US cooperation, 115
  multilateral work, 107
  Permanent Mission of India (PMI), 108
  tense stand-off, 111
  transfer to, 103

Nizami, Farhan, 253
Nizami, Khaliq Ahmad, 13
Nizami, Khusro Shah, 129
NMC Special Reports, 167
Nomani, Maulana Manzoor, 35
Non-Aligned Movement (NAM), 61, 66, 69, 71, 112, 125, 252–54, 263, 267
Non-Aligned Nations, 254
Non-cooperation, 3–4
Noorani, A.G., 326–29
Noori, Hojjat-ul Islam Ali Akbar Nateq, 104
Northern Alliance, 81
Nuriya (second child), 47, 58, 78, 90, 92, 151, 185, 246, 331

Obama, Barack, 316
Oberoi, Dinesh, 82, 89
objective of minority rights. *See* National Commission for Minorities
Observer Research Foundation (ORF), 62, 156–62
  democracy in non-Arab Asian societies, 159
  focus of work, 157
  intellectual and organizational space, 160
  Iran Today: Twenty-five Years after the Islamic Revolution, 158
  The Islamic Boomerang in Saudi Arabia, 157–58
  Makkah Dialogue (2003), 158
  ORF Studies in Contemporary Muslim Societies IV, 159
  ORF Studies in Muslim Societies: III, 158
  Revolution and Creativity, 158
ochlocracy, 335
Oil and Natural Gas Corporation (ONGC), 19
oil crisis of 1973, 47, 49, 52

O'Malley, 73
Omar, Mullah, 127
One Life Is Not Enough, 69
One Village, One Product Programme of Malawi, 245
Oommen, T.K., 152, 336
Operation Desert Storm, 98n63
Orbán, Viktor, 266
O'Reilly, Bill, 76
Organisation of Islamic Cooperation (OIC), 49, 98, 109, 124–28, 164–65
Organization of the Petroleum Exporting Countries (OPEC), 47
Osman, 41, 58, 78, 90, 93, 116, 160, 185, 331–32
Oufkir, Gen. Muhammad, 50
Outlook, 183
Oza, Bhupat, 20

Pachachi, Adnan, 56
Pachauri, Rajendra, 98
Packer, Kerry, 76
Padgaonkar, Dileep, 165, 170–71
Padma Awards, 69
Padma Bhushan, 69
Padma Shri, 69
Paghman Valley, 89
Pahlavi, Ashraf Princess of Iran, 95
Pahlavi, Reza Shah, 15
Pal, Bipin Chandra, 302
Panchsheel, 253–54
Panda, Baijayant 'Jay', 209
Pande, Kamal, 145
Pandey, Captain, 82
Pant, Girijesh, 138, 160
Paolo Cotta-Ramusino, 154, 156
Paranjpe, Raghunath Purushottam, 73
Partition (1947), 134, 140, 291, 321
  trauma and bloodshed of the aftermath of, 6
Parvez, Athar, 14

Pasha, A.K., 138
Pasha, Azzam, 35
Passport (Entry into India) Act, 1920, 220
Patankar, A.C., 160
Patel, B.R., 46
Patel, Vallabhbhai, 4
Pathak, Gopal Swarup, 191
Patil, Pratibha Devisingh, 183, 214
Patil, Shivraj, 238
Pawar, Sharad, 184
Pax Britannica, policy of, 42
Pearson, Michael, 129
People's Democratic Party of Afghanistan (PDPA), 85–88, 91
People's Republic of China (PRC), 15
People's Union for Civil Liberties, 210
Permanent Court of International Justice, 174
Persia, 93, 100, 101, 310–11
Persian Gulf Security: Past Perspectives, Future Prospects, 138
Persian Gulf, emerging strategic scenario in, 160
Personal Narrative of a Pilgrimage to Al-Madina and Meccah, 34
Peshawari, Abdul Rahman, 2
pessimism of the intellect, 301, 308
Peters, F.E., 129
Phillips, Kevin, 160
Pinto, Michael, 165
The Pioneer, 183
Pious Passengers, 129
Places of Worship (Special Provisions) Act, 1991, 7
Plato, 14
Pluralism in Muslim Societies, 155
pluralism, 155, 224, 311–12
  impingement of, 336
  realization of the objectives of, 314
pluralistic society, benefits of, 282
Pluralistic Theory of the State, 18

Permanent Mission of India (PMI), 108, 118, 250
PM's Relief Fund, 21
Pokhran nuclear tests (1998), 127
political Arabism, failure of, 318
political mobilization, 324, 329
Politics in South Asia: Salience of Religion and Culture, 153
populism, success of, 335
post-Godhra riots, 149, 152, 168, 189
post-Khomeini Islamic Republic, 95
Power and Diplomacy, 327
Prasad, Rajendra, 4
Preparing for the Twenty-First Century, 299
Prevention of Terrorism Act (POTA) 2002, 153
Prevention of Torture Bill, 206
Problem of Palestine: Diplomacy and its Limitations, 154
professional and personal counts, objections on, 91
protocol ritual, 70
Provisional Constitution, 53
public addresses
    135th anniversary of the Kerala Legislative Assembly (September 2013), 293–94
    150th Birth Anniversary of Lala Lajpat Rai, 302–3
    Ambedkar Memorial Lecture (December 2012), 287
    All India Muslim Majlis-e-Mushawarat, 291–93
    All India Whips Conference in Mumbai (February 2008), 273
    AMU convocation (May 2014), 298–301
    Asia Centre Lecture, Bangalore (Feb., 2013), 290
    Asiatic Society, Kolkata, (October 2016), 305–7
    Association of Indian Diplomats (AID) (Feb., 2008), 279
    at IDSA Conference (January 2016), 290–91
    Bhimsen Sachar Memorial Lecture (December 2012), 287
    Conference of the Konkan Muslim Education Society in Thane (November 2013), 297–98
    Convocation address to the National Law School of India University, Bengaluru (2017), 311–15
    Convocation of the Indian Law Institute, New Delhi, 271
    Convocation of Jamia Millia Islamia, (2007), 270–71
    D.D. Kosambi Memorial Lecture in Goa (February 2008), 273–74
    D.P. Kohli Memorial Lecture of the CBI (April 2008), 274–76
    Fakhruddin Ali Ahmad Memorial Lecture, 325, 336
    Field Marshal KM Cariappa Memorial Lecture (Oct., 2009), 279
    Foundation Day Lecture of the University of Calcutta (December 2010), 282–84
    Foundation Day Lecture at the Rajiv Gandhi Centre for Contemporary Studies in Mumbai University (March 2008), 276
    G. Parthasarathi Memorial Lecture at JNU (March 2013), 286–87
    Hindu Huddle in February 2017 in Bengaluru, 308
    'Human Rights and Human Wrongs', 295
    IDSA Foundation Day Lecture (October 2007), 271–72
    Indian Ocean Naval Symposium (February 2008), 278–79
    Iran Research Institute of Philosophy, 101

Khuda Bakhsh Memorial Lecture in Patna (December 2009), 282
at Khuda Bakhsh Oriental Public Library (2003), 153
Maulana Azad Memorial Lecture of the ICCR (November 2014), 289
Prof. Mohammad Mujeeb Memorial Lecture, 180
Mohammad Quli Qutub Shah Lecture at the Maulana Azad National Urdu University, Hyderabad (April 2017), 308–11
Ninety-third Convocation of the Banaras Hindu University in March 2011, 284
Nizam Lecture at the University of Delhi in January 2012, 285
P.N. Haksar Memorial Lecture in Chandigarh (November 2007), 272–73
Pune Security Conference (December 2015), 291
R.N. Kao Memorial Lecture (January 2010), 280
Radhakrishnan Memorial Lecture (November 2009), 280–82
Sardar Patel Memorial Lecture (November 2012), 285–86
Twenty-second Justice Sunanda Bhandare Memorial Lecture (November 2016), 301–2
University of Kota Convocation Address (May 2008), 276–77
V.M. Tarkunde Memorial Lecture (November 2014), 288–89
at Yerevan State University, 269
World Summit of AMU Alumni (October 2008), 277–78
public interest litigation (PIL), 206
public–private partnership (PPP), 213–14
Pugwash General, 156

Punjab Provincial Political Conference, 302
Puri, J.N., 20
Puri, Y.K., 31

Qand-e Parsi, 100
Qasim, Abd al-Karim, 24
Question Hour, 193, 194–96, 198–99
  noise-making in, 198
  whose principal objective, 196
Quraishi, Shamim, 86
Qureshi, Shafi, 54
Qureshi, Shuaib, 2
Qutb Shahi courts, 100

Rabat, 31–33
  Arab and Islamic impact, 32
  impact of 'psychic dualism', 32
  Maghrebi identity, 32
  phraseology 'exigencies of service', 33
  work as commercial secretary of the mission, 31
Rabat Islamic Summit, 39, 40n28
Radhakrishnan, Sarvepalli, 186, 216, 226
Radhakrishnan's lecture (1942), 280
Rae, Ranjit, 250
Rafsanjani, Hashemi, 61, 94–95, 98–99, 104–6
Rahman, Asadur, 8
Rahman, Ataur (Ishi), 44
Rahman, Hakim Zillur, 143
Rahman, M.A. (Ishi), 266
Rahmon, Emomali, 250
Rai, Lala Lajpat, 4, 302
Raja, D., 202
Rajagopalachari, C., 4
Raje, Vasundhara, 143
Rajya Sabha at Work, 190
Rajya Sabha (Chairman)
  absolute power of the Speaker, 188n130
  Advisory Committee of the House, 193

allocation of 2G spectrum, 210
'black money' problem was being discussed, 191
'called in agony and distress', 197
calling attention, 199
Constitution (One Hundred and Eighth) Amendment Bill, 2008, 205–8
Department-related Parliamentary Standing Committees, 193
distress over the disruption of proceedings, 185
Ethics Committee of, 272
General Purposes Committee, 190, 193
Golden Jubilee Resolution of 1997, 199
Indo-US nuclear deal, 202
inviolability of the Question Hour, 195
Judges (Declaration of Assets and Liabilities) Bill, 2009, 203
Land Acquisition, Rehabilitation and Resettlement (LARR) Bill, 213
learning process in this new responsibility, 190
legislative business of, 200
Lokpal and Lokayuktas Bill, 2011, 207
Mines and Minerals (Development and Regulation) Bill, 2011, 209
money bills, 219
no control over the editorial content of, 219
norms of the functioning, 317
parliamentary sessions, 195
practice of two Zero Hours, 216
proceedings of, 199
proceedings or happenings in, 195
Question Hour, 193, 196, 198–99
Rajya Sabha Fellowships, 195
removal of a Calcutta High Court Judge, 204
Right of Children to Free and Compulsory Education Bill, 203
right to food campaign, 210
rules Committee, 193, 198
rules, procedures and precedents, 190
Dr S. Radhakrishnan Chair, 195
select committee of, 201
short duration discussions, 202–3, 222
special economic zone (SEZ) in Nandigram, 202
special mentions, 199
'spreading undercurrents of fairness', 200
swearing-in, 189
time-restricted normal sessions of, 201
unique features of Rajya Sabha, 188
Whistle Blowers Protection Bill, 2011, 207–8
Zero Hour, 193, 198
Rama Devi, V.S., 190
Ramgarh Congress session, 115
Rampur State, 5
Rantzu, Graf Zu, 116
Rao, C.N.R., 147
Rao, P.V. Narasimha, 84, 99, 103–4, 107, 110
Rao, Vidyasagar, 238
Rasgotra, M.K., 60
Rasheed, Shaikh Abdul, 13
Rashiduzzafar, 9
Rashtriya Janata Dal (RJD), 194
Rau, B.N., 187
Rauf, Abdul, 2
Razali, Ahmad, 116
reciprocity, principle of, 66
Reddy, B. Sudershan, 204
Reddy, Neelam Sanjiva, 59, 63
Re-forming India: The Nation Today, 328
Rehman, Mujibur, 326, 328
Rekhta Foundation, 285
religious conservatism at home, 120
religious endowments (*Awqaf*), 277
religious minorities, 311

Research and Analysis, 68
Rethinking Pluralism, Secularism and Tolerance, 327
Reza, Sheikh Mohammad Ali, 36
Right of Children to Free and Compulsory Education Bill, 203
Right to Food campaign, 210
Right to Freedom of Religion, 171
Right to Information Act, 275
right-wing extremist, 316
Riot Act, 66
Risalahila al-Muwatineen, 34, 41
Rise of Saffron Power, 328
Riyadh (Saudi Arabia), 117–36
   10-point programme of reforms, 120
   attack in Makkah, 118
   basic law of governance, 121
   budgetary pressures on social spending, 123
   community schools, 131
   concerns about the Taliban regime in Kabul, 127
   conclusion of assignment, 136
   dimensions of the Hajj exercise, 128–29
   establishment of a Shura Council, 120
   establishment of a Special Care Centre by Salma, 131
   explanatory memorandum of advice, 122
   first assignment in Jeddah, 131
   future markets for Saudi crude oil, 125
   impact on the management of foreign policy, 123
   Jaswant Singh's visit (Jan 2000), 128
   National Guard killed four US nationals (June 1996), 123
   procedural incorrectness, 121
   region of concentration is the holy cities of Makkah and Madina, 133
   regulatory system for the issue of fatwas, 120–21
   religio-political discourse, 117
   religious police or mutaween, 131
   rigidity with regard to other faiths, 131
   role of women, 121
   social and economic justice, 121
   visible signs of social change, 132
Rizvi, Mehdi, 143
Rizvi, Tahir, 14
Rodrigues, S.F., 238
Role of Women in Making a Humane Society, 319
Roshanara Club, 18
Rousseau, 14, 295
Roy, Raja Ram Mohun, 100
Royal Military Academy, 20
The RSS, 328–29
Rule of Law, 271, 282, 288, 290, 300, 324–25, 328, 335, 338, 341
Rules of Allegiance and Obedience: The Misconduct of Rulers, 119
Rulings and Observations from the Chair 1952–2008, 193

Sab Ka Saath, Sab Ka Vikas, 292
Sabine, George, 14
Sachar Committee Report, 173, 175, 282, 291
Safavi, Azarmi Dukht, 158
Safia (sister), 1, 12, 19
Sahni, Yogeshwar, 23
Saikal, Amin, 321
'salad bowl' approach, 314
Salahuddin, Mohammad, 41
Saleha (sister), 1
Salim, Ali-Quli, 100
Salisbury Doctrine, 217–18
Salma (wife), 7, 18, 28, 30–33, 39, 43, 45, 47–48, 57–58, 63, 72, 78, 82, 90, 93, 104, 107, 116, 128, 131, 137, 148, 151, 160, 185, 227–29, 240, 246, 252, 260, 267–68, 330–31

alumna and president of Women's
  College Union, 148
appendicitis operation in Rabat, 31
community welfare activities, 131
confinement and childbirth, 47
confinement to Edith Cavell clinic,
  47–48
establish a school for community
  children, 39
established the Embassy school, 131
gall-bladder surgery, 72
initiating a weekly open house, 58
organized a charity bazaar, 105
Salve, N.K.P., 76
Samajwadi Party, 184
Sankalp Patra (2019), 337, 340
Sankaranarayanan, K., 238
Santoshi, Pyare Lal, 31
Sappal, Gurdeep, 190
Saqqaf, Sheikh Omar, 40, 134
Sarkaria Commission, 339
Sarwari, Asadullah, 86
Sathe, Ram, 60
Satow, Ernest, 59
Sattar, Abdul, 108
Saud, Ibn, 38, 130
Saudi Arabia, 15, 34, 42, 44, 53, 57, 61,
  64, 92, 114, 117–22, 125–27, 130, 143,
  255
  Bangladeshi Hajj pilgrims, 55
  defence spending, 120
  dress norms, 61
  inclined to invest in India, 126
  Kingdom is a kafir regime, 123
  Mrs. Gandhi's visit (1982), 61, 125
  recovered from domestic turmoil, 34
  Saudi-Pak relations, 128
  telecom blackout (1979), 57
  10-point programme of reforms, 120
  tensions with Egypt, 36
  See Riyadh
Saudi Arabian National Guard, 118

Saudi Memorial, 36
Saulat un-Nisa, Begum, 38
Schooling, 5–9
  first division in the high-school
    (1952), 9
  Harcourt Butler School, 6
  haziest recollections of that period, 5
  Kailash Sood classmates, 8
  Minto Circle, 9
  Pramod Kapoor (classmate), 8
  St Edwards School, 8
Schotsman, Janine, 47
The Secret History of the Mongols, 263
Secular States, Religious Politics, 327
secularism, 153, 234–35, 261, 270, 277,
  288, 303–5, 313, 314, 319–20, 327,
  335, 340
  anti-secular vision of, 304
  basic principles, 313
  definitive pronouncement on, 313
  disappeared from the government's
    official vocabulary, 340
  impingement of, 336
  realization of the objectives of, 314
Security in the Persian Gulf, 137
Sehgal, Amar Nath, 47
Seminar, 323
Sen, Amartya, 296
Sen, Soumitra, 204
Sengupta, Arjun, 162
73rd and 74th Amendments, 306
Shabbir, Mohsin Bin, 22
Shafqi, Abdu Rahman, 87
Shah, Hasmukh, 237
Shah, King Nadir, 92
Shah, Prakash, 20, 110
Shahabuddin, Syed, 33, 48, 139, 149
Shahidi, Jaafat, 97
The Shahnama of Firdausi, 150
Shamim, Khwaja, 9
Shand, Tonia, 73
Shanghai Cooperation Organisation, 241

Sharia, 38, 121–22, 180
Shariati, Ali, 105
Sharif, Nawaz, 256
Shaw, George Bernard, 105
Shayba, Banu (traditional custodian of the Kaaba), 50
Shehr-e-Aashob, 180
Sheikh, Farooq, 131
Shekhawat, Bhairon Singh, 182
Sheriff, Shumsher, 190
Sherman, Roger, 228
Shervani, Saleem, 126
Shikhar trips, 8
Shiv Sena, 203
Short Duration Discussion, 202, 222–23
Shraddhanand, Swami, 4
Shura Council, 120, 122–23
Siddiqi, Abdul Rahman, 2, 5
Siddiqi, Rasheed Ahmad, 14
Siddiqi, Zubair, 6, 12
Silk Letter Conspiracy, 3
Sinai, Peter, 23
Singh, Amar, 82–83
Singh, B.P., 238
Singh, Badan, 82
Singh, Desh Raj, 16
Singh, Dinesh, 108
Singh, Gajendra, 20
Singh, Giani Zail, 59, 65, 70–71, 146
Singh, Gunmeen, 160
Singh, Gurbachan, 40
Singh, J.P., 20
Singh, Jaswant, 128, 194, 216
Singh, K. Natwar, 155
Singh, Karan, 195
Singh, Manju, 83
Singh, Manmohan, 112, 125, 172, 176, 182, 194, 216, 241
Singh, Nagesh, 191
Singh, Natwar, 60, 67–69
Singh, Prithi, 43
Singh, R.P., 143
Singh, R.U., 20
Singh, Randhir, 46–47
Singh, Rina, 60
Singh, S.K., 62, 78, 83
Singh, Sanjay, 179
Singh, Sardar Joginder, 20
Singh, Sujata, 249
Singh, Surendra Pal, 42
Singh, Swashpawan, 191
Singh, Tarlochan, 65
Singh, Zorawar Daulet, 326–27
Sinha, Yashwant, 202
Sins and Sinners: Where Did It Go Wrong?, 325
Six-Day War of 1967, 36, 125
Snoussi, Ahmed, 116
Solanki, Madhav Singh, 99
Somalia, 112, 114
Somavía, Juan, 116
Some Dichotomies of Our Times, 325
Sorabjee, Soli, 168
Soviet state, impending collapse of, 91
Special economic zone (SEZ) in Nandigram, 202
special mentions, 199
Srinivas, M.N., 231
Stalin, Joseph, 12
State of Denial: Bush at War, Part III, 181
The Statesman, 315
Steele, Jonathan, 81
Stewart, Cynthia, 28
'strategic partnership', 250
Strategies of Group Mobilization, 138
The Streets of Makkah, 132
Studies in a Dying Culture, 9
Subramanian, T.S.R., 20
Sukarnoputri, Megawati, 255
Sulaiman, 21, 32–33, 43, 48, 50, 58, 73, 77–79, 89, 104, 116, 185, 330–31
Sultan, Sheikh, 55
Sunbul, Shaikh Salim, 48

Suroor, Aal-e-Ahmad, 14
Suwaidi, Ahmad Khalifa Al, 54
Swaraj, Sushma, 164, 253
Syed, Ayub, 16
Sykes-Picot Agreement, 289
syncretism, 311, 327
Syriac Orthodox Church, 56

Taghut, 97
Tagore, Rabindranath, 246, 266
Talabani, Jalal, 27
Talal, Al-Waleed bin, 125
Talbot, Philip, 114, 228
TAPI [Turkmenistan–Afghanistan–Pakistan–India] gas pipeline, 240
Tara Chand, 96
Tarkunde, V.M., 147, 288, 313
Tashkiri, Hojjatul-Islam Ali, 96
Tata Africa Holdings, 244
Tehran (Iran), 93–107
    antipathetic atmosphere, 94
    economic relations, 98, 103
    bilateral relations, 104
    cultural relations, 101
    expensive alternate accommodation, 96
    farewell by Indian community, 105
    housekeeping problems, 96
    'imperialist' associations and Baha'is, 97
    imprint of the revolutionary period, 96
    India's relations with Iran, 93
    informal channels in interstate relations, 95
    Iranian approach as 'CHOKER', 106
    Narasimha Rao's visit, 104
    official perceptions on the situation in J&K, 97
    Rajiv Gandhi's visit, 98
    reaction of Babri Masjid destruction, 103–4

state of bilateral relations, 93
    visa policy, 101
    visa problem, 95
The Telegraph, 183
Telemetry Tracking and Telecommand Station, 257
Telugu Desam, 194
Tennyson, Alfred, 334
tension-laden communal situation, 162
Thakur, Rameshwar, 238
Thakur, T.S., 204
Thapar, P.N., 83
Tharoor, Shashi, 116
Three Presidents and an Aide, 41
Tilak, Bal Gangadhar, 302
Timur, Amir, 251
Tito, Marshal of Yugoslavia, 71
Tonki, Syed Mohammad, 9
Touré, Ahmed Sékou, 63
Toynbee, Arnold, 289
'Track 1.5' Asia-Middle East Dialogue (AMED), 155
Transcendental Meditation, 48
Travelling Through Conflict: Essays on the Politics of West Asia, 180
Traxl, Herbert, 229
trickle-down model of growth, 308
Tripathi, Deepak, 90
Tripathi, G.P., 79
Trivedi, R.K., 20
Trotsky, Leon, 26, 158
Trucial States, 42
Tumhari Amrita, 131
Tung, Mao Tse, 14
Tunis–India Parliamentary Group, 261
Twelver J'afari School, 97
2G spectrum, allocation of, 210
Two Obligatory Isms, 224
Tyabji, Badruddin, 42, 137

ulema, 119, 121–22, 132, 135

UN Commission on Human Rights (UNCHR), 104, 110
UN Convention against Corruption (2003), 287
UN Convention against Torture, 206
UN peacekeeping operations, 112
  activism on, 113
UN resolutions on J&K, 128
Union and Provincial Constitution Committees, 188
United Arab Emirates (UAE), 52, 54–57, 164, 269
United Nations Development Programme (UNDP), 82, 85, 88–90, 275, 326, 336
United Nations Educational, Scientific and Cultural Organization's (UNESCO), 27
United Nations Security Council (UNSC), 53, 107, 241, 246, 258
Universal Declaration of Human Rights, 171, 230
UPA government (2004)
  common minimum programme, 165, 201
  legislative agenda, 201
Urban middle-class activism, 307
The US Approach to the Islamic World in Post 9/11 Era, 159
Usman, Mohammad, 21, 227
Usmani, A.A., 96
Usmani, Maulana Shabbir Ahmad, 4

Vahanvati, Goolam, 271
Vajpayee, Atal Bihari, 55, 62, 109–10, 133, 152, 176, 228
Vala, Vajubhai, 238
Velayati, Ali Akbar (Foreign Minister of Iran), 98–99, 103, 229
Venkatachaliah, M.N., 150
Venkataraman, R., 228
Venkatraman, Muthu, 69

Verghese, B.G., 270
Verma, J.S., 152
Vice presidency
  61st Convocation of the Panjab University, 230
  ceremonial and functional duties of, 228
  chancellor of the universities of Delhi, Punjab and Pondicherry, 229
  Conference of Governors, 232–37
  ex officio functions of, 229
  foreign visits, 238–69
    Afghanistan (2014), 255
    Algeria, 266
    Armenia (2017), 268
    Ashgabat (2015), 256
    Australia (2011), 246–47
    Bangkok, 257–58
    Bangladesh (2011), 246–47
    Botswana (2010), 244–45
    Brussels (2010), 246
    Cambodia (2015), 255
    China, 253–55
    Croatia (2010), 245–46
    Cuba (2014), 249–50, 252–53
    Czech Republic (2010), 245–46
    Hungary, 266
    Indonesia (2015), 255
    Kazakhstan (2008), 240–42
    Kuwait (2009), 243
    Malawi (2010), 244–45
    Maldives (2008), 242
    Mali, 264–66
    Mongolia, 262–63
    Morocco, 259–61
    Myanmar (2009), 242–43
    Nigeria, 264–66
    Peru (2014), 249–50, 252–53
    Poland (2017), 268
    Republic of South Sudan, 247
    Rwanda (2017), 267–68
    Saudi Arabia (2014), 255

South Africa (2009), 244
South Sudan (2011), 246–47
Tajikistan, 249–51, 256
Tunisia (2016), 261–62
Turkey (2011), 246–49
Turkmenistan (2008), 240–42
UAE (last visit), 269
Uganda (2011, 2017), 246–47, 267–68
Uzbekistan (2014), 249–51
Vietnam (2014), 249–50
Venezuela, 263
Zambia (2010), 244–45
invited by the Academic Research Centre of the University of Delhi, 229
public address as, 334–35
record of daily engagements, 228
visits to states, 237–38
  Dras, 238
  Kashmir, 237
  Mizoram, 237
  Mumbai, 238
  Rann of Kutch, 237
Vienna Conventions on Diplomatic and Consular Relations, 59
Visvanathan, Shiv, 317
Vivekananda, 294–95, 314
  unveiled a statue of, 294
Vohra, N.N., 238
von Gierke, Otto, 18
Vorontsov, Yuli, 88, 116
'vote buying', phenomenon of, 276
Voter Verifiable Paper Audit Trails (VVPATs), 222

Wada-e-fardaa (Promise of Tomorrow), 92
Walker, Julian, 53
War of Succession, 311
War Remnants Museum (earlier named War Crimes Museum), 250

War, Peace and Hegemony in a Globalised World, 180
Warrant of Precedence, 61
Wasey, Akhtarul, 180
'Washing of the Kaaba' ceremony, 50
Washington, George, 187
'way of life' argument, 304
Well of the House, 196
West Asia and North Africa (WANA) division, 41–42
Westrip, Joyce, 249
Whistle Blowers Protection Bill, 2011, 207–8
Who Rules Iran? The Structure of Power in the Islamic Republic, 156
Widodo, Joko, 255
Willingdon Cricket Pavilion, 17
Women's Reservation Bill, 198
The Wonder That Was India, 75
Woodward, Bob, 181
Working group on J&K, 175–79
  awareness about it among civil and military functionaries, 177
  centre–state relations, 176, 178–79
  confidence-building measures, 176
  dimensions to the problems of J&K, 176
  economic development, 176
  ensuring good governance, 176
  general amnesty to minor under trial, 178
  rehabilitation package, 178
  rehabilitation policy for Kashmiri Pandit migrants, 178
  relief to victims of militancy, 178
  strengthening relations across the Line of Control, 176
World Bank, 131
The World of Tomorrow, 269
World Press Freedom Index, 324
World Social Summit for Social Development, 108
World Value Surveys, 159

World War I, 3, 24, 26, 129
World War II, 5, 42, 65

Yaacobi, Gad, 116
Yadav, Mulayam Singh, 215
Yazdi, Ebrahim, 98
Yechury, Sitaram, 182
Yellow Fever certificate, 63
Yogi, Maharishi Mahesh, 48

Zahedi, Ardeshir, 44

Zakaria, Tan Sri, 77
Zakia (sister), 1, 12, 19
Zambia Electricity Supply Corporation, 244
Zamiruddin, 16
Zayed, Sheikh, 54–57, 269
Zero Hour, 193, 198–99, 216
   three-minute rule, 198–99
Zia, Begum Khaleda, 247
Zionist, 322
Zoroastrian, 86, 97